Perceptual
and Motor
Development

Harriet G. Williams
University of South Carolina

Perceptual and Motor Development

PRENTICE-HALL, INC., ENGLEWOOD CLIFFS, NEW JERSEY 07632

Library of Congress Cataloging in Publication Data

WILLIAMS, HARRIET G.
  Perceptual and motor development.

  Includes bibliographies and index.
  1. Perceptual-motor learning.   2. Perception in
children.   3. Physical education for children.
I. Title.
BF723.M6W56   155.4′12   82-5408
ISBN 0-13-656892-0   AACR2

Editorial production/supervision by Peter Roberts
Cover design by Ray Lundgren
Manufacturing buyer: Harry P. Baisley

Printed in the United States of America

10 9 8 7 6 5 4 3 2 1

ISBN 0-13-656892-0

Prentice-Hall International, Inc., *London*
Prentice-Hall of Australia Pty. Limited, *Sydney*
Prentice-Hall Canada, Inc., *Toronto*
Prentice-Hall of India Private Limited, *New Delhi*
Prentice-Hall of Japan, Inc., *Tokyo*
Prentice-Hall of Southeast Asia Pte. Ltd., *Singapore*
Whitehall Books Limited, Wellington, *New Zealand*

To Mom, Dad, and Jerry,
who were my silent authors and wrote many words
with their unwavering love and support.

CONTENTS

CHAPTER 2

Growth and Development of the Nervous System: Selected Topics *34*

CHAPTER 3

Sensory-Perceptual Development: An Overview of Visual Perception Processes *68*

CHAPTER 4

Characteristics of Visual Perception Development
in Young Children   *87*

CHAPTER 5

Intra-Sensory Development: Tactile-Kinesthetic
and Auditory Abilities   *127*

CHAPTER 6

Intersensory Integration   *142*

PART 2

Motor and Physical-Related Aspects of Perceptual-Motor Development

CHAPTER 7

Development of Fine Motor Control in Young Children   *171*

CHAPTER 8

Development of Gross Motor Skills in Young Children   *200*

PREFACE

This text on perceptual-motor development in young children is divided into two parts: neural and sensory-perceptual considerations in perceptual-motor development, and motor and physical-related aspects of perceptual-motor development.

Part 1 describes, from both a theoretical and behavioral point of view, the nature of the relationship between perceptual-motor, perceptual, and cognitive development. The role of the nervous system in perceptual-motor development is examined in Chapter 2: The emphasis is on the importance of the relationship between brain growth and development to the overall development of the child and the factors that affect such growth. In Chapter 3, an overview of sensory-perceptual development in the young child is presented, and an attempt is made to outline the processes and mechanisms that regulate visual perception. Important behavioral aspects and developmental characteristics of selected visual-perceptual abilities in young children are described in Chapter 4, as well as the contribution of visual perception to the skillful movement of children. Developmental changes in tactile-kinesthetic and auditory abilities and their significance to perceptual-motor development are discussed in Chapter 5. Chapter 6 is devoted to a description and analysis of intersensory integration abilities of young children. The focus is on the development of visual-auditory, auditory-tactile, and visual-tactile/kinesthetic abilities, and the implications for perceptual-motor and cognitive functioning in normally and slowly developing children.

Part 2 opens with a discussion of the factors involved in, and the developmental characteristics associated with, the mastery of fine-motor or eye-hand coordination skills (Chapter 7). Chapter 8 examines the "concept of the physical self"—how it develops in the young child, and the nature of the role of body awareness in perceptual-motor development. A model of balance abilities and sex- and age-related differences in balance task performances are described in Chapter 9. The final chapter presents a theoretical and behavioral analysis of the development of gross motor skills in young children. The difference between intertask and intratask motor development is discussed, and sex- and age-related changes in process and product characteristics of fundamental motor skill performance in young children are outlined. A series of checklists that can be used for simple evaluation of gross motor skill performance are provided.

It is my intent to present and discuss both theoretical and practical issues of importance to professionals who work with young children in a variety of fields, so that better and wiser decisions might be made about the lives of children everywhere.

Harriet G. Williams

ACKNOWLEDGMENTS

The author wishes to acknowledge permission to use the following material:

Table 1-1, on page 24 is reprinted by permission of the publisher from Belka, D., and Williams, H., Prediction of later cognitive behavior from early school perceptual-motor, perceptual and cognitive performances. PERCEPTUAL AND MOTOR SKILLS, 1979, 49, 131–141, Table 1.

Perceptual
and Motor
Development

PART ONE
THEORETICAL AND SENSORY-PERCEPTUAL CONSIDERATIONS IN PERCEPTUAL-MOTOR DEVELOPMENT

CHAPTER ONE
THE RELATIONSHIP BETWEEN PERCEPTUAL-MOTOR, PERCEPTUAL, AND COGNITIVE DEVELOPMENT

The purpose of this introductory chapter is to provide a broad overview of theoretical and practical concepts relevant to perceptual-motor development (PMD) and its role in or contribution to the total development of the young child. This chapter sets the tone for the discussion of the more specific topics related to perceptual-motor development that follow.

A THEORETICAL MODEL OF PERCEPTUAL-MOTOR FUNCTIONING

To thoroughly understand the concept of perceptual-motor development and its relationship to the total development of the child, we must first understand something about the processes that underlie or subserve perceptual-motor development and the learning or performance of perceptual-motor skills. A simple schematic of perceptual-motor functioning is given in sections A and B of Figure 1.1. In its simplest form, perceptual-motor functioning may be thought of as a continuous cycle of four basic events—*sensory-perceptual decisions* that are prerequisite to and necessary for the formulation of *motor decisions* that are in turn prerequisite to the actual execution of a motor or *movement behavior itself*. Last are the *reafference or information-feedback events* that are used to evaluate and/or modify both the

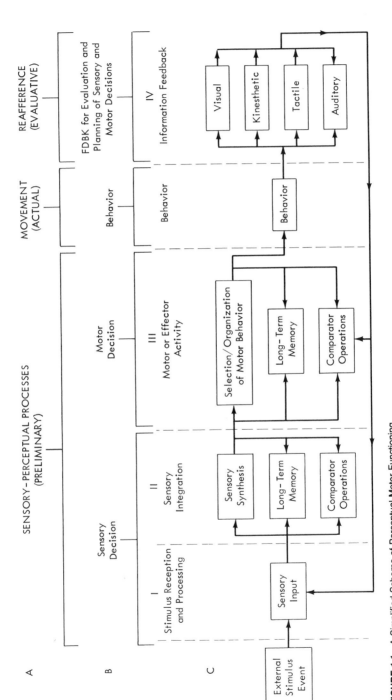

FIGURE 1.1 A Simplified Schema of Perceptual-Motor Functioning

movement behavior and the underlying sensory-motor processes that sub-serve that behavior.

To understand perceptual-motor functioning in a little more detail (section C of Figure 1.1) we need to set a task around which to focus the discussion of this model. For convenience sake, let us make the task that of returning the shot of an opponent on the tennis court. According to the model, then, this perceptual-motor task is begun with an "external stimulus event"—the ball being hit by an opponent.

Step One: Stimulus Reception and Processing

The first step in the long chain of events that eventually leads to the perceptual-motor behavior of returning the tennis ball to the opponent is a process that involves *stimulus reception and processing* of that information. In this case, the individual sees the ball being hit and coming toward him through space. Immediately, he fixates on the ball and tracks it through space, so that specific information concerning the flight of the ball (e.g., its speed and direction) is picked up by the system to be processed further. This implies, of course, that the performer has blocked out extraneous or irrelevant aspects of the visual environment and is selectively attending to specific elements of the environment pertinent to returning the ball. The highly skilled performer probably watches both the flight of the ball and the movement of his opponent, whereas the individual who is just learning to play tennis needs to place his attention solely on the flight of the ball in order to track it efficiently and to accurately process information regarding its flight. At any rate, the initial step involved in the perceptual-motor act of "returning the opponent's shot on the tennis court" is one of picking up and processing specific sensory information—in this case information concerning the flight characteristics of the oncoming ball (Williams, 1968).

Step Two: Sensory Integration

We know that the nature and extent of an individual's prior experience in a given situation can affect in very subtle ways the manner in which he perceives or interprets (and thus reacts to) that situation. This is equally true for the judgment that the performer makes on the tennis court. His *past experience* in such situations strongly influences his ability to fixate and track the moving object in space and to process information that is relevant to making a decision about how to move on the tennis court. This process is referred to as *sensory integration*. It involves three elements: sensory synthesis, long-term memory (LTM), and comparator operations. In sensory synthesis, present (incoming) and past (stored) sensory information relevant to "judging the ball and/or the opponent's movement on the tennis court" is shared or integrated. Sensory synthesis is inherently linked to long-term memory, for it is in long-term memory that information from the individual's past experience with similar "skill situations" is stored. Thus the initial sensory information picked up by the system simultaneously activates both sensory synthesis and long-term memory processes and allows for a mixing or comparing of present incoming information with information stored in the performer's memory. This makes possible a more precise analysis of the nature of present environmental demands (Williams, 1968).

Sensory integration may also involve a comparator function that is concerned (a) with monitoring what is happening in sensory synthesis and long-term memory and (b) with providing information to the system about current changes in the environment of the performer (e.g., has the flight of the ball changed due to backspin, has the opponent changed his position on the court, etc.?). In this way the system is kept up to date about changes that have taken place most recently in the environment. This allows the ongoing analysis of the information originally picked up by the system (brain) to be both more precise and relevant to the situation in which the individual *now* finds himself.

When a decision about "what is happening out there in the environment" (a sensory decision) is made, it is sent to the effector activity unit where the motor behavior itself is outlined and organized. This so-called sensory decision is also kept or maintained in the system via the comparator mechanism until sometime after the behavioral act is completed. When (and if) the ball is struck, this original *sensory decision* becomes a part of long-term memory and is stored in the system to be called upon for use in future sensory decisions on how to return a ball on the tennis court.

Step Three: Effector Activity

Once the decision about what is happening in the environment is made, the selection and organization of an appropriate motor behavior can begin. The decision about how, when, and where to move is guided by and based upon the sensory decision provided to the motor or effector mechanisms. Thus initial sensory-perceptual processes are integral to the organization of an appropriate motor response. The final selection of the motor behavior involves both long-term memory (in this case motor memory) and comparator operations. The nature and extent of the performer's past experience with moving on the tennis court is again an important factor in determining how smoothly and quickly the player can organize and set a response into action. The determination of how, when, and where to move, then, is based largely on available motor-memory stores (e.g., the nature and number of motor programs that the individual has acquired through experience and training) and on the immediately preceding sensory decision. Intricately intertwined with this final selection process is the comparator activity, which constantly keeps the system (brain) informed about changes in the position of the performer's body in space. Such current information is used to modify or redirect the selection of the up-and-coming movement behavior so that the final overt behavior is as appropriate for present environmental conditions as is possible. Once the behavior has been decided upon—that is once a motor decision has been made—a command for a specific set of movements is sent out to the muscles of the body and the performer begins to move. In this case we might assume that the movement command is one that says "move quickly to the left rear of the court and hit a sharp cross-court shot to the opponent's backhand." We then would observe the player moving back and to the left of the court where he would meet and hit the oncoming ball (Williams, 1968).

Step Four: Information Feedback

As soon as the performer begins to move, information feedback occurs. Information feedback (information about the nature of the ongoing behavior) continues as long as the individual is moving and for a period of time after the player has stopped moving and has either won, lost, or prolonged the playing of the point. Information feedback in this case may consist of:

1. proprioceptive and kinesthetic information derived from the movement of the body and/or body parts through space;
2. touch information that is derived from the actual contact between the hand and the racket and any other external factors acting upon the touch receptors of the body as the individual moves;
3. visual information derived from the changing images of objects in the visual field of the observer as they are reflected on the retina of the eye;
4. auditory information derived primarily from the sound of the racket contacting the ball (Williams, 1968).

The system (brain) uses this feedback information to judge the overall success of the motor act and to evaluate the adequacy of the processes that have contributed to the formulation of the behavior. This judgment, it is suggested, is made by comparing the information in the original sensory and motor decisions with the information fed back into the system after the behavior has been initiated and carried out by the performer. If the two sources of information are coincident (e.g., there are minimal or no discrepancies between the two), the behavior is judged as adequate and no further adaptation or modification is deemed necessary. If, however, there is an identifiable discrepancy between what was "ordered" and what "happened" (e.g., "a" was supposed to happen but "b" is what actually took place), the system immediately recognizes that an error has been made (e.g., the player hit the ball too short) and that some modification or adjustment of the movement order is called for. In this instance modification would occur in some future situation that the performer might face on the tennis court. The importance of feedback information to this whole series of events is that it is the primary way that sensory and motor decisions are corrected or modified so that learning (more effective adaptation to the environment) can take place. The use of feedback information in the whole schema of perceptual-motor functioning suggests that perceptual-motor functioning is a dynamic process—one that depends in large part upon the ability of the individual to rapidly and continuously pick up and analyze information pertinent to making decisions about the environment in which he finds himself.

This model of perceptual-motor functioning can be used equally easily to analyze what a child has to do to learn to catch a ball or to understand how a child develops the ability to use scissors to cut a picture from a book. The nature of the processes involved in the sensory and motor decisions of both of these skills is essentially the same; only the nature and details of the information to be processed are different. Thus in cutting out a picture, for example, the initial step required for the child to be successful in such an act is for him to fixate or attend to the figure to be cut out. The child thus picks up and begins to process information about the size, shape, and position of the figure on the page (stimulus reception and information processing). The accuracy of this analysis is, of course, influenced by both his level of development and his past experience in such activities (sensory integration). Once he has gathered this information, the original sensory decision can be made and he can proceed to make a motor decision about how to organize the cutting action (effector activity). This decision is based upon the original sensory decision, upon past information about how he has moved in such situations before (long-term motor memory), and upon information about his present position in space (e.g., the relative position of the arms, hands, fingers, head, and trunk). When the motor decision is made, the child begins to cut (overt behavior). Information feedback from the movement itself (how he is holding the paper, how he is grasping the scissors, and what movements he is making with the hands and fingers) and from new or changing visual input that occurs as the cutting action takes place is used to determine the adequacy of the ongoing behavior and to establish the basis for making the next, most immediate sensory and motor decisions that have to be made if the cutting behavior is to be continuous, smooth, and skillful.

Just as the model describes some of the basic processes that are involved in the perceptual-motor act of cutting, it also indicates a number of points at which the cutting behavior (e.g., perceptual-motor functioning) may break down. These include: (a) the initial pick-up of information where, perhaps due to faulty eye movement control and/or underdeveloped selection/attention habits, the child does not attend to or get the "right" information into the system; (b) the analysis or interpretation of this basic sensory information where, due to general lack of development of the sensory systems themselves or poor long-term memory or both, the child makes inadequate decisions about what present environmental demands are like; (c) the selection and organization of the motor behavior where, perhaps as a result of faulty sensory decisions, poor long-term motor memory, general lack of development of the motor systems, etc., the child plans and/or carries out the cutting movements inappropriately; and (d) the use of information feedback where, due to any one or a combination of the foregoing, the child is unable to modify or correct his behavior so that it more successfully meets the demands of the environment. Remediation of any perceptual-motor deficit, therefore, must be based on a careful consideration of all possible underlying sources of the problem. This is no simple task and requires a careful and logical step-by-step analysis of the child's behavior on the part of the teacher, parent, or clinician.

A Theoretical Definition of Perceptual-Motor Development

Theoretically, then, what is perceptual-motor development? Perceptual-motor development is that part of the child's development that is concerned with changes that take place, with age, in the movement behavior of the young child—changes that represent improvements in sensory-perceptual-motor and reafference processes that underlie such behavior. The focus of perceptual-motor development is on the development of the child's capacity to make sensory and motor decisions and to use feedback to modify and/or eliminate errors from his behavior and from these decision-making processes. Learning/development occurs primarily as reafference is used by the child to evaluate and modify those underlying sensory and motor decision-making processes. Thus perceptual-motor development is a direct manifestation of the quality of perceptual-motor functioning and is concerned with the total scope of the processes outlined in Figure 1.1. Motor development has traditionally been thought of as the study of age changes in the development or refinement of the movement behavior component of the schema.

PERCEPTUAL-MOTOR DEVELOPMENT: A PRACTICAL APPROACH

In order to be able to learn about and/or solve problems presented to him by his environment, the child must be able to take in information from that environment; process or analyze it quickly and accurately; decide when, how, and what action to take; and then perform or execute that action.

When the child is dealing with the concrete, physical dimensions of the environment—when he is asked to interact with or use scissors, pencils, balls, bats, etc.—he is usually said to be using or developing perceptual-motor skills, skills that provide the means by which he learns to deal with and master his physical environment in a very direct way. On the other hand, when the child is asked to process or use abstract information (e.g., when he has to read or use words and/or numbers) and make decisions about his environment or his behavior on the basis of this kind of information, he is said to be using or developing intellectual or cognitive abilities. These abilities are important if the child is to be able to function effectively in school and/or in a society that emphasizes the use of symbolic, logical, and rational thinking (Williams, 1974).

Perceptual-motor development may perhaps best be thought of in practical terms as that domain of behaviors or basic, foundational skills that provide the child with the means to deal effectively (and in a direct way) with the concrete or physical realities of the environment. What specifically are these perceptual-motor skills or behaviors that provide this basic foundation for learning and/or adaptation to the environment? To help bring order to a somewhat chaotic and still sparse field of knowledge, we suggest that there are four basic categories of behaviors that can be identified as foundational perceptual-motor behaviors. These include:

1. Gross motor control   Gross motor control has to do with the skillful use of the total body in large muscle or gross motor activities that require intricate temporal and spatial coordination of movement of a number of body parts or segments sequentially or simultaneously. Gross motor control skills generally include such skills as walking, running, hopping, skipping, jumping, throwing, catching, striking, balancing.

2. Fine motor control   Fine motor control may be defined as that dimension of behavior that involves the use of individual body parts, especially the hands and fingers, in manipulating and/or controlling small objects in precision acts. Fine motor control behaviors are frequently referred to as eye-hand coordination or visuo-motor integration behaviors and include such skills as cutting, coloring, writing, pasting, etc. The defining feature of fine motor control is that it involves a close functional relationship between the use of the eyes and the small muscle masses of the hands and fingers (or feet).

3. Simple auditory, visual, and tactile-kinesthetic behaviors   In general, perceptual behaviors as we have identified them involve the detection, recognition, discrimination, and interpretation of simple stimuli received through individual sensory modalities.

4. Body awareness Body awareness behaviors are perhaps best described as those behaviors that involve the recognition, identification, and differentiation of the parts, dimensions, positions, movements, and spatial location of the body. These skills are ones that provide the foundation for the child's awareness of the physical dimensions or capacities of his body and his understanding of the relationship between his body and the movement of his body and the surrounding environment (Williams, 1974).

It is believed that most children develop these fundamental skills during the early years through natural, spontaneous interaction with their environment. All organisms seem to have a natural biological drive that leads them to seek stimulation from the environment, and therefore they tend to actively explore and examine the physical environment as well as their own bodies. It is through this active exploration that they gradually build the foundation of basic skills that they need for dealing with more complex, abstract dimensions of their world. Many children, for a variety of reasons (e.g., a slower rate of development, nutritional deficiency, emotional instability, lack of opportunity, etc.) do not develop these fundamental skills to the degree that they should. These children then become the focus of attention of teachers and parents, because they are the ones who have difficulty complying with simple environmental demands found in the home or at school.

If we think of the total growth and development process of the child as one that is concerned with the building of a ladder that provides the means by which the child climbs up to and reaches over into the world of abstraction, symbolic reasoning, and thinking, then we can think of perceptual-motor skills as being the materials of which the lower rungs of the ladder are constructed. These lower rungs provide the foundation upon which strong, stable rungs higher and higher up on the ladder are built— a building process that eventually leads to higher-order thought processes.

PERCEPTUAL-MOTOR THEORY
AND PERCEPTUAL-MOTOR AND
COGNITIVE FUNCTIONING

The basic premise of the general theory underlying perceptual-motor development is that early perceptual-motor experiences and cognitive or intellectual development are intimately related. This theory suggests that the development of the child is hierarchical in nature and that three basic levels of this hierarchy can be identified: an early base level of development that is dominated by perceptual-motor functioning; an intermediate stage or level of development that is manifested in more independent and refined perceptual functioning; and the highest level of development that is re-flected in higher-order symbolic or abstract thinking. The theory proposes that functioning at each level higher up on the hierarchy is to some degree dependent upon the development and/or refinement of at least a limited set of skills or abilities at each of the immediately preceding lower levels of functioning. Thus to function efficiently in a cognitive mode (e.g., to think or reason symbolically), the theory suggests that the child must have developed certain minimal perceptual-motor abilities and must have at-tained some degree of advanced refinement of visual, auditory and tactile-kinesthetic perception capacities. (For a review of theories see Belka and Williams, 1979b.)

PERCEPTUAL-MOTOR AND COGNITIVE DEVELOPMENT: A PIAGETIAN POINT OF VIEW

To examine these proposed relationships further, let us take a brief look at Piagetian theory (Piaget 1963, 1967, 1969, 1973). Piaget has suggested that there are four basic stages of development in the child's growth toward mature intellectual functioning.

Sensory-Motor Period

The first of these stages he labels the sensory-motor period. This stage of development spans the period from birth to two years of age and is characterized by the appearance and development of basic sensori-percep-tual, motor, and language capacities. During this sensory-motor period, the child acquires skills and behaviors—sensori-motor schemas—that help him in the process of organizing and adapting to the immediate, concrete external environment into which the child has been thrust. Significantly, the child during these two years:

- builds a basic repertoire of "later-to-be-perfected" *manipulative* and *locomotor* skills;
- learns to organize and *use sensory information skillfully;*
- learns to *recognize functional invariants of objects* and events in the external world;
- develops *goal-directed behavior* and learns to put together two or three actions that will lead to a specific end goal;
- develops primitive *notions of self, of space, of time, of causality.*

As a result of these important behavioral acquisitions, people, objects, and events in the child's external world take on an identity and permanence of their own. Few of these acquired behaviors or operations, however, are accompanied by true cognitive or conceptual understanding.

The child initially develops this repertoire of sensori-motor schemas in conjunction with and as a result of his own physical activity—by and through active bodily movement in and exploration of his environment. Thus the sensory-motor child functions almost totally in the physical, immediate, concrete realm of the present. This period is perhaps most succinctly characterized by the observation that *actions (behaviors) exist and are executed independently of the guidance of true thought or cognitive processes.*

Preoperational Period

The sensory-motor period is followed by the preoperational stage of development. These years, two to seven, mark the beginning of true cognition and/or conceptualization. During this period the child begins to operate symbolically for the first time. The basis for this primitive symbolic functioning is, of course, laid down during the earlier sensori-motor period but will require, if these processes are to reach their ultimate level of refined abstraction, further nurturing and development during the years of the preoperational period.

The child, during this time, begins to establish an internal, conceptual picture of the external world, with its objects and events and their many laws and relationships. This early cognitive mapping of reality begins in a kind of piecemeal way, in that in the beginning it is merely—to use Piaget's words—"an internal copy of sensori-motor schemata." Thus the child begins to carve out a system of symbolic functioning through active physical involvement with his environment—through concrete and motor examination of the many dimensions of the external world. The primary tools used in this masterful sculpturing of the early stages of cognitive development are *imitation, symbolic play,* and *language.* Imitation and symbolic play are, of course, highly concrete and motoric in nature, and it is through these active physical processes that the child begins to internalize information about external reality. This information—derived from the child's active, physical interaction with the environment—provides the data base for building more complex conceptual representations of reality and for supporting the elaboration of these conceptualizations (conservation, change, number, perspective, etc.) into higher-order, abstract thought processes. It might be said of this period that *action is thought and thought is action,* for the two do not seem to exist or to operate independently of one another.

Concrete and Formal Operations

The concrete operations period follows after and builds upon the experiences of the preoperational stage. During this time span (7-11 years of age) formal thought processes (abstraction) are operative and cognitive development becomes more stable and rational. The child can now perform elementary logical operations and can make elementary groupings of classes and relations. He develops concepts of conservation (substance, length, weight, volume, etc.) and of reversibility. Still he is very much tied to the "concrete" dimensions of reality and cannot isolate, conceptually, variables that will lead directly to the solution of a problem. When compared to the previous period of development, behavior during this time is characterized by the fact that *thought can now precede and guide action but does not ordinarily function independently of it.*

The last stage of development is the *formal-operations period,* 11 years of age and older. Logical thought processes are now operable—the child can deduce implications and understands and can use the scientific method. Thus we note the characteristic appearance of hypothetical, deductive reasoning and the recognition of the reversibility between reality and possibility. *Thought can now operate independently of action*—although the two never become, even in the optimally functioning adult, completely separate or independent of one another.

The two earliest stages, sensori-motor and preoperational, are often referred to as the period of sensori-motor intelligence—a period of development during which foundations are being laid for the future development of the more complex cognitive functions of the concrete and formal operations periods (higher-order intelligence).

Piaget provides data to show that the young child develops from being the kind of organism that operates on and within his environment primarily via concrete, sensori-motor-based processes, into one who approaches adaptation to his environment on a more representational, abstract or conceptual basis. Thus the child, as he grows and develops, learns to solve problems and to adapt to his environment first by simply "acting or behaving" in the environment and then observing the consequences of his behavior, and later by thinking about and analyzing the conditions that contribute to the formulation of solutions to those problems.

The Process of Symbolization

The process that is perhaps most instrumental in the child's metamorphosis from more primitive levels of concrete—sensori-motor and preoperational—levels of functioning to those of a higher, more abstract level (concrete and formal operations) is the symbolization of objects and events and their relationships. The initial stages of this process are begun in the early sensori-motor period but are built upon and nurtured to significant levels of refinement during the preoperational period. The years from 2 to 7 thus become a vital part of the total cognitive growth cycle of the child.

There are three levels of the symbolization process. The first of these is the concrete reality/index level. This stage of development of the cognitive process requires that the child deal with the environment he is to master in a direct way. It requires that he manipulate objects, that he actively use and explore his environment. This active interaction is necessary so that the child can acquire a well-defined knowledge and understanding of the many facets of his external world. Motor activity is vital to this level of the symbolization process, for it provides the raw data upon which the child will begin to build an information base for the structuring of higher levels of the symbolization process. Thus the young child must gather raw data from his environment in the early stages of his development if he is to function easily at later stages of development. He achieves this goal primarily through the effective use of his perceptual and motor capacities.

The next level of the symbolization process is the "symbol" level. This stage of cognitive development, although also nonverbal in nature, is one in which more abstract, conceptual bases for the representation of objects and events in external reality are developed. These concepts are developed primarily through:

1. the use of the body to represent objects and events—*imitation* (gross motor activity);
2. the use of objects to represent other objects—*symbolic play* (fine and gross motor activity);
3. the construction of objects in two and three dimensions—*modeling, drawing, cutting* (fine motor activity);
4. the recognition and use of pictures as representing objects and events—*visual perception;*
5. the use of sounds to characterize objects and events—*auditory perception.*

The child uses all of these semi-concrete methods to construct more advanced concepts about objects and events in the world in which he lives. *Both perceptual and motor capacities are obviously an integral part of this development.*

The highest level of abstraction, then, is the use of language, written or spoken, to represent or describe objects and events in the immediate or not so immediate environment. This level of operation follows after and is based upon the earlier developments in symbolic functioning that have preceded it. Development of the use of words and sentences to represent reality proceeds more easily and with more meaning to the child if he has built a strong sensori-perceptual-motor foundation upon which to base these abstract, verbal conceptualizations. Thus, from a Piagetian point of view, the development of adequate sensori-perceptual and motor abilities is a vital part of the total cycle of the child's cognitive growth.

THE GUILFORD MODEL OF THE INTELLECT

Another important step in understanding the logic of a possible relationship between perceptual-motor and cognitive functioning requires some analysis of the nature of human cognitive function (the human intellect). Probably the most widely accepted and most useful description of the intellect is that provided by J. P. Guilford (1967). It is to a discussion of this model of the intellect that we will now direct our attention. A schema of Guilford's model is given in Figure 1.2. Guilford (1967) views intelligence (cognition) as an information-processing system that organizes, stores, cross-files, and retrieves information. The intellect, according to this model, has two primary components: content and process. The content of intellect is concerned with the *kind* of information used in intellectual activity, whereas the *process* of intellect is concerned with the nature of the operation performed on the information involved in the cognitive or intellectual act.

The Content of Cognition

The content of intellect has three basic forms: figural, symbolic, and semantic. Figural content is best described as concrete material that represents reality directly (e.g., the things we see, feel, and hear). Its focus is on physical dimensions of the environment (e.g., a brown dog, a red truck) that do not represent anything other than themselves. Figural content is typically thought of as basic sensory information that is perceived directly and immediately through the senses themselves. Symbolic and semantic information are more uniquely human components of intellectual content. Symbolic information is composed of numbers, letters, and other conventional signs that are organized in a general system and that usually have

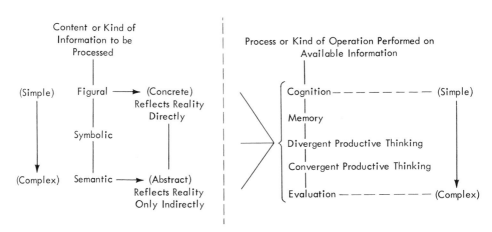

FIGURE 1.2 The Nature of the Intellect (After Guilford, 1967)

16

a figural base. The figural base, however, is superficial, for the very purpose of symbolic content is to represent reality indirectly and to communicate more extensive information in a succinct form. Semantic content builds on symbolic content and takes the form of verbal meanings; semantic information thus is used to communicate about reality in an even more sophisticated and indirect way.

The Process of Cognition

The process aspects of the intellect (e.g., the methods of thinking or operating on figural, symbolic, or semantic information) have five primary forms: cognition, memory, divergent productive thinking, convergent productive thinking, and evaluation. Cognition is an awareness or possession of information in the present. It is the recognition or attachment of meaning to stimulus information. Memory may be a more sophisticated operation in that it involves the storage of information. It involves the retention and recall of information and may have several dimensions including: intentional, incidental, short-term, and long-term processes. Divergent productive thinking is the expansion and use of information in new applications; it is the generation of logical possibilities. Convergent productive thinking, on the other hand, is a synthesizing operation in which diverse bits of information are united. Finally, Guilford's highest intellectual operation is that of evaluation—the assessment of the validity, goodness, or correctness of information. It is the means by which the person judges whether or not the criteria for making a decision or responding in a situation have been satisfactorily met.

The Nature of the Intellect

Intellectual or cognitive functioning, then, is concerned with processing both concrete (figural) and abstract information (symbolic/semantic). The *kind of information* processed dictates the *kind of intelligence* involved in solving a problem. Thus there may be two kinds of intelligence: (a) *concrete intelligence,* which depends heavily on the processing of figural or concrete information; and (b) *abstract intelligence,* which depends uniquely on the use of symbolic or semantic information.

The process or nature of the operation performed on the content of intellectual activity (e.g., what the individual is asked to do with the figural or symbolic information) determines the *level of intellectual functioning.* In this case convergent productive thinking or the synthesizing of a large body of information represents a higher level of cognitive functioning than simple recognition or recall of that same information; similarly, evaluation of information represents a higher level of cognitive functioning than convergent productive thinking (see Figure 1.2). Therefore intellectual or cognitive functioning might be most simply described as the ability of the individual to efficiently *process different kinds* of information (figural versus symbolic or semantic) at different levels of complexity (recognition versus synthesis or evaluation of information). Although Guilford (1967) does not state this directly, his use of the model implies that more complex modes of cognitive functioning (e.g., the use of abstract information in evaluative activities) may be to some extent dependent upon (or supported by) adequate development of lower levels of functioning (e.g., efficient recall of concrete or figural information). Thus, according to Guilford's formulation there may be two kinds of intelligence and five levels of intellectual functioning.

THE LINK BETWEEN PERCEPTION AND COGNITION

In our previous discussion of perceptual-motor functioning, perception was described as a set of sensory-perceptual processes concerned with the pick-up, processing, and analyzing of information about sensory and motor events taking place in the immediate environment. It is evident from this description that perception may be thought of as a part of an information-processing system that is primarily concerned with the handling or processing of concrete or figural information. Thus we might think of perception and cognition as making up two ends of a continuum of information processing, a continuum that deals at one end with concrete or figural information and at the other end with more abstract forms of information (see Figure 1.3). If this is indeed the case, the distinction between perception and cognition is a fine one—one that has more to do with the *kind* of information processed than with how or at what level the information is processed. Thus perception may indeed be a rudimentary form of intelligence or cognition, and it might be thought of as a "building block" for the development of the ability to process or use abstract information—the kind of information more uniquely involved in human cognitive or intellectual activity.

There is little doubt that the figural base of letters, words, and sentences (which are the substance of symbolic or abstract thinking) needs to be adequately processed before the words and sentences themselves can become meaningful abstractions. This notion is readily illustrated in the experience that individuals undergo when they are presented a single word tachistoscopically (e.g., the word *sad* is flashed onto a screen for durations of one millisecond each). With the first exposure the individual is aware that something is present on the screen, probably due to variations in brightness seen in the stimulus. However, no particular form or organization can be ascribed to what is seen. Some authors compare this to the

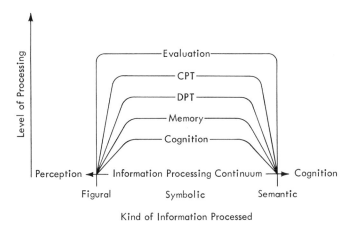

FIGURE 1.3   The Link Between Perception and Cognition (After Guilford, 1967)

process of sensation. On the second flash the individual takes in a little more information and becomes aware that the nature of the stimulus is in the form of lines, although the organization of the lines into letter forms is still not perceived. With about the third flash the observer is aware that the stimulus is composed of letters, and he or she is able to identify one or two of those letters. Most psychologists would agree that perception is now under way if it has not already occurred. The information processing that has gone on to this point has had to do with the processing of figural or concrete information—the number, shape, and relationship of the lines that make up the letters in the word. With the next flash the individual is aware that there are three letters present and that these letters form a word. On the fifth exposure the meaning of the word arises. The last two exposures seem to allow for symbolic and semantic dimensions of the stimulus to be processed and consciously recognized. In this sense perception may overlap and/or precede cognition. That is, the figural base for more abstract meaning or interpretation of stimulus information occurs before the symbolic/semantic meaning of the information arises. Therefore perception may provide the foundation for higher-order, abstract, intellectual operations.

PERCEPTUAL-MOTOR DEVELOPMENT AND PERCEPTION

To take our analysis of the intellect and the relationship between perceptual-motor and cognitive functioning a step further, we must look at the nature of the relationship between perceptual-motor functioning and the process of perception. We indicated earlier that certain sensory-perceptual processes are prerequisite to (provide the foundation for) the formulation and performance of many, if not most, motor acts. This, of course, strongly intimates that there is an integral interrelationship between perception and perceptual-motor functioning at early stages of development. We also know that perceptual-motor functioning affects the development and refinement of perceptual processes *per se*. Several authors (Held and Bauer, 1967; Held and Bossom, 1961; Held and Hein, 1963) have shown that young animals that are restricted in terms of active movement in or interaction with their external environments (such animals are passively moved in or through the environment but are never allowed to move on their own) exhibit difficulty with selected visual discriminations, with visual control of movement, with depth perception, and with visual placing responses. The implications of these studies is that the information feedback or reafference provided by active movement in the environment (an integral part of perceptual-motor functioning) is used by the system (brain) to modify underlying perceptual processes, modifications that eventually lead to more refined perceptual functioning. Thus the use of the senses in or through perceptual-motor activity may provide the stimulus needed for continued growth and/or refinement of the senses.

More dramatic than the foregoing observations are those reported by Dru, *et al.* (1975). In this study rats were trained to discriminate between vertical (|||||) and horizontal (≡) bars. After these discriminations were learned, the rats were subjected to an operation in which one striate (visual) cortex was removed. The striate cortex is a part of the brain directly concerned with the reception and simple analysis of visual input. When the animals had fully recovered, one group was allowed to move actively in a visually stimulating environment. The second group was moved passively about the same environment. All the animals were then subjected to a second operation in which the remaining striate cortex was removed. Generally when the full striate cortex is removed, organisms are for all intents and purposes functionally blind (Doty, 1971). In this instance, however, the animals that had been allowed to move actively in their environment retained some of their original ability to discriminate between vertical and horizontal bars and were able to relearn that discrimination to its original level. The animals that were moved passively lost this capacity and could not relearn it. The authors suggest that, for whatever reason, the stimulation (information feedback) derived from active movement of the animals through their environment provided a means by which nonvisual areas of the brain were able to take over functions that were previously under the control of the visual system. In an indirect but dramatic way, these data suggest that one of the consequences of active movement is an increased capacity for perceptual functioning.

THE LINK BETWEEN
PERCEPTUAL-MOTOR AND
COGNITIVE FUNCTIONING

The link between perceptual-motor and cognitive functioning seems to be an indirect one. Perceptual-motor functioning, through its emphasis on and concern with the development of sensory and motor processes associated with active movement and physical exploration of the external environment, probably provides the basic foundation for the development of a higher-order information processing system upon which more sophisticated perceptual and cognitive processes can ultimately be built. Evidence clearly suggests that the reafference provided to the growing, developing organism as a result of its active interaction with the environment is a stimulus for continued perceptual growth. Evidence that perception and cognition may be but slightly different dimensions of the same basic information processing system further suggests that the proposed link between perceptual-motor and cognitive functioning and/or development is at least a logical possibility and should not be totally ignored. It should remain foremost in the minds of the readers, however, that this link, if it exists, is at best a tenuous and indirect one.

A HEBBIAN PERSPECTIVE

Can the connection/relationship among perceptual-motor development, perception, and cognition be made on any basis other than that previously proposed? Is there neurological or biological support for such proposed linkages? For a slightly different perspective, let us turn to the work of D. O. Hebb. Hebb (1949), in his *The Organization of Behavior,* suggests that there are two major factors at work in intelligent and/or adaptive behavior: (a) innate potential, or "intelligence A", which is best described as the possession of a good brain and good neural metabolism; and (b) "intelligence B", or the functioning of a brain in which some development has occurred. This development, he proposes, consists of permanent changes in the organization of the brain that are due primarily to experience. The development of the individual's intelligent or adaptive behavior thus proceeds to the limit set by heredity or the environment, whichever is lower. Given a perfect environment, heredity sets the limits for the ultimate development of adaptive behavior; given the heredity of a genius, the environment sets the pace for such development. Thus more than 30 years ago Hebb clearly suggested that one's innate potential for development was not a guarantee that such development would occur; rather he asserted that environmental conditions had to be appropriate to stimulate or promote optimum development.

It seems clear that Hebb (1949) equates intellectual development with central nervous system (CNS) development or optimum neurological functioning. Since there are abundant data available to support such a notion, the question that must be asked of Hebb's proposal is, "What are the conditions that are necessary for optimum development of the CNS and thereby intelligent or adaptive behavior?" There is considerable evidence from animal studies that one ingredient that is necessary for continued growth and development of the CNS in young organisms is sensory stimulation—in particular sensory stimulation provided to the animal via natural or enriched sensory-motor experiences. In support of this notion, numerous studies have reported that the brains of animals that have had such enriched environmental experiences are identifiably different from those that have not had such experiences. The brains of sensory-enriched animals show important changes in anatomical and biochemical parameters—parameters that are thought to be indicative of a more efficiently functioning brain. Hebb's approach might lead one to speculate that sensory stimulation, provided by early sensory-motor experiences (e.g., active interaction of the growing organism with its external environment), influences the functional development of the nervous system. If intellectual or cognitive development is in any way a reflection of optimal brain function and development, then it would seem that sensory-motor experience, similar to those integral to perceptual-motor functioning, would be at least one important contributor to the development of adequate cognitive behavior. The practical connection between brain function and perceptual-motor development is again a loose, indirect one, but one that must be given some consideration. It seems logical that the sensory-motor experiences the young child undergoes as he grows and develops must provide some of the stimulation needed for continued functional brain growth.

BEHAVIORAL STUDIES OF PERCEPTUAL-MOTOR AND COGNITIVE FUNCTIONING

Numerous studies have been devoted to studying the nature and extent of the relationship among the behavioral domains of perceptual-motor development, perception, and cognition (e.g., Belka and Williams, 1979a, 1979b; Chissom et al., 1972; Thomas and Chissom, 1972, 1973, 1974). Most of these studies have reported positive but minimal support for the general notion that perceptual-motor development, perception, and cognition are interrelated facets of behavior and that perceptual-motor development may provide an important foundation for the development of more sophisticated perceptual and cognitive functioning. Many studies, however, have reported little or no relationship among the three behavioral domains. For example, Chissom, Thomas, and Biasiotto (1972) found a canonical correlation of .70 between two measures of perceptual-motor development (Shape-O-Ball and the Frostig tests) and four criteria of academic success in kindergarten children (e.g., reading readiness and verbal and quantitative ability). Chissom and Thomas (1974) showed in another study that two selected measures of perception and perceptual-motor development (Shape-O-Ball and Frostig) were moderately good predictors of academic readiness in preschool children whereas two others were not (a balance task and a general test of motor development). When Chissom and Thomas (1973) examined the relationship between perceptual-motor and cognitive domains in disadvantaged preschool children, they found little or no relationship between these two behavioral domains. In addition, Singer and Brunk (1967) studied the interrelationships among academic achievement, physical characteristics, and perceptual-motor abilities in third and sixth-grade children using simple correlation techniques. The children studied had an average I.Q. of 116.5 and were achieving at a level approximately two grades higher than their grade placement. Results indicated that there was little or no relationship between perceptual-motor abilities, physical and motor characteristics of these children, and measures of intellectual achievement. This was true for both third- and sixth-graders. This finding could, in part, be a result of the fact that all of the children included in the study were over 8 years of age and, in addition, were advanced in intellectual functioning—both of which conditions could contribute to a masking of interrelationships among the behaviors studied.

The most recent and comprehensive set of studies that has looked at relationships among perceptual-motor development, perception, and cognition is that by Belka and Williams (1979a, 1979b). These investigators looked first at the canonical correlation among clusters of behaviors representing each of the perceptual-motor, perceptual, and cognitive behavioral domains in 180 children ranging in age from 57 months to 92 months (there were 63 children from each of prekindergarten, kindergarten and first-grade levels). The perceptual-motor domain was defined as that domain of behaviors that predominantly involved overt motor behavior but that required the reception and analysis of specific sensory-perceptual information for skillful or controlled regulation of the motor act.

Two subdomains were identified: (a) gross perceptual-motor behaviors, defined as motor behaviors that predominantly emphasized or involved skillful movement or coordination of the total body (running, jumping, etc.); and (b) fine perceptual-motor behaviors, defined as motor acts that predominantly involved or required the use of the hands and fingers in producing precision movements.

The perceptual domain was defined as those behaviors that primarily emphasized the reception, analysis and/or interpretation of concrete sensory data. The motor component in such behaviors was minimal and was used only as a means of obtaining a measure of the adequacy of the perceptual behavior. Two subdomains were outlined: (a) visual perception, defined as the ability to identify and/or discriminate among various kinds of concrete visual stimuli; and (b) auditory perception, defined as the ability to discriminate among different basic sounds, the ability to retain or remember auditory information, and the ability to solve auditory figure-ground problems.

The cognitive domain was defined as that domain of behaviors that required the processing and interpretation of symbolic and/or semantic information in order to arrive at a solution to a problem. No attempt was

TABLE 1-1 Evaluative Instruments Used to Measure Behaviors Representing Perceptual-Motor, Perceptual, and Cognitive Domains

	SUBDOMAINS	
BEHAVIORAL DOMAIN	GROSS MOTOR*	FINE MOTOR
Perceptual-Motor	Controlled Catching Overarm Throw Modified Stork Stand Plank Walk (Balance) Agility	Shape-O-Ball Bender Gestalt Frostig Eye-Motor Coordination
	VISUAL	AUDITORY
Perceptual	Frostig Figure-Ground Frostig Position in Space ITPA Visual Reception ITPA Visual Sequential Memory ITPA Visual Closure	ITPA Auditory Reception ITPA Auditory Sequential Memory ITPA Auditory Closure Wepman's Auditory Discrimination
Cognitive	Prekindergarten—Boehm Test of Basic Concepts Kindergarten—Metropolitan Readiness Tests First Grade—Primary Reading Profiles California Test of Mental Maturity	

*From Cashin's Test of Motor Development, 1974

Source: After Belka and Williams, 1979a. See Preface for full credit line.

Table 1-2   Summary of Results of Study of Relationships Among Perceptual-Motor, Perceptual, and Cognitive Behavioral Domains

BEHAVIORAL DOMAINS	AGE OF CHILDREN		
	PREKINDERGARTEN	KINDERGARTEN	FIRST GRADE
Perceptual-Motor to Perceptual	Relationship Sig; Rc = .754	Relationship Sig; Rc = .735	Relationship NOT Sig; Rc = .722
Perceptual to Cognitive	Relationship Sig; Rc = .795	Relationship Sig; Rc = .843	Relationship Sig; Rc = .787
Perceptual-Motor to Cognitive	Relationship NOT Sig; Rc = .626	Relationship Sig; Rc = .728	Relationship NOT Sig; Rc = .645

Source: After Belka and Williams, 1979a

made to evaluate the total scope of cognitive behaviors in these young children. Instruments used to measure behaviors within each of the domains are described in Table 1-1.

Results of the study are summarized in Table 1-2 and indicate that there was a significant relationship between perceptual-motor and perceptual-behavioral domains for five- and six-year-olds but not for children 7 years or older (first-graders). This suggests that the close association that existed between these two behavioral domains for younger children is diminished or reduced in older children. The relationship between perceptual and cognitive domains was fairly high and significant for all ages. This suggests that a strong link, at least in terms of selected behavioral measures, may exist between perception and cognition for five-, six-, and seven-year-old children. Interestingly, other authors (e.g., Chang and Chang, 1967; Dibner and Korn, 1969; Birch and Belmont, 1965) have reported decreasing relationships between perceptual and cognitive behaviors with increasing age. This work, however, was done with children who were older than seven.

The correlations between perceptual-motor and cognitive development were the lowest of all reported. Only for kindergarteners was the relationship between the two behavioral domains significant (Rc = .728).

These observations suggest that there is a more tenuous, less direct linkage between perceptual-motor and cognitive development than between perceptual-motor and perceptual and between perceptual and cognitive behavioral domains. This is not a surprising finding, for perceptual-motor theory would predict that, because of the hierarchical nature of development, the relationship between the foundational level of perceptual-motor development and the highest level of cognitive or intellectual functioning would not be as great as the relationship between any two adjacent levels of development. These data thus tend to lend some support to the notion that there are small but identifiable interrelationships among perceptual-motor development, perceptual, and cognitive functioning in young children (5-7 years of age). Equally important is the rather consistent finding throughout the study that fine motor behaviors were the most important contributors to whatever relationship existed between perceptual-motor development and perception and between perceptual-motor development and cognitive functioning at all age levels. Gross motor behaviors, on the other hand, although moderately correlated with fine motor behaviors, were relatively unimportant at any age in terms of a significant contribution to such relationships. This suggests that fine motor control may be an important dimension of behavior to pay attention to in the young preschool and early school-age child.

Subsequent to this original study, Belka and Williams (1979b) conducted a follow-up study, one year later, using the same children. The purpose of the follow-up study was to determine whether or not later cognitive development could be predicted from knowledge about earlier performances on perceptual and perceptual-motor tasks. All of the children were reevaluated one year later using the original tests that represented the cognitive behavioral domain. Regression equations were developed. Results indicated that cognitive development at kindergarten level could be predicted from knowledge of the child's performance on perceptual-motor and perceptual tasks at prekindergarten levels. Prediction of cognitive functioning at first or second grades from knowledge of earlier perceptual-motor and perceptual functioning, however, was not as accurate. Generally, prediction of cognitive performance at first grade, and particularly at second grade, was best when it was based on information about earlier cognitive functioning. These observations clearly suggest that beyond the age of 5-6 years, whatever linkages may exist among the three behavioral domains become more tenuous and less readily identifiable. Overall, behavioral studies suggest that although there may be some intricate interrelationships among perceptual-motor, perceptual, and cognitive functioning in young children, these relationships undergo important changes with increasing age and are quite small, if existent at all, after 6-7 years of age.

PERCEPTUAL-MOTOR, PERCEPTUAL, AND COGNITIVE FUNCTIONING IN SLOWLY DEVELOPING CHILDREN

Any discussion of the nature of perceptual-motor, perceptual, and cognitive development in young children would be incomplete without some mention of the nature of such functioning in children whose development is known to be different from that which is generally associated with so-called normal development. For simplicity's sake we will refer to such children as slowly developing children. A large number of studies have been conducted that have attempted to look at differences and similarities between slowly and normally developing children in terms of their perceptual-motor, perceptual, and cognitive development. A typical study is that of Williams, *et al.* (1978a). These authors compared performances of 32 slowly developing children (average chronological age 9 years) with those of 109 normally developing six- and eight-year-olds on (a) 15 measures of sensory-perceptual functioning; (b) two simple perceptual-motor tasks; and (c) three cognitive tasks (paired-associate learning tasks). The slowly developing children were of normal intelligence and were enrolled in learning and behavior disorders classes in the public schools; all of the slowly developing children showed a one- to two-year discrepancy between their level of intelligence and their level of achievement in school. The test battery used to evaluate the sensory-perceptual abilities of these children is summarized in Table 1-3.

In general, the slowly developing children, even though chronologically older, performed at a level similar to six-year-olds on visual-perception tasks and intermediate to six- and eight-year-olds on most of the other auditory, tactile-kinesthetic, and intersensory integration tests. A profile of the sensory-perceptual abilities of the three groups of children, based on standard scores, clearly shows this (See Figure 1.4). If one looks closely at these profile data, one immediately notices that their most striking feature is the relatively even profile of performances across all tasks for normally developing six- and eight-year-olds. In contrast to this is the much more jagged, uneven profile of the older slowly developing children, who seem to hover between the six- and eight-year-olds in terms of their level of development. The major difference between normally developing six- and eight-year-old children seems to be one of level of development and not of the pattern or shape of development *per se*. Overall these observations suggest that slowly developing children (e.g., children with some minimal developmental delay) tend to function more like children who are 1-2 years younger than they are in terms of their basic sensory-perceptual abilities. In addition, because they also tend to show a more jagged profile of per-

TABLE 1-3   Tasks Used to Evaluate Sensory-Perceptual Functioning in Slowly and Normally Developing Children

	MODALITY			
	VISUAL	AUDITORY	TACTILE-KINESTHETIC	INTERSENSORY INTEGRATION
T A S K S	Figure-Ground Perception (Ayres, 1966)	Auditory Discrimination (Wepman, 1973)	Tactile Localization (Ayres, 1966)	Tactile-Visual Integration, (Williams et al., 1978b)
	Visual memory (Williams et al., 1978b)	Auditory Attention Span— Unrelated Words (Barber and Leland, 1958)	Tactile Integration (Williams et al., 1978b)	Auditory-Visual Integration (Birch and Belmont, 1965)
	Dynamic Depth Perception (Williams et al., 1978b)	Auditory Attention Span—Related Syllables (Barber and Leland, 1958)	Movement Awareness (Temple and Williams, 1974)	Auditory-Tactile Integration (Williams et al., 1978b)
	Visual Discrimination (Williams et al., 1978b)	Auditory Sequential Memory (Kirk et al., 1968)	Spatial Orientation (Williams et al., 1978b)	

Source: After Williams et al., 1978a

ceptual development, one might predict that they would have greater difficulty mastering tasks that require the use of or reliance on several different perceptual abilities.

These same children were asked to perform two simple perceptual-motor tasks, one involving fine eye-hand coordination and the other involving gross motor control. In general, slowly developing children performed similarly to six-year-old children on both of these perceptual-motor tasks. Normally developing eight-year-olds were significantly superior to both of the other groups in terms of their ability to learn and/or perform the two tasks. When the three groups of children were asked to perform a series of paired-associated learning tasks (selected to represent one aspect of higher levels of cognitive functioning), results again indicated that older slowly developing children performed at a level similar to that of normally

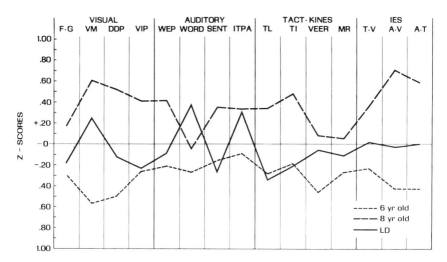

FIGURE 1.4   Profile of Sensory-Perceptual Abilities of Young Normally and Slowly Developing Children

developing six-year-olds. Performances of normally developing eight-year-olds were, as with the perceptual-motor tasks, significantly superior to both of these groups of children. Overall these data suggest that perceptual-motor, perceptual, and cognitive functioning in children with minimal developmental delays may be at lower levels than is true for normally developing children of similar chronological ages. Broadly interpreted, these observations could be construed to indicate that there is some inherent link among perceptual-motor, perceptual, and cognitive behavior in young children, and when one aspect of that development is delayed or altered, the other related dimensions of the child's development also show some delay. Thus behavioral studies on slowly developing children lend indirect support to the notion that there may be some as yet not clearly defined interrelationship among perceptual-motor, perceptual, and cognitive functioning.

SUMMARY

1. Perceptual-motor functioning may be thought of as a continuous cycle of four basic events. These include *sensory-perceptual decisions* that are prerequisite to and necessary for the formulation of *motor decisions* that are in turn prerequisite and necessary for the actual performance of the motor or movement behavior itself. Last are the *information-feedback events* that are used to evaluate and/or modify the sensory-perceptual and motor decisions that led to the original movement behavior.

2. *Perceptual-motor development* is that part of the child's development that is concerned with the changes that take place with age in the movement behavior of the young child—changes that represent improvements in or modifications of the underlying sensory-perceptual-motor-feedback processes involved in perceptual-motor functioning.

3. From a behavioral point of view, perceptual-motor development may be thought of as the acquiring of those basic, fundamental skills that provide the child with the means for dealing effectively with his or her physical environment.

4. Perceptual-motor skills include gross-motor-control behaviors, fine-motor-control behaviors, body awareness behaviors, and simple perceptual skills.

5. Most children develop these fundamental perceptual-motor skills naturally; however, many need help in acquiring optimum levels of functioning in these areas.

6. Perceptual-motor development is believed to be intricately interrelated with perceptual and cognitive dimensions of development.

7. Piaget suggests that this relationship exists in the following forms during the early developmental years: (a) in the *sensory-motor period* (0-2 years), actions exist and are executed independently of true thought or cognition; (b) in the *preoperation period* (2-7 years), action is thought and thought is action; (c) in the *concrete operations period* (7-11 years), thought precedes and guides action but does not function independently of it; and (d) *formal operations period* (11 years and older), thought operates independently of action.

8. Guilford further suggests that perception is a form of concrete intelligence and that perception should be thought of as a building block for the development of cognitive and/or intellectual activity.

9. Movement (perceptual-motor behavior) is integral to the development and refinement of the basic sensory systems that are vital to the development of effective perceptual skills.

10. Most recent behavioral evidence suggests that there are small but important interrelationships among perceptual-motor development, perception, and cognitive functioning in young children 4-7 years of age. These relationships are stronger for four- and five-year-olds than for older children.

11. There is some evidence to suggest that for slowly developing children, there is an important link among perceptual-motor, perceptual, and cognitive behavior, and when one aspect of that development is delayed, other related dimensions of the child's behavior may also show some alteration or delay.

1. Using "kicking" as an example, describe and/or show how the following are related:
   a. sensory-perceptual decisions
   b. motor decisions
   c. reafference
   d. perceptual-motor functioning
2. Give an example of the kind of information feedback that might be available to a child when she/he is walking a balance beam.
3. Define perceptual-motor development. How does it relate to perceptual-motor functioning?
4. Describe and give examples of the four basic categories of perceptual-motor behaviors.
5. How is perceptual-motor development related to perceptual functioning? To cognitive development? What evidence is there to support these proposed relationships?
6. Piaget suggests that the process of symbolization ties perceptual-motor development to cognitive development. How does he explain or justify this?
7. Guilford suggests that the intelligence is composed of two components: content and process. Define each of these, give examples, and show how he uses these components to suggest that "perception is a form of concrete intelligence."
8. Using Guilford's model as a basis, define perception and cognition.
9. Describe from Hebb's point of view how "movement experiences" may be connected to intelligent or adaptive behaviors.
10. Explain what behavioral studies suggest about:
    a. the relationship between perceptual-motor development and cognitive functioning in normal children;
    b. the relationship between perceptual-motor development and perceptual functioning in normal children;
    c. the relationships among perceptual-motor, perceptual, and cognitive development in slowly developing children.

REFERENCES

AYRES, A.J. *Southern California Sensory-Motor Integration Tests.* Los Angeles, Western Psychological Corporation, 1966.
BARBER, L., AND LELAND, B. *Detract Tests of Learning Aptitude.* Indianapolis, IN: The Bobbs Merrill Company, Inc., 1958.
BELKA, D., AND WILLIAMS, H. Canonical relationships among perceptual-motor, perceptual and cognitive behaviors in young, normal children. Unpublished paper, University of Toledo, 1978.

BELKA, D., AND WILLIAMS, H.   Prediction of later cognitive behavior from early school perceptual-motor, perceptual and cognitive performances. *Perceptual and Motor Skills.* 49 (1979): 131-141.

BIRCH, H., AND BELMONT, I.   Auditory-visual integration, intelligence and reading ability in school children. *Perceptual and Motor Skills.* 20 (1965): 295-305.

CASHIN, G.   *The Reliability of Selected Tests of Motor Performance in Prekindergarten Children.* Unpublished master's thesis, Bowling Green State University, Fall, 1974.

CHANG, T.M.C., AND CHANG, V.A.C.   Relation of visual-motor skills and reading achievement in primary grade pupils of superior ability. *Perceptual and Motor Skills.* 24 (1967): 51-53.

CHISSOM, B.S., THOMAS, J.R., AND BIASIOTTO, J.   Canonical validity of perceptual-motor skills for predicting an academic criterion. *Educational and Psychological Measurement.* 32 (1972): 1095-1098.

DIBNER, A., AND KORN, E.   Group administration of the Bender-Gestalt test to predict early school achievement. *Journal of Clinical Psychology.* 25 (1969): 263-268.

DOTY, R.W.   Survival of pattern vision after removal of striate cortex in the adult cat. *Comparative Neurology.* 143 (1971): 341-370.

DRU, D., WALKER, J.P., AND WALKER, J.B.   Self-produced locomotion restores visual capacity after striate lesions. *Science.* 187 (1975): 265-266.

GESCHWIND, N.   Later changes in the nervous system: an overview. In Stein, Rosen, and Butters, *Plasticity and Recovery of Function in the CNS.* New York: Academic Press, 1974.

GOLDMAN, P.S.   Developmental Determinants of Cortical Plasticity. *Acta Neuro-biologiae Experimentia.* 32 (1972): 495-511.

GREENOUGH, W., FASS, B., AND DEVOOGD, T.   The influence of experience on recovery following brain damage in rodents: hypothesis based on developmental research. In Walsh and Greenough, *Environments as Therapy for Brain Dysfunction,* pp. 10-50. New York: Plenum Press, 1976.

GUILFORD, J.   *The Nature of Human Intelligence.* New York: McGraw-Hill Book Company, 1967.

HEBB, D.O.   *The Organization of Behavior.* New York: John Wiley and Sons, Inc., 1949.

HELD, R., AND BAUER, J.   Visually-guided reaching in infant monkeys after restricted rearing. *Science.* 155 (1967): 718-720.

HELD, R., AND BOSSOM, J.   Neonatal deprivation and adult rearrangement: complementary techniques for analyzing plastic sensory-motor coordinations. *Journal of Comparative and Physiological Psychology.* 54 (1961): 33-37.

HELD, R., AND HEIN, A.   Movement produced stimulation in the development of visually-guided behavior. *Journal of Comparative and Physiological Psychology.* 56 (1963): 872-876.

KIRK, S.   *Illinois Test of Psycholinguistic Abilities.* Urbana, IL: University of Illinois Press, 1968.

PIAGET, J.   *The Child and Reality.* New York: Grossman Publishers, 1973.

PIAGET, J.   *The Origins of Intelligence.* New York: W.W. Norton and Company, Inc., 1963.

PIAGET, J., AND INHELDER, B.   *The Child's Conception of Space.* New York: W.W. Norton and Company, Inc., 1967.

PIAGET, J., AND INHELDER, B.   *The Early Growth of Logic in the Child.* New York: W.W. Norton and Company, Inc., 1969.

ROSENZWEIG, M.R.   Effects of environment on development of brain and of behavior. In Toback, Aronson, and Shaw, eds. *The Biopsychology of Development,* pp. 303-342. New York: Academic Press, 1971.

ROSENZWEIG, M.R., AND BENNETT, E.L.   Cerebral changes in rats exposed individually to an enriched environment. *Journal of Comparative Physiological Psychology.* 80 (1972): 304-313.

ROSENWEIG, M., BENNETT, E., AND DIAMOND, M.   Brain changes in response to experience. *Scientific American.* 226(2) (1972): 22-30.

SINGER, R.N., AND BRUNK, J.W.   Relation of perceptual-motor ability in elementary school children. *Perceptual and Motor Skills.* 24 (1967): 967-970.

THOMAS, J.R. AND CHISSOM, B.S.   An investigation of the combination of a perceptual-motor test and a cognitive ability test for the purpose of classifying first-grade children into reading groups. *Psychology in the Schools.* 10(2) (1973): 185-189.

THOMAS, J.R., AND CHISSOM, B.S.   Prediction of first grade academic performances from kindergarten perceptual-motor data. *The Research Quarterly.* 45(2) (1974): 148-153.

THOMAS, J.R., AND CHISSOM, B.S.   Relationships as assessed by canonical correlation between perceptual-motor and intellectual abilities for preschool and early elementary age children. *Journal of Motor Behavior.* 4(1) (1972): 23-29.

WEPMAN, J.   *Auditory Discrimination Test.* Chicago, IL: Language Research Associates, 1973.

WILLIAMS, H.   Neurological concepts and perceptual-motor functioning. In *New Perspectives of Man in Action*, edited by Cratty, B., and Brown, R. Englewood Cliffs, NJ: Prentice-Hall, Inc., 1968.

WILLIAMS, H.   Perceptual-motor development in young children. Unpublished paper, University of Toledo, 1974.

WILLIAMS, H., TEMPLE, I., AND BATEMAN, J.   Perceptual-motor and cognitive learning in the young child. *Psychology of Motor Behavior and Sport II.* 1978, Human Kinetics Press, Champaign, IL.

WILLIAMS, H., TEMPLE, I., AND BATEMAN, J.   A test battery to assess intrasensory and intersensory development of young children. *Perceptual and Motor Skills.* 48 (1979): 643-659.

CHAPTER TWO
GROWTH AND DEVELOPMENT OF THE NERVOUS SYSTEM: SELECTED TOPICS

An awareness of some of the simpler aspects of the growth and development of the nervous system is vital to the total understanding of the nature and importance of perceptual-motor development in young children. The intent of this chapter is to help the reader become familiar with some of the more current and significant facts about the structural and functional growth of the nervous system, the factors that affect such growth, and the relationship between the development of the nervous system and the early development of motor behavior in the young organism. Since some of the language and concepts related to the study of the CNS will not be familiar to many readers, a glossary of basic terms is provided at the end of the chapter.

EARLY DEVELOPMENT OF THE NERVOUS SYSTEM

What are the beginnings of the development of the nervous system? It would appear that six major events are associated with early CNS development. First there is the generation of immature neurons themselves (cell proliferation). These neurons become specified as to general type (e.g., pyramidal versus nonpyramidal) and as to their final destination or location within the nervous system. Different cell types then migrate to different sites remote from their place of birth and orient themselves in proper relationship to other cells making up those structures (cell migration). The final position of the neuron in the nervous system is related to its time of origin, so that early generated neurons, for example, occupy deeper layers of the cerebral cortex, and later generated neurons occupy outer layers. Once the cells have reached their final position in the nervous system, they begin to elaborate axons and dendrites and become ready to accept synaptic input (cell differentiation). The last event to occur in early brain development is the occurrence of myelin sheaths along pathways linking neurons in different parts of the brain. The process of myelination helps to ensure the speed and fidelity of nerve impulse transmission. At different times during this series of events, waves of glial cells (structural and functional support cells of the CNS) are generated, and redundant neurons die and are removed. It is believed that the CNS originally possesses many more neurons than it needs to complete the building of its structures, and that an important part of early development is the paring away of those neurons not needed to complete the structural make-up of the brain. Thus normal brain development seems to depend on a rather exact sequence of integrated biological events including cell proliferation, migration, differentiation, myelination, and cell death (Cowan, 1978; Herschkowitz and Rossi, 1972; Purpura, 1974).

There is considerable evidence to suggest that the early development of the CNS (embryonic and fetal) is largely hereditarily determined. For example, if embryonic brain cells are removed from a living organism and are dissociated (via a centrification process) and placed in a cell culture, within 24 hours these cells reassociate, form cell aggregates, and show a high degree of cellular organization. There is within this time period a 20-fold increase in the number of cells (cell proliferation), just as in vivo (e.g., in the living organism). Within 5 to 15 days, these brain cell cultures undergo cell migration (cells move to different parts of the culture) and begin a process of differentiation during which biochemical and enzymatic properties of the cells begin to be outlined. From 17 to 33 days, identifiable morphological changes take place; thus asymmetrical and narrow synaptic junctions can be seen; there are a few synaptic vesicles present but no evidence of myelination. After approximately 33 days these morphological changes are more definite. Some myelination has occurred; there are increasingly larger numbers of synapses with wide synaptic gaps; there are more synaptic vesicles present and for the first time mitochondria (bodies that help to provide energy needed for neuronal activity) can be seen (Cowan, 1978). These processes are nearly identical to those observed in brain development in vivo. If, then, brain cell cultures act like true brain growth processes, early prenatal and embryonic brain development must be regulated to a great degree by rather specific, predetermined hereditary programs. Such programs, however, do seem to be modifiable to some extent by prevailing hormonal, metabolic, nutritional, and experiential conditions (Purpura, 1974, 1977).

Axonal Growth

During or right after cell migration formation of specific cell structures occurs. Neurons grow axons and dendrites and form synaptic interconnections. (A neuron consists of the cell body and its axons and dendrites.) Glial cells are formed and differentiate into two kinds of cells: astroglia and oligodendroglia. The latter type of glia are important for they provide the basis and support for the development of myelin.

Specification of neurons as to type is probably biochemically set. Basically neurons may be categorized as sensory, motor, and central or internuncial neurons. As tissues etc. are formed, they are innervated by nerve fibers. Newly formed sensory neurons send out axons that often travel long distances to reach their terminal endings. Each axon follows a more or less specific path to its final location in the nervous system. Thus axons of sensory neurons have a high degree of biochemical specificity and ultimately match up with sensory end-organs or tissues that have a similar biochemical profile. This specificity seems to be present early in development and cannot be changed even by surgical rearrangement, for when certain cells (e.g., pyramidal) are inverted, the axon will grow a short distance and then turn abruptly through an appropriate angle and grow in the direction of its predetermined end-target destination (Cowan, 1978).

Although the terminal targets of motor neuron axons seem not to be quite as specific as for sensory neurons, there is still a great deal of specificity involved in this growth process. The growth of motor neuron axons is guided in part by the chronological order in which they mature and differentiate as well as by the biochemical properties that they possess. In the case of motor neuron innervation of muscles, when the axon of a motor neuron makes contact with a muscle, biochemical specificity is induced into the muscle, so that the two (the axon of the motor neuron and the muscle it innervates) match up biochemically. Once biochemical specificity of the neuromuscular junction is established, sensory and central neurons form their synaptic connections with the motor neuron on the basis of matching biochemical characteristics. This completes the important neuronal connections between the peripheral musculature and the CNS.

Cell Death

There is a sizeable elimination of neurons during early development of the nervous system. In some organisms cell death involves 40% to 75% of the original number of neurons generated. Most neuronal death seems to occur when cells are establishing their synaptic connections. It may be that the outgrowing cell processes compete with each other for a limited number of synaptic sites or for some function that is essential for their maintenance. Those that do not compete successfully die. Such cell death helps to bring about functional stabilization of synaptic contacts (Cowan, 1978; Herschkowitz and Rossi, 1972).

Cell DNA and RNA

The evolution of RNA and DNA in human brain development is important, for these nucleic acids carry genetic information and are fundamentally important in controlling multiplication, migration, association, and differentiation of developing neurons. The amount of DNA in the nervous system increases 20 to 25 fold from 4 weeks to the end of gestation; postnatally DNA increases only two to three fold and reaches adult values by one year. RNA increases similarly to DNA during prenatal development but continues to increase more rapidly postnatally, so that by maturity it has increased some ten fold (Mandel *et al.*, 1974).

THE DEVELOPMENT OF SYNAPSES

The importance of synapses to the early development and later functioning of the brain is seen in the fact that deficits or abnormalities in synapses seem to be the underlying problem in many kinds of mental deficiencies in man (Cragg, 1974; Purpura, 1977). (A synapse is essentially a junction or connection between two neurons.) One possible explanation for retardation has been that synaptic connections between neurons in the cerebral cortex are greatly reduced or that for some reason cortical neurons are synaptically connected during development into "incorrect" neuronal circuits. The effectiveness of communication between neurons and thus among widespread parts of the nervous system depends on the number and individual strength of synapses (connections) formed during development (Cragg, 1974).

The course of synaptogenesis or development of synapses has been established via electron microscopic studies on animals. Synapses develop initially on dendritic shafts (the major extension of the dendrite) and later on dendritic spines (smaller outgrowths of the shaft) and neuron cell bodies. The maturation of synapses follows a fairly uniform pattern: First, presynaptic cells (cells before the synapse) develop a few synaptic vesicles (these contain the neuro-transmitter, a substance needed for nerve impulse transmission); next thickenings appear in the membranes of the two cells that form the synapse (e.g., the pre- and post-synaptic cells); and finally more synaptic vesicles appear in the presynaptic cell. Gradually there is an increase in synaptic density. All of these events take place as early as 8.5 weeks of gestation, so that by that time the fetus has approximately five synapses per mm² of nerve tissue. The number of synapses increases rapidly throughout the period of gestation. True synapses are usually not seen in the cerebral cortex until approximately 23 weeks of gestation. It has been estimated that there is an average of 30,000 synapses to one axon in the adult human cortex. If the presence of synapses indicates anything about the functional maturity of the brain, then cortical activity is just beginning to develop toward the end of the gestational period. Thus we see that some aspects of neuronal circuitry are established very early in life (Cragg, 1974; Molliver *et al.*, 1973).

The development of some synapses is independent of sensory stimulation; others, however, cannot or do not form without appropriate sensory input. Studies by Lund and Lund (1972a, 1972b) provide some specific details about the development of synapses in the visual system in lower animals (rats) and about the influence of sensory stimulation on the development of such synapses. There appear to be three stages in synaptic development in selected parts of the rat's visual system. These are:

Stage I: a prefunctional stage during which synaptic contacts are first being made; this stage occurs without visual stimulation;

Stage II: a first functional stage that follows immediately after eye-opening and involves myelination of the optic nerve and transmission of visual information through the nerve; this stage seems to be coincident with a proliferation of synapses throughout the visual system and with the development of more complex synaptic arrangements; and

Stage III: a second functional stage that is marked by the additional formation of intrinsic synapses and by the refining of response characteristics of neurons of the system; this stage is dependent upon patterned vision; after this stage the system no longer forms synaptic connections.

Stages I and II can be observed in visually deprived animals; Stage III, the stage dependent on visual stimulation, cannot. Thus when afferent input (sensory stimulation) to the brain is cut off (as in the case of suturing closed the eyelids of a newborn animal), the number of synapses normally developed in the brain of such an animal is reduced by half in just six weeks (Cragg, 1974). Lack of patterned stimulation results not only in a reduction of the number of synapses formed but also in a lack of specificity or refinement of responses of the neuron itself. The ultimate effect of such lack of refinement may be manifested in deficits in the learning of more complex perceptual tasks. Stage III is believed to occur postnatally in the human infant.

DEVELOPMENT OF NEURONAL DENDRITIC SYSTEMS

Normal neuronal operations depend upon the orderly development of appropriate synaptic relationships. Closely related to the development of synapses is the development of dendritic systems of neurons. The number, distribution, and functional types of synapses on different dendritic systems have long been viewed as essential criteria for building adequate integrative processes within the CNS. In addition, the major event in cortical neuronal differentiation is the elaboration of dendritic systems, for dendrites of cortical neurons provide more than 95% of the targets for transmission of information through the nervous system.

Scheibel and Scheibel (1977) suggest that dendritic systems of neurons are extrasensitive indices of pathology in the brain and that spine loss (which occurs for pathological reasons) is a harbinger of more profound, possibly irreversible changes in brain function. They describe four conditions that occur within the brain that are indices of potential danger to optimum brain development. These include spine loss (seen in many forms of mental retardation and in individuals with chronic seizures), nodulation or development of nodules along both mature and immature cortical cells, distortion of parts of the dendritic tree (bizarre curling and/or shrinkage of dendrites as often is seen in cases of Down's syndrome), and proliferation of glia (increased numbers of glia may crowd and overtake space needed for neuronal and synaptic development). Such disturbances in the proper development of dendritic systems can be expected to produce a wide spectrum of disorders ranging from mild learning disabilities to profound mental retardation.

At 6 months of gestation, dendritic systems in the human cerebral cortex are very poorly developed (e.g., at this time there are no dendritic spines on neurons in the visual cortex). By 8 months of gestation, however, thick dendrites with conspicuous spines are present on most cells in the visual cortex. Thus the 24th to the 32nd week seems to be an important period of development for neuronal dendritic systems in the human fetus (visual cortex). Changes in the dendritic system of the human fetus correlate closely with the early development of visually evoked potentials seen in the visual cortex at this time.

In general, although there seem to be some differences in the timetable of development of dendritic systems in different parts of the cerebral cortex (e.g., structures deep within the cerebral hemispheres and the motor cortex are more advanced in dendritic growth than the visual cortex), the major feature of dendritic development whenever it occurs is the appearance of dendritic spines (small processes that extend from the dendrites themselves and that provide for additional area for receiving synaptic input). At 18 to 22 weeks of gestation, only a few very thin spinelike processes are present anywhere in the cerebral cortex. By 30 to 36 weeks of gestation, the number of long, thin spines has greatly increased and there are now also present a number of short, stubby, mushroom-shaped spines. By 6 months postnatally the number of short, stubby spines has multiplied, and the number of long, thin spines has been greatly reduced. The period from $7^{1}/_{2}$ months prenatally to 6 months postnatally thus seems to be an important period for dendritic growth in the human infant. Interestingly, cortical neurons of human infants who were born at 7 months gestation and who lived five to six weeks after birth tended to show a reduced number of dendritic spines as well as identifiable alterations in dendritic structures in general. Most dendrites on cortical neurons of such infants were very thin and short and frequently had no true spines. Since these infants all suffered cardio-respiratory and/or metabolic disorders, it might be assumed that such conditions drastically affect the course of dendritic development that is usually achieved postnatally. Some authors (e.g., Purpura, 1974) have shown that the brains of mental retardates tend also to possess cortical neurons that have undergone dendritic spine dysgenesis (e.g., they have a reduced number of dendritic spines with only a few abnormally long, thin spines present). Spine development probably exerts profound effects on integrative operations of dendritic systems, which means that cortical neurons are not as effective as they should be in receiving synaptic input meant to reach them.

THE PROCESS OF MYELINATION

One rather universal way of looking at the course of growth and development of the brain is through the study of patterns of myelination that occur during prenatal and postnatal development. Most of the fast conducting pathways of the CNS are myelinated; that is, they develop a protein covering called a myelin sheath that helps to preserve energy in nerve impulse conduction and to maintain a nerve impulse conduction velocity that is almost independent of axonal diameter (Schulte, 1974). Thus myelin serves to help keep nerve impulse conduction velocity fast in spite of the increasing distances that impulses must travel as the body continues to grow. The process of myelination seems to have two overlapping components: (a) a *maturational* component that consists of a gradual thickening of the sheath at its existing length; and (b) a *growth* component that consists of the appearance of myelin in conjunction with continued growth in nerve fiber length (Dobbing and Sands, 1973). The process of growth in the CNS thus can be estimated by the amount and location of myelin present in the system at different points during development.

The time course of myelin development for a few selected structures and pathways within the CNS is outlined in Figure 2.1. Myelin formation begins in the spinal cord during midfetal life and continues throughout postnatal years. The final thickness of the myelin sheath is attained sometime during postnatal development. At about the fourth or fifth year the rate of myelination slows down but continues into adolescence. In general, fiber tracts appear to become completely myelinated at about the time they are functionally mature (Davison, 1974; Moore, 1973).

In general, the motor roots (motor or ventral horns of the spinal cord) are the first parts of the CNS to develop myelin, a process that begins about the fourth fetal month. Sensory roots (sensory or dorsal horns) show a rapid increase in myelination about one month later. Motor mechanisms of the spinal cord appear to be fully myelinated and thereby nearly functionally mature by the end of the neonatal period (one month); sensory mechanisms of the spinal cord continue to show myelin growth until approximately 6 months postnatally.

The major sensory pathways to the cortex (visual or optic radiation, tactile-kinesthetic or somesthetic radiation, auditory radiation) appear to become functionally mature at slightly different times. The higher somesthetic pathways show an increase in myelin growth about the eighth prenatal month, and at birth these pathways are myelinated all the way to the cortex. As a result the newborn infant is quite sensitive to touch information. Major growth in the somesthetic pathways continues until approximately $1^1/_2$ to 2 years. Although such myelination takes place before birth in the visual pathways, the major period of growth for the visual system in humans is between birth and 5 to 6 months. At 6 months myelin growth in the visual system has far surpassed that in the touch pathways and the visual system is nearly functionally complete at this time. The auditory system is the latest developing of the three major sensory systems. Increased growth in myelin in the auditory pathways begins about the time of birth and continues into early childhood (approximately 4 years). At this time the auditory system is nearing functional maturity (Dekaban, 1970; Rorke and Riggs, 1969; Yakovlev and Lecours, 1967).

The major motor pathways from the cortex (the pyramidal tracts) undergo rapid myelination during the last month of gestation and show rather complete myelination at two years. Thus voluntary motor pathways seem to be functionally mature at about 2 years of age. In general, it seems that the motor mechanisms of the CNS become myelinated (e.g., functionally mature) somewhat in advance of the sensory mechanisms that feed into them. It is almost as if nature wants to be sure the effector or motor

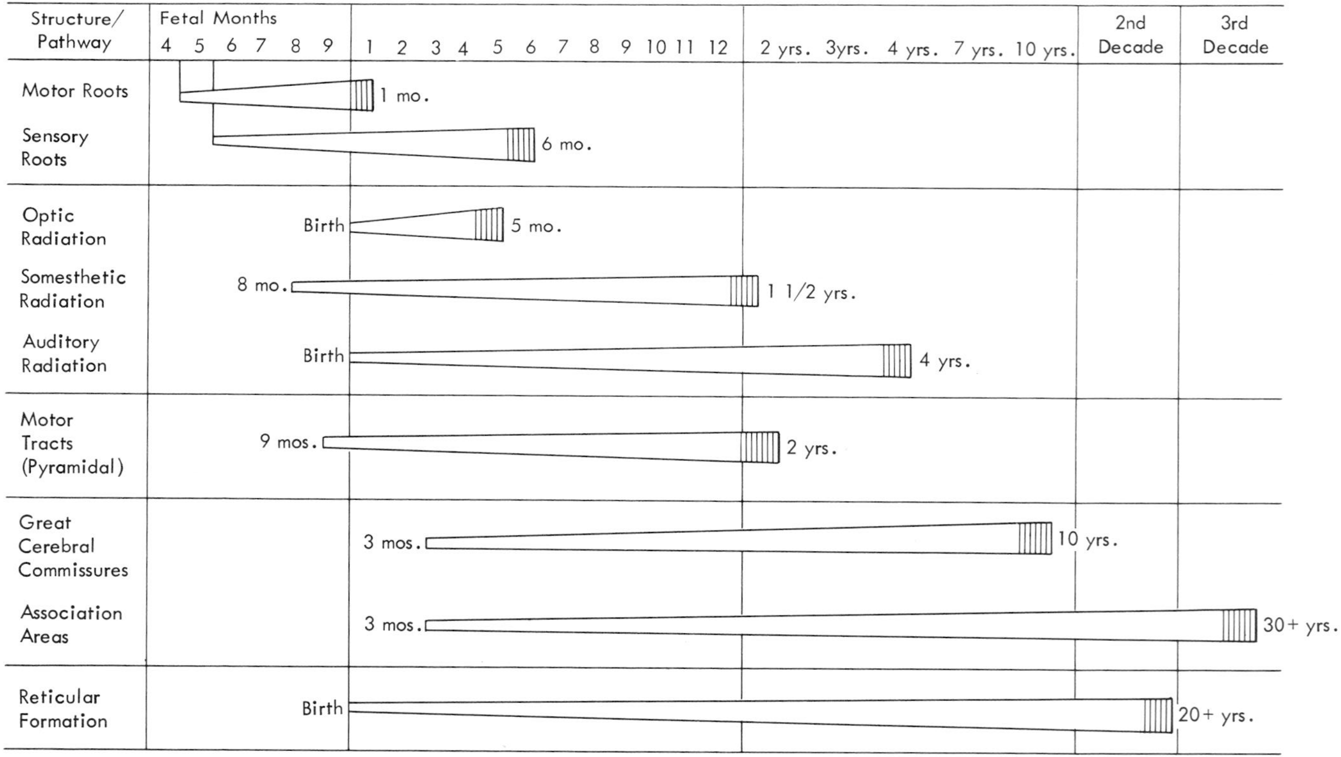

FIGURE 2.1 Course of Myelination of Selected CNS Structures/Pathways (After Rorke & Riggs, 1969; Dekaban, 1970; Yakolev & Lecours, 1967.) By permission of Blackwell Scientific Publications, Ltd., Oxford, England.

*Width and length of bars indicate increasing density of myelination; blacked-in areas at end of bars indicate approximate age range of completion of myelination process.

systems are set and ready to go when the sensory-perceptual processes that support their activity are mature and ready to function.

Those parts of the CNS that are concerned with storing (memory or association areas) or integrating information (cerebral commissures) are the last brain structures to undergo myelination. There is a rapid increase in myelin in these structures about the third postnatal month; this process continues into (and beyond) the third decade of life. The reticular formation, a structure known to be integrally involved with conscious wakefulness and attention processes, begins to undergo rapid myelination at birth; this process is not complete until sometime in the twenties, a good indication that selective attention processes are still capable of being modified throughout late childhood and early adulthood. Taken together these observations suggest that although parts of the CNS reach functional maturity very early in development, other structures and pathways continue to mature throughout the growing years and into adulthood (Dekaban, 1970; Rorke and Riggs, 1969; Yakovlev and Lecours, 1967). This is especially true of structures that subserve higher order functions of attention, memory, and integration and that to a great degree are dependent upon environmental experience. In general, the rate of myelination decreases with age as a negative monotonic function.

The appearance of myelin is frequently associated with the appearance of certain sensory or motor behaviors in the young fetus and infant. A summary description of the general course of myelin development and the accompanying behaviors that can be elicited in the fetus or young infant is given in Table 2-1. Interestingly, prior to the appearance of myelin, behavior (movement) can sometimes be elicited from the fetus but it is thought to be *myogenic* in nature. That is, it is thought to be due to direct stimulation of the muscle and not to stimulation that arrives at the muscle through some intervening neural structure. At about the fourth fetal month, as indicated previously, myelin appears in the spinal cord for the first time and movement can now be elicited through the motor neuron's connection with the muscle. Behavior at this point is said to be *neurogenic,* that is, it is effected through a neural structure. At six months myelination is more complete in the spinal cord and true *reflex arcs* appear. The fetus at this stage in development can receive sensory input and reflexly translate it into a behavior or movement response of some kind. Thus stimulation (touching) of the palms of the hands may give rise to a primitive grasp reflex, whereas stimulation of the soles of the feet may give rise to a Babinski. By the seventh and eighth fetal months the spinal cord is nearly fully myelinated, and myelin growth has proceeded upward toward higher brain regions (e.g., much of the medulla and midbrain are nearing functional maturity). At this point in development stimulation of the medulla results in respiratory movements and primitive sucking. Moro, tonic neck, and other righting responses can also be elicited.

TABLE 2-1   The Course of Myelination in the CNS and Accompanying Behaviors

AGE	MYELINATION	BEHAVIOR
Fourth fetal month	first appearance of myelin; process not complete until puberty very sparse confined to spinal cord	*neurogenic* reaction to stimulation; the motor neuron is functioning, thus stimulation of motor neurons results in muscle contraction before fourth month, movement (muscle contraction) is largely myogenic in nature
Sixth fetal month	cervical region of spinal cord almost fully myelinated myelin decreases as move toward lumbar region motor roots myelinated to greater degree than sensory roots tracts involved with coordination of head with body well myelinated motor tracts from cortex to spinal cord *not* myelinated	onset of *reflex* reactions; sensory connections with muscle have been made and true reflexes appear; behavior has its real genesis various reflex behaviors appear, e.g., grasp reflex, Balunshi reflex; stroking upper/lower lip causes contralateral flexion of neck and upper trunk
Seventh fetal month	myelination in medulla and midbrain evident reflex arcs of spinal cord are well myelinated pathways concerned with vital functions (B.P., respiration) are myelinated parts of cerebellum differentiated six layers of motor cortex recognizable	stimulation of medulla results in respiratory movements and premature sucking mass muscular responses are dominant, e.g., touch mouth, entire body moves more behavior reflexes are present, e.g., moro, righting, tonic neck, diagonal

TABLE 2-1   (continued)

AGE	MYELINATION	BEHAVIOR
Eighth fetal month	motor tracts in spinal cord well myelinated some evidence of myelination of motor tracts to higher centers sensory tracts in spinal cord better myelinated than before; some evidence of myelination to the thalamus	stimulation of the cervical cord results in energetic elevation of shoulders and flexion of arms stimulation of lumbar cord results in movement of legs tendon reflexes appear, e.g., patellar, achilles
Birth (neonatal month)	motor pathways myelinated to cortex sensory pathways slightly less well myelinated; only somato-sensory pathways are myelinated to cortex in cortex, somato-sensory cortex most advanced; motor cortex next in maturity; visual cortex and auditory cortex less mature association areas show little myelin	motor responses are reflex in nature; they include motor, TNR, righting, grasp, sucking, stepping, swimming, etc. tactile-kinesthetic responses are such that the infant reacts to touch anywhere on the body; touch cheek, get sucking response; touch nose, get closing of eyes visual responses include pupillary reflex, visuo-palpebral reflex, pursuit and fixation movements; some form and stereopsis reactions auditory responses are primarily gross reaction to sharp, loud sounds

At birth, motor pathways are myelinated to the cortex (awaiting the onset of voluntary behavior). Somato-sensory pathways are the most advanced of the sensory tracts. Thus at birth the young infant will respond by sucking if he is touched on the cheek, by closing the eyelids if touched on the nose, and so on. He is, in general, sensitive to tactile stimulation and reacts to touch on almost any part of the body. Visual responses are slightly less mature but include fixation and pursuit movements of the eyes and some form and depth perception reactions. The myelination of the auditory system as noted before proceeds a little more slowly, and therefore auditory responses at birth are primarily gross reactions to sharp, loud sounds. It is not until about one year postnatally that fibers to auditory areas of the brain become more fully myelinated (Dekaban, 1970; Rorke and Riggs, 1969; Yakovlev and Lecours, 1967).

Nerve Conduction Velocity

Another indicator of the stage of brain development, and closely related to the myelination process, is that of nerve conduction velocity, or the rate at which nerve impulses are transmitted along nerve pathways. As the thickness of myelin surrounding a nerve fiber increases, so does the speed with which nerve impulses can be transmitted. During the final weeks of gestation (8 to 9 months), nerve conduction velocity increases by about one meter per week (e.g., in the ulnar nerve). This suggests that there is a rapid accumulation of myelin during this period of fetal development. Even so, nerve conduction velocities are still much slower in the newborn than they are in the adult. Increments in nerve conduction velocity are large during the first year of life, the exact increase differing from nerve to nerve. Nerve conduction velocity in some nerves reaches maturity at 3 to 4 years (e.g., tibial nerve), whereas conduction velocity in other nerves continues to increase until 11 years of age (e.g., the median nerve). However, the rate of nerve impulse conduction in eleven-year-olds is still generally slower than it is in adults, an indication that myelination must continue into adolescence and perhaps even into adult years (Martinez *et al.,* 1978; Schulte, 1974).

BRAIN WEIGHT: ANOTHER DIMENSION OF BRAIN GROWTH

Another way of looking at or tracing neural development in the young fetus and infant is to study the pattern of increasing brain weight as the organism grows older. Increases in brain weight are a reflection not only of increases in the amount of myelin accumulated in various structures and pathways but also of increased growth of dendritic spines, increased vascularization, and increased numbers of glial cells—to mention but a few. A summary of selected age-related periods of brain growth in terms of increase in brain weight is given in Table 2-2. In general, increases in brain weight follow a negatively accelerated growth curve, with major increases in weight occurring during the first two years of life. This is followed by a gradual deceleration in accumulation of brain weight until 6 years of age,

TABLE 2-2   Brain Growth as Reflected in Increases in Brain Weight

BRAIN WEIGHT	AGE	COMMENTS
335 gms.	0 mos.	Convolution more marked Cerebellum small
516 gms.	3 mos.	Advancing vascularization Lobes/convolutions increased in size Grey vs. white matter now distinguishable
750 gms.	9 mos.	Temporal lobe nearing adult normal proportions Convolutions still increasing
925 gms.	12 mos.	Frontal lobe close to adult proportion Convolutions still increasing Brain weight tripled since birth
1024 gms.	18 mos.	Lobes and convolutions much like adults
1064 gms.	24 mos.	Color of brain changing Important changes in cerebellum Motor cortex increasing in thickness
1140 gms.	36 mos.	Consistency of brain increasing (firmer) Basal ganglia now distinguishable Cerebellar growth continuing
1190 gms.	48 mos.	Important growth in auditory pathways

1235 gms.	60 mos.	Important changes in motor cortex
		   (now 3.94 mm. thick)
		6 layers of the motor cortex well
		   differentiated

1245 gms.	72 mos.	Brain weight slightly less than adult weight of 1350 gms.

Source: After Dekaban, 1970

when brain weight appears to reach near-adult proportions. Interestingly, brain weight is nearly tripled in the first year, and another 139 grams is added during the second year as important growth takes place in major motor mechanisms of the CNS (the motor cortex, cerebellum, etc.). About one-half the increase in brain weight seen from 1 to 2 years is seen in the year from 2 to 3 (approximately a 76 gram increase). From 3 to 5 years, there is an increase in brain weight each year of approximately 50 grams. From 5 to 6 years, only ten grams are added to the weight of the total brain. Thus the six-year-old child's brain weighs approximately 105 grams less than that of the adult (average weight of the adult brain is 1350 grams). This suggests that although brain growth, as shown in increases in brain weight, greatly decelerates after 5 to 6 years, there is still considerable growth in terms of brain weight before the child's brain achieves full maturity. The increase in brain weight after 6 years probably largely reflects changes in maturity of association and integrative mechanisms that underlie higher-order learning processes (Dekaban, 1970; Dobbing and Sands, 1973).

GROWTH AND DIFFERENTIATION OF THE CORTICAL REGIONS

A brief review of the growth and development of the cerebral cortex seems in order at this point, for it is the coming to full, functioning maturity of the cerebral cortex that is the hallmark of the total cycle of brain growth and development. It is with the maturing of the cortex that more elaborate learning, thought, and reasoning processes in the human are made possible, for it is the cerebral cortex that truly sets the human brain apart from the brains of other organisms. There seem to be three major phases in the early development of the cerebral cortex. These include:

1. a period of *general cortical differentiation* that occupies the sixth to the sixteenth fetal week; this is a time when the cortex itself becomes distinguishable from subcortical structures and the six-layered appearance of the adult cortex begins to be clearly established;

2. a period of *divisional cortical differentiation* that spans the eighth to the thirty-second week of gestation; during this period different parts or divisions of the cortex become structurally defined (e.g., neocortex versus paleocortex, etc.); although the cellular structure of the cortex is still fairly immature, major landmarks on the surface of the cortex appear (e.g., the Sylvian fissure at about 6 months and the central fissure at about 8 months); and

3. a final period of *local cortical differentiation* that begins as early as the twenty-fourth fetal week and continues into the postnatal years; this is a period during which cells of various areas of the cortex take on an orderly arrangement and organization that is ultimately reflected in the highly specialized areas of the adult cortex (e.g., motor cortex, visual cortex).

At five months (early divisional cortical differentiation) the cerebral cortex is smooth; only the main fissures are recognizable. The major lobes (frontal, parietal, occipital, and temporal) are also now fairly well defined. The average thickness of the cortex at this time is 2.5 mm. At 7 months (the beginning of local cortical differentiation) the external configuration and pattern of fissures is similar to the adult brain. Subsequent to this time, the different layers of the cortex undergo rapid differentiation and by $2^1/_2$ months postnatally some parts of the cortex (e.g., motor cortex) have reached adult levels of thickness. They do, however, continue to mature in terms of internal complexity. It is important to note that the formation, development, and maturation of the cerebral cortex is to a great extent dependent upon the arrival and termination of sensory or afferent fibers from adjacent subcortical structures (Marin-Padilla, 1970a, 1970b).

Different lobes of the cortex undergo changes in development at different times. Data from Rabinowitz (1974) indicate that growth of the temporal lobe (auditory and memory functions) is slow from the eighth fetal month to 1 month postnatally but increases rapidly at about 6 months postnatally and remains accelerated until about 6 years. In contrast, the parietal lobe (somato-sensory functions) begins to undergo rapid growth 7 to 8 months prenatally; this continues until the fifteenth postnatal month, at which time growth slows down but continues until 2 years. Parietal lobe growth appears to accelerate once again from 4 to 6 years. The period of most rapid growth for the occipital lobe (visual functions) is from birth to 6 months. After this time growth seems to slow down considerably and the occipital lobe reaches nearly its adult status by 1 year of age. Growth of the frontal lobes (motor and memory functions) is the slowest of all lobes.

In terms of increasing thickness, the area of the frontal lobe controlling hand movements increases rapidly in size during the eighth and ninth prenatal months. After this period of rapid growth the rate of increase in thickness slows down (birth to 15 months); this is followed by a period of irregular growth from 15 months to 6 years. There is then a period of rapid increase in thickness from 6 years to adulthood. This suggests that hand movements involved in fine motor control may undergo rapid development and refinement during the first 15 months of life and again after 6 years of age. The period from 15 months to 6 years may represent a time when the neurological framework that will ultimately subserve fine motor control or eye-hand coordination is being laid down. Interestingly, the growth in thickness of the frontal association areas is fairly rapid from the prenatal period to 2 years of age; the rate of increase in thickness of this part of the cortex after 2 years is slow but steady until (and perhaps throughout most of) adulthood. The frontal association areas are ones integrally concerned with more elaborate thought and memory processes.

In general, it would seem then that the growth and differentiation of the human cerebral cortex is one that begins early in prenatal life and continues throughout childhood and into at least early adult years. Different areas of the cortex mature at different rates, but in general, structures concerned with motor expression or activity are more advanced than those areas concerned with related sensory functions. Association areas and those areas concerned with memory and learning seem to be the last to reach full maturity. In order of increasing maturity early in development, the occipital lobe matures most quickly, the parietal lobe is second, and the temporal and frontal lobes are the slowest to reach full functional maturity.

THE BRAIN GROWTH SPURT

The brain growth spurt (BGS) is a period of rapid brain growth and development that begins in humans during the third trimester of gestation and continues into postnatal life (to at least the third or fourth year and possibly longer). It is a period of time during which there are large increases in brain weight and during which a number of other processes, including glial cell proliferation, myelination, dendritic and synaptic growth, and refinement of certain enzyme systems proceed at a very rapid rate. It is now known that the brain growth spurt is predetermined to occur at a given chronological age, even when conditions are not favorable for its support, and that restriction during this developmental growth spurt universally results in a permanent and irreconcilable reduction (not just simply a delay) in the extent of brain growth. Since the brain has a "once only" opportunity for laying down its foundation for optimum development, the brain growth spurt represents a period of great vulnerability for elaboration of neural processes and potential brain function (Dobbing, 1972, 1974, 1976).

Because the brain is obviously important to behavior, it makes the understanding of the brain growth spurt very important to those interested in child growth and development. Such questions as "When does this growth spurt occur?" and "What are the detectable consequences of interference with such growth?" need to be answered. Although most of the data on the brain growth spurt come from animals, the pattern of brain development is very similar across mammalian species, the major difference being one of *when* the brain growth spurt occurs and not *how* it occurs. First, when does the brain growth spurt occur? A simplified schema of structural brain development and its relationship to the brain growth spurt is given in Figure 2.2. The brain growth spurt occurs immediately after neuroblast multiplication, a period of time in which cells destined to become nerve cells (neurons) undergo rapid division. At this point in development, nearly the full complement of neurons that will make up the adult brain is present. The first part of the brain growth spurt is given over largely to glial cell multiplication; the last and largest part of the spurt is concerned with the process of myelination. In man the most functionally significant part of the brain growth spurt is the myelination process and, indirectly, the development of dendritic systems and synaptic connectivity. These latter two processes are important because it is through the arborization of dendrites and the development of synapses that neurons are connected together in complex circuits that provide the basis for elaborate neurological func-

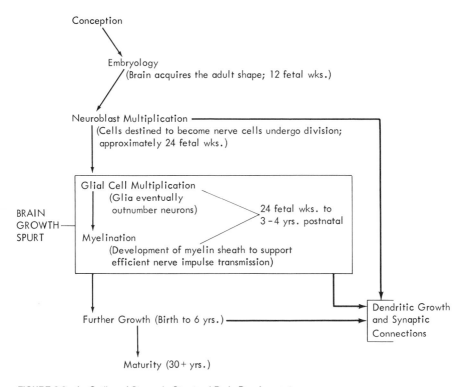

FIGURE 2.2   An Outline of Stages in Structural Brain Development

tioning. The time course of the brain growth spurt is clearly one that begins somewhere around midpregnancy and continues until at least the third or fourth year of postnatal life (Dobbing, 1974, 1976; Dobbing and Sands, 1973).

What are the effects of restriction or interference with such processes on growth and development of the brain? The deficits or distortions in brain growth that occur after restriction during this vulnerable period of development include:

1. *a permanent reduction in brain size* (or true microcephaly); this reduction in brain size, however, is not uniform across all parts of the brain, for the cerebellum (an important sensory-motor integration mechanism) is more affected than other parts of the brain;

2. *a reduction in total number of brain cells;* again, some types of brain cells are more affected than others; for example, glial cells are more reduced in number than neurons; and special neurons in the cerebellum and those in the deep layers of the cerebral cortex are more affected than neurons making up the medulla or midbrain;

3. *deficits in quantity of myelin present in the brain;* the amount of myelin in the system is reduced, and thus the myelination process and ultimately the functional capacity of the brain is greatly affected;

4. *a reduction in the amount of dendritic branching and the number of synaptic connections;* in some parts of the cerebral cortex, dendritic spines are so reduced that there may be as many as 10% fewer synapses per individual neuron;

5. *distortion of brain enzyme systems;* many of the enzyme systems that help to regulate important brain reactions are disturbed; for example, there is a permanent alteration in the activity of ACH-esterase, an enzyme needed to help regulate nerve impulse transmission;

6. *a permanent alteration of reflex ontogeny and later behavior;* there is a tendency on the part of organisms that have been restricted during the brain growth spurt to be clumsy, to overreact to stressful situations, and to show deficits in learning and memory; and

7. *some stunting of somatic growth;* animals undernourished during the brain growth spurt show permanent body stunting, a phenomenon that seems to be greater for males than for females (Davis and Dobbing, 1966; Dobbing, 1972, 1974, 1976; Dobbing and Smart, 1974).

With these possible consequences in mind, it is important to note that the timing of the brain growth spurt cannot be altered; it is prescribed to occur at a predetermined time. Thus conditions must be good at that time for the proper foundations for brain growth to be laid down. There is little, if any, possibility of full recovery of function if this "once only" opportunity for brain growth is missed or severely interfered with. The human growth spurt, as indicated before, begins in fetal life (approximately 24 weeks). This means that radiation, viral infection, abnormal metabolic processes, nutritional deficiencies, and other conditions experienced by the pregnant mother could interfere with the early foundational development of the brain. The first two years of postnatal life seem, however, to be the most significant ones in terms of promoting optimal brain growth and remediating problems that might be associated with growth restrictions that occur during the fetal period.

Nutritional Influences on Brain Growth

One of the major sources of support for the production of energy and "materials" needed for the brain growth spurt comes from the nutrition of the developing fetus or young infant. The human brain accumulates 25% of its mature weight prior to birth, reaches a peak rate of growth at birth, and achieves some 75% of its adult brain weight by the end of the first year (Chase, 1973). Malnutrition, either prenatal or postnatal, has been shown to significantly affect brain weight in general and, more specifically, the weight of the cerebellum. Animals rehabilitated after postnatal malnutrition always have lower brain weights than animals that have not suffered from such malnutrition. This same kind of phenomenon holds true for humans as well (Brown, 1966). For example, malnourished Ugandan children had significantly lower brain weights than nonmalnourished children at all ages from 2 to 15 years (Brown, 1966). Although the effects of malnutrition (in terms of achieving full brain growth) seem to be greatest if malnutrition occurs during late fetal or early infancy development, malnutrition that occurs in later developmental years can still act to inhibit optimal intellectual and personality growth (Brown, 1966; Dobbing *et al.*, 1971).

At the cellular level several studies (Cragg, 1972; Dobbing *et al.*, 1971; Dobbing and Smart, 1973) have clearly shown that undernutrition during early brain development, particularly during the brain growth spurt, results in maturational deficits in brain size, in numbers of cells formed, in the amount of myelin developed and in general enzymatic activity of the brain. Chase (1973) specifically found a 22% reduction in brain weight, significantly fewer glial cells, and a reduction of 38% to 41% in axon terminals on individual neurons in animals that were malnourished during early development. These deficits persisted even after long periods of nutritional rehabilitation had been provided to the animals.

At a behavioral level there is some indication that effects of early malnutrition are also long-lasting. In general, early nutritionally deprived animals exhibit less exploratory activity and appear to be behaviorally more clumsy than animals that have not undergone such nutritional deficits. These animals also tend to show an exaggerated response to food (they eat and spill more food than normal animals), to overreact to stressful situations (they press a lever more often than normal animals to postpone a shock), and to show slightly poorer performances on learning tasks. It is interesting and important to note that a good quality diet and proper nutrition in the second generation of offsprings of such malnourished animals does not eliminate all of the effects of this ancestral malnutrition (Dobbing and Smart, 1973).

Looking at children who had suffered from protein malnutrition sometime during early childhood, Canosa (1974) reported that these children were significantly poorer than normal children on tests of memory for digits as well as tests of memory for sentences. These children were also significantly poorer than nonmalnourished children on tasks that involved intentional and incidental learning. Thus it would appear that some of the effects of early malnutrition found in animals may also hold true for humans. With regard to rehabilitation, Chase (1973) reported that if children who had been malnourished sometime during the first year of life were treated before 4 months of age, a great deal of recovery was possible. However, those who were rehabilitated after 4 months showed little change or catch-up in behavior.

In summary it would appear that nutrition can and does have an important and long-lasting effect on brain growth and development in both animals and humans. The long-lasting effects may be seen in permanent deficits in motor, intellectual, and emotional growth as well as in underlying neural mechanisms that support such behavior.

HYPOXEMIA, ISCHEMIA, AND
BRAIN DEVELOPMENT

Brain injury due to hypoxemia and/or ischemia may be the single most important neurological problem associated with the perinatal period. Such injuries account for more of the nonprogressive neurological deficits seen in children than any other type of injury and include mental retardation and seizures as well as a variety of motor deficits ranging from spasticity to ataxia (Volpe, 1974).

Asphyxia (hypoxemia) is a condition that results from disturbance of the cardio-respiratory mechanism. It might be likened to a state of suspended animation due to a lack of oxygen in the blood. However, the blood of an asphyxiated newborn may not only contain virtually no oxygen, it may also contain large amounts of carbon dioxide and lactic acid. Ischemia is a condition in which there is a diminished amount of blood flowing through the brain and/or other tissues (Windle, 1969; Volpe, 1974).

Why should CNS or brain function fail when the brain is deprived of oxygen? First, the brain has relatively low energy reserves coupled with a relatively high metabolic rate. Second, in the young brain the rate of cerebral blood flow and oxygen consumption is almost five times that of the adult brain. Thus when the much needed supply of oxygen is eliminated or greatly reduced in the young brain, energy sources for brain functioning are quickly depleted and brain function immediately affected (Volpe, 1974). If prolonged, such oxygen deprivation contributes to the onset of irreversible functional and structural deficits.

How long or short a period of asphyxia/ischemia is compatible with survival of brain function? Windle (1966) reports that monkeys asphyxiated for six minutes at birth showed only minimal structural brain damage. Monkeys deprived of adequate oxygen for periods from 8 to 12 minutes showed a loss of cells in certain lower brain centers (e.g., the brainstem, midbrain, thalamus) but not in others (e.g., spinal cord and cerebellum). These animals tended to show abnormal neurological signs after resuscitation; they could not right themselves very easily and limb movements were highly uncoordinated. These abnormalities, however, soon disappeared, often within a few days and usually no longer than a few weeks. The EEGs of such animals also became normal very quickly. The structural damage to the system, even though clinically noticeable for only a short time, was permanent. Windle (1969) suggests that it is difficult to know what the effects of such damage might be for the young organism as it grows and develops, and that these monkeys, deprived of oxygen during the birth process, might be comparable to human infants who encounter some degree of asphyxia at birth or who have low Apgar scores (an index of the infant's general condition at birth) but who recover without any apparent neurological deficiencies.

Asphyxia lasting more than 12 minutes at birth caused more extensive damage to the brain and thus more pronounced functional deficits. Damage to the brain included more severe cell death in those lower brain centers that tended to be damaged by lesser degrees of asphyxia. In addition there were new centers of destruction (the basal ganglia—important for automatic or reflex-like movements; the cerebellum—an important sensory-motor integration mechanism; and the spinal cord). The white matter of the brain and spinal cord seemed to be less directly affected than the gray matter. Functional deficits persisted for a longer time in these animals, and many of them required extensive nursing care. The most seriously injured animals had symptoms very much like those seen in human cerebral palsy (Windle, 1969).

Follow-up observations were made on 17 of the monkeys that were asphyxiated for 8 to 12 minutes at birth to determine what happened, with time, to the behavioral symptoms that accompanied the structural brain damage known to occur with such oxygen deprivation. A summary of some of these behavioral changes is given in Table 2-3. Immediately after asphyxia all animals were comatose, and even a week later they still slept a disproportionately large amount of the time. The most striking symptoms of brain damage at this time were motor related. These animals were muscularly weak and unsteady, with definite ataxia of the limbs. Locomotion in particular was delayed, awkward, and uncoordinated. In addition, these animals were extremely slow in learning to drink milk from a bottle (they required 50-125 trials), a task that most normal animals learn quickly (within 24 trials). At one month, these animals showed some indication of general recovery: EEG's were normal; they could suck, swallow, and right themselves rather easily. However, the animals still showed distinct signs of retardation in comparison to normal animals. At this point in development, normal monkeys are alert, emotional, and active; they run, jump, and climb with considerable facility. The asphyxiated animals were dull, unemotional, and lacked curiosity; their activity levels were also generally very low. In particular the motor behavior of these animals was quite abnormal; forelimbs and hindlimbs were poorly coordinated and ataxia was still present in the forelimbs. They often used strange modes of moving and dragged and scuffed their feet. By 2 months most of the animals seemed overtly normal at first glance. Most were still slow in feeding, had equilibrium difficulties, and were clumsy and unwilling to enter into normal monkey activities. A striking feature of their behavior was the inability on the part of many to execute controlled reaching and grasping movements.

Adjustment to the imposed neurological deficits continued until approximately 4 years, after which time few additional behavioral changes took place. Casual observation of the animals at this point revealed very little clinically that would indicate the presence of brain damage. The major deficits that were present (but in very subtle form) were reduced manual

TABLE 2-3 Behavioral Symptoms Accompanying Recovery in Young Brain-Damaged (Asphyxiated) Monkeys

	IMMEDIATELY AFTER ASPHYXIA	1 WK.	1 MO.	2 MOS.
BEHAVIORAL SYMPTOMS	Animals are comatose, hyporeactive, hypoactive; impaired sucking, swallowing, and righting responses	Animals sleep most of the time; there is ataxia of the limbs with seizures in trunk and extremities; locomotion delayed, uncoordinated, slow; unable to track moving objects; no sound localization; takes 2–5 times longer than normal to learn to drink milk from a bottle	Animals able to suck, swallow, and right themselves; seizures no longer observed; EEG's normal; however, animals distinctly retarded (facial expression dull; activity level low) with abnormal motor behavior (e.g., random chewing movements, imperfect coordination between forelimbs and hindlimbs, etc.)	Many animals seem overtly normal but clumsy; will not enter into normal monkey activities; most have balance problems, are slow in feeding and show an inability to reach and grasp objects skillfully

1–3 YRS.*	3–4 YRS.*
Adjustment so advanced animals seem overtly normal in behavior, with the exception that they *lack* manual dexterity and are docile, unemotional, and somewhat hypoactive.	Adjustment reaches plateau; EEG and most behavior normal; only remaining symptoms are decreased manual dexterity and a reduced level of spontaneous activity.

*At this time, casual observation revealed little overtly abnormal behavior in these animals.

dexterity and generally diminished levels of spontaneous activity. The monkeys had by this time acquired reasonably good coordination between forelimbs and hindlimbs, but control of the wrists, ankles, and digits was still far from well developed. These behavioral characteristics persisted even in eight- and ten-year-old animals.

The important thing to note here is that most of the overt behavioral signs of brain damage gradually disappeared with time; only very subtle indicators of such damage were present after 4 years. Still, there was little or no evidence of structural repair neurologically when the brains of these animals were examined. The original damage appeared as shrunken scars or even cavities in the brain. In addition, there was some evidence in these animals that secondary brain damage had occurred. That is, there was a widespread depletion of nerve cells in parts of the brain that had not been initially affected by the asphyxiation procedure. This was particularly true of the cerebral cortex. Thus even though the clinical/behavioral signs of abnormal brain function disappeared, the damage to the brain was still there. These animals were also shown to have lasting learning/memory deficits.

Windle (1969) suggests that the symptoms these animals exhibited are comparable to those seen in human neurological disorders (including cerebral palsy), and that the whole syndrome may be relevant to the problems encountered in human infants as a result of stressful conditions surrounding the birth process. He reports that some 1.5% of all infants born in 14 different U.S. medical institutions participating in a nationwide study were found to have neurological deficits at the end of their first year. These children were followed for a period of time and it was noted that most of the children appeared to be normal by 3 to 4 years of age. Windle (1969) suggests that "it may be wishful thinking to conclude that all is well with such a child because he does not have a physical handicap" (p. 83).

PLASTICITY OF THE NERVOUS SYSTEM: BRAIN CHANGES IN RESPONSE TO EXPERIENCE

There is now available strong evidence to support the belief that there is room for considerable modification of the brain early in development and that some regions of the brain permanently retain this power of *adaptive plasticity*. The fact that adults can learn and remember new and complex concepts and can master sophisticated psychomotor tasks without great difficulty suggests there is some form of modifiability of the CNS even in the mature organism. It is clear, however, that the most obvious changes in the organization of the brain take place early in prenatal and postnatal life. What are some of the changes in the organization of the brain that depend on and occur with experience? Numerous studies have been reported on animals who have been exposed to a variety of enriched environmental experiences including enrichment from both sensory and social stimulation (e.g., Creutzfeldt and Heggelund, 1975; Mayers *et al.*, 1978; Rosenzweig *et al.*, 1972). In general, such studies agree that the following are characteristic of changes that take place in the brain with experience:

1. an increase in the weight and thickness of the cerebral cortex;
2. an increase in the number of glial cells;
3. an increase in the size of the cell body and nuclei of the neurons;
4. an increase in RNA/DNA ratios;
5. an increase in the ratio of cortex to subcortex;
6. an increase in the biochemical activity of cortical neurons;
7. an increase in synaptic density;
8. an increase in the number of dendritic spines; and
9. an increase in the amount of axonal myelination.

All of these changes in the structural organization of the brain are ones that are thought to be integral to a more efficiently functioning brain and thus represent important dimensions of the total growth and development of the brain. Animals that are not provided with such environmental experiences do not show comparable brain changes. It should be noted that differences in these parameters between "enriched" and "non-enriched" organisms are *small* but highly consistent; differences in the weight and thickness of the cerebral cortex, for example, have been found in at least 16 different replications of the original study. It should also be made clear that environmentally based changes in the brain are more common in the cerebral cortex than in subcortical structures (Goldman, 1974).

The effect of environmental experience on the development of the CNS is perhaps most clearly shown in what happens to visual functions in animals that have had "selected" kinds of visual experiences. For example, in the normal adult cat cortex, every cell is selectively sensitive to the orientation of moving edges; many cells are also directionally sensitive (they respond to movement in a specific direction, up-down, right-left, etc.), and 85% are sensitive to and depend on input from both eyes (e.g., they are driven binocularly). In cats that are deprived of early visual experiences (the animals are not exposed to patterned light during the first 16 days of life), only 41% of the cells in the visual cortex develop orientational, directional, and binocular sensitivity. In other words, more than one-half of the cells in the cortex do not develop their "normal" characteristics of responding. In fact, 27% of such cells do not respond at all to visual stimuli as a result of this lack of early visual experience. Importantly, most of these animals suffer moderate to severe (and persistent) deficits in their visual behaviors including placing responses, visual discriminations, etc. (Blakemore, 1975; Mayers *et al.*, 1971).

When animals are exposed to unusual modifications of visual stimulation (e.g., they are allowed to use only one eye or they are made artificially strabismic), the effects on neuronal functioning and on behavioral activity are dramatic. When artificial strabismus is created (one eye is made to deviate in terms of alignment with the other eye), the end result is that cells in the cortex lose their binocularity; that is, they respond only to input from one eye. Input from the other eye is nonfunctional. The same thing happens in monocular deprivation (animals are allowed to use only one eye to see). In most cases acuity, discrimination, and visuo-motor coordinations common to normal animals are greatly decreased in these animals. Only slight improvement occurs with long periods of appropriate binocular stimulation.

A vivid example of the influence of environmental experience upon the development of functional properties of the CNS is seen in animals reared in an environment that consists only of vertical and horizontal lines (e.g., |||| and ≡), but no diagonals. The effect of such experience is to create two kinds of cells, those that are sensitive to horizontal lines and those that are sensitive to verticals. The behavioral result is that discrimination of diagonals is greatly reduced; there is little sensitivity to and/or visual recognition of obliques in these animals (Blakemore, 1975). These observations clearly suggest that at least some aspects of the functional properties of certain CNS systems and the behaviors that they subserve are dependent upon appropriate environmental experience.

The question that needs to be asked is: Do these changes in organization of the brain have an effect on the organism's capacity for learning? Evidence has already been cited that indicates that such experiences do affect selected aspects of behavior. However, although there is some evidence to suggest that such changes do accompany changes in capacity to learn, such effects seem to be short-lived and depend on a variety of factors including the measure of learning used, the age at which enrichment takes place, and the type of task to be learned. Thus the effects of early environmental experience may be very task-specific and not necessarily manifested in a general or overall improvement or deficit in learning capacity of the individual.

NEURAL PLASTICITY: EFFECTS
OF EARLY BRAIN DAMAGE

There has been for many years some general consensus of opinion that CNS injury in infancy or early childhood produces fewer and less severe effects on behavior than similar injury at maturity. The belief has been that the immature brain is endowed with mechanisms for making compensatory adjustments that the adult brain does not have. Recent data from clinical and experimental studies of developmental processes in neural plasticity suggest the following about neural plasticity in the form of recovery of function after CNS injury:

1. if cerebral injury occurs during the developmental years (up to 8 or 9 years), impairment of function generally occurs, but in milder form; if such injury occurs during the first year of life, little or no deficit in behavior may be detectable;

2. recovery from cerebral injury depends not only on the age at which the injury occurred but also on the locus of the damage;

3. recovery of function also depends on the functional maturity of the other brain structures that remain intact after the injury and that are related to or associated with the damaged area;

4. functional recovery occurs most commonly with those behaviors that have a high level of automatization before injury (e.g., behaviors that are well learned by and/or "second-nature" to the individual);

5. motor functions seem to be impaired by early or late occurring brain damage and are affected by lesions in eight right or left cerebral hemispheres; thus those parts of the brain concerned with motor activity may be most vulnerable to cerebral injury;

6. simple somato-sensory functions seem generally *not* to be impaired by early brain damage, but such functions are affected by injury occurring later in development; complex somato-sensory functions are impaired by either early or late occurring cerebral injury;

7. recovery of language function is possible if injury occurs early in life; however, this recovery may come at the expense of a somewhat lowered general level of intellectual functioning due to "crowding" of functions in one cerebral hemisphere (Eidelberg and Stein, 1979; Goldman, 1974).

It is generally believed that recovery of function or neural plasticity may involve a number of processes or mechanisms. These include sprouting, redundancy of connections, and disappearance of diaschisis (Eidelberg and Stein, 1977). Sprouting has to do with the growth of new fibers (e.g., dendritic spines) that create "rearranged" neural circuits. There is some evidence that newly sprouting fibers do occur after brain damage and that such fibers do have important functional properties.

With regard to redundancy of connections, it has been suggested that more complex nervous systems may start out with populations of neurons that possess the potential for several alternative functions. Learning or development in such systems takes the form of selecting one or a limited number of functions to be subserved by individual neurons. This means that the number of connections that a given neuron has may be many times more than is really needed to carry on its normal functions. Thus in brain injury, this redundancy or excess of connections serves as a basis for recovery. Connections not previously used or needed for a given function may take over in light of damage to other connections that were once a part of normal functioning—and thus behavior is spared.

Some experts believe that recovery from cerebral injury essentially represents recovery from diaschisis (shock or depression of neuronal functioning). Immediately after injury (and often for long periods of time thereafter) there is decreased response in neurons both near to and distant from the site of injury. This is believed to be due to the release of an active inhibitory mechanism that raises the threshold for responding in large populations of neurons. With time this inhibitory process is reduced, and functioning in widespread populations of neurons returns to normal. Accompanying this return to normal functioning of intact neurons is the recovery of normal behavior. Which of these processes is actually responsible for recovery of function (neural plasticity) is not really known, but as has been pointed out, it is likely that a combination of all of these plus other undiscovered processes subserve what we ordinarily think of as recovery of function.

The most common effects of early or late occurring brain injury in animals or humans are deficits in motor control or motor functions (Rudel *et al.*, 1974). For some reason motor mechanisms appear to be highly sensitive to injury occurring to the CNS at any age, and thus deviations in motor behavior are often taken as signs of impaired neurological functioning. Deficits in motor control typically seen with cerebral injury in children are:

1. inability to perform alternating movements of the extremities (e.g., heel-toe alternation; arm/hand supination/pronation); 58 of 63 children between the ages of 7 and 18 years who had mild brain damage exhibited this deficit;
2. abnormal posture in upper extremities with gait; 55 of these same 63 children possessed this deficit;
3. inability to track moving objects and to coordinate head and eye movements; 52 of these children displayed this deficit;
4. facial dyspraxia (e.g., inability to close the eyelids against pressure, puff up the cheeks alternately, or make rapid tongue movements laterally and vertically); and
5. inability to move body parts independently of one another (synkinesia).

All of the 63 children evaluated in this study had one or more (usually more) of the above motor control problems. In addition, most of the children had difficulty recognizing objects through the sense of touch; they also could not perform tasks of spatial orientation (route finding via maps) and tended to display diminished intersensory integration abilities (including visual-tactile and auditory-visual deficits). These deficits persisted for considerable periods of time. Such observations clearly suggest that sensory and motor functions (but especially motor functions) are indeed profoundly disrupted by early brain damage and may require long periods of time to recover if, in fact, they ever do. The degree of recovery, as noted previously, depends a great deal on a variety of factors including age and the extent and location of the damage to the brain.

SUMMARY

1. The development of the nervous system of the child is integral to his overall development. Early development of the nervous system seems to be hereditarily based, and later development of the brain is dramatically affected by the environmental experiences that the organism is exposed to.

2. The process of myelination has been the important method of describing the course of growth and development of the brain during both prenatal and postnatal periods.

3. Motor pathways and mechanisms of the CNS seem to become myelinated (e.g., functionally mature) before sensory pathways and mechanisms. Those parts of the CNS concerned with storing or integrating information are the last structures to undergo myelination. Myelination of these parts of the brain can and does continue into the third decade of life.

4. Brain weight, another dimension of brain growth, increases dramatically during the first two years of life. This is followed by a gradual deceleration in accumulation of brain weight until 6 years of age when brain weight appears to reach adult proportions. Increase in brain weight after 6 years may largely reflect changes in association and integrative mechanisms that underlie complex learning and reasoning processes.

5. The brain undergoes a period of rapid growth and development from the third trimester of gestation to the third or fourth year of postnatal life. This period of rapid growth is known as the "brain growth spurt."

6. Restriction of or interference with factors (especially nutrition) that affect brain growth during the "brain growth spurt" can result in defects and/or distortions in the development of the brain that cannot be remediated.

7. Brain development can also be affected by conditions that affect the availability of oxygen to brain cells. The degree of the brain and/or behavior deficits that result when there is deprivation of oxygen are directly related to the length of time the organism is exposed to reduced or restricted supplies of oxygen.

8. Most overt behavioral signs of brain damage due to mild oxygen deprivation disappear with time; however, the brain itself (especially the cerebral cortex) may remain scarred. When severe oxygen deprivation occurs, brain and/or behavior deficits remain for life.

9. The effect of environmental experience on the development of the brain is well documented. There is clear evidence that the brain may be modified by sensory experiences early in life and that some regions

of the brain retain this adaptive plasticity throughout the lifespan of the individual.

10. Typical changes that take place in the brain with experience include: increase in the weight and thickness of the cerebral cortex; increase in the numbers of glial cells; increase in the size of the cell body of the neuron; and increases in synaptic density as well as numbers of synaptic spines. These changes are all thought to contribute to a more efficiently functioning brain.

11. The visual system and the cerebral cortex seem to be more subject to experiential changes than other systems or parts of the nervous system.

12. In general if cerebral injury occurs during the early developmental years (up to 8 to 9 years), impairment of function is milder than if such injury occurs later in life.

13. It would appear that those parts of the brain that are concerned with motor activity may be most vulnerable to cerebral injury. Motor functions seem to be impaired regardless of whether injury occurs early or later in development.

STUDY QUESTIONS

1. What are the six major events associated with early CNS development?
2. What is a synapse? How do they develop? Describe the three stages in synaptic development in the visual system. Of what importance is synaptic development to the growth of the individual?
3. Describe the growth of neuronal dendritic systems. Of what significance are they to normal development?
4. What is myelination? What purpose does it serve? Describe the time course of myelin development for the major structures of the CNS.
5. Differentiate among the terms myogenic, neurogenic, and true reflex arc. Be specific.
6. How is the process of myelination related to the development of overt behaviors?
7. How is nerve conduction velocity related to myelination? How does nerve conduction velocity change with age?
8. How is brain weight related to development?
9. Describe the major patterns of growth and differentiation of the cortical regions.
10. Define and discuss the brain growth spurt. Be specific. What is its importance to the developing organism?
11. What are the major deficits that result from interference with the brain growth spurt?
12. How does nutrition affect brain growth?

13. Differentiate between hypoxemia and ischemia. How does each affect brain development?
14. Describe the time course and nature of recovery of organisms exposed to severe asphyxia.
15. Define the term "adaptive plasticity." How *does* the brain change in response to experience?
16. What are the effects of early brain damage on neural plasticity?
17. What are the typical deficits in motor control that accompany cerebral injury in children?

REFERENCES

BLAKEMORE, C.   Development of functional connections in the mammalian visual system. In Brazier, ed., *Growth and Development of the Brain,* pp. 157-169. New York: Raven Press, 1975.

BROWN, R.   Organ weight in malnutrition with special reference to brain weight. *Developmental Medicine and Child Neurology.* 8 (1966):512-522.

CANOSA, C.   Early nutrition and mental performance. In Berenberg, Caniaris, and Mosse, eds., *Pre and Postnatal Development of the Human Brain.* New York: S. Karger, 1974.

CHASE, H.   The effects of intrauterine and postnatal under-nutrition on normal brain development. *Annals New York Academy Science.* 205 (1973):231-244.

COWAN, W.   Aspects of neural development. In Porter, ed., *Neurophysiology,* III, 17. Baltimore, MD: University Park Press, 1978.

CRAGG, B.   Plasticity of synapses. *British Medical Bulletin.* 30 (1974):141-144.

CRAGG, B.   The development of cortical synapses during starvation in the rat. *Brain.* 95 (1972):143-150.

CREUTZFELDT, O., AND HEGGELUND, P.   Neural plasticity in visual cortex of adult cats after exposure to visual patterns. *Science.* 188 (1975):1025-1027.

DAVISON, A.   Myelination. In Berenberg, Caniaris, and Mosse, eds., *Pre and Postnatal Development of the Human Brain.* New York: S. Karger, 1974.

DAVISON, A., AND DOBBING, J.   Myelination as a vulnerable period in brain development. *British Medical Bulletin.* 22 (1966):40-49.

DEKABAN, A.   *Neurology of Early Childhood.* Baltimore, MD: Williams and Wilkins, 1970.

DOBBING, J.   Human brain development and its vulnerability. *Biologic and Clinical Aspects of Brain Development.* Mead Johnson Symposium on Perinatal and Developmental Medicine, no. 6, 1974, 3-12.

DOBBING, J.   Vulnerable periods in brain growth and somatic growth. In Roberts, and Thomson, eds., *The Biology of Human Fetal Growth.* New York: Halsted Press, 1976.

DOBBING, J.   Vulnerable periods of brain development. In Elliot, and Knight, eds., *Lipids, Malnutrition and the Developing Brain.* Amsterdam: Elsevier Publishers, 1972.

DOBBING, J., HOPEWELL, J., AND LYNCH, A.   Vulnerability of developing brain: VII. Permanent deficits of neurons in cerebral and cerebellar cortex following early mild undernutrition. *Experimental Neurology.* 32 (1971):439-477.

DOBBING, J., AND SANDS, J.   Quantitative growth and development of human brain. *Archives of Diseases of Childhood.* 48 (1973):757-767.

DOBBING, J., AND SMART, J.   Early undernutrition, brain development and behavior. In Barnett, ed., *Ethology and Development (Clinics in Developmental Medicine, No. 47)*. London: Heinemann, 1973.

DOBBING, J., AND SMART, J.   Vulnerability of developing brain and behavior. *British Medical Bulletin*. 30 (1974):164-168.

EIDELBERG, E., AND STEIN, D.   Possible mechanisms of functional recovery: an overview. *Neurosciences Research Program Bulletin*. 12(2) (1977):275-279.

GOLDMAN, P.   An alternative to developmental plasticity. In Stein, Rosen, and Butters, eds., Heterology of CNS Structures in Infants and Adults. In *Plasticity and Recovery of Function in the CNS*. New York: Academic Press, 1974.

HERSCHKOWITZ, N., AND ROSSI, E.   Critical periods in brain development. In Elliot, and Knight, eds., *Lipids, Malnutrition and the Developing Brain*. Amsterdam: Elsevier Publishers, 1972.

LEMIRE, R., LOESER, J., LEECH, R., AND ALBORD, E.   *Normal and Abnormal Development of the Human Nervous System*. Hagerstown, MD: Harper and Row, Pub., 1975.

LUND, R., AND LUND, J.   Development of synaptic patterns in the superior colliculus of the rat. *Brain Research*. 42 (1972a):1-20.

LUND, K., AND LUND, R.   The effects of varying periods of visual deprivation on synaptogenesis in the superior colliculus of the rat. *Brain Research*. 42 (1972b): 21-32.

MANDEL, P., BIETH, R., JACOB, M., AND JUDES, C.   Changes in nucleic acids during brain maturation. In Berenberg, Caniaris, and Mosse, eds., *Pre and Postnatal Development of the Human Brain*. New York: S. Karger, 1974.

MARIN-PADILLA, M.   Prenatal and early postnatal ontogenesis of the human motor cortex: a golgi study II. The basket-pyramidal system. *Brain Research*. 23 (1970a): 185-191.

MARIN-PADILLA, M.   Prenatal and early postnatal ontogenesis of the human motor cortex: a golgi study I. The sequential development of the cortical layers. *Brain Research*. 23 (1970b):167-183.

MARTINEZ, A., FERRER, M., BONDE, P., AND BERNACER, M.   Motor conduction velocity and H-reflex in infancy and childhood II. Intra and extrauterine maturation of nerve fibers: development of the peripheral nerve from 1 month to 11 years of age. *Electromyography and Clinical Neurophysiology*. 18 (1978):11-27.

MAYERS, K., ROBERTSON, R., RUBEL, E., AND THOMPSON, R.   Development of polysensory responses in association cortex of kitten. *Science*. 171 (1971):1038-1040.

MOLLIVER, M., KOSTOVIC, I., AND VAN DER LOOS, H.   The development of synapses in cerebral cortex of the human fetus. *Brain Research*. 50 (1973):403-407.

MOORE, K.   *The Developing Human: Clinically Oriented Embryology*, p. 313. Philadelphia: W. B. Saunders, 1973.

PURPURA, D.   Factors contributing to abnormal neuronal development in cerebral cortex of human infant. In Berenberg, ed., *Brain Fetal and Infant Development*, pp. 54-78. The Hague: Martinus Nijhoff Medical Division, 1977.

PURPURA, D.   Neuronal migration and dendritic differentiation: normal and aberrant development of human cerebral cortex. *Biologic and Clinical Aspects of Brain Development*. Mead Johnson Symposium on Perinatal and Developmental Medicine, No. 6, 1974, 13-27.

RABINOWIZ, T.   Some aspects of the maturation of the human cerebral cortex. In Berenberg, Caniaris, and Mosse, eds., *Pre and Postnatal Development of the Human Brain*. New York: S. Karger, 1974.

RORKE, L., AND RIGGS, H. *Myelination of the Brain in the Newborn.* Philadelphia: J. B. Lippincott Company, 1969.
ROSENZWEIG, M., BENNETT, E., AND DIAMOND, M. Brain changes in response to experience. *Scientific American.* 226 (1972):22-29.
RUDEL, R., TEUBER, H., AND TWITCHELL, T. Levels of impairment of sensorimotor functions in children with early brain damage. *Neuropsychologia.* 12 (1974): 95-108.
SCHEIBEL, M., AND SCHEIBEL, A. Specific threats to brain development: dendritic changes. In Berenberg, ed., *Brain Fetal and Infant Development,* pp. 302-315. The Hague: Martinus Nijhoff Medical Division, 1977.
SCHULTE, F. Nerve conduction velocity. In Berenberg, Caniaris, and Mosse, eds., *Pre and Postnatal Development of the Human Brain.* New York: S. Karger, 1974.
SCHULTE, F. Neurophysiological aspects of development. In *Biologic and Clinical Aspects of Brain Development.* Mead Johnson Symposium on Perinatal and Developmental Medicine, No. 6, 1974, 38-47.
STRYKER, M. The role of early experience in the development and maintenance of orientation selectivity in the cat's visual cortex. In Poppel, Held, and Dowling, eds., *Neurosciences Research Program Bulletin.* 15(3) (1977):454-462.
VOLPE, J. Perinatal hypoxic-ischemic brain injury. In *Biologic and Clinical Aspects of Brain Development.* Mead Johnson Symposium on Perinatal and Developmental Medicine, No. 6, 1974, 48-59.
WINDLE, W. Brain damage by asphyxia at birth. *Scientific American.* 221 (1969):77-84.
YAKOVLEV, P., AND LECOURS, A. The myelogenetic cycles of regional maturation of the brain. In Minkowski, ed., *Regional Development of the Brain in Early Life.* Philadelphia, PA: F.A. Davis Co., 1967.

GLOSSARY

Acetylcholinesterase: a chemical substance (enzyme) that acts to destroy acetylcholine (Ach) released at the synapse; deactivation or destruction of Ach is necessary for proper synaptic activity.

Ataxia: disordered or awkward voluntary movement.

Axon: the long, thin process or extension of the neuron leading away from the cell body.

Central Nervous System: the CNS; includes the brain and the spinal cord.

Central Neuron: associative neuron or interneuron that may act as a link between sensory and motor neurons; central neurons make up the bulk of the CNS.

Cerebellum: brain structure responsible for the regulation of motor activity at all levels of the CNS; it contributes importantly to smooth, coordinated, purposeful movement and to the maintenance of equilibrium and balance.

Dendrite/Dendritic Spine: a dendrite is a direct extension of the cell body of the neuron; it has many branches; the smaller branches have many projections that are called spines; spines aid greatly in the transmission of nerve impulses.

Diaschisis: depression of neuronal function due to injury or trauma to the nervous system.

Extrapyramidal Tracts: the efferent or motor pathways responsible for nonvoluntary, rather automatic and crude movements of the body including posture and balance.

Frontal Lobe: one of the four lobes or divisions that make up the cerebrum; the frontal lobe contains important *motor* and *memory centers.*

Glia: cells of the brain; they outnumber neurons and act as the supporting tissue of the nervous system; they aid in the forming of myelin sheaths and help to support neuronal metabolism; they may also be involved in memory.

Mitochondria: structures found in neurons that provide *energy* for the support of neuronal activity.

Motor Cortex: an area in the frontal lobe that is responsible for initiating voluntary movements.

Motor Neuron: large nerve cells found in the spinal cord that connect with or innervate the muscles of the body.

Motor or Ventral Horns: that part of the spinal cord (anterior) where large numbers of motor neurons are found.

Myelination: the process by which myelin sheaths are formed.

Myelin Sheath: the protein covering found on many nerve fibers; it acts as an insulator of the nerve fiber and aids in fast conduction of nerve impulses.

Neuron: nerve cell; smallest functional unit of the nervous system; the brain itself is an aggregation of hundreds of thousands of neurons; the neuron has three parts—the cell body, the axon, and the dendrite.

Neurotransmitter: any one of a number of substances that act to effect the transmitting of nerve impulses across the synapse; a common one is acetylcholine.

Occipital Lobe: one of the four lobes or divisions of the cerebrum; it contains the major centers for vision.

Parietal Lobe: one of the four lobes or divisions of the cerebrum; it contains important sensory-motor centers concerned with the perception of bodily sensations and the regulation of eye-hand coordination.

Pyramidal Tract: the major efferent or motor pathway from the cerebrum to the spinal cord; this tract is designed for precise control of complex, voluntary movement.

Sensory or Dorsal Horns: that part of the spinal cord (posterior) where axons of sensory neurons are found.

Sensory Neuron: neuron whose cell body lies outside the spinal cord; it is responsible for transmitting sensory impulses into and upward through the central nervous system.

Somesthetic Pathways: those pathways that carry touch and other information about the body's position and movement in space; they extend from the periphery to the higher centers of the brain.

Sprouting: the process by means of which dendritic spines are formed.

Strabismus: squint due to imbalance in action of muscles that move the eye.

Synapse: region at which two neurons make close contact with each other; the neurons are separated by a gap or space; this space may be thought of as the synapse.

Synaptic Vesicles: small globular bodies in the terminals of neurons that contain neurotransmitter substance.

Temporal Lobe: one of the four lobes or divisions of the cerebrum; important auditory, language, and memory centers are found here.

Visual Cortex: an area in the occipital lobe that receives visual information and aids in the perception of complex visual forms.

Visually Evoked Potentials: electrical activity occurring in the visual cortex when the eye takes in visual information.

Glossary sources: Mountcastle, V. *Medical Physiology.* St. Louis, MO: The C. V. Mosby, Company, 1974.

Peele, T. L. *The Neuroanatomic Basis for Clinical Neurology.* New York, NY: McGraw-Hill Book Company, 1977.

CHAPTER THREE
SENSORY-PERCEPTUAL DEVELOPMENT: AN OVERVIEW OF VISUAL PERCEPTION PROCESSES

In order to build a comprehensive understanding of visual perception functioning and the development of basic visual perception skills in young children, it is important first to understand that visual perception is but one aspect of the total sensori-perceptual development of the young child. What do we mean by sensori-perceptual development? Sensori-perceptual development, in general, has to do with the refinement of afference or sensory processes (discussed in Chapter 1) that allow the young child to steadily improve his ability to pick up, process, and evaluate more complex kinds and quantities of sensory information. In other words, sensori-perceptual development is intricately tied to age-related changes in the ability of the child to pick up or take in information from the external and/or internal environment.

The initial pick-up of information, whatever modality may be involved, is essentially the job of sensory receptors whose primary function is to pick up raw sensory information and send it into the nervous system for further processing by the higher centers of the brain. This information pick-up is a necessary prerequisite to perception, because perception and ultimately behavior have to be built upon *something* and that something is, in large part, the sensory information taken in by the sensory receptors and processed by the system. Thus the child always perceives, reacts, behaves, or moves in relationship to "something," and the nature of that "something," and thus of perception (and possibly the behavioral act that follows), is defined to a great extent by the kind and amount of information picked up by the sensory receptors. Behaviorally, information pick-up, which is the beginning of sensori-perceptual functioning, is most often described as the individual's fixating on or attending to a set of visual stimuli in the environment—hearing a sound or series of sounds emanating from the environment or the kinesthetic experience of a sequence or series of bodily movements.

A second aspect of sensori-perceptual development is the age-related changes that occur in the analysis, interpretation, or evaluation of the sensory information picked up by the sensory receptors and sent into the nervous system. Once information, whether it is visual, auditory, or tactile-kinesthetic, has been picked up by the sensory receptors, it is transmitted to the higher regions of the brain where it is evaluated, interpreted and/or compared to information already stored in the brain—information that is stored in the brain as a result of the child's past experiences with similar stimulus conditions (see Chapter 1). This comparative-evaluative process is a very important part of sensori-perceptual development, for if such internal judgments or decisions are efficient, the child is more likely to experience success in his attempts to adapt to or solve problems related to the processing of such information. For example, a child's skill in catching a ball or walking a balance beam is, at least in part, a result of the effectiveness with which he processes (picks up and analyzes) the sensori-perceptual information related to the execution of those motor acts. Thus afferent processes and sensori-perceptual development become an integral part of the chain of events leading to skillful, adaptive behavior.

DEVELOPMENTAL CHANGES IN SENSORI-PERCEPTUAL PROCESSES

Although developmental changes in sensori-perceptual processes are described in slightly different language by different authorities, there is some general agreement that there are three major changes that gradually occur in sensori-perceptual processes as the child grows and develops. These changes include: (a) a shift in the hierarchy of the dominant sensory systems; (b) an increase or improvement in intrasensory discrimination; and (c) an accompanying improvement in intersensory integration (Williams, 1973).

The Shift in Dominance of the Sensory Systems

The first of the developmental changes in sensori-perceptual processes is seen in the consistently and universally observed shift from the dominance or preeminence of the use of sensory input from tactile-kinesthetic or proximo receptors to use of input from teloreceptors, mainly the eyes, for the control and/or modification of behavior (Williams, 1973). Sensori-perceptual development in the young child thus is characterized by a shift in the reliance on tactile-kinesthetic or somato-sensory information to a primary reliance on information from the visual system as a basis for regulating or modifying motor acts (behavior). This move to dominance by the visual system represents a shift from the use of input from sensory systems with relatively elementary or crude information-processing capacities to the use of input from a sensory system that has much more highly refined information-processing capacities. The visual system is, of course, the most advanced of all the sensory systems with regard to the speed and precision with which it can supply information to the individual about his surrounding environment.

There appears to be some evidence to suggest that, at maturity, man is a visually dominant organism. That is, man uses the visual mechanism and visual information in preference to other sensory modalities whenever possible. The young child, however, is not a visually dominant organism and, during development, only gradually moves away from a somato-sensory base of functioning to one where vision plays a major role in behavior. When the child finally achieves the mature level of *visual*-motor functioning, the visual mechanism dominates in the regulation of perception, movement, and behavior. Dominance does not mean that the other senses are not used. They *are* used, but vision seems to be naturally relied upon because it provides, more frequently than the other senses, the most easily accessible and precise information about the nature of the object, event, or stimulus to be acted upon. In reaching this mature level of functioning, the child passes through an intermediate stage called *motor*-visual functioning. This is a stage in which vision plays a supporting role in behavior, but great reliance is still placed by the child upon somato-sensory or motor-based information (Williams, 1972). For example, in this intermediate motor-visual stage, the child seems to need to actively interact (via involvement of the body) with the visual stimulus before he can respond with a completely adaptive behavior. When a young child is shown a complex geometric form, he may not immediately be able to verbally name it as a particular form unless or until he traces the outline of the form with his finger or hand, thus involving the somesthetic-motor systems. Also some children, when first learning to read, seem to have to follow the written word on the page with the finger. It is almost as though in order to read effectively, the child has to orient the visual mechanism through the use of the body. It has been suggested that when adults are learning any new task, especially one in which the visual cues have been changed, they too tend to revert back to this *motor*-visual stage. Only gradually do they move to the point where they can regulate their performances through the use of visual cues.

Behaviorally, a good example of this change in the preeminence of the sensory systems is seen in the young child's attempts to jump rope while two adults turn it for him. If one observes a four-year-old under such circumstances, it becomes obvious immediately that the child simply cannot coordinate his bodily movements to the movement of the rope. In other words the child is not able to use, in any precise way, the visual information derived from the swinging of the rope to initiate and/or carry out a successful jumping response. To perform successfully in this situation, the child has first to establish his own rhythm or pattern of jumping. Once this rhythm or pattern of movement is established, the rope can be added, but the movement of the rope must always be coordinated by the rope turners to coincide with the pattern of movement already established by the child. This suggests, of course, that the four-year-old is still quite dependent on tactile-kinesthetic (bodily) cues in performing motor acts and that the child cannot as yet effectively use specific visual cues to successfully initiate or regulate his behavior (Williams, 1973).

In contrast to this, the child of 7 or 8 years, when faced with a similar situation, does not have to be led into the skill of rope-jumping by first establishing his own pattern of bodily movement. This child has little or no difficulty in coordinating his rope-jumping behavior with visual cues derived from the movement of the swinging rope. This suggests that there is a shift from reliance on tactile-kinesthetic cues to the use of visual information in the initiation and regulation of the rope-jumping act by the eight-year-old.

Neurologically, there is some evidence to support the notion that there is indeed a hierarchical shift in dominance of the sensory systems. These data come from studies on the early development of the central nervous system. At birth, for example, the somato-sensory areas of the neocortex, as indicated by the observed patterns of myelination, are the most highly developed. The auditory area shows the next most advanced pattern of myelination, while the visual areas show the least advanced myelin development. By the sixth postnatal month, however, cortical visual areas have reached a level of development equal to that of the somato-sensory areas and both are advancing rapidly. The auditory areas are less well developed at this stage. After the first year, visual areas of the neocortex show the most mature levels of myelination; somato-sensory areas are slightly behind and the auditory areas are again the least well developed (Rabinowitz, 1974; Rorke and Riggs, 1964). On this basis it might be speculated that the infant is, at this point in development, beginning to enter into the *motor*-visual stage of development where vision and visual information play a more important role in the regulation of behavior but where tactile-kinesthetic or bodily sensations are still of primary importance. From a behavioral point of view, numerous studies have shown that during the age range from 3 to 8 years, the child uses vision much more efficiently than somato-sensory in identifying various shapes or forms. This could be an indication that the child is now in the *visual*-motor stage of development. Reliance on visual cues, of course, allows the child to make more rapid and precise judgments about the environment to which he must adjust. This, in turn, means that the child is capable of more refined, better coordinated behavior—partly because he *can* make better use of sensory information available to him from his environment.

Improved Intrasensory Discrimination

The second major change that occurs in the sensori-perceptual development of the young child is an increase in or refinement of the discriminatory powers of the individual sensory systems themselves. In other words, during the early and middle years of childhood, individual sensory systems undergo differentiation and refinement and thus develop a greater capacity for handling sensory information peculiar to that system. This improved intrasensory functioning is clearly reflected in the child's increasing ability to see more and more "detail" in various visual stimuli he experiences in his environment. To go back to our rope jumping example, it is partly due to improved intrasensory discrimination that the child is now able to make more precise discriminations about the speed, direction, and pattern of movement of the swinging rope, and thus that he is better able to coordinate the movement of his body to the movement of the rope. As a consequence, his rope jumping behavior improves (Williams, 1973).

It is universally observed that during the age range of 3 to 6 years, individual sensory systems undergo rapid and significant changes in their discriminatory powers. This means that the child begins to be able to detect finer and finer differences and/or similarities in visual stimuli he encounters in his everyday surroundings. He is also more efficient at recognizing and localizing sounds and is more capable of differentiating among a variety of patterns and sounds. The child during this time also develops significantly greater tactile-kinesthetic sensitivity. Thus he is better able to identify shapes, sizes, and textures as well as other characteristics of objects through the sense of touch. He is also more keenly aware of where the body is in space, in what position the various limbs are in space, and just when, how, and in what direction the body is moving. As a result of all these improvements in individual sensory systems, the child is much better able to process available sensory information from the environment and to regulate or control his overt behavior. He thus becomes much more skillful in solving problems and in adapting to the many variations in environment that he faces daily. It is to a discussion of this aspect of sensori-perceptual development, specifically with regard to the visual system, that Chapter 4 will be devoted. Auditory and tactile-kinesthetic perception will be discussed briefly in Chapter 5.

Improved Intersensory Communication

A third clearly observable change in sensori-perceptual processes in the young child is that of improved intersensory functioning or intersensory integration. This implies that as the child grows and develops he is increasingly better able to simultaneously integrate or match up information from several sensory systems. This topic will be dealt with in greater detail in Chapter 6.

VISUAL PERCEPTION

Visual perception may be defined simply as a pick-up and analysis of sensory information from the external environment through the use of the visual mechanism. Visual perception thus defined becomes an identifiable series of processes that involve the pick-up, transmission, and interpretation of information by peripheral and central (cortical and subcortical) nervous system structures. Visual perception is in large part a learned phenomenon. That is, man learns to use his eyes, to attend to relevant aspects of visual stimuli, to make discriminations, and to interpret available cues in specific experience-related ways. In this sense, visual perception is learned.

A Neuro-Conceptual Model of Visual Perception

It is useful in attempting to understand the processes involved in visual perception to think of the visual system as consisting of three functionally distinct but operationally integrated sets of networks: a primary visual system (PVS) that is basic to and necessary for the perception of visual patterns; a more primitive secondary visual system (SVS); and the pathways for the control of eye movements. Let us consider the secondary visual system first (Bronson, 1974).

The secondary visual system is phylogenetically older than the primary visual system and is directly concerned with the processing of visual information that falls on the more peripheral areas of the retina. It is believed that this system plays a central role in the automatic moving or directing of the eyes toward a target of "interest" that is in the peripheral parts of the visual field. In other words this system picks up the information that causes the eyes ultimately to move and focus on salient stimuli falling on the periphery of the retina. Thus the secondary visual system primarily provides information about the directional location of peripheral visual stimuli and contributes little, if anything, to the actual analysis of the detail

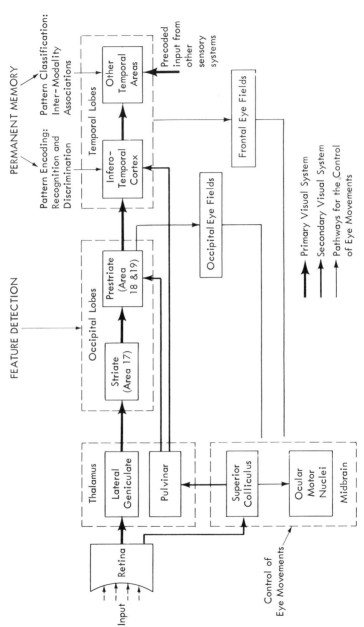

FIGURE 3.1 A simplified representation of information processing in the human visual system (**After Bronson, 1974**).

or content of such stimuli. This is the earlier developing of the two visual systems, as we shall see later, and appears to be present and functioning in the newborn infant. This system is represented in Figure 3.1 by small arrows. Neurologically it consists of the superior colliculus of the midbrain, the pulvinar of the thalamus, Areas 18 and 19 of the occipital lobe, and the inferotemporal cortex in the temporal lobe (Guyton, 1977). Table 3-1 contains a brief summary of the neural structures thought to be involved in each of the three visual networks as well as some of their known functions in or contributions to visual perception.

TABLE 3-1   Summary of Functions of Brain Structures Involved in Visual Perception

Retina (PVS, SVS)	Responds to spatial differences in intensity of light stimulation, especially at contrasting border areas.
	Provides basic information that says there is a "light" area here and a "dark" area there.
Oculo-Motor Nuclei (SVS, EMC)	Responsible for automatic conjugate eye movements: lateral, vertical, convergence.
	Regulates position of eyes in relation to position of head.
	Receives most of its information from the superior colliculus.
Superior Colliculus (SVS, EMC)	Involved in automatic coordination of simple visual input with motor responses.
Lateral Geniculate (PVS)	Receives and integrates binocular information at a simple level.
	May contribute to crude depth perception.
	Projects directly to Area 17.
Pulvinar (SVS)	Receives visual and auditory information and sends it to Area 17 and parts of temporal and parietal lobes.
	Involved in integration of somatic and special senses information, especially visual.
Area 17 (PVS)	Responsible for pattern vision and basic discrimination.
	Contains specialized cells that respond to specific characteristics of visual stimuli: e.g., shape, orientation, location, movement, speed and direction of movement.

TABLE 3-1   (continued)

Areas 18 and 19 (PVS, SVS, EMC)	Contributes to higher order analysis of visual information.
	Important in accurate spatial localization of objects, accurate judgments of size and length, accurate perception of speed and direction of movement, normal visual attention to or awareness of objects in the environment, and identification of meaning of words.
Occipital Eye Fields	Responsible for pursuit and fixation movements of the eyes (lateral, vertical, oblique) induced by visual stimuli.
Inferotemporal cortex and other Parts of Temporal Lobe (PVS, SVS)	Important in intellectual functions (e.g., comprehension of thoughts expressed in the written word).
	Involved in interpretation of different sensory experiences (visual, auditory, somatic).
	Houses long-term memories of complex visual and extravisual events.
Frontal Eye Fields (EMC)	Center for voluntary scanning movements of the eyes.
	Requires information from Area 17 to initiate movement of the eyes.

Source: Guyton, A. *Textbook of Medical Physiology*. Philadelphia, PA: W. B. Saunders and Co., Philadelphia, 1977. Truex, R., and Carpenter, M. *Human Neuroanatomy*. Baltimore, MD: Williams and Wilkins Co., Baltimore, 1971.

The primary visual system, which becomes refined later in development than the secondary visual system, is more directly concerned with the analysis and encoding (interpretation) of complex visual patterns (words, pictures, etc.). This system processes information received from the central area (fovea) of the retina. More refined analyses are possible in this system because neural units involved in the primary visual system become successively more selective in terms of the specificity of the stimulus characteristics to which they respond. This specificity of sensitivity to unique stimulus characteristics begins in the retina itself but is more refined as the information is processed in Areas 17, 18, and 19 of the occipital lobe. Here individual cells respond to very specific features of the stimulus, e.g., size, shape, orientation, and movement. This selective response to specific features of visual configurations is referred to as "feature detection." Feature detection is an important aspect of visual perception, as it allows for the identification of unique characteristics of the visual stimulus that ultimately make it classifiable. Output from these feature detector units provides the necessary information for recognition of complex visual patterns and ultimately for the classification of these patterns. Thus the occipital areas and the processes that they subserve are important parts of visual perception processes. Neural units in both the thalamus and the occipital lobes that are sensitive to stimulation from near-corresponding loci on the retinae of each eye may also be responsible for abstracting and integrating binocular information so that the third dimension is added to the analysis of the visual input (Bronson, 1974).

Before perception is completed, two additional processes must take place. First the visual information picked up by the system must be encoded, that is, it must be identified as having a specific set of features (pattern encoding). Next this information must be classified according to its relationship to or association with other previous or concurrent information or events, visual or extravisual (pattern classification). At this point perception as we know it probably occurs. Essentially, pattern encoding has to do with the recognition of a recurrently experienced visual configuration, whereas pattern classification has to do with the assignment of meaning or significance to that configuration in light of its association or relationship with other present or past sensori-perceptual events. From a behavioral point of view, these two processes are highly interrelated and are essential to the event or condition that we so universally refer to as "perception." Neurologically, pattern encoding and classification are thought to involve widespread areas of the temporal lobes, where a large percentage of multisensory information is stored, and where many permanent memory functions are housed (Bronson, 1974). The primary visual system is shown in Figure 3.1 by large arrows.

A third and integral aspect of efficient visual perception is that of eye movement control (EMC). Efficient processing and analysis of visual information requires an effective search for and fixation of visual stimuli to be analyzed (Maurer and Salapatek, 1976). Only then can the pick-up of information to be used by the system for perception be sufficient to allow for accurate analysis or interpretation of events in the external visual world. Eye movement control is concerned with: (a) moving the eyes toward a salient peripheral stimulus; (b) maintaining a steady focus on small detail within a visual configuration; and (c) maintaining fixation of moving visual stimuli. For the most part control of eye movements, pursuit and/or fixation, is the product of both automatic and learned processes. To be fully adaptive, of course, a system of eye movement control must provide a means by which the child can override any of the above reactions and voluntarily shift attention to and/or focus on an object with acquired/learned significance (Bronson, 1979). However, if the eye cannot maintain accurate, steady fixation on a picture, for example, or if the eye cannot be moved easily and smoothly along the lines of a printed page, the processing of visual information contained therein becomes much more difficult—if not impossible. Let's see how the eye movement control system works in visual perception.

The movement of the eyes to fixate on a visual stimulus in the periphery of the visual field and the smooth following of a moving visual field may be mediated by subcortical parts of the secondary visual system. That is, they may be functions of lower brain structures. Figure 3.1 indicates that information provided to the midbrain (superior colliculus) by the secondary visual system may be passed directly on to the oculo-motor nuclei of the midbrain. These nuclei provide for an automatic shifting or moving of the eyes in a given direction through their connections with the 6 pairs of muscles that are responsible for the actual movement or positioning of the eyes (Truex and Carpenter, 1971). Thus the appearance of a "novel" visual stimulus in the periphery of the visual field or the movement of the entire visual field itself may bring about an automatic reaction that moves the eyes according to the demands of the environmental situation with which the individual is faced. It is possible (but far from clearly established) that the cortical occipital eye fields may also be involved in this reaction. In this instance, more specific analysis of the visual stimulus would most probably take place before the eye movement reaction would occur. This would mean that only stimuli with more salient, new, or unique features would elicit or initiate this automatic fixation and/or pursuit movement of the eyes. Although it is at best speculative at the present time, it is possible that early in development, the subcortically mediated, midbrain eye movement control pathways dominate the visual perception process. Thus any gross feature of a moving or peripheral visual stimulus would elicit these responses. With increasing development, however, the occipital eye fields in association with Areas 17, 18, and 19 may become more dominant and thus override or regulate this subcortical eye movement control pathway. This would allow then only for the more refined aspects of a stimulus configuration to set fixation and/or pursuit movement patterns into action. This refinement in information needed to elicit such reactions could be an important aspect of the development of attentional processes in the young child. That is, as the system becomes more refined, the child is not drawn off by just any new or different moving or peripheral visual stimuli.

The more sophisticated eye-movement-control process of keeping fixation accurately centered on small detail within a visual configuration is believed to be controlled by the features detecting elements of the primary visual system that are located in the occipital lobe and mediated by the occipital eye fields (Bronson, 1974). Evidence of the involvement of this system in such fixation processes comes from the observation that following damage to the occipital eye fields, an individual's gaze oscillates widely around the intended locus of fixation. That is, the individual cannot maintain a steady, easy focus on a small visual target. Persons without efficient central (foveal) vision also do not exhibit the minute readjustments of fixation shown by the person with normal central vision, and generally they can only maintain an unstable fixation that is characterized by continuous "hunting" movements of the eyes, which sweep rather widely about the fixated target stimulus.

The last of the eye movement control processes, the voluntary direction of gaze to an object or stimulus of acquired interest or learned meaning, is important to adaptive behavior and skillful visual perception because its activity is thought to be based upon information provided by the pattern-encoding and classification units of the temporal lobes (Bronson, 1974). This makes *them* more available to control by higher-order cognitive or thought processes. These voluntary eye movements, because they are activated by information related to pattern recognition and classification, would be important in the regulation of eye movements involved in reading or in the general exploration of the external environment that is so characteristic of the young, developing child.

Voluntary eye movements are thought to be mediated by the frontal eye fields located in the frontal lobes adjacent to the major motor areas of the brain (Guyton, 1977). In general, bilateral damage to the frontal eye fields causes the individual to experience difficulty in "unlocking" his gaze from a current object of fixation. In other words, a person finds it very hard to shift his attention or fixation at will (voluntarily). Thus although his capacities for following a moving visual field and for maintaining accurate fixation of a stable target remain undisturbed, the individual with frontal eye field damage cannot smoothly, easily, or voluntarily shift his focus of attention from one visual target to another.

Neurologically, it is believed (based on patterns of myelination) that the peripheral components of the three visual networks begin to mature at an earlier age (completed by the first postnatal month) than the central components (occipital, temporal, and frontal lobe areas) that undergo maturation some months after birth and that continue to mature throughout the first decade of life. In general the sequence of maturation of the neocortical regions involved in the primary visual system roughly approximates the order in which information is processed in the proposed model (Bronson, 1974). Conel's (1963) histological studies of neuronal growth within the infant cortex provide some of the data base for such observations. At birth, visual areas of the occipital and temporal lobes are relatively undeveloped. By 3 months these areas have entered into a period of rapid development. During this period of development, Area 17 is more advanced in myelination than Areas 18 and 19, and those areas are better developed than the temporal lobe areas involved in visual perception. Thus evidence from neuronal growth studies suggests that the brain develops in a sequence that could underlie the appearance of more sophisticated visual perception and eye-movement-control processes.

It is generally assumed that the primary visual system develops later than the secondary visual system and that as the primary visual system develops, eye-movement-control processes become more refined and *vice versa*. Histological studies suggest that the foveal or central vision area of the infant is rather undeveloped at birth but undergoes rapid development soon after and reaches the adult level of maturity by 4 months (Bronson, 1974). This would suggest that the secondary visual system, because of its concern with peripheral visual stimulation, is indeed dominant during the first months of life. That this is the case is also suggested by studies of "visual-evoked responses." In such studies electrodes are placed on the surface of the occipital area of the skull of the infant or child. A light or some visual stimulus is then flashed in front of the eyes of the child. The response the brain makes to this visual information is recorded through an ink-writing system that picks up information through the electrodes placed on the head. Such responses usually have two gross components: a short-latency positive wave and a long-latency negative wave. The short-latency wave occurs first and seems to represent the brain's response to information provided by the primary visual system; the longer-latency wave is believed to represent information provided to the brain by the secondary visual system. In humans this long-latency, secondary visual system response can be elicited in the unborn fetus, whereas the short-latency, primary visual stimulus response is just beginning to appear at birth in full-term babies and is probably not adequate at that time for processing complex visual patterns (Bronson, 1974). Thus, overall, there is reason to believe that in humans the secondary visual system and its accompanying eye movement control develop in advance of the primary visual system and its associated eye movement patterns. The primary visual system, however, undergoes rapid development during the early postnatal years and begins to dominate in terms of visual perception functioning, and it continues to be refined throughout the first decade of life. This means, of course, that visual perception and associated eye movement control patterns will show continued changes throughout early and middle childhood years.

THE STRUCTURE OF VISUAL PERCEPTION

Visual perception as we ordinarily think of it from an educational and/or behavioral point of view has three major dimensions or facets. The processes that constitute or make up what we commonly know as visual perception are referred to as its structure. Thus the structure of visual perception is multidimensional in nature and includes three major abilities. These are: (1) *discrimination,* or the ability to differentiate, to varying degrees of precision, similarities or differences in the characteristics, arrangements, sequences, and/or organization of single or groups of visual stimuli; (2) *visual memory,* or the ability to recall, with or without external help, the above characteristics of visual stimuli; and (3) *integration,* or the ability to coordinate specific visual input with a specific motor output or response (Williams, 1972).

Developmentally, discrimination abilities appear first and seem to provide the foundation upon which the other abilities are built. Integration is the next aspect of visual perception to appear and it undergoes refinement throughout early and middle childhood years. Visual memory processes, although the last to be highly refined, appear early in development and continue to undergo refinement over several decades. Memory processes include both short-term (often nonconceptual) recall or recognition of information and long-term (often conceptual) memory abilities (Williams, 1972).

Developmental Changes in the Structure of Visual Perception

A direct perspective of the nature of visual perception functioning in young children is provided by studies that have been concerned specifically with defining the structure of visual perception in children of different ages (e.g., Boyd and Randle, 1970; Chissom and Thomas, 1971; Corah and Powell, 1963; Leton, 1972). Most of the studies have used factor analysis, because such techniques provide a convenient and acceptable way of defining the structure of complex behavioral constructs. Briefly, factor analysis is a statistical technique in which a large number of tests are intercorrelated. Such tests all represent what the investigator logically or theoretically determines to be important aspects of the construct under study. These intercorrelations are then analyzed mathematically and those test performances that are most highly related cluster together on what are called "factors." These factors are interpreted and/or used to aid in the description of the structure or components that statistically appear to make up the construct that is being studied.

Let us look first at a factor analytic study of the DeHirsch Reading Readiness Predictive Index (Adkins *et al.,* 1971). This study looked at the factor structure of the performances of five-year-old children on eighteen visual perception items included in the DeHirsch Index. The authors report that all of the items in this Index collapsed onto one general factor—that is, they all clustered together and accounted for 84% of total performance variance. This *unidimensional* factor structure was best defined by the following 4 of the 18 tasks:

1. *Word Reproduction:* a task in which the child is asked to reproduce from memory as much of the words "boy" and "train" as possible;
2. *Horst Reversal Test:* a task in which the child is asked to match letter combinations to a model set of letters;
3. *Categories Task:* a task in which the child is asked to categorize three groups of three words; and
4. *Bender Gestalt:* a task in which the child is asked to reproduce different geometric forms.

These data, the authors suggest, indicate that the most important dimensions (and perhaps the only measurable dimension) of visual perception processes in the five-year-old are those concerned with discrimination. They argue that although this visual perception capacity seems to take a slightly different form in each of the four tasks that define the factor, in reality it is the basic ability to discriminate among visual stimuli under different circumstances that provides the key to successful performance on each of the tasks. This suggests that visual perception functioning in the five-year-old may be essentially unidimensional in nature—that is, the ability that dominates visual perception at this age is basically one of discrimination.

It is interesting to note that although these four tasks all clustered together, there seems to be an element of both of the other dimensions of visual perception functioning present in these tasks. For example, the dimension of integration seems to be a definite part of the Bender Gestalt task, whereas memory is an important component of both the Categories and Word Reproduction tests. One might speculate that it is because the visual perception processes of the five-year-old are relatively immature that these other dimensions of visual perception do not appear as a part of the factor structure. This hints again at the possibility that visual perception processes in the five-year-old are unidimensional in nature.

As the child grows and develops, however, the visual mechanism becomes more highly refined and/or functionally differentiated, and this unidimensional base of perception changes and becomes multidimensional in nature. For example, McKinney (1971), in a factor analytic study of the performances of six-year-old children on the Frostig Developmental Test of Visual Perception and the Metropolitan Readiness Test, extracted three factors that best described visual perception functioning in six-year-old children. These included a *psychomotor dimension,* which was described as the ability to coordinate visual and motor information. This factor was clearly defined by Frostig Eye-Motor Coordination and Metropolitan Copying tasks. The second factor or dimension identified was that of *perceptual organization.* The defining tests were the Frostig Figure-Ground and Position in Space tasks. This dimension, the author suggests, represents the ability to organize figural information according to figure-ground and whole-part relationships. The last dimension was a *cognition of figural transformation* factor, which was described as the ability to visualize how a stimulus figure would appear after transformation or rotation in space. This factor was largely defined by the Form Constancy test of the Frostig Developmental Test of Visual Perception.

These last two factors seem essentially to involve discrimination abilities, for both require the identification or discrimination of a specific visual stimulus within a context of other confusing or distracting stimuli. The major difference among the tasks that define the two dimensions seems to be the amount or degree of distracting visual information that has to be filtered out before an adequate discrimination response can be made. If this interpretation is at all correct, then the base of visual perception functioning in the six-year-old—in contrast to the five-year-old—may be three-dimensional in nature: (a) one dimension that involves integration abilities and (b) two dimensions that involve different levels of basic discrimination abilities. Thus at 6 we could expect to find greater differentiation of the basic discrimination dimension present in five-year-olds as well as the appearance of a new dimension of visual perception, that of integration, or the coordination of visual information with motor output.

When the child reaches 7 or 8, the structure of visual perception seems to change once again. This time numerous factor analytic studies of performance of seven- and eight-year-olds on the Frostig Developmental Test of Visual Perception and a variety of other visual perception tests suggest that visual perception functioning in children of this age is essentially three-dimensional in nature: (a) one dimension involving an eye-motor or *integration* dimension (best described by performances on the Frostig Eye-Motor Coordination and Spatial Relations Subtest); (b) a *discrimination* dimension, which is most accurately defined by figure-ground and form-constancy tasks; and (c) a *memory* dimension, which is directly related to the child's ability to recall various forms of visual information (Boyd and Randle, 1971; Chissom and Thomas, 1971; Corah and Powell, 1963; Ward, 1970).

The new discrimination dimension seems to represent a collapsing of the previous two-dimensional visual discrimination factors in the six-year-old into a single, more comprehensive visual discrimination dimension in seven- and eight-year-olds. This, of course, hints at increased refinement of visual discrimination abilities in the older child. Thus visual discrimination tasks that were difficult for the six-year-old become essentially simple problems for seven- and eight-year-olds.

Although far from complete, all of these data do seem to suggest that the structure of visual perception is different for children of different ages. That is, visual perception seems not to be a single unitary process that can be measured by the administration of one simple test for all age groups. This means, of course, that any analysis, assessment, or attempt at enriching visual perception abilities in young children must necessarily take into account the chronological age of the child involved and the structure of visual perception functioning that is common for children of that age.

SUMMARY

1. Sensori-perceptual development in the young child is characterized by three major changes: a shift in the hierarchy of the dominant sensory systems, an increase in intrasensory discrimination, and an improved intersensory integration.

2. The shift in the hierarchy of the dominant sensory system is reflected in the fact that vision becomes, for most individuals, the dominant system used for picking up information about the environment for purposes of decision making.

3. An increase in intrasensory discrimination is manifested in the child's improved capacity for accurately observing detail in the environment through the use of individual sensory systems.

4. An increase in intersensory integration is reflected in the improved ability of the child to simultaneously use information from several senses (vision, audition, touch) to make judgments about his or her environment.

5. Visual perception is an important part of the sensori-perceptual development of the child and is subserved by three fundamentally distinct but operationally integrated systems: the primary visual system, which is necessary for patterned vision; a more primitive secondary visual system, which is concerned with helping the child move its eyes toward a target of interest; and an eye-movement-control system, which is responsible for fixation and tracking movements of the eyes. These systems involve well-identified structures within the CNS.

6. At a behavioral level, visual perception may be thought of as consisting of three major abilities: discrimination, memory, and integration.

7. Discrimination abilities appear first in development.

8. Integration (the ability to coordinate visual input with a specific motor response) appears shortly thereafter and undergoes refinement for several decades.

9. Memory processes are the last to appear and to be refined.

10. Factor analytic studies indicate that discrimination, integration, and memory abilities change with age and assume different degrees of importance in the visual perception process at different points in development.

STUDY QUESTIONS

1. Define sensori-perceptual development.
2. What role do sensory receptors play in sensori-perceptual development?
3. What is "information pick-up"?
4. Describe the role of the "comparative-evaluative" process in sensori-perceptual development.
5. What are the three major changes that occur in sensori-perceptual processes with age? Define and give an example of each.
6. Differentiate among and give examples of somato-sensory, *motor*-visual and *visual*-motor functioning.
7. What evidence is there to support the notion that the child moves gradually from a level of somato-sensory functioning to one of *visual*-motor functioning?
8. Define visual perception.
9. Describe the neuro-conceptual model of visual perception. Include a discussion of the primary, secondary, and eye-movement-control systems and the underlying neural structures involved.
10. Differentiate between pattern encoding and pattern classification. How are these related to perception? To the neuro-conceptual model of visual perception?
11. Differentiate between pursuit and fixation eye movements. Where is each controlled? What are eye movement fields? Oculo-motor nuclei?
12. Define and describe the three major dimensions or facets of visual perception.
13. How do these aspects of visual perception change with age? Be specific. What significance does this have for remediation of perceptual-motor difficulties in young children?

REFERENCES

ADKINS, P., HOLMES, G., AND SCHNACKENBERG, R. Factor Analyses of the De-Hirsch Predictive Index. *Perceptual and Motor Skills.* 33 (1971): 1319-1325.

BRONSON, G. The postnatal growth of visual capacity. *Child Development.* 44 (1973): 461-466.

BOYD, L., AND RANDLE, K. Factor analysis of the Frostig Developmental Test of Visual Perception. *Journal of Learning Disabilities.* 3 (1970): 253-255.

CHISSOM, R., AND THOMAS, J. Comparison of factor structures for the Frostig Developmental Test of Visual Perception. *Perceptual and Motor Skills.* 33 (1971): 1015-1018.

CONEL, J. *The Postnatal Development of the Human Cerebral Cortex.* Cambridge, MA: Harvard University Press, 1963.

CORAH, H., AND POWELL, B. A factor analytic study of the Frostig Developmental Test of Visual Perception. *Perceptual and Motor Skills.* 16 (1963): 59-63.

LETON, D. A factor analysis of ITPA and WISC scores of learning disabled children. *Psychology in Schools.* 9 (1972): 31-36.

MAURER, D., AND SALAPATEK, P. Developmental changes in the scanning of faces by young infants. *Child Development.* 47 (1976): 523-527.

McKINNEY, J.   Factor analytic study of the Developmental Test of Visual Percep-
tion and the Metropolitan Readiness Test. *Perceptual and Motor Skills.* 33
(1971): 1331-1334.
RABINOWITZ, T.   Some aspects of the maturation of the human cerebral cortex.
In Berenberg, Caniaris, and Mosse, eds. *Pre and Postnatal Development of the
Human Brain.* New York: S. Karger, 1974.
RORKE, L., AND RIGGS, H.   *Myelination of the Brain in the Newborn.* Philadelphia: J.
B. Lippincott Company, 1969.
WARD, J.   The factor structure of the Frostig Developmental Test of Visual Per-
ception. *British Journal of Educational Psychology.* 40 (1970): 65-67.
WILLIAMS, H.   Perceptual-motor development in young children. In Corbin, ed.,
A Textbook of Motor Development, pp. 111-150. Dubuque, IA: W. C. Brown,
1973.
WILLIAMS, H.   Visual perception: a general discussion of research methodology.
In *Proceedings from the Symposium in Research Methodology on Perceptual-Motor
Development,* pp. 43-55. Springfield College, 1972.

CHAPTER FOUR
CHARACTERISTICS OF VISUAL PERCEPTION DEVELOPMENT IN YOUNG CHILDREN

The topic of developmental characteristics of visual perception in young children is far too broad and complex to be covered comprehensively in a single chapter. Therefore, the following discussion centers around selected aspects of visual perception development that the author feels would be of most significance to persons working with young children in educational and/or clinical settings. These topics include: developmental characteristics of performances on the Frostig Developmental Test of Visual Perception; development of basic discrimination capacities in children; whole-part relationships and figure-ground perception; perception of spatial orientation; perceptual constancy; general characteristics of visual information-processing in children; selected aspects of visual memory; depth perception; perception of movement; visual acuity and eye-movement-control processes. The chapter concludes with a discussion of the relationship between visual perception development and motor and cognitive performance in young children.

CHARACTERISTICS OF PERFORMANCES ON THE FROSTIG DEVELOPMENTAL TEST OF VISUAL PERCEPTION

Marianne Frostig, a pioneer in the study of the behavioral description and assessment of visual perception in young children, recognizes five basic processes that are important in the child's early visual perception development (Frostig, 1966). These are:

1. *eye-motor coordination:* the ability to coordinate the use of the hands and eyes skillfully;

2. *figure-ground perception:* the ability to see a figure as distinct from a less clearly defined background;

3. *form constancy:* the ability to recognize a shape as the same shape regardless of the context in which it is seen;

4. *position in space:* the ability to recognize differences in the position of objects or forms in space; and

5. *spatial relationships:* the ability to recognize the relationship between two or more objects in space.

Although there is considerable controversy as to whether or not the processes identified by Frostig (1966) truly represent separate and distinct dimensions of visual perception functioning, normative data from children's performances on the Developmental Test of Visual Perception are important to an overall understanding of developmental changes that occur in visual perception in the young child. Information from Frostig's work on the standardization of the Developmental Test of Visual Perception (1966) clearly show that the age span from 3 to 6 years is a time of both rapid and significant change in visual perception abilities (See Table 4-1). Important improvements in perception of figure-ground relationships and position in space occur primarily from 4 to 6 years; the period from 5 to 7 years is one of rapid growth in the perception of spatial relationships. All of these visual perception processes then seem to decelerate and finally reach an asymptote in growth about 9 or 10 years of age (Frostig, 1966). More recent data on developmental changes in performance on the Developmental Test of Visual Perception provided by Williams *et al.* (1977) are described in the following pages.

Eye-Motor Coordination

Age-related changes in performance on the eye-motor coordination subtest of the Frostig Developmental Test of Visual Perception for boys and girls are plotted in Figures 4.1 and 4.2, respectively. Variability of performance is shown by the hatched vertical bar. In general there is a steady, almost linear improvement in this integrative aspect of visual perception from age 5 to 10 years. Although the range of scores varies from age to age for both sexes, there are essentially no differences between boys and girls at any given age.

Overall, boys as a group tend to be more variable than girls in this visual perception ability. Therefore, boys at any given age may show a wider range of scores than girls, and consequently boys may be more likely to exhibit extreme levels of performance on this task (e.g., very high or very low scores). Both boys and girls are more variable at 5 and 6 years of age than they are at ages 8 and 9. A definite decrease in group variability

TABLE 4-1   Developmental Trends: The Frostig Developmental Test of Visual Perception

SUBTEST	AGES	DEVELOPMENTAL TRENDS
Eye-Motor Coordination	3-5	rapid growth
	5-7	decelerated but still rapid improvement
	7-9	slows down; only slight improvement
	9-10	levels off; asymptotes
Figure-Ground	3-4	steady, noticeable improvement but not great
	4-6	rapid growth; large changes
	6-7	stabilized but still improving
	7-8	slight spurt
	8-10	steady asymptote
Form Constancy	3-6	steady increase in ability
	6-7	growth spurt; dramatic changes
	7-8	slows down but still improving
	8-9	steady; levels off
Position in Space	3-4	minimal change
	4-6	rapid growth
	6-7	levels off
	7-9	asymptotes
Spatial Relations	3-4	cannot perform at all
	4-5	gradual improvement
	5-7	rapid growth; large changes
	7-8	levels off but improves until about 10 years

on this integrative task is evident for both sexes at 8 years of age. This may mean that both boys and girls are reaching, at age 8, a peak in development of eye-motor coordination.

Figure-Ground Perception

Age changes in figure-ground perception for both boys and girls are plotted in Figures 4.3 and 4.4. Variability of performance is shown by the hatched vertical bar. There is a steady improvement in figure-ground perception for girls from 5 to 8 years of age. Boys, however, show a large improvement in figure-ground perception from 5 to 7 but little change from 7 to 8 years. After age 8 there is little observable improvement in figure-ground perception for either boys or girls. Thus children seem to

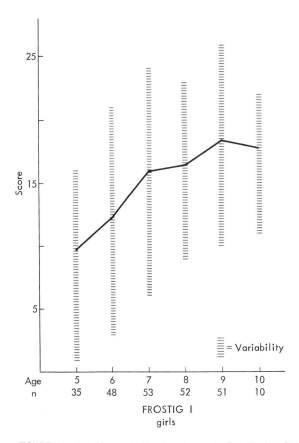

FIGURE 4.1   Age Changes in Frostig I, Eye-Motor Coordination: Girls

reach a plateau in simple figure-ground perception by 8 years of age. There are few, if any, differences between the sexes at any age. However, at 6 years girls seem to be slightly more advanced than boys in this visual perception ability.

With regard to variability of performance, both boys and girls show a sharp decrease in group variability from 5 to 8 years. At this point in development, variability of performance seems to level off, or *plateau*. Thus the range of dispersion of scores is dramatically reduced with increasing age. In general all children gradually improve in figure-ground perception with age and become more homogeneous in terms of their ability to perform such tasks.

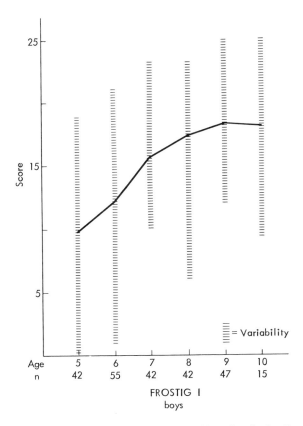

FIGURE 4.2   Age Changes in Frostig I, Eye-Motor Coordination: Boys

Form Constancy

Age changes in form constancy are shown in Figures 4.5 and 4.6. Variability of performance is also given. Overall, there is a steady improvement in form constancy with age. Girls show dramatic increases from 5 through 8 years, followed by a plateauing of performance at 9 and 10 years. Boys tend to show more gradual improvement in form constancy perception from 5 to 7 years, with a slight plateauing of performance from 7 to 9 years. This slow period of growth is then followed by another increase in performance between 9 and 10. It would appear that girls reach their peak of development in form constancy sooner than boys.

Girls show a gradual decrease in variability of performance with age.

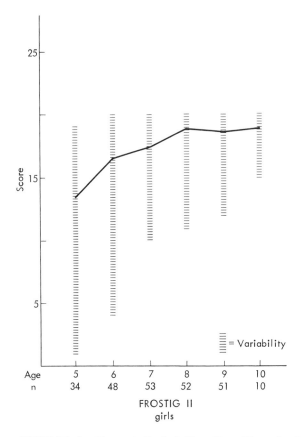

FIGURE 4.3   Age Changes in Frostig II, Figure-Ground Perception: Girls

In contrast to this, boys' performances are much more erratic and tend first to decrease and then increase in variability with increasing age. Boys, in general, tend to be more variable than girls at all ages in form constancy perception.

Position in Space

Age changes in the perception of spatial orientation or position of objects in space are plotted in Figures 4.7 and 4.8. Performance variability is shown by the hatched vertical bar. As with the other Frostig subtests, there is an overall steady improvement in perception of spatial orientation of objects with age. Boys and girls seem to progress at about the same rate, each reaching a plateau in performance at approximately 9 years of age.

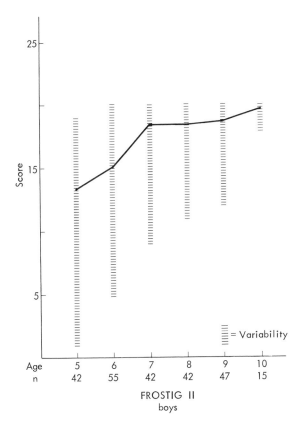

FIGURE 4.4 Age Changes in Frostig II, Figure-Ground Perception: Boys

Variability of performance is great for both boys and girls at the younger ages (5 and 6) but decreases dramatically at 7 years and doesn't change noticeably thereafter. Changes in this visual perception ability primarily involve improvement in level of performance at 5 and 6, whereas changes after 7 or 8 are related to both improvement in level of performance and decreases in group variability.

Spatial Relations

Age changes in the perception of spatial relations for girls and boys are plotted in Figures 4.9 and 4.10, respectively. In general there is a steady improvement in spatial relation performances with age. Boys show an almost linear trend in performance from 5 to 10; girls seem to show an

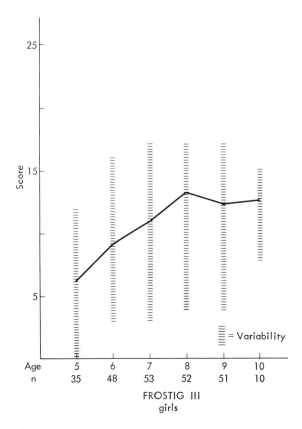

FIGURE 4.5   Age Changes in Frostig III, Form Constancy: Girls

improvement up to age 8 but little, if any, change thereafter. Both boys and girls perform at approximately the same level throughout the age range from 5 to 10. As with the perception of orientation of objects, variability of performance is greater at younger ages (5 and 6) than at older age levels. Boys show a steady decrease in performance variability across age; girls, on the other hand, show a decrease from 5 to 8 but a slight increase thereafter.

DEVELOPMENT OF BASIC DISCRIMINATION CAPACITIES IN CHILDREN

In a comprehensive and unique study of discrimination abilities in young children, Farnham-Diggory and Gregg (1975) asked the question: What features form the basis for discrimination and ultimately classification of

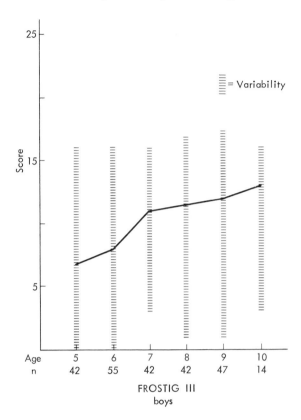

FIGURE 4.6   Age Changes in Frostig III, Form Constancy: Boys

visual stimuli? That is, if a child decides that a cow and a bird are both living things, what cues his judgment? There is some support for the notion that perceptual features (e.g., form, color) provide the basis for early word generalization. That is, the child notices the form (or another specific feature) of the object and then applies to the object as a whole the name he has associated with that particular feature. So for a time everything that is round is a "ball." It is known that the young child also discriminates and classifies objects on the basis of their actions and functions (e.g., what they do). Another question of importance is: If an object has several pertinent features (form, color, function), will one be preferred over another for purposes of classification? Does the feature preferred vary with age?

To answer these questions, Farnham-Diggory and Gregg (1975) looked at five different kinds of discrimination or matching activities in young children (5 years) and adults (college juniors). The tasks themselves, and developmental differences according to the kind of discrimination to

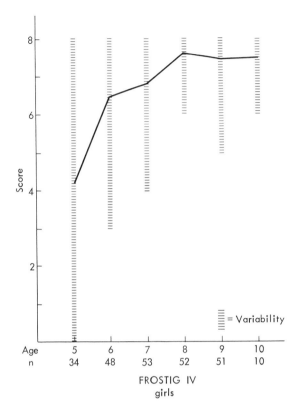

FIGURE 4.7   Age Changes in Frostig IV, Position in Space: Girls

be made, are described in Table 4-2. Identity-matching is the simplest of all discriminations for both children and adults. 63% of all five-year-olds made no errors on identity-matching tasks, and adults made only 4 errors in all. Children took significantly longer to make these matches than did adults. Interestingly, adults tended to spend most of their time looking at the stimulus figure to be matched and always looked at the stimulus figure first before looking at possible responses. Children, in contrast, often began by looking not at the stimulus figure but at one of the possible responses.

Children make more errors on color matching than on identity matching. Only 12.5% of the five-year-olds did not make errors in color matching; 50% of adults had errorless performances. Children again are slower than adults in matching stimuli on the basis of color. Interestingly, however, matching on the basis of color is significantly slower for both children and adults than identity matching.

Errors for children were very high on form matching; every child made some error on this task. However, 63% of adults had errorless per-

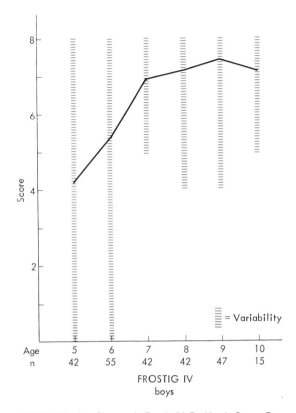

FIGURE 4.8   Age Changes in Frostig IV, Position in Space: Boys

formances. Children were three times slower than adults in matching on the basis of form. Although adults matched figures on the basis of color and form at about the same rate, children took much longer to match on form than on color.

When asked to match items based on functional characteristics, children made fewer errors than when they matched on form. Adult errors on this task were the same as for form matching. Children were twice as slow as adults in function matching. Errors for both children and adults on equivalence matching were fewer than those on form, color or function matching activities. These matches were also slower for children than for adults, but children made equivalence judgments as quickly and accurately as they did form and function matches.

In general then, for both children and adults, identity matches are simpler than color matches, which are in turn simpler than form discriminations. There are some important differences between the young child and the adult in terms of certain kinds of discriminations. For five-year-

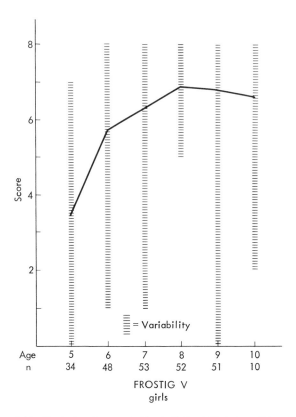

FIGURE 4.9   Age Changes in Frostig V, Spatial Relations: Girls

olds function and equivalence discriminations are about equal in terms of difficulty. They are, however, simpler than form matches. For adults, equivalence and form matches are equally difficult but less so than function matching (which happens to be the most complex judgment of all for adults). Overall, the simplest discriminations for children are identity discriminations; they are followed by color, function, and equivalence judgments, in that order. The most difficult discrimination of all for children is that based on form. The simplest to most difficult matches for adults are: identity, color, form, equivalence, function.

The fact that adults classify objects more easily on the basis of form than function suggests that, with age and experience, the basis for deciding the nature of the similarity between two objects broadens, so that multiple features are considered when determining possible function classifications for objects. Function-matching thus becomes a more difficult task for adults than for children. An adult may have to develop several categories of function before making a decision as to what function two objects do have

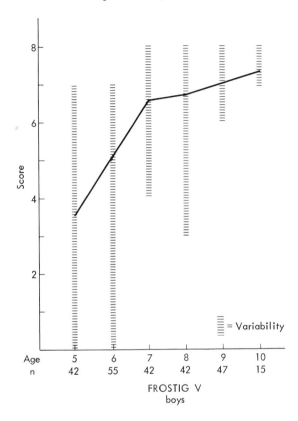

FIGURE 4.10   Age Changes in Frostig V, Spatial Relations: Boys

in common. For the child, function classification may be simpler because he has less information on which to base his decision, and so the answer is arrived at more simply and directly.

WHOLE-PART RELATIONSHIPS AND FIGURE-GROUND PERCEPTION

One concept that is used to describe the development of discrimination abilities in visual perception is that of whole-part relationships. Early in development the child focuses on the whole, whereas later in development he focuses on the parts and, in particular, on the parts as they make up the whole (Lowe, 1973). Visual perception development in young children is, in general, characterized by a change from "diffuse perceptual organization," where the whole is relatively undifferentiated, to a level of re-

TABLE 4-2 Basic Discrimination Capacities of Children and Adults

KIND OF DISCRIMINATION	SAMPLE SLIDE	INSTRUCTION	DEVELOPMENTAL AND TASK DIFFERENCES
Identity Matching	Cat Cat Book	"Touch the picture that's exactly like the top picture."	Simplest of all discriminations for both children and adults. Children significantly slower than adults.
Color Matching	Red Truck Red Brown Apple Book	"Touch the picture that has the same color as the top picture."	Second simplest of all discriminations. More errors made by both children and adults. Children significantly slower than adults.
Form Matching	Wiggly Rope Wiggly Book Snake	"Touch the picture that's about the same shape as the top picture."	Most difficult discrimination of all for children. Adults match color and form equally easily. Children 3 times slower than adults.
Function Matching	Truck Airplane Book	"Touch the picture that does about the same thing as the top picture."	Simpler for children than form matching. More difficult for adults than form matching. Children twice as slow as adults.
Equivalence Matching	Cat Dog Book	"Touch the picture that's most like the top picture."	Simpler for children than form matching. Simpler for adults than function matching. Children slower than adults.

Source: After Farnham-Diggory and Gregg, 1975.

finement at which the parts of the whole become more defined and are ultimately integrated into a precise or articulated whole.

Development of whole-part perception may also be thought of as perceptual schematization. That is, perception of visual stimuli becomes schematized with age. Schematization is a process that involves a shift from the perception of *figurative* wholes to *operative* wholes (Piaget, 1963). Figurative wholes appear early in development and are the result of the child's centering on one single or dominant aspect of the visual field to the exclusion of other dimensions of that field (e.g., he notices the shape but not the orientation of geometric forms). Operative wholes, which develop later, are largely the outgrowth of the child's attending to or integrating several aspects of the stimulus field into one unified perception (e.g., he notices both the shape and orientation of geometric forms).

Observation of performances of children ages 4 to 9 years who are shown the items depicted in Figure 4.11 indicate that there is a definite change in the way such children perceive the parts and the wholes of these stimuli with age. Most five-year-olds, for example, respond to such stimuli with either "I see a man" or "I see some fruit." They report figurative wholes that center on one aspect of the stimulus figure. Seven- and eight-year-olds report that they see both the parts (the fruit) and the whole (the man) but cannot or do not perceive or report them simultaneously. They might say, "I see a man; no, I see fruit; no, I see a man," but they rarely report seeing a "man made of fruit." Thus these children seem to see parts and wholes alternately but not simultaneously. Generally, part-whole integration is mature in nine-year-olds (75%) who say in response to the stimulus configuration, "It's a man made of fruit." This suggests that, by

FIGURE 4.11   Some of the seven items used in the Perceptual Integration Test (After Elkind, Koegler, and Go, 1964)

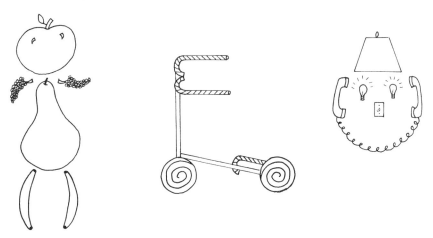

9, children have formed operative wholes and can integrate several dimensions of the visual stimulus into a meaningful, differentiated whole (Elkind, 1975; Elkind *et al.*, 1964).

A similar trend in whole-part perception is seen in children's drawings of human figures. Five-year-olds draw human figures with a distinct body, head, and limbs but more often than not the parts have no obvious relationship to the whole. Children younger than 5 tend to draw more global forms with little differentiation, if any, of body, trunk and/or limbs. Seven-, eight-, and nine-year olds, however, draw figures with distinctive parts and, in contrast to five-year-olds, draw parts that have a direct relationship to the whole (Elkind *et al.*, 1970; Zaporozhets, 1965).

It is possible that both young children and adults "read" visual configurations in a sequential manner (e.g., seeing parts, then the whole, or vice versa), but that the speed with which the child processes information is so slow that the constructive process of perceiving parts and wholes alternately is more obvious than it is with the faster information-processing capacities of the adult. Thus it may be that what happens in more mature perception is that the temporal process involved in perceiving the parts and the whole of a stimulus sequentially is so speeded up that it appears, in adult perception, that the two are perceived simultaneously (Goodglass, 1971).

If visual perception is a constructive process, then it follows that the faster information can be processed the more quickly a perception can occur. There is considerable evidence to suggest that this constructive process does, in fact, take longer in young children than in older ones. For example, the forms in Figure 4.11 were shown to children ages 3 to 12. The children looked at each of the figures for .10, 1.0, 5.0, and 10.0 seconds. In general, as would be expected, more operative wholes were reported by older children. For any given age, however, the number of operative wholes reported was greater when the child viewed the figure for longer periods of time (Elkind, 1975). Young children (4 years of age) reported seeing integrated wholes only when they had viewed the forms for the maximum time (10 seconds). Interestingly, six-year-olds required about the same length of time for stimulus viewing to see integrated wholes as did four-year-olds. In contrast, nine-year-olds as well as older children reported integrated figures under all viewing conditions. They were, of course, better at longer durations. Twelve-year-olds reported significantly more integrated wholes at all stimulus durations than other children. In general then, perceptions do require time to be constructed. The constructive process in the case of whole-part perception seems to be slower in younger children than in older ones. Important changes in the speed of this process, however, occur throughout the age range from 3 to 12 years (Elkind, 1975). Interestingly, twelve-year-olds performed best, not when they viewed the stimulus for the maximum duration, but when they viewed it for 5 seconds.

Thus it is possible that at maturity there may be an "optimum" time for the construction of a perception.

There is some evidence to suggest that early in development, when the child operates primarily at a figurative whole level, the overall nature of the "whole" of the stimulus configuration seems to exert an important influence on the child's growing perception of the parts of that whole (Lowe, 1973). For example, kindergarten and second-, and fourth-grade children who are shown a large, square stimulus figure made up of small rectangles and asked to select a rectangle that is the same as the ones making up the larger square, tend to select rectangles that are *less* elongated than the actual rectangles. Five-year-olds thus select rectangles that are more like the larger whole (square) and less like the smaller part (rectangle). In contrast, eight-year-olds tend to select rectangles that are more elongated than the rectangles that actually make up the square. In this case the presence of the larger square seems to influence the young child's perception in the opposite direction, and so the child selects rectangles that are even more elongated than the ones to be matched. The ten-year-old is not influenced by any interplay between the large square and the smaller rectangles, and the child selects rectangles that are very nearly identical to the ones making up the larger square. Thus a five-year-old child's perception of parts of a stimulus configuration takes on some of the characteristics of the more dominant whole. Eight-year-olds are also influenced by the presence of the whole, but in such a way that the perception of the parts of that whole seems to be exaggerated in favor of the part. By 10 years of age whole-part relationships seem to have taken on mature form, and judgments about the parts of a whole become rather independent of the whole itself (Lowe, 1973).

Figure-Ground Perception

Another aspect of whole-part perception has to do with the ability of the child to extract relevant or pertinent detail from contexts that contain irrelevant or distracting information. Embedded figures (figure-ground tests) are frequently used to assess this visual perception ability. Using the Figure-Ground Test of the Southern California Sensori-Motor Integration Test Battery, Williams *et al.* (1979) report data on five-, six-, and eight-year-old children. They note that when figure-ground perception involves familiar items, six- and eight-year-olds are significantly more advanced than five-year-olds in their ability to separate the relevant figure from an irrelevant background. There is, however, little or no difference between six- and eight-year-olds in the performance of this task. When figure-ground problems involve more *abstract* geometric forms, there are no differences among the three age groups. Thus five-, six-, and eight-year-olds are equally able (or unable) to discriminate figure from ground when abstract or less familiar shapes are used. In general, children at all ages are better at identifying *familiar* figures imbedded in distracting backgrounds than they are at picking out *unfamiliar* or more abstract ones from similar backgrounds. Group variability decreases with age, so that figure-ground perception performances are more homogeneous in older children. Thus eight-year-olds tend, as a group, to be more alike in figure-ground ability than five-year-olds. Other data suggest that there is a marked refinement of figure-ground ability between 8 and 13, and that in some instances figure-ground perception continues to improve through 17 or 18 years (Williams, 1973).

PERCEPTION OF SPATIAL ORIENTATION

Perception of spatial orientation refers to the ability of the child to recognize, identify, or simply be aware of the position or orientation of objects in two- or three-dimensional space. Most adults immediately notice differences in spatial orientation of objects and either pay attention to or disregard such differences according to their importance or relevance to the situation at hand. Young children do not possess this facility and first have to learn to recognize the spatial orientation of objects in their external environment and then to ignore such characteristics if they are irrelevant (Gibson, 1966; Pick, 1979).

Perception of spatial orientation seems to begin with the child becoming aware of the basic dualisms that bisect all of space. At 3–4 years, children become much more aware of spatial dualisms and learn such spatial opposites as in/out, vertical/horizontal, top/bottom, front/back, high/low, over/under, etc. Until the child begins to develop some sensitivity to these spatial opposites, he is as likely to get things inverted, reversed, or rotated as he is to get them properly positioned in space. Thus, for the three- or four-year-old who is just defining his space world, shapes that are tilted or rotated to one side are often copied in an upright position (Williams, 1973).

An important part of the development of awareness of spatial dualisms is the mastery of spatial direction. Children appear to master spatial directions in a fairly orderly sequence, moving from mastery of the vertical to the horizontal to the diagonal or oblique. Children at 3–4 years of age can readily distinguish verticals from horizontals and thus are very aware of the vertical orientation of objects, often remarking that "this is upside-down" or "this is right-side up." This child, unlike the two-year old, is more likely to want the story book in the proper upright position when looking at it. Mirror images (left-right reversals) and oblique lines have yet to be conquered by these children. By 8 years of age all children have mastered verticals and horizontals, and in most cases can distinguish among obliques that are oriented differently in space. The six-year-old can discriminate between horizontal and oblique lines (— /) but has some difficulty with vertical-oblique (| /) and oblique-oblique (/ \ ) discriminations. These latter two spatial-orientation problems are usually mastered by the age of 8. However, it is not unusual to find eight-year-olds who still have difficulty with right-left or mirror image reversals. Children at these young ages also find it more difficult to make right-left discriminations when the figures are adjacent (e.g.,☐ ☐) than when they are placed one above the other (e.g.,☐). The same holds true for up-down discrimination where ⊔ ⊓ judgments are simpler for the child than ☐ judgments. It would appear then that the ability to easily perceive spatial orientation of objects undergoes refinement throughout the early and middle childhood years and does not reach maturity until some time after 8 years of age. (Jeffrey, 1967; Naus and Shillman, 1976; Williams, 1973).

PERCEPTUAL CONSTANCY

Perceptual constancy refers to the relative invariance of perceptual judgments despite wide variations in the sensory representation of stimulus properties at the receptor level. Constancy is important, for it represents perceptual stability and underlies the ability of the individual to interpret the environment consistently and accurately. Although perceptual constancy can be measured in many ways, Collins (1976) has developed a technique that is unique and intrinsically interesting to young children. Children are seated before two sets of two parallel train tracks extending in the sagittal plane. On each of the tracks is a small train car with a pointer attached to it. The first set of tracks is used as a model. The two cars are placed at different distances (120–600 cm.) from the child, with the cars themselves always separated by a constant distance (30 cm.). The child tries to move or place the cars on his set of tracks in the same position (same spatial separation) as those on the model track. In general when these kinds of perceptual constancy judgments are assessed, children of all ages are found to make progressively greater overestimations of the spatial separation between the two cars when the model cars are placed farther away from them. Thus a spatial separation of 30 cm. between two objects is judged to be greater and greater as the objects are positioned farther and farther away from the child. In general, however, there is an increase in accuracy of this kind of perceptual constancy with increasing age. Adults are quite accurate in estimating the spatial separation between the two cars regardless of distance. Nine-to eleven-year-olds, although a little less accurate than adults, show much more perceptual constancy than five- to seven-year olds. Thus up to age 7, the child's ability to judge distance consistently is affected by the absolute distance at which the objects to be judged are located. This suggests that perceptual constancy, an indicator of increasing stability of perception, undergoes important changes during early childhood, and that after the age of 7, perception becomes much more stable and may be relatively mature by the age of 11.

Another indication of the development of perceptual constancy or stability of perception in young children is found in their judgments of the *sizes* of objects placed at different distances from them. Piaget (1963) refers to judgments of this kind as "perceptual transport." That is, the child has to "transport" his judgment of size across different spatial distances, a form of perceptual constancy. When children are asked to compare vertical lines of equal and unequal lengths that are different distances from them, one finds that successful size judgments are more frequent at short spatial distances (when the lines are closer to the child). This ability improves with age, and older children are much more able to make accurate judgments about differences in the size of stimuli at different spatial distances than are young children. In fact young children are often unable to make accurate size judgments at all when the stimuli are placed at a distance from them.

A variation of this procedure is one in which children are shown pairs of geometric figures of different sizes. In this case the figures themselves are separated by different distances. That is, the forms to be judged are separated from each other by distances ranging from 2.54 cm. to 22.86 cm. When two shapes are separated by large spatial distances, size judgments are, in general, much more difficult for children at any age than when the forms are closer together. The ability of the young child to determine which shape is larger is very poor at large spatial separations. This ability, however, increases with age and adults have little, if any, difficulty making such judgments even when the two shapes are separated by large spatial distances. An important characteristic of mature perception is its constancy or invariance (Elkind, 1975).

GENERAL CHARACTERISTICS OF VISUAL INFORMATION-PROCESSING IN CHILDREN

Connolly (1970) investigated visual-information processing in its simplest form by having children of different ages sort cards according to color. In the simplest task the child had to decide between two *colors* and sort them; in the most difficult situation, he had to decide among 8 different colors and sort them accordingly. There were always 24 cards regardless of whether there were 2, 4, 6, or 8 color choices involved. In general the ability to process visual information was less well-developed in six-year-olds than in older children. Eight-, ten-, twelve-, and fourteen-year-olds performed at about the same level on all of the information-processing tasks. According to Connolly (1970), changes in simple visual information-processing capacities of children seem to occur at two principal times in development: between 6 and 8 years, when the first major improvement occurs; and between 14 years and adulthood, when a second significant change in efficiency of information-processing takes place.

A variation of the Connolly card-sorting task was used by Williams *et al.* (1979) to study basic shape-information-processing characteristics of younger children (5, 6, and 8 years old). These children were asked to sort cards according to *shape* when the color of the shape was constant and when the color of the shape was varied. When 4 different shapes were used and color was constant, five-year-olds took much longer than six- and eight-year-olds to process shape information. Six-year-olds were also significantly slower than eight-year-olds in processing shape information under these conditions. This suggests that basic visual-information-processing capacities of the young child are undergoing important developmental changes during the period from 5 to 8 years and that such capacities are much more refined in eight-year-olds than in five- or six-year-olds.

It is interesting to note that when children sorted *shapes* of different colors, there were no differences among the three age groups. That is, five-, six-, and eight-year-olds took equally long periods of time to process shape information when the *color* of the shape was varied. The time required by six- and eight-year-olds to process shape under these conditions was significantly longer than under "color constant" conditions. Thus it would appear that when an irrelevant dimension of a stimulus (e.g., color) is varied and included as a part of the basic information processing task, six- and eight-year-olds cannot completely disregard this aspect of the stimulus and consequently process information at a level comparable to five-year-olds. In contrast, five-year-olds process shape information at the same rate regardless of whether the color of the shape is constant or varied. Why the addition of the irrelevant dimension of color to a shape discrimination task should erase basic developmental differences in information processing capacities of five-, six- and eight-year-olds is not totally clear. It does suggest that such capacities are still being refined in young children.

When children were asked to distinguish among 6 different shapes, there were again few, if any, differences among the three age groups in terms of the efficiency with which such information was processed. This was true whether color was held constant or varied randomly across shapes. The time required to process information under a 6-choice situation was significantly longer than the time required to process similar information under a 4-choice situation. Such observations suggest that the ability of the young child to cope with large information processing demands (e.g., those associated with 6-choice tasks) is limited.

Williams *et al.* (1979) also studied developmental differences in information-processing capacities in young children using *size* as the relevant dimension of the stimulus to be processed. Five-, six- and eight-year-olds were again asked to sort cards on which were drawn four different sizes of a single shape (a triangle). The color of the shape was held constant in one case and varied in another. In general, although young children can make simple size discriminations, the five-year-old children in this study could not perform the task at all. Both six- and eight-year-olds were successful in making such size discriminations. Eight-year-olds were significantly faster in processing *size* information than six-year-olds. Neither the six- nor the eight-year-olds were affected in their processing of size information by the presence of color as an irrelevant dimension. The processing of size information was, in general, more difficult (took significantly more time) for all children than was the processing of shape information. The time required by both six- and eight-year-olds to process size information was more than double that needed to process shape information. The fact that five-year-olds could process shape and not size information under these conditions suggests that size discrimination processes are undergoing significant refinement during these early years (6–8) and that they are not nearly as well developed in five-, six-, and eight-year-olds as are information processing capacities associated with shape.

SELECTED ASPECTS OF
VISUAL MEMORY

Age changes in visual memory as measured by a digit span task are shown in Figure 4.12. In this task the child attempts to recall increasingly longer series of digits flashed on a screen for 5 seconds. Overall, visual memory shows a rather linear increase in the size of the digit span from 7 to 12 years of age. Developmentally, seven-year-olds show an average span of 4 digits; this increases to 5 digits at age 10 and to 5½ digits at age 12. Since the average memory span for digits in adults is 7 ± 2, these data indicate that short-term memory processes are still undergoing change and refinement even at the age of 12. There are few, if any, differences between boys and girls in performances on this memory task across ages. Data on children younger than 7 are generally not available, since digit-span tasks are often beyond the capacity of five- and six-year-olds (Williams *et al.*, 1977). Thus although visual memory processes are obviously present and operative in young children, they are difficult to assess accurately. Refinement of short-term memory is a gradual process that continues throughout at least the early and middle childhood years.

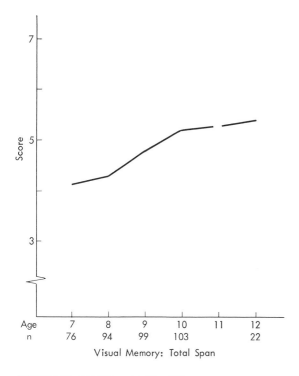

FIGURE 4.12   Age Changes in Visual Memory

More recent data on developmental changes in visual memory processes in young children indicate that there are significant differences in
such abilities among five-, six-, and eight-year-olds (Williams *et al.,* 1979).
The task used by these authors was simpler than the digit span task previously described. In this case familiar geometric shapes were flashed onto
a screen for 5 seconds. The child was then asked to circle on a page in
front of him the figures he had just seen on the screen. Thus, with some
help in probing their recall, young children are able to perform memory
tasks. In general, five- and six-year-old children showed good memory for
shapes when the number of shapes was small (e.g., 3 or 4). However, eight-
year-olds were significantly better than five- or six-year-olds in remembering longer sequences of shapes (e.g., 7 or 8 figures). Developmentally, five-
and six-year-olds seem to be similar in terms of short-term visual memory
processes. Eight-year-olds give evidence of having much more refined
short-term visual memory. Variability of performance, interestingly, increased with age so that eight-year-olds, although performing at a higher
level than five- or six-year-olds, were also more variable as a group than
the younger children.

DEPTH PERCEPTION

To discuss visual perception development in young children without some mention of the development of depth perception would be at best an oversight. However, normative data on such abilities are virtually non-existent in the literature. Depth perception can be defined as the ability to judge how near or how far away one or more objects are from one's person. Depth perception may be considered "static," as when the individual is asked to judge the depth of stationary objects, or "dynamic," as when the individual is asked to judge moving objects in space. This latter aspect of depth perception is discussed in the section on perception of movement.

In general it is believed that some primitive type of depth perception exists even in the very young infant (Van Hofsten, 1977; Walk, 1978). Numerous studies on infants have clearly documented the fact that as early as 2 to 6 months, infants are aware of and pay attention to depth dimensions of their space world and prefer three-dimensional over flat objects (Fantz and Fagan, 1975; Schwartz, Campos, and Baisel, 1973). True binocularity (the ability to use the two eyes together and to fixate accurately on an object) appears at about 2 months, and this may represent the onset of the development of more refined depth perception. Even before this time, however, there is abundant evidence that some depth perception capacity exists in the young infant. By 6 months infants clearly pay attention to depth cues and, as reported in the famous "visual cliff" study, will not crawl to their mothers (even if coaxed) if they have to cross the deep end of the visual cliff. As reaching and grasping behaviors develop, the child's attention to depth in the environment is seen in the observation that invariably the child reaches out for near objects but not for far ones. Thus it is evident that the young child has at least some crude awareness of depth in his environment.

Binocularity improves throughout early childhood (2–5 years) and so do the depth perception capacities of the young child. Still, four-year-olds frequently fail to see differences between two-dimensional and three-dimensional slides. Five- and six-year-olds, in contrast, rarely, if ever, fail to perceive depth in the three-dimensional slides (Jahoda and McGurk, 1974; Yonas *et al.*, 1978). By 6 or 7, the child can judge depth as accurately with monocular cues as with full binocular cues. This suggests that depth perception is nearing maturity. Although complete data on the development of static depth perception in children are scarce, Williams (1968) reports that twelve-year-old boys are as accurate in making static depth judgments as are sixteen- and twenty-year-old males. Taken together then, these data suggest that static depth perception capacities develop rapidly in the early years of childhood and are nearly refined and/or mature by 12 years of age.

PERCEPTION OF MOVEMENT

One of the most important visual perception abilities that the individual possesses is that of the perception of movement. The importance of this capacity for the human organism is seen in the fact that from birth onward, the child is aware of and fascinated by movement in his environment (Haith, 1966). There are, however, few experimental or comprehensive descriptive studies that have dealt with the development and refinement of the child's ability to perceive movement in space. Thus not a lot of information is available with regard to how young children perceive moving objects. A summary of basic developmental characteristics generally associated with the early refinement of perception of movement in the young child is given in Table 4-3.

Data reported by Williams (1967, 1968) and Williams *et al.* (1979) provide important information concerning the nature of the young child's perception of moving objects in space. The results of Williams' 1967 study of the perception of moving objects by children suggests that accurate perception of movement continues to develop well into the upper elementary years (10–12 years). Children in this study were asked to judge the speed and direction of a moving object. They did this by moving as quickly as possible to the spot where they thought they should be in order to catch a moving object were it not interrupted in its flight by a canvas placed over the children's heads. In general children, regardless of age and sex, tended to respond to the moving object equally fast. That is, all of the children tended to start moving fairly soon after the ball was projected into the air. The main difference was in the accuracy of the judgment made by children of different ages. For example, fourth, fifth, and sixth graders were significantly more accurate in judging the flight of the moving object than were first, second, and third graders. The average error of these younger children was 22 feet. Thus six-, seven-, and eight-year-olds misjudged the flight of the moving object and went 22 feet beyond where they should have been to intercept it. The mean error of the older children was only 2½ feet. This suggests that sometime during the course of the upper elementary school years, the child begins to develop a more refined capacity for making complex judgments or perceptions about moving objects in his environment.

Data from the study also suggested that an interesting sequence of changes occurred during the course of development of these behaviors. It would appear that although a child in the early grades (6, 7, 8 years of age) responded quickly to the moving object, the child was *not* able to use the information about its flight to accurately direct his motor behavior. In other words it was as though the young child were simply aware that the object was moving fast and that was all. Thus he proceeded to move as

TABLE 4-3   Developmental Characteristics of the Perception of Movement

AGE	DEVELOPMENTAL CHARACTERISTICS
Birth to 1 mo.	Infant (3-5 days) responds to intermittent movement of a visual stimulus. Follows dangling ring through 90° arc. Fixation and pursuit movements are unrefined.
2-4 mos.	Follows moving objects through greater distances. Reverses pursuit movements more smoothly. Fixation processes much more refined.
5-10 mos.	Becomes more aware of his own bodily movement. Fascinated by movement of his hands. Notices small movements of persons around him. Tracks a ball as it moves toward him or horizontally across his visual field. Entranced with anything that moves.
2-5 yrs.	Ability to track moving objects improves. Eye movements become more controlled. More aware of movement in the periphery of the visual field. Does not like movements that are directly toward him.
5-12 yrs.	Tracking of movement of objects in the horizontal plane is well developed. By 7, tracks objects moving downward more easily than those moving upward. Is influenced in his judgments of range or speed of movement by the total context in which the movement occurs. At 6, 7, 8, does not judge moving objects effectively. By 9, makes accurate judgments about moving objects in space. By 12, makes quick and accurate judgments about moving objects in space.

quickly and as far as possible in the allotted time. It is almost as though the visual mechanism of the child at this age is not functioning at a high enough level to permit the visual information received from the flight of the moving object to be quickly and accurately translated into an appropriate motor response. Therefore a completely adaptive behavior by the young child in this particular situation may not be possible.

During the upper elementary school years, there appears to be a period of transition. Children in the fourth grade show an almost complete reversal of the behavior shown by their younger counterparts. The perceptual judgments that the nine-year-old made about the moving object were very precise. That is, nine-year-old children were quite accurate in judging where the object was going and thus in determining where they should go in order to catch it. The limiting factor was that it took them a very long time to make this judgment. It seems that although this child was able to use the available visual information to guide his motor behavior, the processing and translating of this visual input into a motor behavior still remained a slow operation.

In the fifth grade a greater interplay between the visual and motor mechanisms seems to occur. This is revealed by the fact that the ten-year-old child was a little less accurate in his judgment of the flight of the moving object but that he made the judgment much more quickly. Thus at 10 years we see an increase in the rate at which visual information is processed and used, but concomitantly there is a slight sacrifice in the accuracy of the judgment made. This suggests that the visual and motor systems of the ten-year-old are becoming more interrelated but still have not reached a mature or adult level of functioning.

Children in the sixth grade made their decisions about the moving object both quickly and accurately. That is, they seemed to process the incoming visual information *quickly and accurately,* and their motor responses followed easily and smoothly. This suggests that the interplay between the visual and motor systems of the eleven-year-old may be nearly complete; the result is a smooth and skillful behavioral response to moving objects in space.

More recent information about perception of moving objects or dynamic depth perception characteristics of young children suggests that five-, six-, and eight-year-olds are equally unskilled at making such judgments (Williams *et al.,* 1979). Children were asked to watch on film the trajectories of a number of tennis balls. They saw, as before, only the first portion of the ball's flight (all flights were viewed at least to the high point of the trajectory). The children were then asked to indicate on a target diagram where they thought the ball would have landed if they had been able to see its entire flight. All children, regardless of age, were relatively inaccurate in making precise judgments about the overall trajectory of the moving tennis ball. Variability of performance was quite large, and children of all ages were extremely inconsistent in their judgments of where the moving object in space was going. These observations are in complete agreement with the earlier observation of Williams (1968) that children in the early elementary years simply do not possess a refined facility for judging moving objects in space.

Other data indicate that the ability to quickly and accurately judge moving objects in space does mature by approximately 12 years of age. In a study in which twelve-, sixteen-, and twenty-year-old males were asked to judge the flight of tennis balls projected into the air at different speeds and vertical and horizontal directions, it was observed that twelve-year-olds as a group were as skillful in making such judgments as sixteen- and twenty-year-olds. This would suggest that this visual perception ability is relatively mature at 12, with very little refinement occurring after that age (Williams, 1968).

VISUAL ACUITY

Acuity refers to the capacity of the visual system to detect or perceive detail clearly. Although a separate capacity, acuity is clearly related to basic discrimination processes involved in visual perception, and, as such, improvements in acuity with age and/or experience often accompany an increase in the child's capacity to make more refined visual discriminations. Visual acuity may be classified as static or dynamic. Static visual acuity (SVA) has to do with the ability of an observer to detect detail in a stationary configuration/object, whereas dynamic visual acuity (DVA) refers to the ability of the individual to pick out detail in a moving object/configuration (Whiting, 1974). Miller and Ludvigh (1953) have suggested that DVA is a reflection of the capacity of the central nervous system to estimate the direction and velocity of the movement of an object and of the eye movement or oculo-motor system to catch and hold its image on the fovea long enough to permit resolution of its detail. In tests of DVA, checkerboard targets with different degrees of grid precision (10.0 mins. to 0.6 mins. of arc) are flashed on a screen and made to travel a horizontal path from left to right at a variety of speeds (60°/sec., 90°/sec., 120°/sec.). The child is asked to indicate when he no longer sees the "small checks" in the stationary or moving target.

Developmentally, static acuity shows little or no change after 10 years of age. In general, five- and six-year-olds have much less well developed static visual acuity than older children (7–12 years). There is, however, a period of rapid improvement in static visual acuity from 5 to 7 years; this is followed by a period of relatively little change from 7 to 9 years. There is again a sharp increase in acuity between 9 and 10 years. This increase is once again followed by a plateauing of visual acuity between 10 and 12 years. Static visual acuity at age 12 is nearly equivalent to that of the average adult (Burg and Hulbert, 1961; Cratty, 1973).

With regard to dynamic visual acuity, developmental trends seem to be, in part, a function of the speed at which the stimulus is moved. For example, dynamic visual acuity at slow speeds (e.g., 60°/sec.) follows a trend in development that is very similar to that just described for static visual acuity. The major difference between the two seems to be that while static visual acuity plateaus at 10–12 years, dynamic visual acuity continues to undergo refinement between 11 and 12 years. For dynamic visual acuity at faster target speeds (e.g., 120°/sec.), there is a sharp increase in acuity between 5 and 6 years of age with little or no change during the period of 6 to 9 years. A second stage of refinement in dynamic visual acuity takes place between 9 and 10 years and a third one between 11 and 12. Overall then, there appear to be three major periods during development when important changes in visual acuity take place: 5–7 years, 9–10 years, and 11–12 years. Static visual acuity seems to reach maturity before dynamic visual acuity. Interestingly, boys as a group demonstrate superior visual acuity to girls at all ages under both static and dynamic conditions. Thus, boys at any given age are able to detect detail in both static and moving visual stimuli with greater precision than are girls of similar ages. Acuity, both static and dynamic, seems also to be better for children who do not wear glasses than for those who do (Cratty, 1973).

EYE MOVEMENT CONTROL PROCESSES

A very important part of visual perception development is the scanning or systematic exploration of the visual field. Children learn to systematically search or scan their environments for visual information (Elkind, 1975). A series of studies conducted by Salapatek and Kessen (1966) indicate that the eye movement control system of man is functional at birth. However, the attraction to simple elements (lines and angles) of visual stimuli and the general lack of exploratory eye movements implies that the system has not attained its full functional capacity at birth. Such development occurs during the early years.

Eye movement control in young children was studied by Vurpillot (1968), using a task in which children had to decide whether or not pairs of houses painted in black and white were identical. Each house had six windows with different internal designs. The pair of houses was identical when all corresponding windows had the same internal design. The unlike pairs had 1, 3 or 5 windows with different internal designs. Scan paths or eye movement patterns were observed while children 4 to 9 years old made these judgments. As expected, children made an increasingly larger number of correct discriminations with age. Eye movement patterns also changed with age. In general, with increasing age, children used larger numbers of fixations in making judgments about identical houses. Four- and five-year-olds tended to fixate all pairs of houses in precisely the same manner. They used fewer numbers of fixations than older children and tended to fixate on the same windows in all house pairs. Thus whether the houses were alike or different, the same eye movement or search pattern was used by four- and five-year-olds. In contrast, six and a half- and nine-year-olds showed different eye movement patterns according to the nature of the visual display. Older children used the most fixations in making judgments about houses that were identical, the next largest number of fixations for houses that had only one different pair of windows, and the least number of fixations for discriminations that involved houses with 5 different windows. Thus a developmental characteristic of eye movement control is that in older children (6½ to 9 years), the pattern of fixation varies according to the nature of the stimulus display and the kind of judgment that the child has to make.

Similar differences in scan patterns have been observed in even younger children. For example, three- and four-year-olds, like five-year-olds, have been shown to use fewer fixations when viewing most visual configurations than do older children. In addition eye movement patterns of these younger children tend to show little or no relation to the outline of the stimulus figure, and thus when compared to adult behavior, examination of the display is often incomplete. It would appear, overall, that young children may not attend to or fixate on a stimulus array for a long enough time or in the right way to get the information needed for making precise discriminations. By 5 or 6, fixations are more numerous, although frequently of shorter duration. The more mature pattern of tracking the contours of the stimulus appears at 5 and becomes predominant at 6 years (Whiteside, 1974; Zaporozhets, 1965). The tracing of the contours of the stimulus array is, of course, characteristic of adult eye movement patterns.

Elkind (1975) reports some interesting information on the development of eye movement patterns. When young children are presented with an ordered array of visual information (e.g., the items are arranged in the form of a triangle; see Figure 4.13), five- and eight-year-old children read the figures around the triangle starting at the top. However six- and seven-year-olds tend to scan the triangle from left to right and top to bottom, using patterns much like ones used in reading the printed page. In disordered arrays (random arrangement of the same visual items), five-year-olds show no systematic pattern of scanning the array. Under these circumstances six-, seven-, and eight-year-olds all use the left-to-right, top-to-bottom scan pattern. Thus it would appear that older children employ different scanning strategies depending upon the nature of the organization of the visual field; younger children, in contrast, are largely limited to one dominant scanning strategy, a strategy that they use under all circumstances.

Volitional movement of the body is initiated, expanded, and refined to a great degree during the early years of life. We do not know what effect such perceptual-motor experiences may have on the functional development of eye movement patterns, but it certainly seems plausible to suggest that the spatial exploration that the child undergoes as he or she develops various motor skills could have an important influence on the development of adequate ocular or eye movement behavior. That developmental dif-

FIGURE 4.13 The ordered array from the Picture Exploration Test (P.E.T.). The first half of the test, the disordered array, displayed similar common items arranged randomly on a card. (From Elkind, 1975)

ferences seen in eye movement patterns are *not* strictly due to maturational factors is seen in the fact that the nature of the eye movement patterns of children of various ages can be and are affected by the degree of familiarity of the visual configuration that they are asked to scan. Thus more primitive eye movement patterns frequently observed in three- or four-year-olds are often seen in older children when they are presented with an unfamiliar stimulus array to explore. In general, new stimulus configurations tend to elicit, at least initially, the use of more primitive eye movement patterns in all individuals. In contrast, three- and four-year-olds can, when told what to do, track or scan the contours of a visual stimulus as skillfully as older children normally do. Thus although three- and four-year-olds can execute eye movement patterns that are primarily seen in older children, they do not spontaneously use these more mature eye movement patterns. They seem to have to have practice in learning to use them.

One aspect of eye movement control that is frequently of interest to those in clinical situations is that of ocular tracking or simple pursuit movements of the eyes. Generally, ocular tracking is examined for the smoothness and efficiency with which the child can follow a moving target in the vertical, horizontal, and diagonal planes. Although simple tracking movements appear much earlier than 4 years, it is difficult, if not impossible, for most children to separate eye movement from head movement before this age (Bizzi, 1974; Harris *et al.*, 1974). Thus at 4 years most children track efficiently in the vertical plane and naturally separate eye and head movements. They may also track in the horizontal plane for short distances.

After tracking for short distances, however, head movements begin to appear in the tracking behavior of the child. Most four-year-olds find it extremely difficult, if not impossible, to track in the diagonal plane. Efficient convergence movements are observed in approximately 50% of four-year-olds. By 5, nearly 60% of all children show efficient tracking and convergence movements with eye and head movements easily and naturally separated. Six-year-olds track in all planes with nearly the efficiency of the average adult (Williams, 1979).

VISUAL PERCEPTION DEVELOPMENT AND MOTOR PERFORMANCE

That vision and visual perception play an important role in the learning and performance of motor skills is clearly documented in numerous studies on adult motor behavior. Perhaps the most dramatic illustration of this relationship is the situation in which visual cues are distorted or rearranged, and adults are asked to perform a motor task. Without exception under these circumstances, adults show a marked deterioration in their ability to execute learned motor acts. Only with practice and the opportunity to interrelate visual information with specific motor responses does performance begin to show recognizable improvement (Smith and Smith, 1962).

Fleishman (1954) has reported that visual perception abilities are more important early in learning than in later development of motor skills. Learning curves plotted on the basis of the visual perception abilities of learners revealed that those individuals who had superior visual abilities made the most rapid progress in the early stages of skill acquisition. As practice continued and learning progressed, differences in performances due to variations in visual perception abilities were erased. Thus, in later stages of skilled performance the visual perception abilities of the learner seem to be less important. More recently, Temple and Williams (1977) have shown that for eleven- and twelve-year-olds visual perception ability is indeed important in the learning of perceptual-motor skills where the visual components of the task are important to successful performance (e.g., the pursuit rotor task). In such cases children with better developed visual perception abilities (static depth perception, dynamic depth perception, figure-ground perception) began and remained superior throughout learning to other children in terms of their performance on this fine motor task.

That certain aspects of visual perception are important in skilled motor performance is also seen in the results of a study that looked at the ability of skilled and unskilled performers (ages 12, 16 and 20 years) to judge the trajectories of moving objects in space, something that the individual must be able to do if he is to be successful in such skill situations as catching, striking, kicking, etc. (Williams, 1968). Observations from this study clearly indicated that the skilled player was able to make judgments about the moving object in space significantly more quickly and accurately than were unskilled performers. Skilled persons made such judgments, on the average, in .36 seconds; unskilled persons required more than .51 seconds to make similar judgments. The difference in the speed with which these judgments were made could easily mean the difference between success and failure in a whole host of sports situations. In terms of the accuracy of the response, skilled players were more than twice as accurate as unskilled performers in making judgments about the flight of the moving object. On the average, skillful performers misjudged the end point of the flight, by only 22 inches. The poorly skilled individual misjudged the same flight by more than 51 inches. This means that the poorly skilled person judged that he should be in a position that was on the average more than 4 feet from where he should have been in order to successfully interact with the moving object. Thus one of the things that may characterize the development of proficient performance of certain motor skills is the ability to rapidly and accurately process visual information associated with the performance of that skill.

More recently Williams *et al.* (1978) have shown that for six-year-olds visual perception abilities are very important in the learning of gross perceptual-motor tasks. When young children were asked to perform a gross perceptual-motor task that involved interpretation of visual cues and the execution of such gross motor behaviors as hopping, ball bouncing, and foot tapping, these authors found that six-year-olds who had better developed visual perception abilities (dynamic depth perception, figure-ground perception, visual memory, etc.) were significantly superior to six-year-olds with less well developed visual perception abilities in mastering this task. Children with advanced visual perception abilities began and maintained a higher level of performance throughout the learning period. In addition the rate at which improvement occurred was smoother and steadier for children with better developed visual perception capacities than it was for children with less advanced visual perception capacities. When eight-year-olds performed the same task, no differences in performances of children with different levels of visual perception development were observed. This suggests that early in development, visual perception abilities may be important to the learning of motor skills, but that as the child approaches middle childhood years, they assume a role of less importance.

These same children were asked to learn a fine perceptual-motor task that involved the interpretation of specific visual cues and the execution of selected fine motor skills including line drawing, unscrewing a bolt, placing small pegs in a pegboard, etc. Under these circumstances differences between the performances of children with advanced visual perception abilities and those with less advanced visual perception abilities were even more exaggerated than for the gross perceptual-motor task. Performances of children with advanced visual perception development were far superior to those children with less well developed visual perception and, in fact, these children mastered the task in two practices. Learning was much slower for the children with less well developed visual perception, and even after five sessions they had still not reached the level of performance of the other children. Thus in tasks that require more precise eye-hand coordination and manipulative skill, children with well-developed visual perception abilities show greater ease and efficiency in mastering such tasks than do other children. This is true for both six- and eight-year-olds.

The role of visual perception in the development of motor skills is perhaps best described by Gibson (1966), who suggests that from the moment of birth onward there is a covariation of retinal and musculo-tactile stimulation that ultimately becomes attached to or associated with specific movements or motor behaviors. Thus it is only through opportunities for moving and interacting with the visual environment that task-specific patterns of visual-motor stimulation are laid down in the nervous system, and that visual cues ultimately can come to elicit rather automatic behavioral responses.

VISUAL PERCEPTION
DEVELOPMENT AND COGNITIVE
PERFORMANCE

Although there is little doubt that certain basic visual perception abilities are crucial to the development of selected cognitive activities (e.g., reading), the exact role of visual perception in such development is far from clearly understood. For example, children have been shown to be able to visually identify letters that are physically alike (and/or different) before they can name or classify these letters (Henderson, 1974). It would also appear that children tend developmentally to learn to discriminate spatial relationships among objects before they can make such discriminations on the basis of verbal descriptions and before they conceptually understand what such relationships mean. Thus children can copy spatially confusing letters (d-b, p-b) before they can visually match them; they can visually match such letters before they can easily or readily name them. What is not clear is whether or not there is a causative relationship between visual perception abilities involved in matching and conceptual skills involved in naming or classifying. Although it is largely speculative at this point, there is some belief that verbal descriptions and conceptual classifications do proceed more easily for the young child if the basic visual discrimination abilities are already well established.

Williams *et al.* (1978) report data that suggest that in the performance of certain cognitive tasks (e.g., paired-associate tasks that involve the selection of a visual word label for an object that is examined through the tactile-kinesthetic sense) the level of visual perception development clearly separates both six- and eight-year-olds in terms of their ability to master such tasks. Eight-year-olds with advanced visual perception abilities perform at the highest level of all children; eight-year-olds with less well developed visual perception perform at the next highest level; six-year-olds with advanced visual perception abilities show the next most advanced level of performance, and six-year-olds with less well developed visual perception perform at the lowest level of all the children throughout learning. These latter children perform at a level that is significantly below the level of their more advanced six-year-old counterparts. These data suggest that some aspects of cognitive learning may be tied to the level of visual perception development of the child.

Perhaps the most illuminating information available on the relationship between visual perception and cognitive development is that provided by Belka and Williams (1979) in a study of perceptual-motor and cognitive development in young four-, five-, and six-year-old children. These authors present experimental data that clearly show that there is a strong and significant relationship between cognitive development and visual perception ability in four- and five-year-olds. The relationship is not as strong for six-year-olds. In general, visual perception abilities accounted for 51% of performance variance in cognitive tasks for four-year-old children and for 55% of performance variance in cognitive tasks for five-year-olds. Only 36% of such variance was accounted for by the visual perception abilities of six-year-old children. The visual perception abilities that seemed to be the most important contributors to cognitive development for these young children were figure-ground perception and perception of spatial orientation. Importantly, Belka and Williams (1978) suggest that the kind of visual perception ability that is important in cognitive development of the young child changes with the age of the child. Thus although there are not a lot of data available, there is some reason to believe that there may be at least a loose linkage between visual perception development and cognitive performance in early childhood.

SUMMARY

1. Children, in general, show rapid development in visual perception skills from 3 to 6 years.
2. According to data provided by Frostig (1966), figure-ground perception increases rapidly from 5 to 6 years, whereas perception of spatial relations undergoes rapid growth from 5–7 years. In addition, vari-

ability of performance seems to decrease with age. Boys are often more variable than girls in such behaviors.

3. When asked to discriminate among various kinds of visual stimuli, children tend to be better able to make identity discriminations than color discriminations. Form discrimination is more difficult than color discrimination.

4. Development of whole-part perception in children involves a change from perception of relatively undifferentiated wholes to a perception of the parts of the whole to the perception of a more precise, articulated whole with parts. This process occurs gradually from 4 to 9 years.

5. Children process visual information more slowly than adults but improve markedly in such capacities from 6 to 10 years of age.

6. Visual memory in children increases in a linear fashion from 7 to 12 years. Seven-year-olds have an average span of 4 digits; twelve-year-olds have an average digit span of 5½.

7. Perception of depth and of movement also both improve with age. Both seem to reach maturity between 8 and 12 years of age.

8. Visual acuity, static and dynamic, improves with age and undergoes rapid growth from 5 to 7 years. Static acuity seems to reach maturity (10 years) before dynamic acuity (11–12 years).

9. Eye movement strategies (scanning) are relatively undeveloped in the young child but show adult characteristics at 6–8 years.

10. Visual perception behaviors play a key role in the development of skillful motor behavior and seem to be integrally related to cognitive development in four- and five-year-olds. Such relationships are not as strong for six-year-olds.

STUDY QUESTIONS

1. Describe age and sex differences in the following aspects of visual perception (á la Frostig) and define each:
   a. eye-motor coordination
   b. form constancy
   c. position in space
   d. spatial relations
   When (at what ages) do the greatest changes take place?
2. Order the following tasks from simple to more complex for children and adults. Define or give an example of each.
   a. identity matching
   b. function matching

    c. color matching

    d. form matching

    e. equivalence matching

    How do children and adults differ on these? Why?

3. Define whole-part perception. How is schematization involved in the development of whole-part perception? Give an example of the kind of changes that occur in whole-part perception with age. When is whole-part perception essentially mature?

4. Differentiate between figurative and operative wholes.

5. Some people have suggested that visual perception is a "constructive" process. What does that mean? How does it help to explain differences between children and adults in some aspects of perception?

6. Define perception of spatial orientation. Describe its development in the young child. What are "spatial dualisms"?

7. Describe the development of perception of spatial direction in young children.

8. What is "perceptual constancy"? Describe how it has been studied in young children. When does perceptual constancy reach mature levels?

9. What is perceptual transport? How does it relate to perceptual constancy?

10. Describe the basic age changes in visual information processing in young children. How does shape versus size affect this capacity in children? How does the number of shapes or stimuli affect this process? How does the addition of an irrelevant dimension affect this process?

11. Describe the nature of the changes that occur in visual memory with increasing age. At what age is visual memory span essentially mature?

12. Describe basic depth perception processes in young children.

13. What are the important changes that take place in the child's perception of movement during the elementary school years? When does the child first notice or become aware of movement? When does dynamic depth perception reach adult levels?

14. Define static and dynamic visual acuity. How do these capacities change with age in the young child? When are they mature?

15. Describe the research on the development of eye movement control processes in young children. What are scanning strategies? How do they change with age?

16. How does experience affect eye movement control?

17. Describe how "tracking" movements change with age.

18. How does visual perception affect or contribute to skillful movement responses? Cite specific evidence to support your answer.

19. What differences, if any, exist in visual perception capacities of children who are skillful versus those who are awkward in performing gross and fine motor tasks?

20. How is visual perception related to cognitive development? Cite specific evidence.

REFERENCES

BELKA, D., AND WILLIAMS, H.   Canonical relationships among perceptual-motor, perceptual, and cognitive behaviors in young, normal children. Unpublished paper, University of Toledo, 1978.

BELKA, D., AND WILLIAMS, H.   Prediction of later cognitive behavior from early school perceptual-motor, perceptual, and cognitive performances. *Perceptual and Motor Skills.* 49 (1979): 131–141.

BIZZI, E.   Coordination of eye-head movements. *Scientific American.* 231 (1974): 100–106.

BURG, A., AND HULBERT, S.   Dynamic visual acuity as related to age, sex, and static acuity. *Journal of Applied Psychology.* 45 (1961): 111–116.

CONNOLLY, K.   *Mechanisms of Motor Skill Development,* pp. 161–206. New York: Academic Press, 1970.

CRATTY, B. J.   *Dynamic Visual Acuity: A Developmental Study.* Monograph, University of California at Los Angeles, 1973.

ELKIND, D.   Perceptual development in children. *American Scientist.* 63 (1975): 533–541.

ELKIND, D., ANAGNOSTOPONLOU, R., AND MALONE, S. Determinants of part-whole perception in children. *Child Development.* 2 (1970): 391–397.

ELKIND, D., KOEGLER, R., AND GO, E.   Studies in perceptual development: Whole-part perception. *Child Development.* 35 (1964): 81–90.

FANTZ, R. L., AND FAGAN, J. F., III.   Visual attention to size and number of pattern details by term and preterm infants during the first six months. *Child Development.* 46 (1975): 3–18.

FARNHAM-DIGGORY, S., AND GREGG, L.   Color, form and function as dimensions of natural classification: developmental changes in eye movements, reaction time and response strategies. *Child Development.* 46 (1975): 101–114.

FLEISHMAN, E., AND HEMPEL, W., JR.   Changes in factor structure of a complex psychomotor test as a function of practice. *Psychometrika.* 19 (1954): 239–252.

FLEMING, M.   Eye movement indices of cognitive behavior. *AV Communication Review.* 17 (1969): 383–398.

FROSTIG, M., LEFEVER, W., AND WHITTLESEY, J.   *Administration and Scoring Manual: Marianne Frostig Developmental Test of Visual Perception.* Palo Alto, CA: Consulting Psychologists Press, 1966.

GIBSON, J.   *The Senses Considered as Perceptual Systems.* New York: Houghton Mifflin, 1966.

GOODGLASS, H.   Stimulus duration and visual processing time. *Perceptual and Motor Skills.* 33 (1971): 179–182.

HAITH, M.   The response of the human newborn to visual movement. *Journal of Experimental Child Psychology.* 3 (1966): 235–243.

HALTRECHT, E., AND McCORMACK, P.   Monitoring eye movements of slow and fast learners. *Psychonomic Science.* 6 (1966): 461–462.

HARRIS, P., CASSEL, T., AND BAMBOROUGH, P.   Tracking by young infants. *British Journal of Psychology.* 65 (1974): 345–349.

HENDERSON, S.   Speed of letter cancellation, the bases of visual and name identity in young children. *Journal of Experimental Child Psychology.* 17 (1974): 347–352.

JAHODA, G., AND McGURK, H.   Pictorial depth perception: a developmental study. *British Journal of Psychology.* 65 (1974): 141–149.

JEFFREY, W.   Discrimination of oblique lines by children. *Journal of Comparative Physiological Psychology.* 62 (1966): 154.

LOWE, R. C.　A developmental study of part-whole relations in visual perception. *The Journal of Genetic Psychology.* 123 (1973): 231–240.

MILLER, J., AND LUDVIGH, E.　*Dynamic Visual Acuity When the Required Pursuit Movement of the Eye Is In A Vertical Plane.* Jt. Prof. Rep. No. NM001.075.01.02 United States Naval School of Aviation Medicine, Pensacola, Florida, 1953.

NAUS, M., AND SHILLMAN, R.　Why a Y is not a V; a new look at the distinctive features of letters. *Journal of Experimental Psychology: Human Perception and Performance.* 2 (1976): 394–400.

PIAGET, J.　*The Origins of Intelligence in Children.* New York: W.W. Norton and Company, Inc., 1963.

PICK, A. D., editor.　*Perception and Its Development: A Tribute to Eleanor J. Gibson.* Hillsdale, NJ: Lawrence Erlbaum Associates, 1979.

SALAPATECK, P., AND KESSEN, W.　Visual scanning of triangles by the human newborn. *Journal of Experimental Psychology.* 3 (1966): 155–167.

SCHWARTZ, A., CAMPOS, J., AND BAISEL, E., JR.　The visual cliff: cardiac and behavioral responses on the deep and shallow sides at five and nine months of age. *Journal of Experimental Child Psychology.* 15 (1973): 86–99.

SMITH, K. U., AND SMITH, W. M.　*Perception and Motion.* Philadelphia: W.B. Saunders Company, 1962.

TEMPLE, I., AND WILLIAMS, H.　Rate and level of learning as a function of information processing characteristics of the learner and the task. *Journal of Motor Behavior.* 3 (1977): 179–192.

VAN HOFSTEN, C.　Binocular convergence as a determinant of reaching behavior in infancy. *Perception.* 6 (1977): 139–144.

VURPILLOT, E.　The development of scanning strategies and their relation to visual differentiation. *Journal of Experimental Child Psychology.* 6 (1968): 632–650.

WALK, R. D.　Depth perception and experience. In Walk and Pick, eds., *Perception and Experience.* New York: Plenum Press, 1978.

WHITESIDE, J. A.　Eye movements of children, adults, and elderly persons during inspection of dot patterns. *Journal of Experimental Child Psychology.* 18 (1974): 313–332.

WHITING, H.T.A.　Dynamic visual acuity and performance in a catching task. *Journal of Motor Behavior.* 6 (1974): 87–94.

WILLIAMS, H.　Developmental characteristics of eye and head movements in young children. Unpublished paper, University of Toledo, 1979.

WILLIAMS, H.　Effects of the systematic variation of speed and direction of object flight and of age and skill classifications on visuo-perceptual judgments of moving objects in three-dimensional space. Unpublished dissertation, University of Wisconsin-Madison, 1968.

WILLIAMS, H.　Perceptual-motor development in children. In Corbin, ed., *A Textbook of Motor Development,* pp. 111–150. Dubuque, IA: Wm. C. Brown, 1973.

WILLIAMS, H.　The perception of moving objects by children. Unpublished paper, University of Toledo, 1967.

WILLIAMS, H., TEMPLE, I., AND BATEMAN, J.　A test battery to assess intrasensory and intersensory development of young children. *Perceptual and Motor Skills.* 48 (1979): 643–659.

WILLIAMS, H., TEMPLE, I., AND BATEMAN, J.　Perceptual-motor and cognitive learning in young children. *Psychology of Motor Behavior and Sport II.* Champaign, IL: Human Kinetics Press, 1978.

WILLIAMS, H., TEMPLE, I., AND LOGSDON, B.   Developmental differences in selected aspects of perceptual-motor development. Unpublished paper, Bowling Green State University, 1977.

YONAS, A., CLEONES, W., AND PETTERSON, L.   Development of sensitivity to pictorial depth. *Science.* 200 (1978): 77–79.

ZAPOROZHETS, A.V.   The development of perception in the preschool child. *Monographs of the Society for Research in Child Development.* 30 (1965): 82–101.

CHAPTER FIVE
INTRASENSORY DEVELOPMENT: TACTILE-KINESTHETIC AND AUDITORY ABILITIES

Little has been written concerning the development of the tactile-kinesthetic or somato-sensory system in young children. Gibson (1966) suggests that the sense that we refer to as the tactile-kinesthetic sense is best thought of as a combination of subsystems, each of which provides a unique source of information. These include: (1) the *cutaneous* or *touch* subsystem, which provides information about stimulation of the skin and/or deeper tissues when movement is not necessarily involved; (2) the *kinesthetic* or *articular* subsystem, which provides information about movement of the joints (e.g., movement and/or position of various body parts); (3) the *muscular* subsystem (muscle sense), which provides information about the contractile status of the muscle; (4) the *vestibular* subsystem, which provides information about the movement (linear and angular acceleration and/or deceleration) or position of the head in relation to the body; (5) the *haptic* subsystem, which offers a unique combination of information from the touch and kinesthetic subsystems; and (6) the *dynamic touch* subsystem, which handles information from the muscular, kinesthetic, and touch subsystems.

The tactile-kinesthetic or somato-sensory system as a whole provides information about selected aspects of the external environment (e.g., shape, size, angle, texture, etc., of objects or surfaces) as well as about the relative condition of the body (e.g., its position and/or movement in space). Although basic somato-sensory abilities have not been clearly identified or universally agreed upon, there are some tasks that have been accepted as

TABLE 5-1   General Summary of Tactile-Kinesthetic or Somato-Sensory Development: Birth to 6 Yrs.

BEHAVIOR	AGE
Reacts with mass motor activity to tactile-kinesthetic stimulation.	0-2 mos.
Blinks when eyelashes are touched.	0-2 mos.
Delayed response to nociceptive stimuli.	0-2 mos.
Basic proprioceptive reflexes present (sucking, rooting, grasp, supporting, etc.).	0-2 mos.
Shows discomfort when nose is stimulated by touch.	2 mos.
Generalized motor activity to tactile-kinesthetic stimulation diminished.	3 mos.
Produces selective movements of "pricked" limb, some basic proprioceptive reflexes becoming suppressed.	4-5-6 mos.
Moves extremities independently to tactile-kinesthetic stimulation.	
Turns head when touched from behind.	
Latency response to painful stimuli shortened.	
Manipulates toy and brings it to mouth for exploration.	
Enjoys bouncing.	
Supports part of weight in standing position.	
Uses radial palmar grasp predominantly.	7-10 mos.
Directs gaze at part of body touched.	
Pokes objects with index finger.	
Latency response to pain further shortened.	
Pulls himself up to standing position.	
Quite skillful in use of pincer grasp.	11-12 mos.
Slowly releases cube into cup.	
Localizes pinched area with hand.	
Explores objects with hands and eyes.	
Imitates scribble.	
Able to pick up crumbs skillfully.	13-18 mos.
Opens and closes small boxes.	
Further decrease of latency response to pain.	
Further refinement of localization of touch.	
Points to objects wanted.	
Points to eyes/nose on request.	
Shows some hand dominance.	
Builds tower of 2-4 cubes.	
Draws stroke imitatively.	
Opposes middle finger to thumb.	19-24 mos.
Removes pellet from bottle.	
Scribbles spontaneously.	
Turns pages singly.	

TABLE 5-1   (continued)

BEHAVIOR	AGE
Latency response to pain 50% less than in neonate. Localizes accurately site of touch. Arranges 3-4 cubes in line.	19-24 mos. (continued)
Holds pencil with fingers. Latency response to pain 50% shorter than at 2 yrs. Generally correct in recognizing stimulus symmetrical situation (e.g., both hands, both cheeks). Folds paper. Selects heavier of two blocks.	3 yrs.
Blindfolded, points to touched area on leg. Is correct 40% of time on 2 simultaneous asymmetric stimulations (e.g., face-hand).	4-6 yrs.

Source: Dekaban, *Neurology of Early Childhood,* 1970. Used by permission of Williams & Wilkins Co., Baltimore.

good indicators of tactile-kinesthetic sensitivity. Available information on developmental changes in performances on these tasks is described in this chapter. A summary of age characteristics of tactile-kinesthetic sensitivity is presented in Table 5-1.

One Point Discrimination and/or
Tactile Localization

In this measure of tactile-kinesthetic perception, a tactile stimulus (e.g., a pen point) is applied to the hands and forearms of the child, and the child is asked to point to the spot where he has just been touched. This is done without vision. Available data on the development of one point touch discrimination in children (although sparse) indicate that this basic tactile-kinesthetic ability is well developed by 5 years of age. Williams, Temple, and Bateman (1978, 1979) report that there are no differences among five-, six-, and eight-year-old children in the ability to accurately perceive where they have been stimulated using this technique. Ayres (1978) reports data on tactile localization ability of children ages 4 through 8 years. Her observations indicate that although four-year-olds are much less accurate than older children in their ability to localize tactile stimulation on the hands and forearms, five-, six-, and seven-year-olds appear to have achieved similar levels of tactile localization ability. Both of these sets of data suggest that by the age of 5 the young child has pretty much refined the ability to localize single points of tactile stimulation.

Multiple Point Tactile Discrimination

In multiple point tactile stimulation tasks, two or more points are placed simultaneously or sequentially in contact with the skin. In one type of simultaneous two point discrimination task, two points are placed as close together on the skin as possible and then gradually separated until the child becomes aware or senses two points of stimulation. The point at which the child perceives two separate points of stimulation is referred to as the two point tactile discrimination threshold. Two point discrimination thresholds vary with the area of the body involved. For example, the threshold for sensing two points of tactile stimulation is higher for the back, arm, and thigh (mean = 70 mm.) than for the fingertip (mean = 2 mm.) or the tongue (mean = 1 mm.). No information on developmental changes in such thresholds is available (Van Duyne, 1973).

A variation of the two point tactile discrimination task is one that involves the simultaneous or sequential touching of two different body parts (e.g., the hands and face, two different fingers, etc.). Data from performances of such tasks suggest that this tactile-kinesthetic ability may lag behind the development of the child's ability to localize a single tactile stimulus. For example, only 50% of five-year-olds are able to tell consistently when different fingers are touched simultaneously or sequentially (Ayres, 1966).

There is steady improvement in this tactile-kinesthetic ability from 4 to 7½ years. Ayres (1978) also reports data on performances of children 4 through 8 years of age who were asked to report which body part(s) was (were) touched. In this case the cheek and the back of the hand were touched simultaneously. Observations of children's behavior under these conditions indicate that there is dramatic improvement in such tactile-kinesthetic ability between 4 and 6 years of age. There appears, however, to be little change with age thereafter. Thus this aspect of tactile-kinesthetic sensitivity appears to have reached a level of relative maturity by the age of 6 years. If tactile stimulation is applied to the right and left sides of the body simultaneously (e.g., right versus left arm), only young children or children with diminished tactile sensitivity fail to notice or immediately report one or both points of stimulation.

Tactile-Kinesthetic Discrimination and/or Recognition

This aspect of the child's tactile-kinesthetic abilities has to do with the recognition of objects (e.g., shapes, letters, numbers) and their characteristics through tactile-kinesthetic manipulation or exploration. Much more information is available with regard to the development of tactile-kinesthetic recognition of objects than is available on other aspects of tactile-kinesthetic development.

Van Duyne (1973) studied the transfer of information between the tactile-kinesthetic and visual modalities in two-, three-, and four-year-old children. Children were asked to explore objects tactile-kinesthetically and then to identify these "felt" objects from a visual array of several objects. The reverse of this condition was also used. Observations indicated that young children can go from tactile to visual recognition of objects but not from visual to tactile identification of such objects. This suggests that tactile-kinesthetic perception of objects may develop before the ability to visually identify such objects. After the age of 4, however, the use of vision in form recognition tasks is consistently superior to the use of touch. Thus younger children (three- and four-year-olds) may be more reliant on tactile-kinesthetic information for object recognition than older children (five-, six-, and seven-year-olds).

In general, haptic memory for forms improves significantly between 6 and 8 years of age and thus tactile-kinesthetic recognition of objects shows considerable improvement during this time (Northman and Black, 1976). Tactile-kinesthetic exploration of objects also follows an interesting developmental trend in terms of qualitative differences in methods used by the child to explore the object. Tactile-kinesthetic recognition prior to 30 months appears to be more a matter of accident than anything else. Prior to this time there is little true tactile-kinesthetic search or exploration by the hand and thus little basis for systematic or purposeful tactile recognition of objects (McKibben, 1973). At 3 years of age children tend to explore objects tactile-kinesthetically by grabbing the object and/or patting it with their fingers. Although four-year-olds also grab and pat the object, they more frequently move their hands in meaningful exploration. Five-year-olds use both hands to manipulate and/or explore the object and seem to attend to one or two major features of the object as they explore it. By 6 years of age the child explores an object in a systematic fashion, using the fingers to examine special features of the object and to discover relationships among such features (Van Duyne, 1973). It is also interesting to note that in situations where children are asked to indicate whether or not the form they are feeling is one they have felt before, young children are able to identify with greater certainty objects they have not felt before than they are those that they have felt before.

Williams, Temple, and Bateman (1978, 1979) report data on tactile integration performances in five-, six-, and eight-year-old children. In this situation the child was given a geometric form to explore tactile-kinesthetically for 15 seconds. The child was then given three additional forms to feel and asked to tell whether or not each shape was the same or different from the shape he had previously felt. In such tactile-kinesthetic recognition tasks, five-, six-, and eight-year-olds perform at about the same level. Thus five-, six-, and eight-year-olds were similar to each other in terms of the accuracy with which they could identify objects and/or shapes tactile-kinesthetically. Eight-year-olds, however, were superior to both five- and six-year-olds with respect to the speed with which they could recognize shapes tactile-kinesthetically. Thus eight-year-olds were significantly faster than five- and six-year-olds in identifying various shapes through the tactile-kinesthetic sense.

Data from performances of young children on graphesthesia tasks (the child is asked to reproduce designs drawn on the back of his hand by the tester) indicate that there is continued improvement from 4 through 8 years in the child's ability to perceive tactile information of this kind. The most dramatic changes in such tactile-kinesthetic perception occur between 4 and 5 years of age; there is, however, a second period of improvement that takes place between the sixth and seventh years (Ayres, 1978). Little if any change occurs after the age of 8.

Movement Awareness

Movement awareness tasks are used to assess the child's awareness of movement of the limbs (e.g., the extent of movement that has taken place in one or more joints of the body). In most tasks of this kind the child is asked to move an arm or leg through, for example, 90° of the arc without the use of vision. The child is then asked to reproduce this movement as accurately as possible. Available information on the development of this tactile-kinesthetic ability of children indicates that six-year-olds are more advanced (mean error = 24°) than five-year-olds (mean error = 47°) with regard to their sensitivity to range of joint movement (Williams *et al.,* 1979). Eight-year-olds are significantly superior to both five- and six-year-olds in their ability to reproduce a given extent of limb (arm) movement (mean error = 10°). Truyens (1970) reports a similar improvement in movement awareness between 9 and 10 years of age. Thus it would appear that sensitivity to extent of movement of various limbs increases throughout early and middle childhood years.

Another form of movement awareness is that in which the child is asked to place his finger at a point in space where it had previously been placed by a tester. Data reported by Ayres (1978) indicate that although four-year-olds are able to perform this task with only minimal success, there is both steady and rapid improvement in the performance of this task between 4 and 7 years of age. Little improvement in this aspect of movement awareness is seen after 8 years of age.

Spatial Orientation

Spatial orientation, a more global tactile-kinesthetic ability, is often measured by having the child walk a given distance (e.g., 20 feet or more) blindfolded. The task of the child is to walk this distance in as straight a line as possible. The straighter the path maintained by the child as he walks, the better the spatial orientation. Five- and six-year-olds are essentially unable to maintain a "straight path" throughout a 20 foot distance, and deviate on the average a distance of 33 feet. Eight-year-olds are significantly more accurate in their ability to walk a straight line than are five- or six-year-olds and deviate, on the average, 22 feet from that straight line (Williams, Temple, and Bateman, 1977). Although it is difficult at best to say very much about the development of this tactile-kinesthetic ability on the basis of one set of data, it would appear that spatial orientation does improve significantly during the period from 6 to 8 years of age (Williams *et al.*, 1979).

IMPORTANCE OF THE TACTILE-KINESTHETIC SYSTEMS TO OVERALL DEVELOPMENT

Tactile stimulation during infancy is believed to provide the basis for the development of body awareness, for the carving out of the world of "self-ness" and the world of "other-ness." The handling, rubbing, moving, patting, sponging, stroking, etc., that take place during infancy are all important sources of tactile-kinesthetic stimulation that ultimately help the child to define himself as an entity separate from his environment.

There is general agreement that there are two types or categories of tactile-kinesthetic sensitivity. These are the protopathic and epicritic sensibilities. Protopathic sensibility has a marked affective character, that is, it tells something about the affective quality of the stimulus (e.g., is it agreeable and/or pleasant or is it disagreeable and/or unpleasant?) but provides little information about the exact nature or location of the tactile-kinesthetic input. In epicritic sensibility, the discriminative or informational aspects of tactile-kinesthetic input dominate. That is, tactile-kinesthetic stimulation is localized, identified, and integrated into accurate perception of form, size, and texture of objects and surfaces as well as perceptions of extent, direction, and sequence of bodily movements, etc. (Guyton, 1970). It is this aspect of tactile-kinesthetic sensitivity that forms the basis for complex associative and cognitive reactions that are believed to be functions of the cerebral cortex. It should be noted that these two dimensions of tactile-kinesthetic awareness never operate in isolation or independently of one another.

The protopathic system is believed to appear earlier in development than the epicritic system (in fact it may be organized and operative at birth) and to provide for reflexive reactions to tactile-kinesthetic information that constitute the infant's basic defense or survival reactions. The epicritic system develops later and ultimately achieves a position of dominance in the interpretation and use of tactile-kinesthetic information. Thus early in development, tactile-kinesthetic sensations may be interpreted more from a protopathic or affective point of view. Later in development such input is more likely to be interpreted from an informational, evaluative perspective.

The contribution of tactile-kinesthetic sensitivity to the learning and/ or performance of motor tasks by the young child has been speculated about but has not been carefully studied. For example, Ayres (1978) reports a high correlation between level of touch-discrimination development and the ability of the child to plan and carry out sequential motor acts (e.g., motor planning). Data reported by Williams, Temple, and Bateman (1978) indicate that the age of the child is an important consideration in assessing the contribution of tactile-kinesthetic development to the learning/performance of complex motor acts. Six- and eight-year-old children were asked by these authors to learn a gross and a fine perceptual-motor task. Each of these tasks involved the sequencing of several simple motor acts into a longer behavioral chain (e.g., the gross motor task required the child to organize hopping, foot tapping, and ball bouncing movements into a smooth sequence). On both the fine and gross perceptual-motor tasks, the level of development of tactile-kinesthetic abilities was important only for six-year-olds. Thus six-year-old children with more advanced tactile-kinesthetic abilities were superior to six-year-olds with less well-developed tactile-kinesthetic abilities in the performance of both the gross and fine motor tasks. Interestingly, differences in performances on the fine perceptual-motor task were greater between the two groups of children than were those on the gross perceptual-motor task. Eight-year-olds with more advanced tactile-kinesthetic abilities, however, learned both tasks at a rate and level comparable to that of eight-year-olds with less well-developed tactile-kinesthetic abilities. These data suggest (but do not prove) then that the level of tactile-kinesthetic development of the child may be more important in the learning and/or performance of motor tasks by younger children than by older children. These data also hint that by the age of 8, tactile-kinesthetic abilities of normally developing children have reached some optimum level of development and are not necessarily important contributors to the process of motor skill acquisition thereafter. In addition, for younger children, tactile-kinesthetic abilities may be more important in the development of fine motor control than in the development of control of the large muscle masses of the body.

The importance of tactile-kinesthetic functioning in the clinical assessment of the intactness of the CNS is well known. For example, a large number of tests involved in neurological examinations are, in fact, tests of tactile-kinesthetic functioning (Boll and Reitan, 1972). Level of tactile-kinesthetic functioning has been shown to be related to the cognitive, intellectual, and emotional status of brain-damaged adults. That significant differences exist in tactile-kinesthetic abilities of normal and brain-damaged children has also been well established (Reitan, 1971). The role of tactile-kinesthetic functioning in cognitive development of normal children, however, is far less clear cut. Six- and eight-year-olds and twelve- to fourteen-year-olds were assessed on a variety of tactile-kinesthetic tests (tactile localization, form recognition, etc.) and were classified according to their level of tactile-kinesthetic development based on performances on these tasks (Alan *et al.*, 1976). They were then evaluated for reading achievement (WRAT), intellectual development (WISC), and conceptual development (The Category Test). Observations indicated that for younger children (6–8 years), the level of tactile-kinesthetic functioning was not an important factor in the level of achievement gained in reading or in conceptual development. There were significant differences between children with more advanced (IQ = 122) tactile-kinesthetic functioning and those with less well developed (FSIQ = 113) tactile-kinesthetic abilities in level of *intellectual* development. Interestingly, for older children (12–14 years), those with more advanced development of tactile-kinesthetic abilities were superior to those with less well developed tactile-kinesthetic abilities in all areas (reading, conceptual, and intellectual functioning). Williams, Temple, and Bateman (1978) report similar observations on paired-associate learning tasks. Although a viable explanation for why such a relationship should exist is not presently available, it is possible that well-developed tactile-kinesthetic functioning may in some indirect way reflect the integrity of cortical functioning and thus of higher-order cognitive operations. Why differences should be present in older but not younger children might be explained by suggesting that lack of tactile-kinesthetic development may reflect a minimal cortical dysfunction that is not great enough to interfere with acquisition of low level cognitive skills but that could limit the refinement and/or continued development of such skills to higher levels.

INTRASENSORY DEVELOPMENT: AUDITORY ABILITIES

The auditory system is perhaps the most intricate of all sensory systems. Consequently the study and analysis of auditory information processing abilities and the mechanisms underlying such abilities have lagged behind that of the visual and tactile-kinesthetic systems. Although much information has been gained in recent years about auditory functioning in animals and human adults, very little is known about the development of auditory information processing abilities in young children (Doehring and Libman, 1974; Wood, 1975). Because of the complexity of the auditory system and the scarcity of information concerning developmental aspects of auditory information-processing in young children, only a brief and necessarily superficial summary of age differences on common auditory information-processing tasks will be presented. Other age characteristics are presented in Table 5-2.

Auditory Acuity

Auditory acuity involves the detection by the individual of the presence or absence of sound. Thus in auditory acuity tasks, the child is simply asked to indicate whether or not he hears a sound under circumstances in which pure or warbled tones are randomly interspersed with no sound. Little, if any, change in acuity appears to occur during the early and/or middle childhood years (Doty, 1974).

Sound Localization

In auditory localization tasks, sounds emanating from different spatial origins are presented to the child. The child is asked to indicate the direction from which the sound is coming. Sound localization is believed to be important in the overall development of the young child because it helps him to visually link sounds with their sources and thus aids in establishing specific associations between sounds and various environmental objects and events (Jones and Kabanoff, 1975). Although very young children may have difficulty in accurately localizing or indicating the source of a sound, little information is available with regard to developmental changes in sound localization ability during early and middle childhood years.

Auditory Discrimination

Auditory discrimination tasks require the child to differentiate between two acoustic stimuli that vary primarily on one dimension. Such tasks may include discrimination of pitch and loudness as well as various speech sounds. Most auditory discrimination tasks are concerned with discrimination of different speech sounds. Doty (1974) suggests that perception of speech sounds is operating at an early age. For example, one- to four-month-old infants have been shown to be able to discriminate between basic phoneme categories involving synthetic and real labials (e.g., "b," "p," "m") and real dentals (e.g., "d," "t"). Two- to eight-week-old infants have also been shown to demonstrate frequency discrimination of pure tones in single or two tone patterns, and five-month-olds have been shown to be able to discriminate second format transitions (e.g., "b" versus "g"). All of these data suggest that mechanisms for detecting various acoustic patterns are operating in very young infants.

DiSimoni (1975) reports that there is a gradual but steady reduction of errors from 3 to 5 years in tasks that involve recognition, imitation, and

TABLE 5-2   General Age Characteristics of Auditory Perception Development in Young Children

BEHAVIOR	AGE
Starts in response to a sudden loud noise. May diminish activity to a softly spoken voice. Face brightens to pleasing voice. Vocalizes vowel in prolonged ways.	0-3 mos.
Turns head in direction of sound. Modulates voice when cooing. Further perfects vocalization of sounds. Pronounces "m" sound; babbles to people.	4-6 mos.
Recognizes familiar voices. Listens to tick of watch at ear. Uses polysyllables: *ba, ma, da.*	7-8 mos.
Hears watch from distance of 1-2 ins. Says *ma-ma* and *da-da.* Localizes distant noises. Understands a few commands. Understands several words, e.g., *car, dog.*	9-15 mos.
Hears watch 2½ to 3 ins. from ear. Obeys command "Give it to Mommy." May hum a tune frequently heard. Begins to combine words. Brings various objects upon request.	19-24 mos.
Localizes general direction of sound. Repeats 3 digits. Comprehends question and answer. On command, puts ball *on* or *under* chair. Uses plurals.	3 yrs.
Can hum several tunes. Repeats 3 digits. Uses prepositions in speech. Can define functional uses of several familiar objects.	4 yrs.
Can accurately imitate several pure tones. Repeats 4 digits correctly 50% of the time. Describes actions in pictures. Asks the meaning of words. Can be taught a simple tune in one session. Recites numbers up to 30.	5-6 yrs.

Source: Dekaban, 1970. By permission of Williams & Wilkins Co., Baltimore.

spontaneous production of speech sounds. Other observations indicate that four- and five-year-olds are more accurate in recognizing differences in spoken phonemes (e.g., sun-fun; mouse-mouth) than they are in the production of such phonemes. In general, recognition of phonemic differences develops first in young children; imitation of such sounds develops later; spontaneous and correct production of such sounds develops last. Williams, Temple, and Bateman (1978, 1979) report observations on auditory discrimination abilities of young children aged 5, 6, and 8 years. Using the Wepman Test of Auditory Discrimination as a basis, these authors suggest that there is little or no difference between five- and six-year-olds in the ability to discriminate between pairs of spoken words that differ on one sound. Performances of eight-year-olds, however, are significantly better than those of either five- or six- year olds. Thus recognition of differences in speech sounds appears to undergo important changes during the period from 6 to 8 years.

Birch (1976) asked seven-, ten-, and thirteen-year-old children to perform two auditory discrimination tasks. In one task the children had to respond to phonemic similarities or differences in words; in the other task they had to indicate whether selected words described items and/or objects of a given category (e.g., food, animals, etc.). Phonemic discrimination or matching was simpler than category matching for children of all ages. In general, younger children (7 years old) made significantly more errors on both tasks than older children (10 and 13 years old). Although ten- and thirteen-year-olds were equally able to match words on a phonemic basis, thirteen-year-olds were significantly better than ten-year-olds in identifying words that belonged to the same category. Thus processing of auditory information using lower order physical characteristics seems to be well established by the age of 10. Processing auditory information that involves the use of higher-order rules appears to continue to develop through the age of 13.

Auditory Memory

A child may be able to discriminate one sound from another but still have difficulty remembering and/or reproducing long sequences or patterns of auditory stimuli. Such abilities are referred to as auditory memory. Although auditory memory may involve the retention or remembering of either speech or nonspeech sound sequences, common tasks of auditory memory are by and large concerned with the recalling of speech stimuli. There are many standardized tests of auditory memory, each of which has norms for children of different ages. Still, clear documentation of significant age changes in such auditory abilities is not available. Observations from recent studies on auditory memory abilities of young children indicate that there are significant differences among five-, six-, and eight-year-olds in memory span for spoken digits, memory span for unrelated words, and memory span for meaningful or related groups of words (Williams *et al.*, 1978, 1979). In general, eight-year-olds have a significantly better auditory memory for digits, words, and sentences than do six-year-olds; six-year-olds are in turn superior to five-year-olds in these auditory memory abilities. Thus important changes do seem to occur in auditory memory processes during the period from 5 to 8 years of age.

In another study, children from first, fourth, fifth, and ninth grades were asked to learn and then to recall simple eight note melodic auditory patterns (Wohlwill, 1971). Six-year-olds were unable to perform this task. Although fourth and fifth graders were able to learn the 8 sound patterns with greater ease than younger children, it was not until ninth grade that children could recognize and/or recall these melodic patterns with little or no difficulty. Taken together, these data suggest that certain auditory memory abilities may continue to improve throughout middle and late childhood years.

Auditory Figure-Ground

Many children have difficulty in selecting relevant auditory stimuli from irrelevant auditory input. This ability is referred to as auditory figure-ground. Although this particular auditory ability is believed to be an important one in the overall development of adequate language and verbal communication, little is known about age changes in children's performances on such tasks.

SUMMARY

1. The nature of the development of tactile-kinesthetic abilities (the somato-sensory system) is not well documented.
2. The somato-sensory system provides the child with information about the size, shape, texture, etc., of objects or surfaces in the environment as well as about the relative condition of the body.
3. Tactile-kinesthetic abilities that are generally recognized as being important to the young child include: tactile localization, multiple-point tactile discrimination, tactile (haptic) recognition of objects, kinesthetic or movement awareness, and spatial orientation.
4. Most somato-sensory abilities are well developed by 6 years of age.
5. Tactile-kinesthetic stimulation is important to early development of body awareness. It appears that touch discrimination is important in the development of the ability of the child to plan and carry out sequential motor activities.
6. Six-year-olds who were known to have less well-developed tactile-kinesthetic abilities showed lower levels of performance on selected fine

and gross motor tasks than children with more advanced levels of tactile-kinesthetic awareness. These differences in performance were not present in eight-year-olds.

7. The auditory system is perhaps the most intricate of all sensory systems. Auditory acuity changes little from early to middle childhood years.

8. The nature of the development of sound localization is not known.

9. Auditory discrimination skills improve from 3 to 5 years and undergo continued refinement until at least 12 or 13 years.

10. Important changes occur in auditory memory skills from 5 to 8 years. More complex auditory memory skills continue to improve until 14 to 15 years.

STUDY QUESTIONS

1. List and describe the 6 subsystems that make up the tactile kinesthetic sense.

2. Describe the development of general tactile-kinesthetic behaviors from birth to 6 years.

3. Define and describe age-related changes in the following tactile-kinesthetic abilities:
   a. one-point discrimination (tactile localization)
   b. multiple-point discrimination
   c. tactile-kinesthetic recognition of objects
   d. movement awareness
   e. spatial orientation

4. What are graphesthesia tasks?

5. How are tactile-kinesthetic systems important to the overall development of the young child?

6. Differentiate between protopathic and epicritic sensibilities. How are they related in early development?

7. Of what importance are tactile-kinesthetic abilities in motor-skill learning/performance? Cite specific evidence.

8. How is tactile-kinesthetic functioning related to cognitive development or performance in normal individuals? In brain-damaged individuals?

9. Define and describe age-related changes in the following auditory abilities:
   a. auditory acuity
   b. sound localization
   c. auditory discrimination
   d. auditory memory
   e. figure-ground

REFERENCES

ALAN, M., FINLAYSON, J., AND REITAN, R.M. Tactile-perceptual functioning in relation to intellectual, cognitive and reading skills in younger and older normal children. *Developmental Medicine and Child Neurology.* 18(1976): 442-446.

AYRES, A.J. *Southern California Sensory-Motor Integration Test Manual.* Los Angeles, CA: Western Psychological Corporation, 1978.

BIRCH, L.L. Age trends in children's time-sharing performance. *Journal of Experimental Child Psychology.* 22(1976): 331-345.

BOLL, T.J., AND REITAN, R.M. Motor and tactile-perceptual deficits in brain damaged and normal children. *Perceptual and Motor Skills.* 34(1972): 343.

DEKABAN, A. *Neurology of Early Childhood.* Baltimore, MD: Williams and Wilkins, 1970.

DiSIMONI, F.G. Perceptual and perceptual-motor characteristics of phonemic development. *Child Development.* 46(1975): 243-246.

DOEHRING, D.G., AND R.A. LIBMAN. Signal detection analysis of auditory sequence discrimination by children. *Perceptual and Motor Skills.* 38(1974): 163-169.

DOTY, D. Infant speech perception. *Human Development.* 17(1974): 74-80.

GIBSON, J.J. *The Senses Considered As Perceptual Systems.* New York: Houghton Mifflin, 1966.

GUYTON, A. *Textbook of Medical Physiology.* Philadelphia, PA: W.B. Saunders Company, 1977.

JONES, B., AND KABANOFF, B. Eye movements in auditory space perception. *Perception and Psychophysics.* 17(1975): 241-245.

McKIBBEN, E.H. The effect of additional tactile stimulation in a perceptual-motor treatment program for school children. *American Journal of Occupational Therapy.* 27(1973): 191-197.

NORTHMAN, J.E., AND BLACK, K.N. An examination of errors in children's visual and haptic-tactual memory for random forms. *Journal of Genetic Psychology.* 129(1976): 161-165.

REITAN, R.M. Sensorimotor functions in brain-damaged and normal children of early school age. *Perceptual and Motor Skills.* 33(1971): 655.

TRUYENS, J. *Somato-Sensory Development in Young Children.* Unpublished Master's thesis, University of Toledo, 1970.

VAN DUYNE, H.J. Foundations of tactical perception in three to seven year olds. *Journal of the Association for the Study of Perception.* 8(1973): 1-9.

WILLIAMS, H., TEMPLE, I., AND BATEMAN, J. A test battery to assess intrasensory and intersensory development of young children. *Perceptual and Motor Skills.* 48(1979): 643-659.

WILLIAMS, H., TEMPLE, I., AND BATEMAN, J. Perceptual-motor and cognitive learning in young children. *Psychology of Motor Behavior and Sport II.* Champaign, IL: Human Kinetics Press, 1978.

WOHLWILL, J.F. Effect of correlated visual and tactual feedback on auditory pattern learning at different age levels. *Journal of Experimental Child Psychology.* 11(1971): 213-228.

WOOD, C.C. Auditory and phonetic levels of processing in speech perception: neurophysiological and information-processing analyses. *Journal of Experimental Psychology: Human Perception and Performance.* 104(1975): 3-20.

CHAPTER SIX
INTERSENSORY
INTEGRATION

Information from or about one object or event in the environment usually reaches the observer through several modalities. For example, we see a fire glow, hear it crackle, and feel it radiate heat; we see a falling glass break into pieces and hear it crash. When information about an object or event reaches us in one modality, we are likely to seek more information about that object through other modalities. Consequently, if we see an object of interest, we reach for it; if we hear a sudden, loud noise, we look around to locate it. These all involve or are a part of the process of intersensory integration.

What is intersensory integration? Simply defined, it is the ability of the individual to use or integrate multiple sources of sensory information simultaneously to solve problems and/or to aid him in adapting to the environment (Birch and Lefford, 1963, 1967). Evidence suggests that there are three levels or types of intersensory integration: (1) a type that involves simple, low level or automatic integration of basic sensory information; (2) a kind that involves the higher order integration of perceptual features of stimulus information; and (3) a cognitive-conceptual integration process that involves the transfer of ideas or concepts across different modalities. Blank and Bridger (1974) have further distinguished between cross-modal equivalence (CME) and cross-modal concepts (CMC), both of which are viewed as forms of intersensory integration. Cross-modal equivalence involves the recognition of a particular stimulus or set of stimulus features as the same or equivalent when they are presented to two different sensory modalities. Thus evaluation of cross-modal equivalence abilities in young children usually requires the child to judge whether or not the shape of an object presented visually (or tactile-kinesthetically) is the same or different from an object presented in the other modality. Cross-modal concept abilities, on the other hand, involve the utilization of a concept or principle to solve problems that are associated with dissimilar yet analogous stimulus information presented through two different senses (Tyrrell, 1974). Thus a child in this situation might be asked to judge whether or not an object seen and an object heard belong to the same functional category of objects (e.g., animals). This, of course, requires the interrelating of certain cognitive or abstract dimensions of sensory information available from the two modalities. It is obvious that cross-modal equivalence is comparable to what was described earlier as intersensory integration of perceptual features (the second type or level), and that cross-modal concept is identical to cognitive-conceptual intersensory integration (the third type). The first lowest level of intersensory integration is perhaps best described as a set of subcortical processes that are inherent to nervous system functioning and that begin to operate at birth or shortly thereafter.

EARLY DEVELOPMENT OF
INTERSENSORY INTEGRATION

How does the child develop this ability to perceive and/or understand objects/events in the environment using several modalities? This is an important question to ask, for the way in which the child integrates or uses two or more sensory modalities simultaneously has important implications for understanding the growth and development of the young child. A disruption of the hierarchical organization of an interaction among various sensory systems can lead to developmental delays that may have serious consequences. There is little doubt that we do learn to integrate sensory information—that we come to recognize what kinds of sounds accompany a talking face and/or how an object that moves or has certain characteristics actually feels. This process is believed to involve the gradual integration by the child (through countless experiences) of all available stimulus information surrounding a given environmental event into one complex sensory matrix or picture (Gibson, 1966; Gibson, 1969). This matrix of information is then used as a model for interpreting other sensory experiences and/or guiding the processes involved in formulating adaptive behavior. Learning to relate or integrate several sources of sensory information probably involves both the discovery of specific sets of associations among different sources of sensory input as well as the overcoming of any sensory discordance, that is, the making of allowances for any discrepancies between what are normally congruent sources of sensory information. Learning and experience, therefore, are *not* visual *or* auditory *or* tactile-kinesthetic—they are *intermodal and multidimensional.*

It has been suggested that rather than being endowed with a genetic set of rigid perceptual expectations, infants tend innately to explore objects and events in several modalities whenever they gather enough information to guide this exploration. Thus when the location of an object is specified in one modality (audition), infants will seek information about that same object through other modalities (e.g., they look in the direction of the sound; they reach in the direction of the object). Usually multimodal exploration of an object and/or event yields additional information about that object or event (Aaronson and Rosenbloom, 1971). Thus through the process of intersensory exploration, the infant acquires and/or discovers information that she needs to build a clearer picture of the relationship among what she sees, what she hears and what she feels.

In accordance with this, recent research has indicated that visual and auditory information are experienced on a common dimension or in a "common space." That is, auditory and visual information about the direction of an object in space, for example, results in an experience of "spatial direction" on the part of the child that is independent of modality. Thus the child doesn't necessarily experience visual direction or auditory direction but rather experiences "direction" as a single dimension of space, a dimension that is derived from information provided by both visual and auditory systems (Auerbach and Sperling, 1974).

Evidence of early low-level intersensory integration is clearly shown in a study by Bower (1971, 1972) in which polarized lenses and light were used to create the impression of an object within the visible reach of an infant. Infants as young as seven days reached for the projected object, and when they found no object began to cry. This suggests that the "visually perceived" object was expected to have or to be associated with certain tactile-kinesthetic sensations, and when such sensations were discordant, the infant became disturbed. Infants as young as one month have also been shown to be noticeably distressed if, when watching their mothers talk through a window, the face and the voice of the mother appear to come from different points in space. Thus one-month-old infants seem to expect a "seen-and-heard" event to have certain sensory consequences (e.g., to emanate from the same point in space). This suggests the presence of a low level of intersensory integration involving visual and auditory information at a very early age. As before, when this integration is not what it should be (e.g., visual and auditory information are in some way discordant), the infant appears to be aware of the condition very quickly and attempts through his distress to do something about it.

Spelke (1976, 1979) studied intersensory integration in infants 3-4 months old by showing two movies side by side to these infants. The sound track played was appropriate to only one of the movies and came from a source midway between the two films. Generally, infants this age looked at the movie for which the sound was appropriate significantly longer than they did at the movie for which the sound was not appropriate. Infants spent an average of 88.6 seconds looking at the film that was congruent with the sound track and only 47.1 seconds looking at the film unrelated to the sound. In fact, preference for the sound-related film increased as the infant viewed the film for longer periods of time. This suggests that although the young infant may recognize discordance in sensory input rather quickly, it takes time for him to sort out the information he needs to make the judgment that two dimensions of a single event are in fact related. Thus the young infant seems to try to relate the several dimensions of a single environmental event to each other. Because of this, the young infant's visual preferences can be and probably are influenced by the structure of the sounds occurring in the environment in which visual stimuli occur.

The efficient use of multiple-sensory input by the young child represents a move toward a higher-order, more adaptive level of behavioral and neural functioning. When the child can use multimodal information effectively, it is possible for him to modify his response to a given environmental situation to the degree that it is accurately represented in a number of afferent or sensori-perceptual systems. In other words the processing of multiple-sensory integration enables the child to use ancillary information to facilitate the analysis of environmental events surrounding him.

Intersensory integration is a fundamental part of the processing of sensory information by humans. This is, of course, in accordance with phylogenetic evidence which clearly indicates that improved intersensory integration is a critical aspect of the development of refined adaptation to the environment. Neurologically there is strong evidence for the existence and importance of the functions of intersensory integration. For example, there are numerous and widespread areas within the CNS where sensory information from all modalities converge (e.g., the polysensory areas of frontal, temporal, parietal, and occipital lobes; the reticular system, etc.). Without such convergence and integration of sensory information, the human communication system (visual-motor and/or auditory-verbal) could not be functionally realized. In fact, it is the presence of more and more polysensory areas in evolutionary development that separates man (and ape) from lower species (Berenberg *et al.,* 1974; Conel, 1959). Intersensory integration development thus represents an advanced form of brain growth and development. In fact the polysensory areas of the cerebral cortex are the last of the higher brain structures in man to fully mature. It is not until the third decade of life that these areas of the brain reach complete development and/or maturity.

RELATIONSHIP OF
INTRASENSORY DEVELOPMENT
TO INTERSENSORY
DEVELOPMENT

Although it was once believed that refined intrasensory development preceded and was prerequisite to efficient intersensory functioning, it is now known that sensori-perceptual development, in general, follows an asynchronous pattern of growth (Gaines and Raskin, 1970). That is, refinement of both intrasensory and intersensory functions occurs simultaneously and at any given age; certain intrasensory abilities may be more advanced than selected intersensory functions. At other stages, however, specific intersensory abilities may be better developed than certain intrasensory functions. For example, in four- and five-year-olds, visual-visual (intrasensory) matching of forms is much easier (e.g., more advanced) than tactile-visual or intermodal matching of such forms. However at the same age, tactile-visual comparisons of familiar forms are much less difficult (e.g., less advanced) than tactile-tactile matching of such forms (Balter and Fogarty, 1971). Thus there appears to be, during growth and development, a reciprocal interweaving of the pattern of refinement in intrasensory and intersensory integration abilities. This is true for both boys and girls.

Another aspect of the relationship between intrasensory and intersensory development that must be considered is the nature of the spatial and temporal characteristics of the information the child is asked to integrate. In general, spatial patterns of sensory information (whether they are unimodal or intermodal) are mastered and integrated more easily than temporal patterns. For example, if a child is asked to compare two visual patterns presented temporally, she has as much difficulty in matching these unimodal patterns as she does in matching intermodal patterns (e.g., visual and auditory) if they too are presented temporally. Tasks involving temporal patterns of sensory input are thus much more difficult for children than are those involving spatial patterns (Sterritt et al., 1971).

In the sequence of development, children seem also to master the integration of spatial patterns with temporal patterns before they master the reverse (e.g., the integration of temporal with spatial patterns). Thus the refinement of intrasensory and intersensory integration abilities (whether it involves visual, auditory, or tactile-kinesthetic information) is dependent, in part, upon the spatial-temporal characteristics of the input. The order of mastery of such characteristics appears to be spatial-spatial,

spatial-temporal, temporal-spatial, and temporal-temporal patterns (Sterritt *et al.,* 1971).

AGE CHANGES IN AUDITORY-VISUAL INTEGRATION

In general, auditory-visual integration abilities improve with age for all children. A summary of such changes is given here.

AGE CHANGES IN AUDITORY-VISUAL INTEGRATION

1. Children 5 years or younger have difficulty performing auditory-visual integration tasks (Williams *et al.,* 1979, 1979; Goodnow, 1971).
2. A significant increase in auditory and visual integration occurs between 5 and 7 years of age (Birch and Lefford, 1969; Williams *et al.,* 1979).
3. Both auditory-visual and visual-auditory integration abilities improve with age (Jones and Alexander, 1974; Kuhlman and Walking, 1972).
4. The five-year-old performs visual-auditory integration tasks more efficiently than auditory-visual tasks (Jones and Alexander, 1974).
5. Six-year-olds are significantly more advanced in auditory-visual and visual-auditory integration abilities than five-year-olds (Goodnow, 1971b).
6. Seven-year-olds are significantly superior to six-year-olds in visual-auditory integration ability (Goodnow, 1971b).
7. Six- and seven-year-olds are at about the same level of development with regard to auditory-visual integration abilities (Goodnow, 1971b).
8. Eight-year-olds perform better on auditory-visual than on visual-auditory integration tasks (Jones and Alexander, 1974).
9. In children 5½ to 8 years, visual-auditory and auditory-visual integration abilities are intermediate in development to visual integration abilities (most advanced) and auditory integration abilities (least advanced); for children 5-7 years, visual-auditory ability is more advanced than auditory-visual integration ability; after 7 years the difference in these two integration abilities diminishes and is virtually nonexistent (Rudel and Teuber, 1971).
10. Eight-year-olds perform at the same level on visual-auditory, auditory-visual, visual-visual, and auditory-auditory tasks (Jones, 1974).
11. There is a significant improvement in auditory and visual integration between 8-10 years (Birch and Lefford, 1967).
12. Auditory-visual integration continues to improve to 12 years (Birch and Belmont, 1965).
13. Intersensory integration is usually more efficient when the task is presented visually first (Jones, 1974).

Descriptive data available on age changes in cross-modal or intersensory matching of visual and auditory information suggest that children at 5 and

6 years of age operate at chance level with regard to equating auditory with visual input. That is, children at these ages are as likely to be unable to perform auditory-visual integration tasks as they are to be successful at them. By 7 years of age, however, the child is much more efficient at integrating or matching up visual and auditory input. Auditory-visual integration abilities continue to improve through early and middle childhood and are believed to be mastered by the time the child is 11 or 12 years of age (Goodnow, 1971a). Overall, there appear to be two periods of rapid and important growth in visual-auditory integration abilities for the young child, 5 to 7 years and 8 to 10 years.

Williams, Temple, and Bateman (1978, 1979) also report consistent and significant developmental differences among five-, six-, and eight-year-olds in auditory-visual integration abilities. Children in these studies were asked to compare (equate) a rhythmic auditory pattern with a spatial pattern of dots displayed visually and to indicate whether these patterns were alike or different. Under these conditions, eight-year-olds were significantly superior to six-year-olds in matching up such patterns; six-year-olds were in turn significantly more advanced than five-year-olds, who showed considerable difficulty in performing the task. These data suggest that important changes in auditory-visual integration abilities occur throughout the early childhood years. Birch and Lefford (1967) report data on auditory-visual integration abilities in children ages 5 to 11 and suggest that a critical period for refinement of auditory-visual integration occurs between 8 and 10 years of age. Thus the Williams *et al.* (1978, 1979) data suggest that the ability to integrate auditory and visual information undergoes important changes at 5, 6 and 7 years of age, and the Birch and Lefford (1967) data suggest that such abilities continue to undergo refinement through the age of 10. These observations indicate that significant refinement of auditory-visual integration abilities occurs throughout the early and middle childhood years.

How does the child accomplish a task that involves the comparing or equating of visual and auditory information? Only partial answers are available, but in situations where children are asked to reproduce (write out) a pattern of sounds, five-year-olds use "motor spaces" for "auditory spaces." That is, instead of reproducing the temporal pattern with appropriate visual spacing (e.g., · · · ·), the young child simply draws the first dot and then waits a brief period of time before he makes the next three dots, and thus the pattern often looks like · · · · ·. The "spacing" is noticed but is included in a motor form. In contrast, six- and seven-year-olds tend to reproduce such patterns using a "spatial" rule. That is, they equate auditory "spaces" with visual "spaces" and reproduce the pattern to look like · · · · ·. This may reflect an advancement in cognitive growth that is shown in a shift from a kind of "time for time" rule to a "space for time" rule (Goodnow, 1971a).

What about the matching of visual with auditory information? What happens when a child is asked to tap out in time (rhythmically) a spatial pattern of dots or visual items? Young children (6 years and younger), if they can perform the task at all, tend to use the "space" covered in tapping to represent the space interval present in the visual pattern. So the young child taps out the visual pattern in a spatial pattern that is nearly identical to the visual one, and temporal elements seem to be ignored. Children at 7 years of age tend also to use a similar "space" rule but operate in a much smaller space in tapping out the pattern. By 8 years the child has begun to use the "space-for-time" rule and taps out the pattern using temporal intervals and a single space in the reproduction of the visual pattern (Goodnow, 1971a). Thus important age changes occur both in the child's ability to interrelate space and time concepts and in his ability to integrate auditory and visual information.

Interestingly, in tasks that involve simultaneous processing of auditory and visual information, if the information load is increased in both auditory and visual modalities (e.g., the number of items to be processed or remembered is gradually increased from 2 to 16), most individuals (both children and adults) show a tendency to abandon the processing of auditory information in favor of information coming in through the visual channel. Thus when faced with not being able to process adequately all of the information coming in over both visual and auditory channels, vision seems to assume a position of superiority with regard to which source of information is most strongly attended to (Long and Newsome, 1974).

Some studies have reported that in children older than 9 years of age, vision continues to have a facilitating effect on certain auditory behaviors. For example, when children are asked to judge the location (right-left) of a tone, with and without the presence of vision, children of all ages are more accurate in their localization of a sound when vision is present than when it is not. This intersensory effect, however, is much greater for older children (9–12 years) than for younger children ($6^1/_2$ years) (Jones, 1975).

Older children also show a better ability to localize sounds that are not seen than do younger children. It has been suggested that a part of the reason for this is the advanced level of intersensory abilities in older children. That is, visual information helps to put sound into a visual representation of the environment, and throughout growth and development the child undergoes countless events and experiences that involve sound in relation to "sound producers" (visually related cues). Gradually a correspondence is built up between specific auditory stimuli and specific locations in the visual environment with respect to some internal axis. Thus when an older child hears a sound from an unseen source, he has available a more elaborate internal history of auditory-visual integration experience than the younger child. This allows the older child to make a more accurate analysis of sound location even without vision than can the younger child (Warren, 1970).

AUDITORY-TACTILE INTEGRATION

Although little is written about auditory-tactile integration, there is some evidence to suggest that there is some natural interaction between the tactile-kinesthetic and auditory systems. For example, awareness of tactile stimulation has been shown to be more acute when it is accompanied by auditory stimulation (Gescheider *et al.,* 1974). Other authors (Willot, 1973) have reported that processing of auditory information by both children and adults is disrupted by the presence of proprioceptive information, whereas the processing of proprioceptive information seems to be relatively unaffected by the presence of auditory stimulation.

Williams, Temple, and Bateman (1978, 1979) have reported consistent developmental differences among five-, six-, and eight-year-olds in auditory-tactile integration ability. Children were asked to match a verbal label spoken to them with tactile-kinesthetic information derived from an object they were feeling. In all cases eight-year-olds were superior to six-year-olds in their ability; six-year-olds were also significantly more advanced than five-year-olds in such intersensory integration abilities. In addition, older children (eight-year-olds) were less variable as a group than younger children (five-year-olds) in performance of this intersensory integration task. Thus although only scanty information is available, it would seem that, as with other intersensory integration abilities, auditory-tactile integration undergoes important developmental changes during early childhood. There seems also to be a natural or spontaneous interaction between these two sensory systems.

AGE CHANGES IN VISUAL-TACTILE AND/OR KINESTHETIC INTEGRATION

Results of studies on the development of visual-tactile/kinesthetic intersensory integration are very consistent. Visual-tactile/kinesthetic integration abilities improve with age and appear to become refined before those of auditory-visual integration. A general description of the developmental trends in visual-tactile/kinesthetic-integration abilities of young children is given here.

AGE CHANGES IN VISUAL-TACTILE AND/OR KINESTHETIC INTEGRATION.

1. Three-year-olds function at chance level on most visual-tactile/kinesthetic integration tasks (Blank and Bridger, 1974; Jessen and Kaess, 1973).

2. Five-year-olds are superior to four-year-olds in performing visual-tactile/kinesthetic integration tasks involving shape discrimination (Abravanel, 1968, 1972).

3. Visual-tactile/kinesthetic integration abilities involving the recognition of shape are nearly mature by the age of 5 (Blank and Bridger, 1964; Birch and Lefford, 1967).

4. The year from 5 to 6 is a period of important advancement in visual-tactile/kinesthetic integration abilities (Williams et al., 1978, 1979; Goodnow, 1971; Birch and Lefford, 1967).

5. Significant refinement of visual-tactile/kinesthetic integration abilities occurs from 5 to 7 years of age but appears to plateau after that (Birch and Lefford, 1967; Miller and Bryant, 1970).

6. A second period of improvement in visual-tactile/kinesthetic integration ability may occur between 9 and 11 years (Birch and Lefford, 1967).

7. At all ages, visual-tactile/kinesthetic and tactile-kinesthetic/visual discrimination of form is intermediate in development to visual-visual (most advanced) and tactile-tactile (least advanced) discrimination of form (Jones et al., 1972; Rudel and Teuber, 1964, 1971; Jones and Robinson, 1973).

8. With nine- to ten-year-olds integration of visual and tactile-kinesthetic information is more effective when the form is presented visually first; this is not true for younger children (Goodnow, 1971).

Jessen and Kaess (1973) report a study in which three- and five-year-old children were given either visual experience with complex unnamed shapes or visual-tactile experience with the same kinds of shapes. The children were then asked to identify (through vision or touch) the shapes that they had previously had experience with. For both three- and five-year-olds previous visual-tactile experience facilitated tactile recognition of shapes but not visual recognition of shapes. On the other hand previous visual experience facilitated recognition of shapes through vision but not through touch. These data suggest that for very young children there is little integration of visual and tactile information at a perceptual or concrete feature level. Some low-level integration, however, must occur as is evidenced in the observation that, when the child is provided with visual-tactile/kinesthetic experience, there is some minimal facilitation of recognition of shapes through the tactile-kinesthetic sense.

Most information available suggests that the capacity for intermodal matching of visual and tactile-kinesthetic information (in the form of recognizing the object through vision and touch) appears to be relatively mature by the age of 5. Thus, whereas three-year-olds function at chance level on tasks that require intermodal recognition of shape, children at 4 are successful 84% of the time on such tasks. Five-year-olds perform such tasks successfully 95% of the time (Blank and Bridger, 1964).

Birch and Lefford (1963, 1967) report information that suggests that, with regard to integration of visual, haptic, and kinesthetic information, visual-haptic integration abilities are the most well-developed in the five-year-old. (Haptic information is that information provided through active manipulation of an object with the hand and fingers.) Visual-haptic integration ability continues to improve through 8 years of age and seems to level off, or plateau, thereafter.

Kinesthetic information (although difficult, if not impossible, to separate from touch information) is provided by "joint receptors" that are stimulated when movement (active or passive) of any of the joints of the body occurs. In most studies of visual-kinesthetic integration, the hand and/or arm of the child is moved passively through a maze or some other construction of the shape or object that is to be identified visually (Birch and Lefford, 1967). Integration or equating of visual-kinesthetic information, measured in this way, appears in general to lag behind visual-haptic integration. Visual-kinesthetic integration abilities of the young child show rapid improvement from 5–7 years. This is followed by a plateauing from 7–9 years with a second period of improvement from 9–11 years. Thus with increasing age there is an improved ability on the part of the child to integrate or use information gained from visual and tactile-kinesthetic modalities. This represents an important step forward in the overall sensori-perceptual development of the young child.

In a series of studies on intersensory development in young children, Williams, Temple, and Bateman (1978, 1979) showed that important changes do occur in simple visual-tactile and/or kinesthetic integration abilities in five-, six-, and eight-year-olds. Children were asked to pick the form they were feeling from a visual display of 8 different shapes. Six- and eight-year-olds performed this task with equal facility. This suggests that six- and eight-year-old children have developed the capacity to integrate simple dimensions of visual and tactile-kinesthetic information. Although five-year-olds were able to integrate visual shape information with tactile-kinesthetic shape information successfully, they required a significantly longer period of time to do so than did six- or eight-year-olds. Overall this suggests that some important changes in intersensory integration involving the tactile-kinesthetic and visual systems occur between 5 and 6 years of age.

Birch and Lefford (1967) report wide individual variation in visual-tactile/kinesthetic integration abilities in children ages 5 through 11 years. This interindividual variation in intersensory development is quite large in young children but decreases rapidly with age. Thus older children are more alike, as a group, in visual-tactile/kinesthetic integration abilities than are young children. A noticeable increase in interindividual variability is observed at 5½ years of age.

OTHER INTERSENSORY INTERACTIONS

Stimulation of one sense is known to affect the processing or use of information in other sensory systems. The ways in which such stimulation affects processing of information in other systems, however, changes with age. When young children (ages 3 through 9 years) are asked to respond to either a visual or tactile-kinesthetic cue when they have been stimulated simultaneously in the opposite sense, there is in general a significant increase in the time that is required by the child to respond to that cue, whether it is visual or tactile-kinesthetic. Thus young children often do not handle two sources of sensory input as efficiently as they do a single source. The precise nature of the effect of stimulation in one modality upon processing of information in another modality, however, is a function of age. The young child's ability (5 years or under) to process visual information is affected more profoundly by simultaneous tactile-kinesthetic stimulation than is his ability to process tactile-kinesthetic information when there is interpolated visual stimulation. In contrast, six-year-old children show equal slowing of responses under both conditions. Thus six-year-olds are affected as much in their processing of visual information as they are in their processing of tactile-kinesthetic information when there is accompanying stimulation in the opposing channel. For seven- to nine-year-olds, stimulation in the visual system causes a greater decrease in the rate of processing tactile-kinesthetic information than tactile-kinesthetic stimulation does in the rate of processing visual information. Thus interaction among sensory systems seems to be different for children of different ages (Kaufman *et al.*, 1973).

Another indicator of the nature of the changes that occur with age in the interaction among sensory systems is seen in the situation in which children receive prestimulation in a sense that is not directly involved in the response or behavior to be performed. In general, young children (3 to 7 years) show a general decrease in the ability to process information in one modality when they have been prestimulated in another modality. Eight-year-olds show no such effect of prestimulation on the processing of information. Interestingly, nine-year-olds show an increase in the speed of response or rate of information processing when they have been prestimulated in another sense. This suggests that, with development, the child becomes increasingly more able to process multiple sources of sensory information and that in fact, in older children, processing of information in one sensory modality may be facilitated by previous processing of information in another. The mechanisms by means of which this occurs are not clear, but such observations do suggest that the nature of the interaction among various senses changes during growth and development.

It may be that older children are simply better able to treat stimulation in another modality (previous or simultaneous) as an alerting or supporting source of information. Younger children, on the other hand, act as though stimulation of another sense is an inhibitor or distractor to the processing of information. Such differences indicate that an important change in the utilization of multimodal information takes place with age. Of particular importance is the fact that the attentional or supportive value of tactile-kinesthetic and visual information changes with age. For older children visual information has a greater alerting or facilitatory effect (value) than does tactile-kinesthetic information (Kaufman, 1973).

THE RELATIONSHIP OF INTERSENSORY INTEGRATION TO MOTOR CONTROL

Williams, Temple, and Bateman (1978) have looked at the contribution of intersensory functioning to the learning and/or performance of perceptual-motor tasks. Six- and eight-year-old children were asked to learn both a gross and a fine perceptual-motor task that involved the ordering of a series of simple motor acts into a longer, more complex behavioral sequence. The children were classified, on the basis of their performances on three different intersensory integration tasks, into two groups: one with advanced levels of intersensory development and the other with less advanced intersensory development. Six-year-olds with advanced intersensory development were significantly superior in their learning performance to six-year-olds with less advanced intersensory development. Eight-year-olds with different levels of intersensory development, however, showed little or no difference in their ability to master the gross perceptual-motor task. It seems that at younger ages the intersensory-integration ability of the child directly affects his ability to perform a gross perceptual-motor task that involves the sequencing of a series of simple motor acts into a smooth behavioral chain of greater complexity. By the age of 8, the level of intersensory development, or the ability of the child to use multisensory cues (at least at a low level of analysis), seems to have little effect upon the nature of the learning or mastery of such gross perceptual-motor tasks. This may mean that by the age of 8 the normal child has reached a relatively mature level of simple intersensory functioning and thus is fairly efficient in the mastery and/or regulation of simple motor acts.

It is interesting to note that throughout the learning period, children (both six- and eight-year-olds) with less advanced levels of intersensory development were more variable as a group than those with more advanced levels of intersensory functioning. This variability in performance might be an indirect reflection of an unstable, still growing sensori-perceptual system. Since at both 6 and 8 years of age, greater variability in learning and/or performance of the gross perceptual-motor task seemed to be associated with less advanced levels of intersensory development, this may mean that the sensory systems of these children have not yet developed a stable framework within which to process multiple-sensory information. Such children thus show greater variation in performance than do the more advanced children.

On the fine perceptual-motor task, six-year-olds with different levels of intersensory functioning performed at approximately the same level during the early stages of learning. As learning progressed, however, six-year-olds with more advanced intersensory development began to show accelerated improvement in performance and finished the learning session at a level that was significantly superior to that of the six-year-olds with less advanced intersensory development. Thus early in the mastery of the fine perceptual-motor task, the level of intersensory development of the child had little or nothing to do with how he mastered the task, and learning proceeded steadily and smoothly for both groups of children. However as practice continued, children with less advanced intersensory development seemed to show less and less improvement in performance and actually reached a plateau after the third trial. Six-year-olds with more advanced intersensory functioning continued to show steady improvement in performance of the fine perceptual-motor task throughout learning. This may imply that refinement of intersensory integration abilities allows for a continued modification of fine motor control, a modification that is not possible, or at least is not as easily or readily achieved, when the child's ability to process multisensory information is less well-developed.

As with the gross perceptual-motor task, the level of intersensory development of older children (eight-year-olds) had little or no effect upon their ability to master the fine perceptual-motor task. Eight-year-olds learned the fine perceptual-motor task with equal ease, regardless of their level of intersensory functioning. Again, children with more advanced levels of intersensory functioning were less variable in performance than were children with lower levels of intersensory development.

Similar to Williams *et al.* (1978), Douglass and Williams (1976) reported observations of five-, six-, and seven-year-old children who were classified according to their intersensory integration abilities and asked to perform a gross motor task that consisted of a series of four individual motor acts, all of which required the processing of multisensory information for their successful completion. These authors observed that children with advanced levels of intersensory development were superior to those with poorly developed levels of intersensory functioning on all aspects of the learning performance of this gross motor task. For example, the information-processing times of the advanced group of children were significantly faster than those of children with less advanced intersensory development. That is, children with advanced intersensory development processed the multiple sensory cues required for task performance more quickly and efficiently than the children with less advanced intersensory development. On the average, children with low levels of intersensory development required almost twice as long to process task-related multisensory cues as did those children with more advanced intersensory development. They were also less variable, as a group, than children with low intersensory development. In addition the efferent or motor-control processes of children with advanced intersensory functioning (e.g., raw movement times) were also superior. That is, children with more advanced intersensory development were able to execute the actual individual motor acts that comprised the gross perceptual-motor task more quickly and skillfully than the children with less well developed intersensory functioning.

As a whole, children with more advanced intersensory development showed a gradual and steady improvement in performance throughout the learning period. This is in contrast to the children with low intersensory development, who showed a more erratic pattern of learning. Errors were systematically reduced across learning by children with high intersensory development, whereas for children with low intersensory development, performance errors decreased early in learning but showed only minimal changes thereafter. By the end of the learning period, children with less advanced intersensory development were actually making more errors than they had earlier in learning. Overall, children with more advanced intersensory development committed significantly fewer errors throughout learning than did children less advanced in intersensory development. Since feedback about performance errors was provided to each child on an individual basis, these observations suggest that advanced intersensory development may also be reflected in the child's ability to use such feedback information to refine and/or modify his overt motor behavior.

It is interesting to note that the most difficult part of this gross perceptual-motor task for children with less advanced levels of intersensory development was one that involved auditory and motor integration. In this part of the task, the child was required to process visual and auditory information simultaneously with the execution of a simple motor act (e.g., bouncing a playground ball). Most children with less well-developed intersensory development showed a marked cessation in motor activity while auditory cues were being received and processed. Once the auditory information had been processed, this child then proceeded to perform the visual-motor parts of the task. In contrast to this the child with advanced intersensory development simultaneously integrated all of these aspects of the task easily and smoothly. In addition, although children with less advanced intersensory functioning gained some mastery over the individual parts of the gross motor task, few were able to organize the individual motor acts into a smooth, sequential behavioral chain, something that was easily accomplished by the child with advanced intersensory development after one or two attempts.

Birch and Lefford (1967) report data on the role of intersensory integration in acquisition of fine motor control (e.g., freehand drawing) in children ages 5 through 9 years. Children in this study performed three tasks requiring the integration of visual and/or tactile-kinesthetic information and then were asked to draw a number of geometric forms freehand. From 5 through 7 years, the intersensory integration abilities of the child were directly related to the accuracy and ease with which the child drew the geometric forms. At 5 and 6 years, intersensory integration abilities accounted for 41% and 45% of variance in performance on this fine motor task. At 7, intersensory integration characteristics of the child accounted for 68% of the performance variance shown on the task. Thus the contribution of intersensory-integration development to fine motor control was greater at 7 years than at 5 or 6 years. At 8 and 9 years the relationship between intersensory functioning and fine motor control was greatly reduced and accounted for less than 30% of performance variance on such tasks. Thus up to approximately 8 years of age, Birch and Lefford (1967) suggest that the level of intersensory development of the child is an important factor in his acquisition and/or refinement of fine motor behaviors.

Since more mature CNS function is generally associated with effective intersensory integration, it is possible that the child with less advanced intersensory development may have underlying immaturities in associated neurological functioning. This seems reasonable, for it is frequently observed that in less mature stages of development, any more than moderate demands placed on the central information processing mechanism of the child limits the amount of attention (space) that can be given to the processing of other information. Thus the child with less well developed intersensory functioning may be neurologically young and unable to handle the demands of processing and integrating multiple sources of sensory information simultaneously. It would be reasonable to expect that such a child would display an awkwardness or slowness in movement as well as a general inability to master complex perceptual-motor tasks, in part because he cannot handle the multisensory demands of these tasks. The consistent differences in variability of performance between children with advanced versus low levels of intersensory development also suggest that the sensory systems of these young children are immature. The sensory systems of the child with less well developed intersensory integration may only be beginning to undergo important changes in development. For children with more advanced intersensory development, these systems have perhaps already matured and thus are capable of handling multisensory information more efficiently. Consequently such children show less interindividual variation in motor control than do their more immature counterparts. Taken as a whole, available data strongly suggest that intersensory integration is important in the acquisition of refined voluntary motor control, both in terms of control of the large muscle masses of the body (gross motor behavior) and the small muscle masses of the hands and fingers (fine motor behavior).

INTERSENSORY INTEGRATION
AND COGNITIVE DEVELOPMENT

The role of intersensory integration in the cognitive development of the child will only be touched upon briefly here. In general the importance of intersensory integration in the cognitive development of retarded readers, learning disabled children, or minimal brain-damaged children is far from clearly understood. On one side there is evidence that developmentally delayed children are indeed characterized by a lack of refinement of intersensory integration abilities, especially those involved with the integration of auditory and visual information (Bartholomeus and Doehring, 1972; Birch and Belmont, 1964, 1965; Hsia, 1969; McGrady and Olson, 1970). In contrast, equally strong evidence is available to suggest that the discrepancies in intersensory integration of normally and slowly developing children is not as great as it was once thought to be, and that developmental delays in intrasensory functioning may be more important contributors to developmental problems related to cognitive functioning in young children than intersensory factors (Williams et al., 1978).

Recent observations of young children's paired-associate learning (an indicator of cognitive development) suggest that the role of intersensory development in such learning depends both on the age of the child and the nature of the cognitive task to be learned. When the cognitive performance (paired-associate) task relies primarily on information provided by the auditory and visual senses (e.g., relating a visual symbol to an auditory concept), the level of intersensory development has little or no effect on the rate or level at which such a task is mastered by six- and eight-year-old children. All children, regardless of their level of intersensory development, learn such tasks equally efficiently. However, when the cognitive performance requires the use of tactile-kinesthetic information in combination with either visual or auditory information, the level of intersensory development of the child does affect the level at which that task is learned. In general, in these instances children with higher levels of intersensory integration master such cognitive tasks more efficiently than children with less advanced intersensory integration functioning.

There are also some important age differences to be considered. For example, when cognitive performance involves the use of tactile-kinesthetic information in combination with visual information (e.g., relating a felt object to a written descriptor), the level of intersensory development has little or no effect on the learning of this task by eight-year-olds. Thus all eight-year-olds master this kind of cognitive task with relative ease. Six-year-olds, on the other hand, are affected, at least in the middle stages of learning, by the degree of refinement of their intersensory integration abilities. Although six-year-olds begin and end learning at the same level of mastery, those with more advanced intersensory functioning show an accelerated level of learning during the middle portion of task mastery. Children with less advanced intersensory development show a less accelerated rate of improvement during this stage of learning. Thus cognitive learning by the six-year-old child with advanced intersensory development is in some instances more accelerated than that of the six-year-old with less advanced intersensory development.

When cognitive performances involve the use of tactile-kinesthetic and auditory information (e.g., relating a felt object to a concept or word spoken to the child), the opposite age effect is observed. In this instance there are no differences in the learning of such cognitive tasks by six-year-olds with different levels of intersensory integration abilities. In contrast, eight-year-olds with advanced intersensory functioning perform at a higher level than do those with less advanced intersensory development. Since eight-year-old children performed at a consistently higher level of mastery throughout learning than six-year-olds, it would appear that the integrated use of tactile-kinesthetic and auditory information in a conceptual format develops later than does the use of tactile-kinesthetic and visual information in such conceptual activity.

THE DEVELOPMENT OF A
SPATIAL REFERENCE SYSTEM

One important aspect of the young child's intersensory development is that of the development of a spatial reference system, or the ability to systematically and objectively perceive spatial relations. The adult's superior capacity to deal with spatial relations is believed to be due to his having intellectual access to a cognitive representation of such relations. The young child, in contrast, operates primarily with a perceptually dependent reference system. That is, he is to a great degree dependent upon the perceptual cues available to him from the external environment. Thus the young child has difficulty mentally representing spatial relationships among objects in space.

Early in development the child's organization of representative space is egocentric, that is, he judges spatial relations in terms of a self-reference system. For example, whereas children tend to think of objects as being located at certain distances and directions from their persons, adults tend to think of themselves as just another object in the matrix of relationships among all objects in space. However, egocentric thought seems to be the child's first attempt to order relationships that have been previously unordered (Piaget, 1956).

There are three stages in the development of an objective spatial reference system by the young child. The first stage (2-3 years) consists of the ordering of space by topological relations. During this stage the child recognizes objects as being *near* to him or *next* to each other. The child at this age also recognizes that objects are separate—that they can be *beside* each other, *on top* of each other, etc. This child notices enclosure or "surroundingness." He thus will place the eyes of a figure within the head in his drawing of a person. Another characteristic of topological organization of space is that of the awareness of order and continuity. In this instance the child is aware of the fact that hats are *on* heads, roofs are *on* houses, and that legs and arms are located in two different positions on the two sides of the body (Pufall and Shaw, 1973).

In the second stage of the development of an objective spatial reference system (4 to 7 years), both topological and self-reference processes are involved in defining the child's space world. The child at this stage begins to distinguish not only the nearness-farness dimension of space (proximity) but also the right-left dimension of space and tries to integrate the two. Thus by 5 or 6 years of age the child coordinates near-far and right-left in relationship to his person and locates objects in space as "far-right," "near-left," etc. (Pufall and Shaw, 1973).

The third stage in the development of a spatial reference system is one in which the objective reference system of the adult begins to dominate and to operate. This final adult stage is believed to be achieved by the age of 12. It is during this stage that the child discovers that objects other than himself can be used as reference points in space. This of course requires the use of perspective in organizing spatial relations. During this final stage of development then, the center of the reference system of the child shifts or can be shifted outside the body to objects and/or characteristics of objects in space.

The important thing to note is that the move toward an objective spatial reference system by the young child closely parallels changes in his intrasensory and intersensory development (Shilkret and Friedland, 1974; Williams, 1979). A description of the stages in intrasensory and intersensory development and their possible relationship to the acquisition of an objective spatial reference system is shown in Table 6-1. In general the age of onset of a new stage in the proposed spatial reference system development appears to coincide with those periods of development during which the

TABLE 6-1 Development of Sensory Reference System

	AGE	KIND OF DEVELOPMENT	SENSORY SYSTEMS INVOLVED	KIND OF INFORMATION INVOLVED**	SOURCE OF INFORMATION
Stage I (Topological System)	0-5 yrs.	Intrasensory	a. vision* b. tactile-kinesthetic	a. spatial b. spatial c. temporal	a. external b. internal c. external
Stage II (Topological and Self-Reference System)	3-6 yrs. (early)	Intersensory	vision and tactile-kinesthetic	spatial	external/ internal
	4-? yrs (late)	Intrasensory	a. vision* c. audition b. tactile-kinesthetic	a. temporal c. temporal b. temporal	a. external c. external b. internal
Stage III (Objective Reference System)	6-8 yrs. (early)	Intersensory	vision and tactile-kinesthetic	temporal	external/ internal
	8-10 yrs. (late)	Intersensory	vision and audition; tactile-kinesthetic and audition	temporal	external

*Order of most rapid development
**Spatial ≈ simultaneous
Temporal ≈ sequential

child is undergoing the most rapid change and/or improvement in intra-sensory and intersensory functioning. Thus the child's ability to concep-tually represent or organize space seems to coincide with his development of a more refined capacity for integrating sensory information. It also coincides with an increase in the ability of the child to use sequential or temporally based information (in contrast to the use of simultaneous or spatially based information). Accompanying the move toward the achieve-ment of an objective spatial reference system by the child is a tendency on his part to focus on or use external sources of sensory information, that is, to rely on information derived from objects or events that are outside the body (Williams, 1979).

Whether or not there is a causal relationship between changes in intrasensory and intersensory development and the acquisition of an ob-jective spatial reference system is not known. It does not seem unreasonable, however, to suggest that as the young child becomes better able to integrate various sources of sensory information, he concomitantly develops a clearer representation of the relationship among objects in his space world. It follows logically that when objects and events are clearly perceived or ex-perienced, it is easier to objectify, mentally manipulate, and thus to con-ceptualize about them. Thus it would make sense that as the child develops a more elaborate perceptual picture of his space world (through improved intrasensory and intersensory integration), he will also be better able to handle or judge spatial relations among those objects and/or events that make up his external space world.

SUMMARY

1. Intersensory integration may be defined as the ability of the individual to use or integrate several sources of sensory information simulta-neously to solve problems and/or to help him in adapting to his en-vironment.

2. There are believed to be three levels of intersensory functioning: (a) a low-level automatic level of integration, which is built into the nerv-ous system and which is present at birth; (b) a higher order level of integration, which involves analysis of perceptual features and which occurs at a more conscious level; and (c) a cognitive/conceptual level of integration, which involves the transfer of ideas or concepts across different sensory modalities.

3. It is believed that infants inherently tend to explore objects and events in the environment in several modalities (e.g., they look in the direc-tion of a sound they hear or they reach in the direction of an object they see).

4. The efficient use of multiple sources of sensory information by the young child represents a move toward a higher, more adaptive level of behavioral and neural functioning.

5. Children at 5-6 years of age operate at chance levels with regard to integrating or matching visual and auditory information. By 7 years this integration ability has improved greatly but continues to mature until 11-12 years.

6. There appear to be two periods of rapid growth in auditory-visual integration abilities in the young child: 5-7 years and 8-10 years.

7. Although little is written about auditory-tactile integration, there is some evidence that there is a natural linkage between the tactile-kinesthetic and auditory systems. For example, awareness of tactile information is more acute when it is accompanied by auditory stimulation.

8. Significant improvements in the child's ability to integrate auditory and tactile information occur between 5 and 8 years of age.

9. Visual-tactile/kinesthetic integration abilities also improve with age and seem to become refined before those associated with auditory-visual integration. These intersensory integration abilities are relatively mature by the age of 5 years. Three-year-olds function at chance level, whereas four-year-olds are successful 84% of the time. Some aspects of visual-tactile/kinesthetic integration, however, continue to improve and mature until 11-12 years of age.

10. Intersensory integration development appears to be important to the development of skillful movement behavior. It has been shown that six-year-old children with more advanced levels of intersensory integration are superior to five-year-olds with less advanced levels of intersensory development in performance of both gross and fine motor control tasks. Such differences are not as great for eight-year-olds. This suggests that intersensory integration may play a more vital role in the early development of gross and fine motor control than in later development.

11. In general, children with more advanced intersensory development show gradual and steady improvement in performing motor tasks throughout learning; children with lower levels of intersensory development tend to show much more erratic patterns of learning.

12. The role of intersensory integration in the cognitive development of young children is far from clearly understood. There is some evidence that developmentally delayed children are characterized by a lack of refinement of intersensory integration abilities (especially auditory-visual integration). Equally strong evidence is available to suggest that the discrepancies in intersensory integration abilities of normally and

slowly developing children are not as great as they were once thought to be.

13. The role of intersensory integration in learning appears to be somewhat dependent upon the age of the child and the nature of the cognitive task to be mastered.

STUDY QUESTIONS

1. What is intersensory integration?
2. List and describe the three levels or types of intersensory integration.
3. Differentiate between cross-modal equivalence and cross-modal concepts.
4. How are 2 and 3 related?
5. Intersensory integration is believed to be in part a learned process. How does the notion of a "common space" support or negate this belief?
6. Describe the evidence that suggests that some aspects of intersensory integration may be innate.
7. How is intersensory integration related to more-advanced neural functioning?
8. How is intersensory development related to intrasensory development? Be specific and complete.
9. How are intersensory integration abilities studied?
10. Describe the changes that occur with age in auditory-visual integration abilities; visual-auditory integration abilities.
11. In cases of information overload (e.g., too much information), to which kind of information is more attention given—visual or auditory? Discuss.
12. Describe important age changes in auditory-tactile integration abilities.
13. Describe the nature of age-related changes in visual-tactile/kinesthetic abilities in young children. When do they reach maturity?
14. Stimulation of one sense is known to affect the use of information in other sensory systems. Describe how the interaction among sensory systems may change with age.
15. How is intersensory integration related to performance of gross motor tasks? Fine motor tasks? Does this change with age? Be specific.
16. Describe the Douglass and Williams (1976) study on level of intersensory development and the learning of gross motor tasks. What particular significance does this have for the teaching of motor skills to young children?
17. How is intersensory integration related to cognitive development? Cite specific evidence. Does age play a role in this interrelationship? How?
18. What is a "spatial reference system"? Describe the stages of its development in the young child.
19. How is the acquisition of a spatial reference system related to the intersensory and intrasensory development of the young child?

REFERENCES

AARONSON, E., AND ROSENBLOOM, S.   Space perception in early infancy: perception within a common auditory visual space. *Science.* 172 (1971): 1161-1163.

ABRAVANEL, E.   How children combine vision and touch when perceiving the shapes of objects. *Perception and Psychophysics.* 12 (1972): 171-175.

ABRAVANEL, E.   The development of intersensory patterning in regard to selected spatial dimensions. *Monographs of the Society for Research in Child Development.* 33 (1968): 1-52.

AUERBACH, C., AND P. SPERLING.   A common auditory-visual space: evidence for its reality. *Perception and Psychophysics.* 16 (1974): 129-135.

BALTER, L., AND FOGARTY, J.   Intra- and intersensory matching by nursery school children. *Perceptual and Motor Skills.* 33 (1971): 467-472.

BARTHOLOMEUS, B. N., AND DOEHRING, D. G.   Acquisition of visual-auditory associations by good and excellent readers. *Perceptual and Motor Skills.* 35 (1972): 847-855.

BERENBERG, S., CANIARIS, M., AND MOSSE, N., editors. *Pre and postnatal development of the human brain.* New York: S. Karger, 1974.

BIRCH, H. G., AND BELMONT, L.   Auditory-visual integration in normal and retarded readers. *American Journal of Orthopsychiatry.* 34 (1964): 852-861.

BIRCH, H. D., AND BELMONT, L.   Auditory-visual integration, intelligence, and reading ability in school children. *Perceptual and Motor Skills.* 20 (1965): 295-305.

BIRCH, H. G., AND LEFFORD, A.   Intersensory development in children. *Monographs of the Society for Research in Child Development.* 28 (1963): 1-87.

BIRCH, H. G., AND LEFFORD, A.   Visual differentiation, intersensory integration and voluntary motor control. *Monographs of the Society for Research in Child Development.* 32 (1967): 1-87.

BLANK, M., AND BRIDGER, W.   Cross modal transfer in nursery school children. *Journal of Experimental Child Psychology.* 58 (1974): 277-282.

BOWER, T. G. R.   Object perception in infants. *Perception.* 1 (1972): 15-30.

BOWER, T. G. R.   The object in the world of the infant. *Scientific American.* 225 (1971): 30-38.

CONEL, J. L.   *The Postnatal Development of the Human Cerebral Cortex.* Cambridge, MA: Harvard University Press, 1959.

DOUGLASS, M. V., AND WILLIAMS, H.   The relationship of intrasensory and intersensory development to motor control. Unpublished paper, University of Toledo, 1976.

GAINES, G. J., AND L. M. RASKIN.   Comparison of cross-modal and intra-modal form recognition in children with learning disabilities. *Journal of Learning Disabilities.* 3 (1970): 243-246.

GESCHEIDER, G. A., MARTIN, J., KANE, L., SAGER, C., AND RUFFOLO, L.   The effect of auditory stimulation on responses to tactile stimuli. *Bulletin of the Psychonomic Society.* 3 (1974): 204-206.

GIBSON, E. J.   *Principles of perceptual learning and development.* Englewood Cliffs, NJ: Prentice-Hall, Inc., 1969.

GIBSON, J. J.   *The senses considered as perceptual systems.* New York: Houghton Mifflin, 1966.

GOODNOW, J.   Eye and hand: differential memory and its effect on matching. *Neuropsychologia.* 9 (1971a): 89-95.

GOODNOW, J.   Matching auditory and visual series: modality problem or translation problem? *Child Development.* 42 (1971b): 1187-1201.

HSIA, J. J.   Intelligence in auditory, visual and audio-visual information processing. *AV Communication Review.* 17 (1969): 282-292.

JESSEN, L. J., AND KAESS, D. W.   Effects of training on intersensory communication by three- and five-year olds. *The Journal of Genetic Psychology.* 123 (1973): 115-122.

JONES, B.   Cross-modal matching by retarded and normal readers. *Bulletin of the Psychonomic Society.* 3 (1974): 163-165.

JONES, B.   Visual facilitation of auditory localization in schoolchildren: a signal detection analysis. *Perception and Psychophysics.* 17 (1975): 217-220.

JONES, B., AND ALEXANDER, R.   Developmental trends in auditory-visual cross-modal matching of spatio-temporal patterns. *Developmental Psychology.* 10 (1974): 354-356.

JONES, B., AND ROBINSON, T.   Sensory integration in normal and retarded children. *Developmental Psychology.* 9 (1973): 178-182.

KAUFMAN, J., BELMONT, I., BIRCH, H.G., AND ZACH, L.   Tactile and visual sense system interactions: a developmental study using reaction time models. *Developmental Psychobiology.* 6 (1973): 165-176.

KUHLMAN, E., AND WOLKING, W.   Development of within and cross-modal matching in the auditory and visual sense modalities. *Developmental Psychology.* 7 (1972): 365.

LONG, N. R., AND NEWSOME L. R.   Recall of messages presented simultaneously to auditory and visual channels with varying uncertainty and delay of message. *Perceptual and Motor Skills.* 38 (1974): 24.

MCGRADY, H. J., AND OLSON, D. A.   Visual and auditory learning processes in normal children and children with specific learning disabilities. *Exceptional Children.* 36 (1970): 581-589.

MILLER, A., AND BRYANT, P.   Cross-modal matching by young children. *Journal of Comparative Physiological Psychology.* 71 (1970): 453-458.

PIAGET, J., AND INHELDER, B.   *The child's conception of space.* London: Routledge and Kegan Paul, 1956.

PUFALL, P. B., AND SHAW, R. E.   Analysis of the development of children's spatial reference systems. *Cognitive Psychology.* 5 (1973): 151-175.

RUDEL, R., AND TEUBER, H.   Cross-modal transfer of shape discrimination by children. *Neuropsychologia.* 2 (1964): 1-8.

RUDEL, R., AND TEUBER, H.   Pattern recognition within and across sensory modalities in normal and brain injured children. *Neuropsychologia.* 9 (1971): 389-400.

SPELKE, E.   Infants' intermodal perception of events. *Cognitive Psychology.* 8 (1976): 553-560.

SPELKE, E., AND OUISLEY, C.   Intermodal exploration and knowledge in infancy. *Infant Behavior and Development.* 2 (1979): 13-27.

STERRITT, G., MARTIN, V., AND RUDNICK, M.   Auditory-visual and temporal-spatial integration as determinants of test difficulty. *Psychonomic Science.* 23 (1971): 289-291.

TYRRELL, D. J.   Cross-modal transfer of conceptual responding in children. *Bulletin of the Psychonomic Society.* 4 (1974): 269-271.

WARREN, D. H.   Intermodality interactions in spatial localization. *Cognitive Psychology.* 1 (1970): 114-133.

WILLIAMS, H.   Relationship between intrasensory, intersensory development and the conceptualization of space. Unpublished paper, University of Toledo, 1979.

WILLIAMS, H., TEMPLE, I., AND BATEMAN, J.   A test battery to assess intrasensory and intersensory development of young children. *Perceptual and Motor Skills.* 48 (1979): 643-659.

WILLIAMS, H., TEMPLE, I., AND BATEMAN, J.   Perceptual-motor and cognitive learning in young children. *Psychology of Motor Behavior and Sport II.* Champaign, IL: Human Kinetics Press, 1978.

WILLOT, J.   Perceptual judgments with discrepant information from audition and proprioception. *Perception and Psychophysics.* 14 (1973): 577-580.

PART TWO
MOTOR AND PHYSICAL-RELATED ASPECTS OF PERCEPTUAL-MOTOR DEVELOPMENT

CHAPTER SEVEN
DEVELOPMENT OF FINE MOTOR CONTROL IN YOUNG CHILDREN

Fine motor control has been previously defined as the ability to coordinate or regulate the use of the eyes and the hands together in efficient, precise, and adaptive movement patterns. These movement patterns can manifest themselves in a myriad of forms ranging from writing, drawing, and coloring to cutting, pasting, and manipulation of small objects and/or instruments. More universally, these movement patterns are referred to as eye-hand coordination skills. Development of fine motor control or eye-hand coordination skills represents an important and integral part of the total motor development of the young child and clearly reflects the increasing capacity of the CNS to pick up and process visual input and to translate that input into skillful, well-executed motor behaviors—behaviors that are necessary if the child is to be able to interact effectively with the practical as well as the communication aspects of his object-laden school and home environments.

EARLY FOUNDATIONS OF FINE MOTOR CONTROL: ROLE OF REFLEX GRASP MECHANISMS

It is generally held (although not without disagreement on the part of some) that reflex mechanisms play an important role in the early development of voluntary motor behavior in young children. This is especially true of the development of eye-hand coordination skills, which may indeed have their earliest beginnings in reflex grasp mechanisms which provide the initial means that the child has for prehension or interaction with objects in the environment. Although the role of reflex grasping in the development of voluntary prehensile behaviors has not been clearly defined, it is important to our understanding of the total development of fine motor control in young children to be aware of the changes in such reflex movement patterns that occur early in the infant's use of his hands to acquire or interact with objects.

It is believed by most authorities that prehension, a forerunner of fine motor control, doesn't suddenly appear as a "single entity." Its development and expansion is gradual and builds on the reflex mechanisms functioning in that stage of development (Twitchell, 1970). A general overview of the various forms of prehensile or reflex grasping responses, the kind of stimuli that evoke them, and the pattern of movement involved in such responses is given in Table 7-1.

Early grasping responses are elicited primarily by proprioceptive stimulation, so that within the first 8 weeks of life a passive pull on the arms of the infant elicits a "traction" response that consists of flexion at all of the joints of the stimulated limb. Interestingly, these early traction responses are also influenced by the asymmetrical tonic neck reflex (TNR). Thus if the child's head is turned to the right and the right arm is passively pulled, the traction response is diminished or may not occur at all in that arm. However, if in the same right TNR position the left arm is passively pulled, the traction response is facilitated, that is, flexion at various joints in the arm is more energetic. Ultimately the influence of the TNR on these early eye-hand coordination movement patterns is reduced as development of higher cortical control takes place. With increasingly greater cortical control, important changes or refinements occur in the kind of stimulus that will elicit the response as well as in the nature of the response or movement pattern itself. Thus early, crude traction responses soon expand from primarily synergistic limb flexion elicited by a general pull on the arm itself to synergistic limb flexion accompanied by adduction and flexion of the thumb and index fingers ("local reaction"). The eliciting stimulus in this case is heavy pressing of the palm of the hand (Twitchell, 1970, 1979).

From 16 to 44 weeks several important changes occur in the prehensile behaviors of the infant. One is a fractionation (further differentiation) of the movement pattern involved in the grasp reflex. This consists of flexion in individual fingers when they are touched and appears first in the index finger, an important contributor to the whole process of fine motor control. A second and usually overlapping event is the appearance of clearcut orientation of the hand to the stimulus that comes into contact with it. Thus if touched on the thumb side, the hand is turned in that direction (supination); if touched on the little finger side, the hand is turned in that direction (pronation). Such orientation movements are, of course, necessary

TABLE 7-1 Stages of Development of Grasp Response

AGE	TYPE OF REFLEX GRASPING	EVOKING STIMULUS	PATTERN OF MOVEMENT
0-8 wks.	Traction Response I	Passive pull on arm (proprioceptive dominance)	Synergistic flexion at all joints of limb, especially fingers/wrists facilitated/inhibited by TNR
2-8 wks.	Traction Response II	Contact stimulation of palm (heavy pressing)	Adduction/flexion of thumb and index finger (local reaction) plus the above
8-20 wks.	Full Grasp Reflex	Deeply pressing contact to radial respect of palm moving out to proximal parts of fingers	Sudden quick flexion of fingers (catching), sustained flexion of fingers (proprioceptive holding), and dorsiflexion of wrist; little synergistic flexion at other joints*
16-40 wks.	Fractionation of Grasp Reflex	Contact to individual fingers	Individual fingers flex when touched; first seen in index fingers, then in others
16-36 wks.	Hand Orientation	Contact to radial part of hand, then ulnar	Supination of hand toward radial stimulus; later pronation of hand toward ulnar stimulation
20-44 wks.	Full, Instinctive Grasp Reaction	Light stationary or moving contact to any part of hand (exteroceptive dominance)	The above plus palpating movement toward stimulus as it is withdrawn (groping) plus closing of fingers around object

*TNR not effective in altering limb posture.

to allow for adequate contact, grasp, and manipulation of potentially interesting objects that the infant may accidentally encounter. The last change to take place in prehension during this time is a combination of orientation and palpating movements of the hand toward the contact object together with an ultimate closing of the fingers around the object. This is the *full instinctive grasp reaction*. This movement pattern is elicited by *light* contact (stationary or moving) to any part of the hand and represents a shift away from proprioceptive dominance (deep heavy pressure) of basic prehensile movements to dominance by more exteroceptive stimuli (light touch). Thus by 20-44 weeks rather complex sequences of movements needed for "grasping" objects are present in the young infant and can be elicited easily by light exteroceptive touch stimuli (Twitchell, 1970, 1979).

Contact stimulation (e.g., coming into contact with an object) early in development can also cause withdrawal or avoiding responses; in these situations the movement patterns that predominate are ones that cause the child to "reject" or move away from the object touched. The age characteristics of these avoidance reactions are described below. During the course of normal development, contact avoidance and grasping reactions evolve in overlapping fashion and ultimately complement each other as the final product of skillful fine motor control is achieved (Twitchell, 1970, 1979). However at any particular point in early development, avoidance reactions can dominate and thus contaminate eye-hand coordination behaviors. How do avoidance reactions that are undergoing changes at the same time as basic grasping responses influence development of early prehensile behaviors? In general, in early infancy most reaching/grasping movements are biased toward withdrawal reactions. This is seen most vividly in the brain-damaged patient who simply holds his hand by his head and cannot project it toward an object. This is, of course, the most severe form of avoidance-reaction dominance. In less severe forms, the person reaches for the object but keeps the hand "too open" to be able to grasp it. For example, the young child in reaching for a small pellet will keep the hand opened as though reaching for a large ball. Often the fingers also remain too spread for skillful prehension of small objects, and if the hand does succeed in getting hold of the object, it (the hand) may quickly spring away (Twitchell, 1970, 1979).

DEVELOPMENT OF AVOIDANCE REACTIONS

0-4 wks.:	Light contact stimulus elicits slight withdrawal of hand/limb; consists of dorsiflexion and abduction of the fingers.
3-8 wks.:	Above become easier to elicit; added to the movement are pronation of the hand and flexion of the arm.
12-20 wks.:	Contact stimulus to ulnar border of hand elicits pronation/adduction; later contact stimulus to radial border elicits supination and abduction; extension and flexion movements are added; infant "avoids," does not just "withdraw."
24-40 wks.:	Full instinctive avoiding reaction; "avoiding" is accomplished by various combinations of flexion, extension, abduction, adduction, etc.; these movements do not depend on visual guidance but on contact stimulus.

Avoidance reactions seem in one respect to add a source of variety or refinement to the movement patterns involved in the basic grasp mechanism. Their influence is perhaps best understood by looking at what happens when these two forms of reflex patterns are not precisely integrated, e.g., that is, when there is some imbalance between them in terms of one or the other dominating the movement response. In the most severe case, if neither of these reflex behavior patterns is present, true prehension is not possible and never develops. If on the other hand the early traction response dominates (e.g., there is synergistic flexion at all limb joints, especially the wrist and fingers), and this is not properly balanced with the extension/abduction movements of the fingers associated with the early avoidance reaction, the child's movement is dominated by flexion of the fingers. This prevents development of finger-thumb opposition, an important prerequisite to fine motor control. Isolation of individual movements of the fingers is also impaired and this makes manipulation of objects, when and if it occurs, quite clumsy. If later developing aspects of the avoidance reaction are not adequately integrated with the rapidly differentiating grasp reflex movement patterns, fine motor control behaviors are characterized by lack of refinement of the finer aspects of grasping such as poor orientation and adjustment of the hand to the object. These observations suggest that early development of fine motor control is indeed based to a large degree on the integration of both grasping and avoidance reflex movement patterns that are elicited by object contact with the hands. It is important to note that both sets of these reflex movement patterns are basically *not* under the guidance of the visual system. This is seen in the fact that: (a) voluntary prehensile behavior of children with congenital encephalopathy is interrupted even though the visual mechanism is intact, and (b) it is largely through techniques of proprioceptive facilitation that such patterns are trained/learned (if they ever are). These clinical facts attest to the importance of early proprioceptively based reflex movement patterns in the development of fine motor control.

THE ROLE OF VISION IN DEVELOPMENT OF FINE MOTOR CONTROL

It is generally believed that eye-hand coordination and fine motor control require the building of sensori-motor control mechanisms that can locate the hand and object in visual space and then bring them together. The facts of the development of reaching in infants show that there is indeed an underlying fundamental coordination of eyes and hands in space that probably exists at birth. For example, drawings of single movie frames arranged in sequence indicate that, in the young infant, there is a regular "pattern of space-controlled form" to reaching/grasping movements. However these basic eye-hand coordination connections may be further refined and elaborated upon through visuo-motor experience the child has in using the eyes and hands together in a variety of situations (Hein, 1972).

There can be little doubt that full development of fine motor behaviors involves the regulation of movement patterns by visual information. But how and when does such input become important to fine motor control? It is clear from the foregoing discussion that most, if not all, of the movement patterns needed for fine motor control develop early and without the direct help of vision. Hein and Held (1967), however, have shown that the visual placing response is an important part of the reflex strata that underlies the development of reaching/grasping behaviors, and that differentiation of basic visual placing responses requires experience in using the eyes and hands together. Visual placing is an automatic reaction that occurs when animals or young infants are placed in juxtaposition to or moved toward a stationary surface. If an infant is held in the air near a surface and then is moved downward toward that surface (e.g., a table top), the infant will automatically extend the upper limbs to meet the approaching surface. This would seem to be an early form of eye-hand coordination—the eliciting of a certain pattern of hand and/or limb movement in conjunction with specific visual input. This reaction probably represents a built-in connection between the eyes and the hands that does not require any previous experience in using the eyes and hands together in a coordinated fashion. For example, kittens reared under conditions where they do not have the opportunity to use eyes and hands (paws) together (they are not allowed to see the paws as they use or move them) still exhibit this primitive placing reaction—a reaction that is automatically elicited, just as it is in kittens reared under normal conditions. The effect of the lack of opportunity to use eyes and hands together and to see the hands as they are used is seen primarily in the inadequate development of *guided placing responses*. Without appropriate visual experience, young animals cannot guide their limb movements accurately to specific points or parts of the visual environment. For example, monkeys deprived of natural visual-motor experiences cannot immediately reach out skillfully for objects in their environment. They tend instead to look at or fixate on the hand in a fashion similar to the human infant during early stages of eye-hand coordination development and to make gross errors in visually directing these primitive reaching movements. In addition, they also show some deficiency in the tactile control of associated grasping responses. Thus even when contact is made with an object, these monkeys display extremely awkward use of the paw in touch-based grasping, manipulative movements. Normally reared animals do not evidence either of these fine motor behavior difficulties. Accurate reaching movements develop gradually in these deprived animals as they gain experience in viewing the hand and using it in coordination with the eyes (Hein and Held, 1967; Hein, 1974).

It is also important to point out that not only do normally reared animals show a high degree of accuracy and precision in reaching for and manipulating objects, they also show considerable intermanual transfer as well as a ready generalization of such reaching responses to a variety of spatial locations of objects. In other words normal animals can quickly and accurately reach for objects placed in new and different spatial locations without additional practice; they are also able to use a previously unused limb skillfully in reaching for such objects. Animals without this eye-hand coordination experience, on the other hand, show a marked inability to generalize such visually guided reaching responses spontaneously and have to be specifically trained to reach to each new target location in space. They also have to be taught to use the inexperienced limb to perform the reaching behaviors previously learned with the opposite limb. Thus it would seem that development of refined eye-hand coordination behaviors requires the integration of both visual and nonvisual sources of sensory information—a process that requires that the organism simultaneously see and feel the movement of the hands and/or limbs as they are used in interacting with and exploring objects in the environment. If there is a lack of opportunity for the young animal to calibrate the feeling of such reaching movements with appropriate movement-produced visual feedback, some deficiency in visually guided reaching/grasping movements often results (Hein, 1974). In this respect vision seems to be an important regulating element in the development of highly refined fine motor behaviors.

In general, there appear to be four major stages in the early development of eye-hand coordination in humans that strongly involve the visual mechanism. The initial stage of this aspect of eye-hand coordination development includes the period from 0 to 16 weeks and is best described as a stage of *static visual exploration*. The infant, during this stage of development, seems to have a genuine visual predilection for his hands and spends a large percentage of his waking time fixating intently on his hands while he lies in the crib. Typically this infant will look at an object in his crib or playpen and then immediately look back at his hands. At this point the eyes tend to immobilize and fixate on the hands while the arms and legs activate in rather spontaneous activity (Williams, 1973).

The second stage of eye-hand coordination involving vision covers the seventeenth to the twenty-eighth week and is characterized by *active and repeated visual exploration of objects* in the child's environment. This active, visual manipulation of objects seems to be a kind of ocular grasping in which the infant visually picks up an object with his eyes, drops it, and then picks it up again. For example a twenty-week-old infant, lying in a supine position, will intently watch a dangling ring held above him. He looks at the object and then at his hand and then back at the object, and he does this repeatedly. All at once, while the eyes are on the object, all bodily activity stops and shortly thereafter the arms are flung outward in a crude attempt to make contact with the ring as it swings near his hands. Contact may or may not be made (this is not yet under full control of the child), but when it is and the infant actually grasps the object, it goes immediately to his mouth for further exploration. Interestingly, even while the object is in the mouth the infant tries to fixate it visually (Williams, 1973).

The third stage of eye-hand coordination development (28-40 weeks) is one in which the visual mechanism of the child seems to prompt or take the lead in regulating specific grasping and/or manipulative responses. Perhaps the most important characteristic of this stage of eye-hand coordination development is the newly acquired ability of the child to correct his reaching/grasping movements through intensified activity of the visual mechanism. For example, during this stage the child seems first to locate an object or toy with his eyes. He then initiates a movement toward the toy. As he reaches for the object, his visual fixation relaxes. Frequently this initial movement is in error, and when it is the child's visual fixation of the object intensifies and he adjusts or corrects his reaching response. Focus on the toy is maintained throughout this time, and when the hand finally comes into contact with the toy, visual fixation becomes even more intensified. As the object is grasped and manipulated, the eyes continue to explore it visually (Williams, 1973). The final stage of eye-hand coordination development begins at approximately 40 weeks and continues throughout the years of middle childhood. The main feature of this period of development is the acquiring of a more refined control of eye-hand coordination behaviors and the extending of them to the performance of a wide variety of tasks.

Trevarthen (1978) describes the following as characteristic of the early developmental stages of voluntary eye-hand coordination/fine motor control behaviors:

1. at 1 week: (a) infants, if properly supported, try to acquire small objects (2-4 cm. in diameter) in near space (10-20 cm.); they do this first by "visual centering" and then by "aimed" extension of the fingers of one or both hands (toes may also be involved) in the direction of the target object; (b) if objects are moved slowly, they are tracked by the eyes, head, torso, hands, and feet;

2. at 1-2 weeks: (a) reaching and grasping movements consist of finger extension and flexion in anticipation of acquiring the object; these movements are tied to arm extension and withdrawal; (b) some infants show simultaneous movement of mouth and tongue;

3. at 2-3 months: (a) infants have increased control of proximal segments of limbs; concurrently there is decreased control of extension movements of the fingers; (b) grasping movements may be lost, but vigorous jerky arm movements, which are made as the infant intensely fixates on the object of interest, are present;

4. at 5 months: (a) a more controlled form of reaching is present; this is a differentiation of the preestablished eye-hand coordination present at birth; (b) there is now present a regular periodicity of arm movements, the rhythm of which is precisely coordinated with that of exploratory head movements (these are seen for the first time at this age);

5. at 6-12 months: (a) fine adjustment of fingers and delicate prehension occur; this is associated with improved visual fixation and scanning and with increased exploration of objects with the mouth.

In general, Trevarthen (1978) suggests that vision and touch work together to produce complex reaching/grasping movements in the three-month-old infant, but such movements are not used in any purposeful way until about 1 year of age. He, too, believes there is an underlying "motor prewiring" involved in fine motor control that needs to be triggered visually for eye-hand coordination skills to develop fully.

The foregoing descriptive analysis of the role of vision in the early development of eye-hand coordination behaviors suggests that while grasp and avoidance reaction mechanisms are undergoing rapid change, so is the tendency of the child to use the eyes in regulating fine motor control. At a time when grasp patterns are elicited primarily through proprioceptive means, the eyes seem to be used independently to actively explore the nature of the hands and the objects that they will be or are interacting with. Coincident with the time (16-44 weeks) when proprioceptive-elicited reaching/grasping behaviors are becoming more differentiated (individual finger flexion and orientation and adjustment of the hand to the object through touch are occurring), we see the young infant attempting to integrate or use vision to regulate such movement patterns and to correct for errors in reaching/grasping behavior through intense visual fixation. Through trial and error, the infant uses what he sees to guide what he does motorically. Perhaps this is the time when visual dominance of fine motor control begins to assume real significance. After 40 weeks these two systems seem to be, for most children, effectively integrated, so that the child now spends his time expanding and refining the process of adapting his fine-motor-control behaviors to meet increasingly more complex environmental demands. Most important of all, *experience* may be the key word in understanding how these two systems are ultimately integrated in an efficient way in the growing, developing child.

BILATERAL MOTOR COORDINATION

Most manipulative activity requires the controlled use of the two hands and/or limbs in concert with one another. Thus in cutting, for example, one hand manipulates the scissors while the other hand holds and positions the paper that is to be cut. To be successful in cutting, both hands must be skillful and must move in appropriate temporal relationships to each other. As a result, an important part of fine motor control may have its early roots in the development of the integrated and skillful use of the two sides of the body, a neuromuscular phenomenon generally referred to as bilateral motor coordination. Although the development of bilateral motor coordination has not been clearly documented, clinical observations of young children suggest that there is a general overall sequence in which the early foundation for more highly refined bilateral motor coordination develops (Williams, 1979). The following is an outline of this developmental sequence:

1. The child (on command) moves both arms simultaneously on either side of the vertical midline; movement is crude but controlled.
2. The child moves both legs simultaneously on either side of the vertical midline of the body; movement is crude but fairly well controlled.
3. The child moves both arms and both legs simultaneously on either side of the vertical midline of the body; movements are not refined but are reasonably well controlled.
4. The child simultaneously moves the arm and leg on the same side of the body in a controlled manner with no involvement of the opposite arm and/or leg (homolateral control); there may be more refined coordination on the preferred side than on the nonpreferred side.
5. The child simultaneously moves the arm and leg on opposite sides of the body in a controlled manner with little or no involvement of the other arm and/or leg (contralateral control); these movements are more coordinated when the preferred hand is a part of the two-limb combination.

Bilateral motor coordination begins with the child's attempts to move the arms bilaterally in a crude fashion on either side of the vertical midline of the body; this is followed by the development of similar control of the two legs (in accordance with the cephalocaudal law of developmental direction). This early and crude form of bilateral motor coordination is followed by the development of control over homolateral movements, the use of the arm and leg on the same side of the body. Such control obviously involves both the coordination of upper and lower limbs and the isolation of movement activity to one side of the body. Such control places a greater demand on the neuromuscular system of the child and reflects the increasing refinement of neuromuscular mechanisms underlying fine motor control. Last but not least, control of contralateral movements appears. At this point the child must coordinate the use of upper and lower limbs on opposite sides of the body and isolate movement to the specific limbs designated. This represents even greater differentiation and/or refinement of the neuromuscular system and heralds the establishment of the basic foundation for more refined bilateral motor coordination. Although specific ages for acquisition of such control cannot be indicated, it would appear in general that by the time the child is 6, he should show good mastery of all phases of this early aspect of bilateral motor coordination (Williams, 1979).

Ayres (1978) has studied the development of bilateral motor coordination in the upper extremities in young children and has shown that with regard to smooth, skillful integration of the two limbs in simple movements (e.g., clapping out simple rhythms), there is considerable improvement in such control between 4 and 6 years of age but little change or improvement after 6½ years. The most significant gain in bilateral motor coordination, according to Ayres' data, occurs between 5 and 6 years.

On this basic foundation of motor coordination develops the control that ultimately manifests itself in fine manipulative ability displayed in a variety of forms. Again the nature and sequence of such development is really not agreed upon, but some general dimensions of such development can be at least roughly described. These are outlined in Figure 7.1. Overall there seems to be a general trend from early, crude bilateral movements to development of some degree of control or skill in unilateral movements and, finally, a blending of individual unilateral movements into more refined and skillful bilateral patterns of manipulation. Unilateral movement activities contribute to the development of preferred and nonpreferred hands, whereas the later appearing, more highly refined bilateral movement activities culminate in the use of a lead-and-assist hand that is universally seen in the performance of most manipulative tasks (Williams, 1979). There is some suggestion that there may be an inherent or wired-in pattern of development in which the use of the limbs actually changes alternately throughout development from bilateral to unilateral to bilateral activity.

Within this overall framework of fine motor control, there is interwoven another pattern of development, one that involves development of control over discrete or isolated versus sequentially ordered movements of the limb(s). Thus during the course of development, the young child at

FIGURE 7.1. Schema of the Development of Selected Aspects of Fine Motor Control

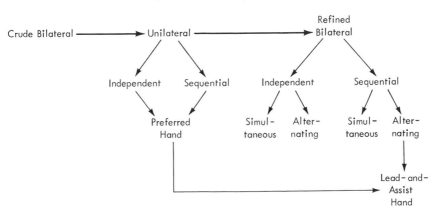

overlapping points in time learns to control isolated movements at various joints of the upper extremities and then learns to organize such movements into appropriate temporal sequences that are used to master various kinds of fine motor tasks with which he is faced. The importance of this aspect of fine motor control should not be overlooked, for it is integral to successful performance of most fine motor tasks that the individual be able to produce specific limb movements in isolation of other limb movements and to order such movements into specific temporal patterns. For example, in cutting it is important at times to be able to isolate movement of the fingers from movement of the wrist and/or elbow; yet it is also important to be able to maintain an appropriate sequence of movements at wrists, elbows, and shoulders in order to accommodate the outline of the figure that is to be cut. Children who cannot isolate individual movements of hands and arms frequently have difficulty learning to cut skillfully (Williams, 1979). Development of this kind of control takes place simultaneously in both unilateral and bilateral activities.

Superimposed upon this aspect of bilateral motor coordination is an additional dimension of fine motor control, that of moving the limbs together (simultaneously) versus moving them in some kind of alternating fashion. In some manipulative tasks both hands/arms must move simultaneously; however in most tasks they must move in some kind of alternately timed relationship to one another. To use the example of cutting, if the child is cutting a picture out of a book or from a piece of paper, the hands must work together in a coordinated alternating fashion. One hand leads in the sense of holding the scissors and performing the cutting action; the other hand assists by holding the paper, maintaining its proper orientation, and moving the paper when and if it is necessary to accommodate the cutting action of the lead hand. Many children have difficulty using the two hands together in this simple, sequential, alternating pattern of movement (Williams, 1979).

AGE CHARACTERISTICS OF FINE MOTOR SKILL DEVELOPMENT

Descriptions concerned with development of fine motor skills usually consist of lists of ages at which various fine motor behaviors are mastered by the young child. Definitive investigations of more sophisticated aspects of age characteristics of fine motor skill development are generally lacking. Only a few studies have looked at object manipulation; most have looked at various dimensions of the development of the child's ability to copy various kinds of geometric forms and other simple shapes.

Object Manipulation

Uzgiris (1967) provides a good description of some general characteristics of the development object use by the young child (6-24 months). He suggests that with increasing age, different schema are used by the child to interact with or use objects in the environment. These schema are listed below:

1. *exploring schema* (6-11 mos.): the initial way children deal with objects (shaking, hitting against surfaces);
2. *examining schema* (6-11 mos.): the child begins to explore objects in many different ways: (tearing, pulling, squeezing, rubbing, turning);
3. *letting-go schema* (6-11 mos.): the child drops and/or throws objects (this allows him to pair visual and auditory cues and to form more advanced perceptual impressions of the object);
4. *showing schema* (11 mos.): the child uses objects to instigate social interaction; he holds objects out to others to get their reaction, but if the individual attempts to take the object, the infant withholds it;
5. *naming schema* (18-24 mos): the child classifies/identifies objects via verbal labeling.

Frey (1979) studied differences in performances of four-, six-, and eight-year-old children on two different object manipulation tasks. One task required the child to place 12 small pegs, one at a time as quickly as possible, into slots in a small pegboard placed in front of the child (Pegs-In Task). The second task was one in which the child had to pick up, turn over, and place back into their original slots slightly larger wooden discs (Pegs-Over Task). This task was a modification of the Minnesota Rate of Manipulation Task designed to be used with young children. The discs themselves were the same size as those in the Minnesota test but only 12 were used. Performances on both tasks were timed to the nearest one-hundredth of a second and four trials were given to each child on each task.

Frey's data indicated that in general there were significant improvements in the performances of children on both object manipulation tasks between 4 and 6 years and again between 6 and 8 years. On the Pegs-In Task the greatest change in performance occurred between 4-6 years, with a smaller increment in performance between 6-8 years. For the Pegs-Over Task the amount of improvement from 4-6 was essentially equal to that which occurred from 6-8 years. Boys continued to show improvement in performance on both tasks from 6-8 years, whereas girls seemed to show more of a plateauing of performance during this same 6-8 year period. The plateauing of performance of girls resulted in a slight but not significant superiority in overall fine motor control for eight-year-old boys. Overall these data suggest that important changes take place in object manipulation skills for both boys and girls during the period of 4-6 years. The period from 6-8 years represents a period of less rapid change in such skills, particularly for girls.

Design or Form Copying

The child's ability to copy and/or draw different designs begins with simple constructive activities that appear about the age of 1 year in the form of scribbling. However, this early scribbling is basically a "motor expression" and is unrelated to any goal or particular visual model. This early "motor copying" gradually evolves throughout the early years and by the time the child is 5, a definite organization in his drawing and/or copying is evident —an organization that is guided by or directly related to a particular visual model. Goodenough (1926) describes very nicely the changes in characteristics of this early development of copying ability, as shown here.

CHARACTERISTICS OF EARLY DEVELOPMENT OF DESIGN COPYING

I.	1 yr.	*Scribbling:* Motor expression unrelated to any goal and undirected by any visual schema.
II.	2 yrs.	*Scribbling:* Still a spontaneous motor production, but now the child is visually responsive to the scribbles he produces; they have post hoc meaning.
III.	$2^1/_2$ yrs.	The child's preponderant response to any request to copy and/or draw is scribbling with inclusion of closed loops and parts of loops.
IV.	3 yrs.	*Copying:* The child begins to pay attention to characteristics of the visual model presented to him to copy.
	4 yrs.	*Copying:* The child begins to make differential drawings that involve *angular* as well as smooth contours.
	5 yrs.	*Copying:* There is a definite organization of drawing in relationship to the visually presented model, but copying is still undergoing refinement.

Ayres (1978) has studied the development of fine motor skill of design copying in children ages 4 to 11 years. Designs or figures of varying complexity (made up of 1-12 horizontal, vertical, and diagonal lines) were presented to over 200 children. The children were asked to reproduce these designs as accurately as possible. In general, results of this study indicated that the child's ability to copy designs skillfully gradually increases from 4 to 9 years. At 9 there is a plateauing of performance with little or no change thereafter. Thus it would seem that the ability to copy forms from visual models of varying complexity is nearly mature at the age of 9. There is a small improvement from 4 to 5 years—similar to that observed by Goodenough (1926), when the child begins to show greater mastery over the construction of angles and contours. The most dramatic increase in this ability occurs between 5-7 years, with equally large improvements between 5-6 and 6-7 years. At 7 there is a gradual deceleration in the rate of change in this fine motor skill. Thus from 7-8 years there is an improvement in the child's ability to copy figures, but this improvement is considerably smaller than that seen in the previous year. The change from 8 to 9 is even smaller. Overall Ayres' data (1978) suggest that the period of major growth for the fine motor ability of design copying is from 5 to 8 years, a time coincident with the early elementary years, when such skills are being emphasized and much time is spent in practicing them.

Birch and Lefford (1967) carried out the most comprehensive study of age changes in form or design copying. Children 5 to 11 years of age drew upright and inverted isosceles triangles (△▽) and equilateral (◇) and elongated vertical (◊) diamonds under three basic conditions: (1) *tracing* (the child traced the outline of the shape); (2) *line grid drawing* (the child copied the figure onto a line grid); and (3) *freehand drawing*. Performance on all three of these approaches to design copying improved with age, but the period of maximal change for most was from 5-6 years. The amount of improvement that occurred during this one year was as great as that which occurred during the next five years (6-11). Variability of performance decreased with increasing age. In general the tracing task was the easiest of the tasks, line grid drawing was intermediate, and freehand drawing was the most difficult for children of all ages. There were some interesting differences in the ages at which children mastered these three forms of design copying. Tracing abilities for all forms (triangles and diamonds) were mature at 6 years; line grid drawing was not mastered until 9 years, and freehand drawing in general tended to improve through 9 years for the triangle forms and through 11 years for the diamond shapes. Interestingly, at 5 years of age, line grids seemed to have an inhibitory effect on design copying, whereas by age 8, they tended to facilitate performance. Thus for five-year-olds line grid drawings were no better than freehand drawings, but at 7-8 years line grid drawings were superior to freehand drawings for most children.

In evaluating the development of children's freehand drawing abilities, Birch and Lefford (1967) essentially looked at four different dimensions of the form reproduced by the child: relative size of parts, spatial orientation, angle formation (size), and straightness of lines.

Relative size of parts of figure For triangles, by 5 years 40% of the children studied drew the two sides and base of the triangle in proper proportion. This dimension of design copying improved with age and by 9, 80% of all children reproduced triangles in appropriate proportions. The greatest change in this aspect of freehand drawing occurred from 5-7 years. For diamonds, only 3 or 4 five-year-olds, at most, could draw the sides of the diamonds in proper proportion. There was little change between 5 and 8 years, and even at 8 years less than 20% of all children drew diamonds properly in this respect. At 9 years, 40% drew the sides of the diamonds in proper relationship. Thus even at 9 years some aspects of design copying were still maturing.

Spatial orientation   Freehand drawings of the upright inverted isosceles triangles with respect to proper spatial orientation were very easy even for young children. Eighty percent of five-year-olds drew triangles in proper spatial orientation; by 6 years 100% of the children drew such forms in proper orientation. The drawing of diamonds in correct spatial orientation was more difficult, and only 50% of the five-year-olds could do this. This ability continued to improve rapidly, and by 7, 75% of the children drew diamonds in correct spatial orientation. By 9 years 80% of children had mastered this aspect of design copying. However, many children were still having difficulty with the spatial orientation of designs.

Angle formation (size)   Triangles were simpler to reproduce in this respect than were diamonds, and children by 6-7 years were able to reproduce triangles with appropriate angularity. For the vertical diamond, at 5 years only 42% of the children drew the shape with appropriate angles. By 9 years all children were able to reproduce the vertical diamond shape with good angle formation. The equilateral diamond was the most difficult of all shapes in terms of angle formation. Only 2 of the five-year-olds could reproduce this figure with appropriate angles, and even at 9 years only one-third of the children had mastered this aspect of freehand drawing of geometric shapes.

Straightness of line   This dimension of design copying was mastered relatively easily by young children, so that by 6 years more than 75% of the children drew shapes using acceptably straight lines. By 9 years, more than 90% of the children drew triangles and diamonds with adequate straightness of lines.

Bernbaum *et al.* (1974) reported that when children copy geometric shapes, they display consistent patterns of "directional" behavior. That is, they start at the top of the figure more often than at the bottom; they start at the left of the figure more often than at the right; and they start with vertical strokes more often than with horizontal strokes. These patterns of directional behavior hold true for both freehand drawing and tracing and appear before the child learns to write. The dominance of these patterns of directional behavior may in part help to explain why some letters and/ or shapes are more frequently "miscopied" than others (e.g., 'd' is reversed more often than 'b'). Interestingly, both right-handed and left-handed children displayed similar patterns of directional behavior in design copying. The least stable pattern of the three, however, was whether the child started at the right or the left of the figure in reproducing it.

Motor Accuracy

Ayres (1978) has accumulated data on children ages 4 through 9 years on a fine motor control task that she calls "motor accuracy." This task is one in which the child is asked to trace on top of a line that is laid out in such a way that the child has to move in a variety of different directions (up, down, forward, backward, etc.). In general, children's performances on this task improved dramatically from 4 to 6 years, with little or no change thereafter. Thus in a fine motor control task that is primarily emphasizing the motor component of performance, the major period of growth takes place before the age of 6 years.

Dynamic Eye-Hand Coordination

A unique form of fine motor control is that associated with the manual tracking of a disc or object moving in two dimensional space—dynamic eye-hand coordination. The typical type of test used to measure this ability is a pursuit rotor task, in which the individual is asked to keep a long stylus, held in one hand, in contact with a small disc as it rotates around a moving turntable. Depending upon the task, the turntable and thus the disc may rotate at different speeds (e.g., 30 rpm. versus 60 rpm.) and in different paths (e.g., circular versus triangular). Using a simple pursuit rotor task (disc speed—30 rpm.; path—circular), Williams *et al.* (1972) studied the development of dynamic eye-hand coordination in young children ages 5 to 12 years. In general, these authors observed an almost linear improvement in pursuit-rotor or dynamic eye-hand coordination performance from 5 to 12 years. (See Figures 7.2, 7.3, 7.4.) Time on target increased from an average of 3 seconds at 5 years to an average of 12 seconds at 12 years. The general increment in performance was 1 second per year. Interestingly, although there were no significant differences between performances of boys and girls at any age, performance discrepancies between the sexes tended to increase with age. Thus by 10 years of age dynamic eye-hand coordination of boys was superior to that of girls the same age. At 11 years there was evidence of a plateauing of growth in this skill for girls; for boys, performance increments continued to occur at a steady rate throughout the eleventh and twelfth years.

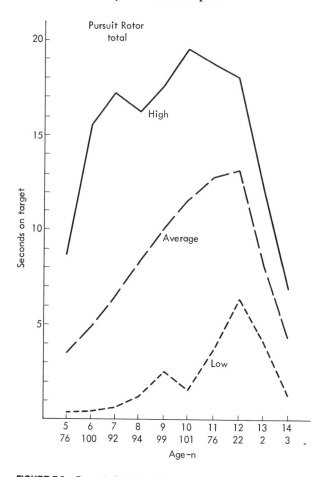

FIGURE 7.2. Dynamic Eye-Hand Coordination as a Function of Age

Other Aspects of Fine Motor Control

Denckla (1973, 1974) has studied the development of some different dimensions of fine motor control in right-handed children ages 5-10 years. She studied changes in the ability of the child to perform the following fine motor control movements: repetitive and successive finger movements, repetitive hand patting, alternating arm/hand supination/pronation, alternating hand flexion/extension, repetitive toe tapping, and alternating heel/toe tapping. Each child was asked to perform each of these movements 20 times consecutively; performances were timed and the rhythm, maintenance of sequence, and presence of synkinetic and/or mirror movements was observed. Such fine motor control tasks represent a major means by

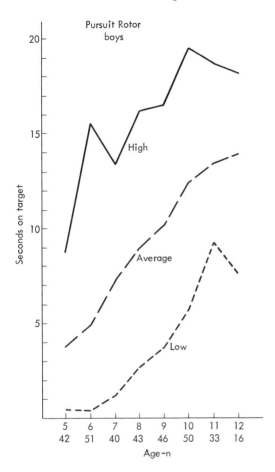

FIGURE 7.3. Dynamic Eye-Hand Coordination as a Function of Age—Boys

which the presence or absence of neurological deficits in motor control in young children is determined (Rapin *et al.*, 1966; Reitan, 1971b).

Finger movements   In these tasks the child is asked either to move one finger repeatedly in tapping as quickly as possible (repetitive) or to touch each finger to the thumb in sequence starting with the index finger (successive). There was significant improvement in all aspects of both repetitive and successive finger movements between the ages of 5 and 7 years. There was little or no difference in such fine motor control at 8, 9 or 10 years. Although there were no differences between right- and left-hand performances on the successive finger movement task, right hand performance was

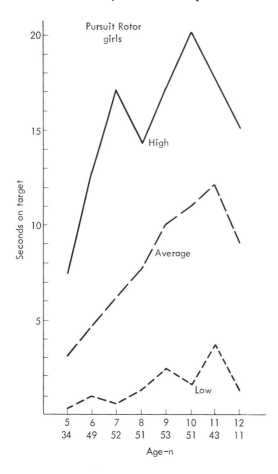

FIGURE 7.4. Dynamic Eye-Hand Coordination as a Function of Age—Girls

significantly superior to left hand performance of repetitive finger movements.

Hand patting   In this task the child is asked to tap the whole hand against a surface 20 times as quickly as possible. The ability to move the hand quickly in this simple repetitive movement gradually increased from 5 to 8 years; a plateau in performance occurred at 8, 9 and 10 years. There was only a slight right-hand superiority for both boys and girls.

Alternating pronation/supination   This movement requires that the child move the hands/forearms into and out of pronation/supination as quickly as possible. Overall there was a significant improvement in the ability of both boys and girls to perform this task between 5-8 years. There was a small but identifiable improvement between 5 and 6 years, a slightly greater change between 6 and 7 years, with the most dramatic change taking place between 7-8 years. There was little or no change in this aspect of fine motor control after 8 years. Again, right hand performances were slightly better than left hand performances.

Alternating hand flexion/extension   The child is asked in this task to move the hand (wrist) into and out of flexion/extension as rapidly as possible. The speed with which this movement could be performed increased significantly between 5 and 7 years, with little or no change thereafter. The period of greatest improvement was between 5-6 years. Right hand performances were superior to left-hand performances.

Repetitive toe tapping   This movement is one in which the child repeatedly taps his toes against the floor while maintaining the heel in contact with the floor. Ability to smoothly execute this movement sequence improved significantly from 5-8 years. There was little or no change in performance after 8 years. The period of most significant change was between 5-6 years. Right foot performances were superior to left foot performances.

Alternating heel/toe tapping   This task requires the child to alternately tap the toe and heel against the floor or some stable surface as quickly as possible. Performance of this task increased with age from 5 to 10 years; the period of most dramatic change was from 5-7 years. Right foot performances were superior to left foot performances.

Overall Denckla's data (1973, 1974) seem to suggest that important changes take place in the fine motor control of simple repetitive and alternating movements of the hands and feet between 5 and 8 years, with the period of most significant change for most tasks being from 5-7 years. For all tasks except successive finger tapping, right hand performance was superior, that is, faster, smoother, and more rhythmical than left hand performance. Denckla (1973, 1974) notes that although this right-left asymmetry exists at all ages, it is more obvious in younger children (5-6 years) than in older children (7 years). The fine motor control tasks for which right-left asymmetry was the greatest (finger and foot repetitive tapping, hand flexion/extension, alternate heel/toe tapping) all involve distal flexion/extension movements, which are known to have stronger contralateral cortical control than do movements of more proximal joints. This suggests that at least for these right-handed children, right-sided function may be established first (by 6 years); this is followed by rapid improvement in left-sided function (6 to 8 years). After 8 years, although right-sided functions are still superior, the difference between the motor control of the right and left sides is quite minimal. This suggests that some aspects of fine motor control may be directly linked to the development of cerebral dominance and/or hemispheric specialization (Reitan, 1971a, 1971b).

THE RELATIONSHIP BETWEEN
FINE AND GROSS MOTOR
CONTROL

It has been hypothesized that since there is but one basic system for controlling movement or motor behavior in humans, the same mechanisms must be involved in the development and refinement of fine motor skills as are involved in the development and refinement of gross motor behaviors. However it has never been clear, in terms of the development of the young child, just how these two aspects of motor control are or might be related to each other. Hein (1974), through his research with young kittens, has recently helped to clarify something about how these two dimensions of motor development may be interrelated during the early years. He suggests that, in general, refined control of motor behavior (gross or fine) develops only when changes in visual stimulation (information) are systematically related to self-produced movement. That is, the young organism has to simultaneously experience seeing and feeling movements of the body as well as the consequences or outcomes of these movements if adequate motor control is to be developed. He proposes that skillful gross motor control (e.g., visually guided locomotion) requires the utilization of a body-centered map of visual space, an internal schema that is acquired by experiencing (via tactile-kinesthetic function) the body as it moves through space and by registering the changes in *visual* stimulation that occur concomitantly with this active locomotor or gross body activity. In other words the young child, through active movement, becomes visually and tactile-kinesthetically aware of the body itself and the gross movements of the body. Even more importantly, he learns to recognize how the body and its movement fit into the specific visuo-spatial framework of his environment (Hein, 1979; Hein and Diamond, 1972).

Visually guided reaching behaviors (fine motor control) develop subsequently to the establishment of this body-centered map of visual space and are based upon the organism's ability to locate the limbs themselves within this visuo-spatial framework. If such a body-centered map has not been established, the limbs cannot be assigned a stable or accurate location in visual space, for there is no basic framework of visual space to use as a guide for making such assignments. As a result precise, well-controlled reaching behaviors are at best difficult to perform (Held and Bauer, 1967, 1974; Held and Hein, 1963). Even if the organism is given the opportunity to use the limbs to develop fine motor control, without the prior establishment of this body-centered map of visual space, development of highly refined reaching or eye-hand coordination behaviors is inadequate. Thus Hein (1974) has proposed that in order to develop skillful fine motor control, the young organism has first to develop a body-centered map of visual space based on movement-produced visual and tactile-kinesthetic feedback derived from active gross motor activity.

To support this theoretical position, Hein (1974) reports the following data that are summarized in Table 7-2. Animals provided only with visual feedback from movement of a forelimb, without benefit of previous or concurrent visual stimulation derived from gross or locomotor movements of the total body in space (the animals were permitted to locomote freely in a totally dark room with a spot of chemiluminescent material placed on the appropriate forelimb so no body-centered map can develop), are deficient in their ability to reach accurately for objects in space. Animals raised under such conditions are able to reach and touch the prongs of an interrupted surface only 44% of the time. Normally reared animals reach and touch such prongs in 95% of all trials.

Interestingly, when such animals are placed in an environment where concomitant tactile-kinesthetic and visual feedback associated with locomotion is available (but where observation of the limbs themselves is not possible), they are able to move easily through obstacle courses that require controlled locomotor behaviors. Animals that are placed in identical visual environments but are restricted in their active locomotion (even though they are moved passively) fail to perform this locomotor task effectively. Thus only those animals given the opportunity to actively locomote in patterned visual environments and allowed to experience related movement-produced visual/tactile-kinesthetic feedback develop refined locomotor or gross motor control.

With regard to visually guided reaching or fine motor control behaviors, both of these groups of animals perform poorly, that is, they perform at chance level. This occurs in the former because, although they have established a body-centered map of visual space, they have not had the opportunity to actually place the limbs into that visual space because they have not simultaneously seen and felt them "being used." The latter group is deficient in fine motor control presumably because the animals still have not established a body-centered map of visual space upon which to begin to build visually guided fine motor control. When these two groups of animals are given the opportunity to experience concomitant visual/tactile-kinesthetic feedback from the movement of a single limb (see Table 7-2), only those animals that have previously developed refined control of gross locomotor behaviors (and established a body-centered map of visual space) are able to perform refined reaching/grasping behaviors successfully. These animals reach and grasp accurately on more than 92% of all trials. Animals that have not previously developed this body-centered map of visual space

TABLE 7-2 Summary of Results of Research on Development of Visually Guided Movement Behavior

	I	II	III
CONDITION	Group 1 and Group 2 both moved freely but experienced only visual feedback from one limb; there was no visual feedback from total body movement.	Group 1 actively *moved* in a normal visual environment but could not see the forelimbs. Group 2 was exposed to normal environment but was not allowed to *move* or to *see forelimbs*.	Both Groups moved freely and experienced visual feedback from opposite limb used in Condition I.
PERFORMANCE	Both Groups failed to develop adequate visually guided locomotor or reaching behaviors.	Group 1 discriminated depth and had good locomotor control in avoiding objects; visually guided reaching was very poor. Group 2 failed to develop any of the above.	Group 1 now displayed visually guided reaching but only with limb for which there was visual feedback after the establishment of visually guided locomotion; the other limb performed at chance level. Group 2 performed visually guided reaching behaviors at chance level with both limbs.

(gross motor control) perform at chance levels on such reaching tasks. These data then provide some strong support for the notion that some degree of refinement of visually guided locomotor behaviors (gross motor control) may be prerequisite to the development of refined visually guided fine motor control (reaching behaviors). If these data can be believed, they point to an important and integral interweaving of gross and fine motor behaviors during the early years of development. Most importantly, it would seem that although later in development the young organism's ability to perform gross motor acts is not very predictive of his ability to perform fine motor tasks skillfully, some experience with and ability to control and move the total body skillfully, early in development, may be a necessary foundation for developing refined control of the use of the hands/limbs in fine manipulative tasks.

RELATIONSHIP OF FINE MOTOR
CONTROL TO OTHER
DIMENSIONS OF DEVELOPMENT

It has been observed with a rather awesome degree of regularity that deficits or lags in fine motor control often accompany difficulties in other aspects of learning and/or behavior in young children. Williams *et al.*, (1978) found that learning disabled children (average chronological age 9 years) learned/ performed a new fine motor control task at about the same level of proficiency as normally developing six-year-olds. The learning disabled children were children who were, on the average, two years behind their grade level in reading. Interestingly, the rate of improvement in performance of the fine motor task with continued practice was much slower for the learning disabled children than for either normally developing six- or eight-year-olds. Although these observations clearly do *not* show a cause and effect relationship between fine motor control and learning disabilities, they do indicate that deficits in fine motor control are much more obvious in children with accompanying learning disabilities than in children without such problems. As might be suspected, these children were significantly poorer than normally developing eight-year-olds in learning/performing this same task.

Belka and Williams (1978) studied the relationship among various measures of perceptual-motor, perceptual, and cognitive behaviors in 189 young, normal children ranging in age from 4 to 7 years. Results of this investigation indicated that there was a significant relationship between fine motor control and the level of perceptual functioning for four- and five-year-olds but not for six-year-olds. In other words performances on a variety of visual and auditory perception tasks were highly correlated with performances on fine motor tasks (accuracy of line drawing, design copying, etc.) for normally developing, young preschool age children. Belka and Williams (1979) conducted a follow-up study using the same children to try to determine whether or not cognitive functioning later in development could be predicted from knowledge about a child's performance on fine motor control and other kinds of perceptual-motor tasks at an earlier age. Prediction equations developed in this study indicated that cognitive performances of children of kindergarten age could be effectively predicted from information about their performances on fine motor control and other perceptual-motor tasks at prekindergarten levels. (Performances on such tasks accounted for 75.1% of the variation in cognitive performances at the kindergarten levels.) Prediction of such cognitive behaviors for older children (first and second grades) was far less accurate. These observations strongly suggest that there may be a close relationship for normally developing children between fine motor control development and other dimensions of development in the early years (4 to 5 years of age), but that such relationships may tend to diminish in later years (6 and 7 years of age). Such relationships, however, may persist in children who are undergoing developmental delays associated with learning disabilities.

SUMMARY

1. Fine motor control can be defined as the ability to coordinate the action of the eyes and hands together in performing skillful, adaptive movements (eye-hand coordination).

2. The early forerunners of fine motor control appear to be the reflex grasp and avoidance reactions that become integrated and refined with increasing age and experience.

3. Vision is known to play an important role in fine motor control as early as birth. Continued visual experience is necessary for refinement and differentiation of early guided-placing responses that are important to refined eye-hand coordination.

4. There appear to be four major stages in the early development of eye-hand coordination behaviors: static visual exploration; active visual exploration; dominance of the visual system in regulation of manipulative responses; and mature eye-hand coordination behaviors. These all appear within the first two years of life.

5. Most manipulative activity requires the use of the two hands in concert with each other. This is referred to as bilateral motor coordination. Bilateral motor coordination follows an identifiable pattern of development and seems to be nearly mature by 5 to 6 years of age.

6. In general, children show the most improvement in simple fine motor control behaviors from 4 to 6 years, whereas more complex ones tend to improve gradually from 5 to 12 years.
7. Isolated finger, hand, wrist, and foot movements tend to improve significantly from 5 to 8 years.
8. During the early development years, fine motor control behaviors seem to be significantly related to several other dimensions of growth. These include gross motor control, perception, and certain cognitive behaviors.

STUDY QUESTIONS

1. Define fine motor control.
2. Describe the role of reflex grasp mechanisms in the early development of fine motor control.
3. Describe the early developmental changes in the grasping response. Include a discussion of:
   a. traction response
   b. fine grasp reflex
   c. fractionation of grasp reflex
   d. hand orientation
   e. full instinctive grasp reaction
4. What are avoidance reactions? How do they affect early fine motor control?
5. Describe the role of vision and visual experience in the development of fine motor control.
6. What are "visual placing responses"? "Guided placing responses"? How are each involved in early fine motor control?
7. What are the four major stages in the early development of eye-hand coordination? Describe each stage and indicate the approximate age at which the child reaches that stage.
8. Describe Trevarthen's (1978) early stages of eye-hand coordination.
9. What is bilateral motor coordination? Describe its development in the young child. Be specific.
10. Differentiate between, give examples of, and discuss the relationship among the following: bilateral and unilateral movements; independent and sequential movements; simultaneous and alternating movements; and lead-and-assist hand. How are these related to the development of fine motor control?
11. Define and describe age-related changes in the following dimensions of fine motor skill development:
    a. object manipulation
    b. design or form copying

   c. tracing, line grid drawing, and freehand drawing

   d. motor accuracy

   e. dynamic eye-hand coordination

12. When do the major changes occur in these fine motor abilities?

13. Describe the major age and sex differences in the following fine motor control movements: finger movements; hand patting; alternating pronation/supination; alternating hand flexion/extension; repetitive toe tapping, and alternating heel/ toe tapping.

14. What significance do these age and sex differences have for early fine motor development?

15. What is the relationship between fine and gross motor control? Be specific and cite evidence in support of your answer.

16. How do normally developing and learning disabled children differ in fine motor development?

REFERENCES

AYRES, A. J. *Southern California Sensory-Motor Integration Tests Manual.* Los Angeles, CA: Western Psychological Services, 1978.

BELKA, D., AND WILLIAMS, H. Canonical relationships among perceptual-motor, perceptual and cognitive behaviors in young, normal children. Unpublished paper, University of Toledo, 1978.

BELKA, D., AND WILLIAMS, H. Prediction of later cognitive behavior from early school perceptual-motor, perceptual and cognitive performances. *Perceptual-Motor Skills.* 49(1979): 131-141.

BERNBAUM, M., GOODNOW, J., AND LEHMAN, E. Relationships among perceptual-motor tasks: tracing and copying. *Journal of Educational Psychology.* 66(1974): 731-735.

BIRCH, H. G., AND LEFFORD, A. Visual differentiation, intersensory integration and voluntary motor control. *Monographs of the Society for Research in Child Development.* 32(21)(1967): serial no. 110.

DENCKLA, M. B. Development of motor coordination in normal children. *Developmental Medicine and Child Neurology.* 16(1974): 729-741.

DENCKLA, M. B. Development of speed in repetitive and successive finger movements in normal children. *Developmental Medicine and Child Neurology.* 15(1973): 635-645.

FREY, C. *The Development of Fine Motor Control in Young, Normal Children.* Unpublished Master's project, University of Toledo, August, 1979.

GOODENOUGH, F. L. *Measurement of Intelligence by Drawings.* Yonkers, NY: World Book, 1926.

HEIN, A. Acquiring components of visually guided behavior. In Pick, ed., *Minnesota Symposia on Child Development,* 6, pp. 53–68. Minnesota: University of Minnesota Press, 1972.

HEIN, A. Dependence of coordination and discrimination upon a body-centered representation of visual space. *Neurosciences Research Program Bulletin.* 15(3)(1979): 462-467.

HEIN, A. Prerequisite for development of visually-guided reaching in the kitten. *Brain Research.* 71(1974): 259-263.

HEIN, A., AND DIAMOND, R.   Locomotory space as a prerequisite for acquiring visually-guided reaching in kittens. *Journal of Comparative Physiological Psychology.* 81(1972): 394-398.

HEIN, A., AND HELD, R.   Dissociation of the visual placing response with elicited and guided components. *Science.* 158(1967): 390-391.

HELD, R., AND BAUER, J.   Development of sensorially guided reaching in infant monkeys. *Brain Research.* 71(1974): 265-271.

HELD, R., AND BAUER, J.   Visually guided reaching in infant monkeys after restricted rearing. *Science.* 157(1967): 718-720.

HELD, R., AND HEIN, A.   Movement-produced stimulation in the development of visually guided behaviors. *Journal of Comparative and Physiological Psychology.* 56(1963): 872-876.

RAPIN, I., TOURK, L., AND COSTA, L.   Evaluation of the Purdue Pegboard as a screening test for brain damage. *Developmental Medicine and Child Neurology.* 8(1966): 45-54.

REITAN, R. M.   Complex motor functions of preferred and non-preferred hands in brain damaged and normal children. *Perceptual–Motor Skills.* 33(1971a): 671-675.

REITAN, R. M.   Sensorimotor functions in brain damaged and normal children of early school age. *Perceptual–Motor Skills.* 33(1971b): 655-664.

TREVARTHEN, C.   The psychobiology of speech development. In Development of Motor, Language, and Cognitive Behavior. *Neurosciences Research Program Bulletin.* 12(4)(1979): 570-585.

TWITCHELL, T. E.   Development of motor coordination in the presence of cerebral lesions. In Development of Motor, Learning and Cognitive Behaviors. *Neurosciences Research Program Bulletin.* 12(4)(1979): 565-569.

TWITCHELL, T. E.   Reflex mechanisms and the development of prehension. In Connolly, ed., *Mechanisms of Motor Skill Development,* pp. 25–62. New York: Academic Press, 1970.

UZGIRIS, J. C.   Ordinality in the development of schema for relating to objects. In Hellemuth, ed., *Exceptional Infant.* 1(1967): 315-334.

WILLIAMS, H.   Gross motor behavior patterns in children. In Corbin, ed., *A Textbook of Motor Development.* Dubuque, IA: Wm. C. Brown, 1973.

WILLIAMS, H.   Clinical observations of fine motor control in young children. Unpublished paper, University of Toledo, 1979.

WILLIAMS, H., TEMPLE, I., AND BATEMAN, J.   Perceptual-motor and cognitive learning in young children. In *Psychology of Motor Behavior and Sport II.* Champaign, IL: Human Kinetics Publishers, 1978.

WILLIAMS, H., TEMPLE, I., AND LOGSDON, B.   Perceptual-Motor characteristics of young children. Unpublished paper, Bowling Green State University, 1972.

CHAPTER EIGHT
DEVELOPMENT OF GROSS MOTOR SKILLS IN YOUNG CHILDREN

The discussion of gross motor development will focus on those skills commonly referred to as "fundamental motor skills." The fundamental skills to be discussed are characteristic of the motor development of the child from 3 to 6 or 7 years of age and include the locomotor patterns of walking, running, jumping, hopping, galloping, and skipping, and the ball handling skills of throwing, kicking, striking, and bouncing. The fundamental motor skills developed during the preschool and early school years appear to be prerequisite to the acquisition of efficient movement skills in general and set the foundation for the development of more specific task-related motor skills that are an integral part of motor performance at all age levels. Most sport and/or game skills are, in fact, some variation, adaptation and/or combination of different fundamental motor skills, the nature of the variation or adaptation being dictated by the requirements of the sport or game.

An acceptable or optimum level of proficiency in performance of fundamental motor skills is often described as a performance in which the process characteristics or "form" of the movement is "mature" or skillful. The term "process characteristic" refers to the way in which the body is moved, that is, the way the child selects a movement as well as the way the joint actions that make up the movement are spatially and temporally organized. The term "mature" implies that the characteristics of skill performance are the same or similar to those observed in the adult or skilled performer. This does not in any way suggest that all aspects of performance by the child are identical to those of the adult, but rather that the spatial and temporal organization of the body is skillful and/or adult-like. Obviously adults can, on the average, throw and kick farther and run faster than children. Still, the movement pattern involved in the execution of the skill itself (e.g., its form or process characteristics) may be essentially the same.

Adequate development of fundamental movement patterns is a function of both maturation and experience. Maturation sets the rate at which fundamental motor skills develop; in contrast most fundamental motor skills cannot and/or do not develop without appropriate practice or experience. Many children simply do not develop mature or skilled patterns of movement without some help. Recent assessments of fundamental motor skill development in prekindergarten children have clearly indicated that one in five children lags behind in the development of one or more fundamental motor skills (Temple, 1979). Thus, without appropriate practice, movement patterns often remain at a rudimentary or early level of development and never reach mature levels (Halverson, 1966).

Before the fundamental motor skills are discussed in detail, let us consider the general, overall development of gross motor skills by looking at a proposed model of motor control and accompanying intertask motor development. Some factors that affect the level of motor control demonstrated by the performer as well as the notion of intratask motor development will also be addressed briefly.

LEVELS OF MOTOR CONTROL: INTERTASK MOTOR DEVELOPMENT

Intertask motor development is concerned with the nature of the development of control over a number of different motor tasks, e.g., how children acquire skills in throwing, catching, kicking, striking, etc. There are essentially two views or theories of intertask motor development: predetermined and probabilistic theories. "Predetermined" theories of intertask motor development suggest that all of behavior, including motor behavior, is predetermined or set by neural growth and differentiation. Consequently, acquisition of motor skills is viewed as automatic, sequential, and invariant and is believed to be the result of maturation of endogenous mechanisms that are relatively unaffected by external influences. Importantly, this view emphasizes the *unidirectional* nature of growth and motor development—that is, that maturational changes in underlying mechanisms are responsible for changes in motor behavior. Thus as mechanisms governing motor control mature, the modified functioning of those mechanisms is seen in the form of advanced motor development. Such approaches would predict that clear, identifiable stages of intertask motor development exist.

"Probabilistic" theories of motor development emphasize that behavior and thus motor development are not automatic and invariant, but rather that much of motor development is determined by exogenous factors that make growth and motor development a *bidirectional* process. Thus although maturation of structures closely involved with motor control is believed to influence the level of motor and/or behavioral development, the actual use of such mechanisms (e.g., through movement) is believed to be necessary for optimum refinement of motor control. This approach to the acquisition of motor skills suggests that there will be some general, observable trends or patterns in motor development across individuals because certain mechanisms involved in the acquisition of such behaviors are endogenously regulated. However individual variations in the rate, pattern and/or sequence of motor skill acquisition will be the rule rather than the exception.

The following model or description of levels of motor control attempts to describe the broad trends in motor development suggested by probabilistic theories. Intertask motor development may in general be thought of as passing through five general levels of control. These levels essentially reflect differences in three factors: the degree of conscious intervention between the environmental input and the motor behavior; the degree of perceptual and/or cognitive analysis involved; and the extent of diversity and/or modifiability of the movements themselves. The levels of the model are not particularly new or dramatic; what holds them together is their conceptual framework—that of the increasing probability of greater involvement of one or more of these three factors.

Level I: Reflexive and spontaneous motor control   This level of motor control involves minimally or *nonconsciously* directed execution of an innate or conditioned simple movement in response to simple environmental events (internal or external). Motor development at this level is characterized by the presence of little or no perceptual analysis of the environment, minimal conscious intervention between the environmental stimulus evoking the motor behavior and the behavior itself, and, in general, rather stereotyped movement responses. Much of the young infant's behavior is reflexive and spontaneous in nature. Important reflexive and spontaneous reactions typical of this level of motor development include the withdrawal crossed extensor and diagonal reflexes as well as the placing, righting, and equilibrium reactions. Structural maturation seems to be the predominant influence in motor control at this level.

Level II: Exploratory motor control   This level of motor control is defined by *deliberate* but unrefined control of movements used to interact with the environment in simple, spontaneous ways. At this level motor development is characterized primarily by the increased suppression of reflex behaviors and an accompanying increase in voluntary control of movements of the upper and lower extremities. This expanding voluntary control is reflected in more adaptable, less stereotyped yet still spontaneous motor responses. The two major accomplishments of this level of motor control are the attainment of upright posture and the appearance and beginning mastery of prehension skills (see Chapter 6). Mastery of upright posture appears to follow a somewhat consistent pattern of development. It begins with mastery of equilibrium in the pivot-prone position; mastery of balance in the prone position on elbows, on all fours, and on the knees (full- and half-kneel) then follows. Last but not least, balance in the upright position is achieved. There is also some evidence of increased perceptual analysis of environmental events at this level of development.

Level III: Examinatory and regulatory motor control Conscious control of movement behaviors used to systematically *examine* both the body and the external environment is the primary feature of this level of motor control. Motor development is characterized by increased perceptual awareness of body and environmental events and by the appearance and use of a wide range of highly regular (predictable) and more modifiable patterns of movement behavior than have been seen before. Visual and tactile-kinesthetic perception skills are advancing rapidly, and most of the so-called fundamental motor patterns (locomotor and ball handling skills) are displayed by the majority of children. There is now conscious assessment of task requirements as well as conscious selection and execution of movement patterns. Exogenous influences are becoming more dominant.

Level IV: Directed, executory motor control Unique combinations of developmental movement patterns and examinatory skills are organized so that the individual can accomplish specific goals and/or tasks dictated or suggested by the environment. This level of motor development is especially characterized by immediate and accurate execution of longer, highly modifiable movement behaviors, a condition that greatly increases the probability of successful mastery of motor tasks. Because of this the individual at this level of development is much more capable of adapting to a wide variety of environmental movement challenges. The key to motor control at this level is diversity and modifiability of motor behaviors.

Level V: Refined, automatic motor control At this level, well-learned motor responses are initiated without much conscious intervention. Motor control is now more automatic and easy. The individual can select, initiate, and regulate long sequences of movements that can (within certain limits) be modified in accordance with changing environmental demands. Unexpected and/or new environmental or bodily events are more easily adapted to, and the amount of conscious involvement in the actual control of the movement is greatly reduced. Cognitive analysis is now more dominant because of the need for the use of movement strategies that will increase success in accomplishing end goals of the motor tasks.

OTHER FACTORS AFFECTING THE LEVEL OF MOTOR CONTROL

There are a number of factors that define or contribute to the underlying complexity of motor skill performance and thus to the level of motor control exhibited during the acquisition of gross motor skills. These factors will be discussed under three headings: phases in the execution of a motor skill; patterns of development of motor control in the extremities; and the nature of the environmental interaction involved in motor task performance.

Phases in the Execution of a Motor Skill

It is generally agreed upon that there are two major phases of control in the execution of a motor skill. The first is a phase that involves postural or positioning movements. During this phase the body and/or body parts are moved to or maintained in a position that is designed to provide an appropriate base of support for the execution of the second phase of task performance. This second phase of performance, the manipulation phase, usually involves the use of one or more of the extremities (often the arms and hands) in moving, maintaining, or interacting in some way with the external environment (e.g., objects). There is little doubt that efficient positioning of the body is important to effective execution of manipulative actions (Broer, 1977; Gavator, 1959; Smith, 1962), and that in intertask skill development, efficient static and/or dynamic body-positioning skills (e.g., balance and locomotor skills) may be prerequisite to development of optimum manipulative skills (e.g., catching, striking, cutting).

Patterns of Development of Motor Control in the Extremities

Patterns of lower limb movements have been shown to follow a rather consistent developmental sequence (McGraw, 1968; Seefeldt, 1971; Williams, 1973; DeOreo, 1973). This sequence is as follows: (a) bilateral simultaneous movement of both limbs (gravity not involved); (b) bilateral alternating movements of both limbs (gravity not involved); (c) bilateral simultaneous movements of both limbs (gravity involved); (d) unilateral movements (e.g., movements of a single limb independently of the other) (gravity involved); and (e) combinations of bilateral and unilateral movements in more complex rhythmic sequences (gravity involved). This sequence of development of lower limb control hints at a somewhat consistent ordering of motor skill acquisition when leg movement patterns are the primary focal point. Walking and running represent variations of bilateral alternating leg movement patterns—gravity involved. The observed pattern of development of leg movements suggests that these skills should appear before jumping skills that involve efficient control of bilateral simultaneous leg movements—gravity involved. Hopping and kicking skills are variations of the more complex unilateral leg movement patterns—gravity involved—and would most likely appear after basic jumping skills are at least minimally mastered. Skipping patterns that reflect the highest level of leg movement patterns, a combination of two lower-limb movement patterns into one skill, are the last to be mastered. This combining of two movement patterns into one typically involves more complex rhythmical and/or temporal co-ordination of movements.

Control of arm/hand/finger movements also appears to follow a somewhat consistent developmental sequence. Gesell (1946) described control of the musculature of the upper extremities as progressing from the center to the periphery of the body (the proximodistal principle of development). Thus control of the arm usually precedes control of the hand, and control of the hand usually precedes control of the fingers. In general, skillful use of the upper limbs requires that the arms/hands/fingers move in a coordinated fashion (e.g., in specific spatio-temporal patterns). Control of upper limb movements appears to occur in the following general sequence: (a) unilateral limb movements that require the use of a single limb independently of the other (e.g., throwing, line drawing, ball bouncing); (b) bilateral limb movements that involve simultaneous use of the two limbs (catching, batting); and (c) bilateral limb movements that require the use of individual limbs in alternating movements and that ultimately result in the appearance of a lead and assist hand (e.g., peg manipulation, cutting).

Movements of the arms, hands, and fingers are usually organized around the manipulation of or interaction with an external object. More often than not manipulative activities require an adequate postural base. As a result, activities involving the upper limbs may be mastered slightly later in development than skills involving the lower limbs. (There are of course exceptions to this rule.) Observations also suggest that children tend to develop control over movement of the total body before they develop control of movement involved in interaction with external objects.

The Nature of the Environmental Interaction

The way in which the body must be used to interact with the environment also provides certain guidelines for understanding the overall sequence of development of intertask motor control. Three performer-environmental states seem to be particularly important: (a) whether or not the performer is in possession of the object with which he must interact;

(b) whether or not the object to be interacted with is moving or stationary; and (c) whether or not the performer must use an implement as an extension of the body in interacting with the object (e.g., catching vs. batting, coloring with a crayon vs. finger painting).

When the performer has possession of the object to be interacted with, the selection of the body movement is more internally controlled. That is, for example, when throwing a ball at a target, although the nature of the external environment (target size, distance of the thrower from the target) may set the general framework for the movement to be performed, the precise spatio-temporal characteristics of the movement are not strictly dictated by it. The child can throw the ball in a variety of ways and still be successful at hitting the target. The ball (object) in this case is considered to be a part of the subjective space of the individual, and the movement is said to be internally paced. If, on the other hand, the object (ball) is outside the performer's possession (e.g., batting), a greater accommodation of the movement to meet the demands of the external environment is inherent in successful performance of the task. Skillful movements performed under these conditions are said to be externally paced because they are more directly regulated by the environment. Adults have been shown to master internally paced tasks more easily than externally paced tasks (Gentile, 1975). If the same principle holds true in the development of motor control by young children, skillful performance of tasks that involve interaction with objects in the possession of the performer (e.g., throwing, ball bouncing) should appear earlier in intertask skill development than those that involve interaction with objects not in the possession of the child (e.g. catching, kicking).

Perception of an object's speed and direction and the anticipation of its arrival at a specific point in space require more complex analysis of the external environment than does perception of the distance, position, or location of a stationary object in space (Gentile, 1975; Williams, 1973). In accordance with this observation, Williams (1968) reports that static depth perception ability stabilizes earlier in development than do dynamic depth perception abilities. In addition skillful control of tracking movements of the eyes has been shown to continue throughout early and middle childhood (Yarbus, 1971). Williams (1967) also reports that older children are faster and more accurate in estimating the flight of a moving object in space than are younger children. These data suggest that the mastery of tasks requiring interaction with stationary objects in space precedes mastery of tasks requiring interaction with moving objects in space.

Using an implement as an extension of the body creates an added dimension that must be considered in the selection and control of bodily movements. For example, the child becomes familiar first with the distance that he can reach with his hands. When or if an implement is added, this distance changes and the child must reorganize or learn to adapt his motor responses to meet new distance demands. Since implements are more commonly used with the upper limbs than with the lower limbs, the use of an implement would mean a new and perhaps more precise coordination between eyes and hands. If this is the case, skills involving the use of an implement should appear later in development than those that do not involve the use of an implement. Using these considerations along with the levels of motor control described earlier, one should be able to apply some logic in assessing the nature and level of intertask motor development in young children.

INTRATASK MOTOR DEVELOPMENT

Intratask motor development is primarily concerned with changes that take place in individual body actions that occur during the acquisition of single motor skills. The notion that "stages of development" exist in intratask motor development of young children has until recently been rather universally accepted. This notion suggests that all individuals exhibit a predictable sequence of changes in overt body actions during the acquisition of given motor skills. Most classic stage descriptions outline the entire body configuration (e.g., movement characteristics of each part of the body) at different stages of development and imply that developmental changes occur in all body parts predictably and simultaneously. Roberton and colleagues (Roberton, 1978; Roberton & Langendorfer, 1980) have provided some strong evidence to suggest that this long adhered to notion of invariant, total body intratask motor development may in fact not hold true. Instead, Roberton (1978) proposes that a "component" approach is a more accurate way to describe intratask motor development in young children and proposes that the term "step" be substituted for the term "stage." (These terms are used interchangeably in this text.) The component model approach suggests that dramatic developmental changes can and do occur in one part of the body (e.g., in the humerus action in the overarm throw) independent of changes in other body parts (e.g., the pelvis-spine or forearm actions in the overarm throw). This is, of course, what everyday observation of children's movement patterns would strongly support.

Since most of the data available to date are on the overarm throw, let us use it as an example for exploring the "component" approach to motor development further. There are essentially three body actions to be considered in observing developmental changes in the overarm throw: action of the humerus, action of the forearm, and action of the pelvis-spine. During development, changes in each of these body actions may occur at different rates (and thus at slightly different ages). Roberton (1978) has shown that pelvis-spine action is initially more advanced than either forearm or humerus actions; when pelvis-spine action stabilizes, the humerus and forearm actions tend to advance. The humerus action then continues to progress to its most advanced step; later, forearm and pelvis-spine actions reach their advanced levels. These observations clearly indicate that total body configuration descriptions may be somewhat limited in their usefulness in analyzing sequential changes in motor development.

It must be pointed out, however, that Roberton's data (1978, 1980) also suggest that the classic "stage" assumptions so prevalent in the literature do, for individual body actions, hold a high probability occurrence across large numbers of children. Since exceptions can and do occur, a probability model may perhaps be the best explanation for individual differences in children's motor development. To use the overarm throw, once again, the high probability (or classic) sequence for humerus action is:

Step 1:   Humerus Oblique
Step 2:   Humerus Aligned but Independent
Step 3:   Humerus Lags

Most children, according to probability theory, will follow this developmental sequence of changes in humerus action. In general, at age 3, Step 3 has a very low probability of occurring whereas Steps 1 and 2 each have a high probability of occurring (50%). With advancing age, Step 3 (humerus lags) increases in the likelihood of its occurrence, whereas the frequency of occurrence of the other two steps decreases. The important thing to note, however, is that for any given individual Step 3 may occur *in* or *out* of this high probability sequence. Thus "whole-body" action descriptions are most useful as a guide for observing general levels of intratask motor development in children and least helpful as a diagnostic tool for use in analysis of precise, intratask motor development characteristics in individual children.

OBSERVATION AND ASSESSMENT OF PROCESS CHARACTERISTICS OF MOVEMENT

Until relatively recently, motor development *per se* and fundamental motor skills in particular were assessed almost solely in terms of achievement scores or product characteristics, that is, how fast the child could run or how far he could throw a ball, and so on (Halverson, 1966). Although product characteristics provide an objective measure of performance and can be used to identify changes in performance that occur over time, assessment of *how* the child moves is not possible if these kinds of measures alone are used. Thus details concerning specific qualitative characteristics of movement (e.g., body position, sequence of movement, presence of extraneous motion) are not accessible from objective achievement scores alone. Meaningful and dramatic changes in the way a young child moves or performs a motor skill may occur without obvious or concomitant change in achievement scores (product characteristics). Halverson and Roberton (1979) reported just such an observation. Kindergarten children who received guided practice in performing the overhand throw showed no greater change in the velocity of the throw (the product measure of throwing performance used) than children who had not received such practice. Yet when qualitative aspects of the movement were analyzed, children who had had practice showed significant changes in the "form" or movement pattern used in throwing; those who had not had practice did not show similar changes (Halverson and Roberton, 1979). Thus a single measure or indicator of fundamental motor skill performance may be inadequate for fully describing the nature and/or level of such performance in young children.

Two-dimensional descriptions or assessments of motor performances provide a much more helpful picture than single-dimensional descriptions or assessments. The two dimensions of assessment should include *how* the child moves and *what* the result of the movement is. Specific descriptions of the way the body is moved are referred to as *process characteristics*. Objective measures of performance, such as the distance of a throw or the speed of a run, assess the result of the movement or *product characteristics*. If the product or result of movement has more than one dimension (e.g., throwing velocity *and* accuracy), these dimensions are referred to as *product components*. The result of the movement or product is a reflection of the movement itself (the process) and, therefore, product measures are valuable measures of performance. If the product measure is specific enough, it may in fact help to identify process errors. For example, if an accuracy measure (product) indicates direction of deviation from the target (as in throwing at a target), information concerning body position at release or contact is available. It is important to note, however, that some movement skills cannot be evaluated in a meaningful way by use of product scores. Catching is a good example. There is no meaningful distance, velocity, or directional component to catching performance. Process characteristics of a movement may be assessed by directly observing that dimension of performance.

Recognizing the need for specific diagnostic information concerning all aspects of a movement, many persons involved in the assessment of motor development in young children have begun to look at process *and* product characteristics of movement performance (e.g., DeOreo, Halverson, Roberton, Williams). In keeping with this approach, the section on information for teachers and parents will focus on identification and discussion of both process and product characteristics of fundamental motor skill performance.

OBSERVING PROCESS CHARACTERISTICS OF MOVEMENT: A CHECKLIST APPROACH

The information presented here has been developed for use primarily by teachers and parents. First, the process characteristics of the mature pattern of individual fundamental motor skills are identified. Process characteristics of various stages or steps that lead to the mature pattern are then presented in the form of a checklist. The checklist presents information on performance characteristics for a given step or age as well as changes that occur in those characteristics from one step to the next in summary form. By looking down the column of Xs on each of the checklists, one can quickly identify major process characteristics that typify certain ages and/or steps of fundamental motor skill development. By looking across the rows of Xs one can quickly see how arm and leg or trunk action changes with age and/or level of development. Ages associated with typical achievement of the mature pattern person and with various developmental steps are also indicated. The ages are approximations and are meant only to serve as general guidelines.

The checklist can be used as an *instrument* for assessing process characteristics of fundamental motor skill performance in young children. To use the checklists simply circle the X that characterizes a particular body action for a child as he performs the skill. Whenever process characteristics are being assessed, the child should perform the skill several times, unless the performance is recorded on film or videotape. Even then the child should repeat the performance at least once. Each time the skill is performed, the observer should focus on different components of the process; replay of film or videotape serves the same purpose. For many tasks, movement of the body should be observed from behind or in front of the child as well as from the side. This is particularly important for observation of locomotor skills.

The illustrations presented with the checklists depict, for each of the steps of development, what the child might look like at specific points in the execution of the skill. The illustrations were developed from 16 mm. films of young children performing fundamental motor skills. They are included as a supplement to the checklists to serve as a pictorial model against which to compare direct observations of children.

Walking

Walking is the first form of locomotion executed in the upright position. The initial stage of development of walking occurs during infancy; the age of the onset of independent walking ranges from 9 to 18 months. Because of this early appearance of walking and because it is the least complex of the fundamental motor skills, the mature pattern of walking is usually achieved by 3 to 4 years of age. The characteristics of the mature walking pattern and the stages leading to it are presented in Table 8-1. Generally, once the characteristics of the mature pattern are present the speed of walking and length of stride increase, while the vertical displacement of the center of gravity decreases (Wickstrom, 1977).

TABLE 8-1 Process Characteristics of Walking

Mature Pattern (mastered by age 4):
        Trunk is erect but not stiff.
        Arms swing freely in sagittal plane.
        Arms swing in opposition to legs.
        Rhythmical, easy swinging stride of legs.
        Smooth transfer of weight from heel-to-toe.
        Foot points in line of direction.

DEVELOPMENTAL COMPONENTS	STAGE 1 (9-18 MOS.)	STAGE 2 (24 MOS.)	STAGE 3 (36 MOS.)
Trunk			
inclined slightly forward	X		
visually attends to feet	X	X	
erect but not stiff		X	X
Arm Swing			
arms held high and abducted; elbows flexed	X		
swing from elbow		X	
swing freely from shoulder in sagittal plane			X
in opposition to leg action			X
Leg action			
wide base of support; toeing out of feet	X		
flat-footed contact	X		
steps high with marked flexion of knees and hips (little ankle action)	X		
heel-toe progression		X	X
foot points in line of direction		X	X
smooth transition from one foot to other			X
Control			
rigid, jerky steps	X		
smooth, rhythmical, coordination pattern		X	X
can stop, start, turn easily			X

The transition from the initial stage of walking—which consists of high, jerky, unstable, flat-footed steps with arms held high—to the smooth, rhythmical transfer of weight with heel-to-toe foot action and rhythmical arm swing in opposition to the leg action occurs without clear demarcation of stages. The changes that occur from the first attempts at independent walking to the adult-like performance seen at approximately age 4 are associated with increased strength, improvement in the balance mechanism, and general increases in neuromuscular control (Espenschade and Eckert, 1980). The base of support gradually narrows, arm muscles relax, excessive muscular contractions of the lower extremities diminish, and length of stride increases. Transfer of weight also occurs more smoothly as the child gains control of his limb actions. As these changes occur the child gains confidence, which in turn affects and helps to improve the walking pattern.

As the mature pattern of walking is mastered, variations in the basic forward walk are attempted. The child begins to walk in different directions (e.g., backward, sideward), varies the rate of walking, and experiments with smaller bases of support (e.g., tiptoes, walks on a line). These variations are often observed as the child engages in spontaneous play activities.

Climbing (ascending to a higher point) is a form of locomotion that is related, developmentally, to walking. Although climbing is not considered one of the fundamental motor skills, it may be considered an extension of or a specialized kind of walking. Achievement of the mature pattern of climbing is characterized by a series of distinct developmental stages. Most research on climbing has focused on the tasks of stair climbing and ladder climbing.

Even before the child can stand alone, she attempts to go upstairs. These first attempts are creeping movements and coincide with the child's efforts to pull herself up onto her feet. Shortly after the child begins walking independently, she tries to ascend stairs in an upright position with assistance and support provided by an older person; shortly thereafter, the child will attempt to climb alone if there is some stationary object (e.g., a handrail) available for support. The movement pattern employed by the child during this first level of climbing in an upright body position is a "mark time" pattern (Espenschade and Eckert, 1980). That is, the child steps up on one foot (lead foot) and brings the other foot (trail foot) up and places it on the step beside the lead foot. The same lead foot is used for each step of the ascent. The age at which this level of stair climbing occurs varies among children; however, a majority of twenty-seven-month-old children have been observed to exhibit this pattern of climbing (Wellman, 1937).

The mark time method of stair climbing persists for several months, until the child gains strength, balance, coordination, and self-confidence. At that time an alternate-foot pattern begins to emerge. Because of increased balance demands with this newly learned alternating foot pattern, the child reverts back to the use of hand support. Cratty (1979) suggests the alternating foot pattern can be observed by the age of 3. The mature, alternating foot pattern without support follows shortly thereafter.

Developmental changes in the ability to descend stairs do not occur at the same time or rate as the ascending progression. In fact the mature pattern of descent—alternating foot pattern without support—usually does not occur until the age of four or perhaps five (Wellman, 1937). When the child first attempts to go down stairs, she usually crawls down backward. The same sequence of developmental levels seen in ascending follows these first attempts to descend.

The age at which ascent and descent of stairs commence and the rate at which proficiency develops are influenced by several factors, foremost of which is the opportunity to practice. For this reason climbing behavior may "lag behind" the development of other locomotor skills. Other important factors that affect stair climbing development are the height of the risers and the length of the flight of stairs. If the risers are too far apart, the small child will have difficulty stepping high enough to place the foot on the step in a mature fashion. Short flights of stairs (two or three steps) do not give the child enough time to practice with each attempt; a long flight of stairs may cause fatigue (or fear), and the child may revert to an earlier developmental stage at which she feels more secure.

The developmental sequence of ladder climbing is very similar to stair climbing. The mark time step pattern precedes the alternating foot pattern and ascent precedes attempts at descending the ladder. The distance between ladder rungs and the angle or steepness of the incline as well as the length of incline are important influences on the rate of development of ladder climbing.

Running

Running has been the focus of much research, perhaps more than any other form of locomotion. Both process and product aspects of running have been investigated in an attempt to determine the changing characteristics of the run associated with the development of locomotor patterns.

Running is an important fundamental motor skill, for without a good fundamental running pattern, the capacity of and/or opportunity for the child to successfully participate in many physical activities is limited. Running and variations of running are essential components of most games and sports. The run is like the walk in that the weight is transferred from one foot to the other. It differs from the walk in that the period of double support, which is characteristic of walking, is replaced in running by a period of no support. This period of no support occurs between the time the back foot pushes off the ground and the forward foot strikes the ground (Broer and Zernicke, 1979).

The basic limb movements in running are like those of walking; the adjustments made from walking to running are associated with increased speed of limb movement. In fact running is so closely associated with walking that a young child may attempt to take running steps before she can walk skillfully. This happens when the child first attempts to move about in the upright, unsupported position and experiences a lack of postural control. Balance is lost and, in order to maintain an upright position, the child moves her feet as rapidly as possible—she runs to the nearest object (furniture or person) for support. These first running steps are more accidental than planned.

Children begin to run shortly after they learn to walk, and by the age of five most children have mastered the skill of running (DeOreo, 1977). The development of a mature running pattern usually takes place without need for specific help or instruction. The process characteristics of the mature running pattern, and the steps of development that lead to it are outlined in Table 8-2. Initial changes in the running pattern are associated with improved balance and general neuromuscular coordination. As general body control and coordination, balance, and confidence increase, the width of stride of the run narrows and the arms drop down closer to waist level (McClenaghan and Gallahue, 1978). This allows the movement and therefore the momentum of the run to be directed forward and reduces lateral or rotary interferences, i.e., swaying of the body left to right and/ or rotation of the trunk and/or recovery leg. As a result the speed of the run increases. With increases in strength and coordination, running skill continues to increase and other changes in the running pattern become evident (Beck, 1965; Brown, 1978; Clouse, 1959; Dittmer, 1962; Fortney, 1964; Smith, 1977).

Specific changes occur in the process characteristics of the running pattern as the child progresses from early to later stages of running. These age-related changes in the process characteristics of the running pattern include:

1. increased length of stride (Brown, 1978; Clouse, 1959; Dittmer, 1962; Smith, 1977);
2. increased length of nonsupport period (Clouse, 1959; Dittmer, 1962; Smith, 1977);
3. increased flexion of the support knee on contact (Dittmer, 1962; Fortney, 1964);
4. more contact time used for propulsion with increased knee extension at take-off (Beck, 1965; Clouse, 1959; Dittmer, 1962);
5. increased knee flexion in the recovery leg (Clouse, 1959; Dittmer, 1962; Fortney, 1964);
6. increased speed and height of swing of the recovery leg thigh (Clouse, 1959);
7. greater horizontal than vertical displacement of the center of gravity.

TABLE 8-2 Process Characteristics of Running

Mature Patterns (mastered reasonably well by age 5):
  Trunk inclined slightly forward.
  Head erect; facing forward.
  Arms swing freely in sagittal plane.
  Arms swing in opposition to legs; elbows flexed.
  Support foot contacts floor, heel first.
  Support leg extends as it pushes off.
  Recovery leg flexed during forward swing.
  High knee lift during recovery.
  Flexion of support leg as it contacts ground.
  Relaxed stride; little elevation.
  Controls starts, stops, and sudden changes in direction.

DEVELOPMENTAL COMPONENTS	STAGE 1 (2 YRS.)	STAGE 2 (3 YRS.)	STAGE 3 (4 YRS.)
Trunk and Head Position			
trunk is erect or inclined backwards	X		
eyes focus on feet	X		
trunk rotation around long axis	X		
trunk inclined slightly forward			X
Arm Swing			
arms stiff, held high	X		
tendency to swing arms outward	X		
swing from elbows		X	
elbows flexed, approximately at right angles			X
swing freely in opposition to legs			X
Leg Action			
wide base of support	X		
receives weight on whole foot; runs flat footed; foot toes outward	X		
heel-toe foot contact		X	X
flexion of support leg as it contacts ground		X	X
complete extension of support leg; push off from ball of foot			X
limited swing forward of recovery leg	X		
recovery foot crosses midline in rear (may not have nonsupport phase)		X	
flexion of recovery leg during forward swing			X
relaxed stride; little elevation			X
Control			
smooth, rhythmical			X
difficulty in controlling starts, stops, and sudden turns	X	X	
little difficulty in controlling stops, starts, and sudden turns			X

TABLE 8-2   continued

STAGE 2: RUNNING

STAGE 3: RUNNING

As the speed and coordination of the leg actions increase, changes in the arm action also occur. At later stages the arms swing in a sagittal plane, unlike the rather random arm movements observed in earlier stages. The arms are also more flexed at the elbow, so that the arm movement through the arc can occur quickly and in timed opposition to the increased speed of leg action. These changes in arm action are a must if proper coordination and timing of the total running pattern is to occur. Importantly, the position of the trunk may be slightly forward of the vertical.

Jumping

Jumping is a fundamental locomotor skill that involves projection of the body into the air and the receiving of the body's weight in landing on two feet; the propulsive force is exerted from one or both feet (Broer and Zernicke, 1979). As early as the 1930s progress in the development of jumping skill by preschool children was described by Bayley, Gutteridge, and McCaskill and Wellman (Wickstrom, 1977). Since that time the process and product characteristics of mature jumping patterns, and the stages by which the child acquires these mature patterns, have been given considerable attention. The two specific forms of jumping that have received the most attention are the vertical jump (as in the jump and reach) and the standing broad jump. The discussion here will focus upon these two forms of jumping.

The development of jumping ability appears to have its beginning about the time the child begins to descend stairs—approximately 18 months of age (Cratty, 1979; Espenschade and Eckert, 1980; McClenaghan and Gallahue, 1978). As the child descends stairs with assistance, she may begin to take an exaggerated step down. This of course is not a true jump, since the landing from the step down is on one foot and contact with the supporting surface is maintained (a jump requires a two-foot landing and a period of flight). However it seems to be a necessary initial stage to what may later become the standing broad jump. For a period of time the child experiments with this exaggerated step down as she gains proficiency in descending stairs. At about the same time the child is often observed jumping up and down in place (bouncing) on the floor. This bouncing up and down may be a forerunner of the vertical jump pattern.

Although the child may jump off the bottom step of a flight of stairs and continue to jump up and down, it is not until she has the leg strength and coordination needed to elevate (project) the body that the actual jump develops. When strength, stability, and coordination (and confidence) are gained, the child jumps from ever increasing heights, begins to use a more vigorous push-off that results in momentary suspension in the air, and lands without losing balance. The two-foot takeoff and landing is observed soon after, at about the age of 2 years (Cratty, 1979). The initial jumping patterns are void of effective arm action. Hillebrandt *et al.* (1961) observed that leg action in the jumping pattern is far more advanced than arm action. In early stages of jumping the arms are not used at all; later they are used for stability, and finally they are used to augment the force of the jumping action.

The vertical jump and the standing broad jump are very similar in terms of process characteristics. Process characteristics for the vertical and standing broad jumps are given in Tables 8-3 and 8-4, respectively. A simple comparison of the information contained in those two tables clearly indicates the similarities in movement patterns of the two skills. In the mature form both involve a preparatory crouch, a vigorous swing of the arms forward and upward to initiate the action, rapid extension of the legs to project the body from the floor, a time in flight when the body is fully extended, and flexion of the hips, knees, and ankles to absorb the force upon landing. The major difference between the two forms of jumping is the angle at which the body is projected into the air and the specific movements associated with that angle of projection; the standing broad jump requires projection of the body forward as well as upward. This additional directional component makes the standing broad jump slightly more difficult to execute than the vertical jump. In order to project the body forward, the center of gravity must be slightly ahead of the base of support at takeoff; this requires a momentary loss of balance. Because of this there is a strong tendency for the young child to step out automatically with one foot to avoid falling forward (Roberton and Halverson, 1977). The coordination of the forward arm swing with the leg extension in the standing broad jump is also somewhat more intricate than in the vertical jump. In addition, because the angle of projection of the broad jump is forward-upward (45°), the trunk is slightly ahead of the legs at takeoff; the jumper therefore must swing the legs forward under the trunk in preparation for the landing. In the vertical jump the legs maintain the same relationship to the trunk throughout the jump.

In general, the child may acquire a mature vertical jumping pattern before he acquires a mature standing broad jump pattern. Adult-like or mature process characteristics of the vertical jump have been observed in children as young as 2 years of age (Poe, 1978). The standing broad jump is usually not mastered until age 6. Although the majority of two-year-olds do not display the mature form, most children are able to jump vertically with a relatively high degree of proficiency by the age of 5.

In general, the following changes characterize the development of mature patterns of jumping:

1. increased depth of preparatory crouch;
2. increased use and effectiveness of arm action;

TABLE 8-3 Process Characteristics of the Vertical Jump

Mature Pattern (mastered reasonably well by age 5):

    1. Preparatory Phase:
    Hips, knees, and ankles are flexed.
    Weight is on balls of feet.
    Trunk is nearly vertical.
    Feet are pointed forward and slightly apart.
    Arms are in backward-upward position behind the body.

    2. Action:
    Arms lead with a vigorous forward and upward thrust.
    Hips, knees, and ankles extend.
    Body remains extended until landing.
    Hips, knees, ankles flex upon landing.
    Feet are apart upon landing.

DEVELOPMENTAL COMPONENTS	STAGE 1 (3 YRS.)	STAGE 2 (4 YRS.)	STAGE 3 (5 YRS.)
Trunk and head position			
1. Preparatory Phase			
trunk erect	X		
trunk inclined slightly forward		X	X
focuses upward	X	X	X
2. Action			
trunk remains extended throughout jump			X
Arm Action			
1. Preparatory Phase			
arms down at sides	X		
swing backward		X	X
2. Action Phase			
reach upward rather than swing	X	X	
swing vigorously upward			X
initiates jump		X	X
Leg action			
1. Preparatory Phase			
feet slightly apart		X	X
limited flexion of hips, knees, and ankles	X		
deep flexion of hips, knees, ankles	X	X	X
weight is on balls of feet		X	X
2. Action Phase			
some extension of hips, knees, and ankles	X	X	
rapid extension of legs			X
legs remain flexed when in air	X		
land stiff legged	X		
hips, knees, ankles flex up on landing		X	X
feet together on landing	X		
feet slightly apart on landing	X	X	X

TABLE 8-3   continued

DEVELOPMENTAL COMPONENTS	STAGE 1 (3 YRS.)	STAGE 2 (4 YRS.)	STAGE 3 (5 YRS.)
Control			
tends to bounce upward rather than jump	X		
balance lost when landing		X	
balance maintained on landing	X		X

STAGE 1: VERTICAL JUMP

STAGE 2: VERTICAL JUMP

STAGE 3: VERTICAL JUMP

TABLE 8-4   Process Characteristics of the Standing Broad Jump

Mature Pattern (mastered reasonably well by age 6):

    1. Preparatory Phase
    Hips, knees, and ankles are flexed; body is crouched.
    Weight is on the balls of the feet.
    Feet are pointed forward and slightly apart.
    Trunk is inclined forward.
    Arms are in backward-upward position behind the body.

    2. Actions
    Arms lead with a vigorous forward and upward thrust.
    Hips, knees, and ankles extend fully for takeoff.
    Body is fully extended as it becomes airborne; approximate angle of takeoff—45°.
    Hips and knees flex until thighs are horizontal as approach to land; knees then extend.
    Feet are apart upon landing.
    Hips, knees, and ankles flex on landing.
    Arms continue to reach forward.

DEVELOPMENTAL COMPONENTS	STAGE 1 (3 YRS.)	STAGE 2 (4 YRS.)	STAGE 3 (5 YRS.)
Trunk and head position			
trunk is erect throughout jump	X		
trunk is inclined forward; focus is forward during preparatory crouch		X	X
body is fully extended as it becomes airborne			X
Arm Action			
1. Preparatory Phase			
no arm action occurs	X		
repeated back-and-forth motion during preparatory phase		X	
held in backward-upward position during preparatory phase			X
2. Action Phase			
swing vigorously forward and upward for takeoff			X
initiate jumping action			X
swing backward during flight		X	X
held high during flight phase			X
continue to reach forward on landing			X
Leg Action			
1. Preparatory Phase			
limited flexion	X		
hip, knee, ankle flexion (crouch)		X	X
weight is on entire foot	X	X	
weight is on ball of foot			X
2. Action Phase			
tend to use one-foot takeoff	X		
vigorous extension of legs at takeoff			X
hips, knees flexed during entire flight	X		

TABLE 8-4   continued

DEVELOPMENTAL COMPONENTS	STAGE 1 (3 YRS.)	STAGE 2 (4 YRS.)	STAGE 3 (5 YRS.)
2. Action Phase (continued)			
thighs are horizontal as approach landing; knees extend			X
feet are apart on landing			X
hips, knees, ankles flex upon landing		X	X
Control			
arm swing and leg action are independent	X		
balance is maintained			X
arms swing and legs are extended in coordinated fashion at takeoff			X
jump is more vertical than horizontal	X		
loses balance upon landing	X	X	

STAGE 1: STANDING BROAD JUMP

STAGE 2: STANDING BROAD JUMP

STAGE 2–3: STANDING BROAD JUMP

TABLE 8-4   Continued

STAGE 3: STANDING BROAD JUMP

3. greater extension of the body at takeoff and during flight;
4. improved landing with increased stability and absorption of force;
5. decreased angle of takeoff (standing broad jump only);
6. increased flexion of legs during flight in preparation for the landing (standing broad jump only).

These changes in the process characteristics of jumping patterns are closely related. The increased crouch (hip, knee, and ankle flexion) during the preparatory phase, together with the more effective use of the arms and greater extension of the body at takeoff, permit a more forceful takeoff. This in turn results in increased time of flight and greater distances jumped. Greater extension of the body at takeoff and during flight requires more hip, knee, and ankle flexion upon landing so that balance is attained and force is absorbed properly. These developmental changes result from increases in leg strength, limb coordination, *and* practice. Thus although the child may be able to jump higher or farther simply because he is older and stronger, effective, coordinated jumping movements require practice. Zimmerman (1956) reported that unskilled college women performing the standing broad jump demonstrated limited arm movements, lack of full extension at takeoff, more vertical angles of takeoff, and a more hurried action of the legs during flight in preparation for landing. Similar immature characteristics were observed by Halverson (1958) in a comparison of good and poor jumpers of kindergarten age. Good or skilled kindergarten jumpers had a greater horizontal angle of takeoff and a greater horizontal thigh position on landing. Thus regardless of the age of the performer, the process characteristics of poor or immature performances are similar. This strongly suggests that practice may be an important contributor to the development of a mature jumping pattern.

Hopping

When the body is projected into the air by the propulsive force of one foot and the subsequent landing is on that same foot, the action performed is a hop (Broer and Zernicke, 1979). Hopping may be done in place or while moving across the floor. A single hop or repeated hops with or without specific rhythm or timing may be executed. The hop may be performed as a single skill or in combination with other skills.

Although hopping is not necessarily a natural, spontaneous extension of jumping, the two locomotor skills have much in common. They both involve projection of the body into the air and therefore many of the process characteristics of the jumping pattern are also present in the hopping pattern. The major difference between the two skills is in the landing; jumping requires a two-foot landing and hopping involves a one-foot landing. This difference makes the hop more difficult to perform, for there is a greater problem of stability or balance when the body's weight has to be received on one foot rather than two. Most children are able to execute at least the basic form of jumping before they demonstrate the skill of hopping. Until the child has adequate strength to project her own body mass from one foot and to receive that body mass on landing, skill in hopping is usually not achieved.

There has been relatively little systematic attention given to the development of hopping, but a small amount of information about process characteristics of mature and immature patterns of hopping is available. Static balance on one foot is prerequisite to hopping; one-foot balance skill is not achieved until the child is approximately 29 months of age (Espenschade and Eckert, 1980). Because the hop is a dynamic task and thus requires regaining balance, it does not usually begin to develop for several months after the child has achieved static balance (Espenschade and Eckert, 1980). By $3^1/_2$ years of age the child can usually hop 1 to 3 steps. The distance and number of hops that the child can perform increases with age. By 5, most children can execute 10 consecutive hops (Cratty, 1979; DeOreo, 1974; Espenschade and Eckert, 1980).

The first attempts at hopping (stationary and moving) involve jerky movements with little extension and flexion of the support leg. This results in a hop with little elevation and flat-footed landings. The arms are used ineffectively, if at all, and the nonsupport leg is often held in a tense, awkward position. The nonsupport foot also may touch the floor frequently, and the overall pattern of movement may be a hop, hop, step; hop, hop, step. As the child's balance, coordination, and leg strength improve, the distance which she can hop without touching the nonsupport foot down increases. With time and practice the hopping movement becomes more efficient due to the increased propulsive action of the legs (extension of knee and ankle) and to elimination of extraneous arm action. A rhythmical transfer of weight from one foot to the same foot is also seen. The process characteristics associated with the developmental stages and the mature pattern of hopping are described in Table 8-5.

Galloping

The gallop is a combination of walking and leaping. Leaping is a locomotor movement that involves a propulsive force resulting in a transfer of weight from one foot to the other. It is similar to the run except that the body is elevated to a greater height and there is a moment of suspension in the leap that does not occur in the run. The element of elevation also makes the leap similar to the hop. The leap is usually not considered one of the fundamental motor skills. It does not appear to develop spontaneously, and it is quite difficult even for adults to execute as a unitary skill. Although the gallop is not considered one of the fundamental motor skills,

TABLE 8-5 Process Characteristics of Hopping

Mature Pattern (mastered reasonably well by age 6 yrs.):
Head and trunk are held erect.
Knee and ankle of support leg extend at take-off.
Landing is on ball of foot with knee and ankle flexion (to absorb force).
Nonsupport foot is held low to ground and behind body; knee flexed.
Arms held in flexed elbow position close to body; assist in elevation of body.
Movement is smooth and rhythmical.

DEVELOPMENTAL COMPONENTS	STAGE 1 (3 YRS.)	STAGE 2 (4 YRS.)	STAGE 3 (5 YRS.)
Trunk and Head Position			
inclined forward upon landing			X
held erect	X	X	
Arm Action			
used in a flailing, jerky manner	X	X	
flexed elbows close to body or out to sides			X
assist in elevation of body			X
Leg Action			
1. Support Leg			
flat-footed landing and propulsion	X		
lands on ball of foot			X
knee and ankle flex on landing and extend for take-off		X	X
2. Nonsupport Leg			
held high in front of body	X		
held near the knee while hopping		X	
held high behind the body		X	
held low behind the body			X
Control			
movement is jerky	X		
movement is smooth and rhythmical			X
steps on nonsupport foot frequently	X		
maintains balance on supporting foot			X

STAGE 1: HOPPING

TABLE 8-5   **continued**

STAGE 2: HOPPING

STAGE 3: HOPPING

it is included in our discussion because it is a locomotor pattern that is performed spontaneously by most young children. The primitive form of the gallop can be observed as early as 3 years of age, as the child periodically introduces a slight leaping step into her run (DeOreo, 1974; Espenschade and Eckert, 1980). The child gradually masters the technique of galloping by "throwing her weight" onto the forward foot (Espenschade and Eckert, 1980) as she moves about using the step-leap pattern in an uneven rhythm. Eventually (by age 5 for most children) a well-coordinated gallop pattern with controlled arm movements and a momentary suspension in the air develops. The process characteristics of developing and mature galloping patterns are given in Table 8-6.

Some locomotor movements of three-year-olds may *resemble* the gallop pattern, but true gallop patterns seem to emerge around 4 years of age. Although gallop movements appear later in development than many other locomotor movements, the child rapidly gains proficiency in galloping. Approximately 50% of four-year-olds gallop (Gutteridge, 1939). By 5 most children can gallop proficiently and begin to introduce variations into the pattern by moving backward and sideward, etc.

TABLE 8-6   Process Characteristics of Galloping

Mature Pattern (mastered reasonably well by age 5 yrs.):
Body is extended and inclined slightly forward.
Arms swing freely from shoulders.
Extension and flexion of both legs during complete cycle.
Heel-toe foot action of lead foot.
Consistently leads with same foot.
Trailing foot moves up but does not pass lead foot.
Momentary suspension in air.
Action is smooth and rhythmical.

DEVELOPMENTAL COMPONENTS	STAGE 1 (3 YRS.)	STAGE 2 (4 YRS.)	STAGE 3 (5 YRS.)
Trunk and Head Position			
erect	X		
inclined slightly forward		X	X
Arm Action			
flailing, jerky	X		
swing freely from shoulder		X	X
Leg Action			
performs a shuffle step	X		
limited leg flexion on landing and extension at take-off	X		
maintains constant floor contact with rear foot	X		
heel-toe action of lead foot		X	X
extension and flexion of both legs			X
rear foot propels body forward with slight elevation			X
allows trailing foot to pass lead foot	X	X	
maintains the same lead foot			X
Body Control			
movement is jerky; irregular rhythm	X		
moves clearly in a forward direction		X	X
movement is smooth and rhythmical			X
there is momentary suspension in air		X	X

STAGE 1: GALLOPING

TABLE 8-6   continued

STAGE 2: GALLOPING

STAGE 3: GALLOPING

Skipping

As with the gallop, the skip is a combination of two basic forms of locomotion and is therefore not considered one of the fundamental motor skills. However skipping is a pattern that is universally performed and used by children in many movement activities and is therefore worthy of some discussion. The skip is a step-hop pattern, performed in an uneven rhythm. (Note: If the step and hop are combined in an even rhythm, as in many folk dances, the resultant pattern is not considered a skip.) The combination of the step and hop in skipping is a complex one. Not only is it performed in an uneven rhythm with the step taking longer than the hop, it is a "double-task pattern" (Roberton and Halverson, 1977). That is, the step and hop are performed by one foot before the weight is transferred to the other foot. To perform a step-hop pattern on one foot requires more skill in timing of sequential movements as well as a considerable amount of balance control. In order for the movement of the skip to be smooth and rhythmical and exemplary of the mature form, the transfer of weight to the opposite foot and the subsequent step-hop must also be a smooth, well-timed, and continuous action. The skip is one of the last of the locomotor skills to appear and may not be observed in mature form until 6 to 7 years of age.

The process characteristics of the skipping pattern are indicated in Table 8-7. The first attempts at skipping may involve a shuffle step (approximately age 3 years) resulting from the child knowing that she is supposed to do something other than walk or run but not quite knowing what to do or how to do it. As proficiency in hopping develops, the child introduces the hop into her walking or running patterns, and the first step toward the mature skipping pattern is initiated. With continued practice, the hopping pattern appears with at least every other step. The child now performs a step-hop-step, step-hop-step sequence of skipping. This is often referred to as a one-sided or half skip, because the skipping action occurs on only one side of the body (usually the preferred or dominant side). As proficiency in the one-sided skip is achieved and balance is no longer a major problem for the child, the hop is included in the action on the other side of the body. At this point the major ingredients in the skipping pattern have appeared. Further development involves refinement of the arm and leg actions, increasing elevation, and the overall control of the skipping pattern.

Throwing (Overhand)

Of all object manipulation and/or projection skills, the overhand throw has been the focus of most interest. The overhand throwing pattern can be traced back to infancy, when the child first releases an object held in the hand (Espenschade and Eckert, 1980). This primitive form of throwing may be observed as early as 6 months of age—about the time when the child is actively exploring objects and developing prehension skills. At this stage of development the throwing action is usually executed from a sitting position and is limited to the use of the arm. The child is not yet able to assume an upright position without support. It is not until the child develops some degree of proficiency in basic locomotor skills (walking and running) that she has the balance and body control to project an object while standing in the upright position. Thus there is a relatively long period of time between the initial appearance of the primitive throwing pattern and the development of a mature pattern of throwing.

Wild's classic study (1938) indicated that the *first* of four identifiable stages of development of the overhand throw is one in which the feet remain stationary, there is no trunk rotation, and the ball is projected primarily by elbow extension. The trunk may flex forward when the ball is released in an attempt to add force to the throw. The major characteristic of this first stage of throwing is that all movement is in the anterior-posterior

TABLE 8-7 Process Characteristics of Skipping

Mature Pattern (mastered reasonably well by age 6-7):
Trunk is erect; focus is forward.
Arms swing freely in opposition to legs.
Knee and ankle extend for take-off.
Knee and ankle flex upon landing.
Nonsupport leg flexes to aid elevation.
Body is suspended in air momentarily.
Continuous alternate step-hop foot pattern.
Movement is smooth, rhythmical, springing, effortless.

DEVELOPMENTAL COMPONENTS	STAGE 1 (4 YRS.)	STAGE 2 (5 YRS.)	STAGE 3 (6 YRS.)
Trunk and Head Position			
trunk is erect	X	X	X
focus is downward	X		
focus is forward		X	X
Arm Action			
move in a jerky fashion or sideways across the body	X		
move freely in opposition to legs		X	X
elbows flex to aid elevation			X
Leg Action			
flat-footed pattern is used	X		
limited flexion and extension on landing and take-off	X		
balls of feet receive weight; ankle and knee flex upon landing			X
knee and ankle extend for take-off			X
nonsupport leg is stiff	X	X	
nonsupport leg flexes to aid elevation			
Control			
skips with one foot while other steps or runs (one-sided skip)	X		
alternate step-hop pattern is used		X	
a shuffle step is executed	X		
movement is jerky and nonrhythmical	X	X	
movement is smooth, rhythmical, and effortless			X
body is suspended in air momentarily		X	X

TABLE 8-7 continued

STAGE 1: SKIPPING

STAGE 2: SKIPPING

plane. The *second* stage is characterized primarily by movement in the horizontal plane; feet remain stationary but rotation of the pelvis and spine now appear. The differentiating characteristic of the *third* stage is the transfer of weight forward. The transfer of weight in this case is onto the foot on the same side as the throwing arm (ipsilateral). Most of the other characteristics of the mature throwing pattern are present in the third stage, e.g., the trunk rotates, the elbow leads, and there is a follow-through. The *fourth* stage involves a weight transfer to the foot opposite the throwing arm (contralateral). These process characteristics identified by Wild (1938) are reflected in Table 8-8.

Two important developmental trends can be seen in Wild's data: (a) movement progresses from the anterior-posterior to the horizontal plane; and (b) movement occurs initially on a static base and then on a shifting base. The general developmental stages identified by Wild (1938) have been verified by several other investigators (e.g., Roberton and Halverson, 1977; Seefeldt, 1972). In an attempt to further define developmental stages in the overhand throw, Roberton (1975) focused on two major components of the overhand throwing action—arm action and pelvic-spinal action. She identified five stages of arm action and eight stages of pelvic-spinal action. She suggests that the action of the various body parts involved in the overhand throw do not all develop at the same rate.

Catching

Catching is a fundamental motor skill that involves controlling or stopping an aerial ball or object by the use of the hands. The importance of proficiency in catching to success in a variety of play activities, games, and sports is obvious. The development of the skill of catching has been the focus of several investigations. From these studies the developmental stages that lead to the mature pattern of catching have been outlined. What is not clear from such studies is the age at which various stages and/or the mature form of catching may be expected. This lack of age-specific information is partially due to individual differences in the rate of development, but is also due to differences in methods used to look at the development of catching skills. Specific process characteristics of the mature and developing pattern of catching are given in Table 8-9. Before the child makes an overt attempt to catch a tossed ball, she may stand with outstretched arms and let the ball bounce off her chest. The child then proceeds to chase the ball to catch it. This "no response" behavior usually occurs when the child is very young, i.e., not developmentally ready to catch. The first attempts at catching an aerial ball (which usually occur at approximately 3 years of age) are characterized by a rigid preparatory position of the arms (outstretched in front of the body with palms up and fingers extended and stiff), trapping of the ball against the chest by flexing the elbows, or "scoop-

TABLE 8-8   Process Characteristics of Throwing (Overhand)

Mature Pattern (mastered reasonably well by age 5):

1. Preparatory Phase
   Fingers are spread around the ball; palm does not touch ball.
   Feet are slightly apart with forward foot opposite throwing arm.
   Trunk is rotated to throwing side and weight is shifted onto rear foot.
   Throwing arm is moved backward; lateral rotation occurs at shoulder joint.
2. Action
   Body rotates forward with hips leading.
   Step forward is taken in opposition to throwing arm.
   Arm lags behind the body rotation; moves forward in horizontal plane.
   Shoulder medial rotation and elbow extension occur just before release.
   Body and arm continue to rotate forward on follow through.

DEVELOPMENTAL COMPONENTS	STAGE 1 (3 YRS.)	STAGE 2 (4 YRS.)	STAGE 3 (5 YRS.)
Trunk and Head Position			
1. Preparatory Phase			
no trunk rotation or hyperextension occurs	X		
trunk rotates to throwing side		X	X
2. Action Phase			
trunk flexes forward	X		
trunk rotates forward		X	X
Arm Action			
1. Preparatory Phase			
ball is held in the palm of the hand	X	X	
ball is held in the finger tips			X
arm swings upward and backward behind the head	X		
arm moves backward in horizontal plane; lateral rotation at shoulder occurs		X	X
2. Action Phase			
arm moves forward with trunk		X	
arm lags behind trunk action; elbow leads			X
shoulder medial rotation occurs			X
elbow extends to release ball	X		X
ball is released too early or late	X	X	
ball is released in line with the target			X
Leg Action			
1. Preparatory Phase			
no weight transfer	X		
weight shifts onto back foot		X	X
2. Action Phase			
there is no weight transfer	X		
step is forward on same foot as throwing side		X	
step is forward on foot opposite throwing side			X
Control			
there is no follow-through	X		
arm continues to rotate forward on follow-through		X	X
action is smooth and sequential			X

TABLE 8-8 **continued**

STAGE 1: THROWING

STAGE 2: THROWING

STAGE 3: THROWING

ing" the ball toward the body as it contacts the hands and arms. The timing of the arm action is poor and frequently the ball is missed completely. An important characteristic of this initial stage of catching is an "avoidance reaction"—the child turns her head to the side as the ball approaches. Success in catching (controlling the ball) at this stage is as much dependent upon the accuracy of the toss as it is on the ability of the catcher. From this first awkward and often unsuccessful stage the child begins to relax the arms in preparation for the toss, tracks the ball more effectively (this results in improved timing of the catching response), and controls the ball with the hands upon contact. These qualitative changes in the child's catching movements set the stage for the adult-like performance in which the catcher: (a) adjusts her body and hand/arm positions to accommodate the trajectory of the oncoming object; and (b) receives the object with coor-

TABLE 8-9   Process Characteristics of Catching

Mature Pattern (mastered reasonably well by age 5):
  Body is in line with approaching ball.
  Feet are slightly apart in parallel or forward stride position.
  Arms are at sides of body; elbows flexed.
  Hands, fingers are relaxed but slightly cupped and pointing in direction of oncoming object.
  Eyes follow the flight of the ball until ball contact is made.
  Hands turn to accommodate high or low trajectory of ball.
  As ball contacts hand, elbows flex to "give" with impact; fingers close around the ball.
  Weight is transferred from front to back.

DEVELOPMENTAL COMPONENTS	STAGE 1 (3 YRS.)	STAGE 2 (4 YRS.)	STAGE 3 (5 YRS.)
Trunk and Head Position			
trunk is erect	X	X	X
head turns away in "avoidance reaction" as ball approaches	X		
eyes follow flight of ball		X	X
Arm Action			
1. Preparatory Phase			
arms are outstretched and straight; fingers stiff	X		
elbows are slightly flexed and in front of body		X	
elbows are flexed and at sides of body			X
hand and/or fingers relaxed—slightly cupped		X	X
fingers point in direction of oncoming ball		X	X
2. Action Phase			
arms remain outstretched; ball bounces off them	X		
arms, hands, and body are used as a single unit to "trap" the ball	X	X	
hands adjust to level of oncoming ball			X
arms swing up as ball is contacted		X	
the ball is caught mainly with the hands and arms			X
hands close around the ball, elbows flex to absorb force			X
Leg Action			
feet are together	X		
feet are slightly apart in side or forward stride			
weight transfers from front to back as ball is caught			
Control			
body remains stationary	X		
adjusts body position to be in line with approaching ball			X

TABLE 8-9 continued

STAGE 1: CATCHING

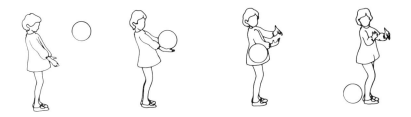

STAGE 2: CATCHING

STAGE 3: CATCHING

dinated, well-timed movements that result in proper absorption of force and skillful control of the ball.

There are some general factors that may affect the catching performance of all children. One of the most important of these factors is the size of the ball. Wellman (1937) found that children were more successful catching a larger ball (16¼-inch) than a smaller ball (9½-inch). This supports the commonly held assumption that the larger ball is easier for the young child to control. However, it has long been observed by people who work with young children that a large ball frequently results in a more elementary form of catching, i.e., the "basket" catch, or trapping the ball against the young child will have difficulty catching (controlling) a very small ball such as a tennis ball, but the action of the catching response to this smaller ball is usually more mature. The best catching performance is elicited by using a ball that the child can cup in her hands but that does not require the fine perceptual-motor control that a very small ball does.

A second set of variables that affect catching performance is the flight characteristics of the ball—the velocity, the angle of projection (both horizontal and vertical), and whether the ball is purely aerial or is bounced toward the child. Bruce (1966) studied the catching performance of second-fourth-, and sixth-grade children using a tennis ball projected from a machine at different horizontal and vertical angles and at different velocities. He found that performance was not adversely affected when the child had to move laterally (horizontal angle of projection). However, children of all grade levels had difficulty moving forward or backward to catch the ball (vertical angles of projection). When the speed of the ball was increased, the catching performance of second- and fourth-grade children deteriorated, but the increased ball velocity did not seem to bother the sixth-grade children. The need for quick, accurate perception of the ball's flight characteristics is evident from Bruce's (1966) work. The younger, less experienced child has difficulty judging the flight of the higher velocity projection in time to respond accurately. Thus when tossing a ball to a young child who is in the process of developing skill in catching, it is important not to throw the ball too fast (i.e., allow time for perceptual judgments to be made) or in such a way that the child must move forward or backward to catch it. Tossing the ball directly to the child will result in her best performance. Bouncing the ball to the child, rather than tossing it, also tends to elicit better catching performance. The bounced ball appears to be easier for the child to track (perhaps because it is not coming straight at her, and/or because of the increased time to "watch" the ball) and is not as likely to elicit the avoidance reaction. Although it seems logical that the bounced ball might be easier for the young child to catch, there has been no research to either support or refute this observation.

Striking

Striking skills are ones in which an object is projected by contacting it with a body part or an implement. The skill can be executed using a sidearm, underhand, or overhand pattern. Following this definition, a variety of skills could be listed as striking skills, among which would be batting, kicking, tennis strokes, volleyball serves, etc. Although kicking may be considered a striking skill, it will be discussed separately. It is considered a fundamental motor skill, and it involves some process characteristics that differ from other striking skills. Most striking skills are performed with a sidearm movement pattern in the horizontal plane (Wickstrom, 1977). Relatively little research has focused on the development of sidearm striking skills. Process characteristics of the developmental stages and mature pattern of striking in the horizontal plane are described in Table 8-10. The characteristics of the mature pattern are very similar to those of throwing. There is rotation away from the target during the preparatory action, weight transference and pelvic and spinal rotation forward during the action phase, arm action that follows trunk rotation, and a follow-through after contact. Available information suggests that the first stage of the sidearm striking pattern develops from a throwing action in the anterior-posterior plane (Espenschade and Eckert, 1967; Wickstrom, 1977). Regardless of whether a paddle, racket, bat, or some other implement is used, or whether the object is stationary or moving toward the striker, the child faces the direction of the intended flight and uses a "chopping" action to contact the object. From that initial stage the child "seems to progress slowly from striking in a vertical plane, downward through a series of increasingly flatter oblique planes to an effective pattern predominantly in a horizontal plane" (Wickstrom, 1977, pp. 145–146).

The development of the striking pattern presents different kinds of problems to the child. One is that a new element has been introduced—an implement. The child now is not only concerned with moving her body but also with coordinating the movement of the implement with the body. Because contact is to be made with an object located away from the body, a visual perception factor is introduced. Even if the object is stationary (e.g., on a batting tee or suspended), there is the problem of positioning oneself appropriately. If the object is projected to the child (e.g., tossed), the problem of positioning is compounded by the need for quick and accurate perception of the flight characteristics of the object, so that the initiation of the response can be properly timed. These all add to the complexity of the striking skill.

Harper and Struma (1973) report case studies of the development of one-handed striking in two youngsters, one male and one female. The developmental sequence for the girl, which spanned one year (3 years, 4

TABLE 8-10 Process Characteristics of Striking (Horizontal plane)

Mature Pattern (mastered reasonably well with stationary ball by age 5):
  1. Preparatory Phase:
    Feet are approximately shoulder width apart in side stride.
    Body position is perpendicular to line of flight of ball.
    Trunk is rotated backward and weight is shifted to rear foot.
    Lead elbow is held up and out from body with implement held off shoulders.
    Eyes focus on ball until just before contact.
  2. Action:
    Trunk rotates in direction of intended hit with hips leading.
    Weight is shifted forward in the direction of the hit.
    Arms swing out away from body.
    Movement continues after ball contact is made.

DEVELOPMENTAL COMPONENTS	STAGE 1 (3 YRS.)	STAGE 2 (4 YRS.)	STAGE 3 (5 YRS.)
Trunk and Head Position			
focus is on object to be struck	X	X	
no trunk action occurs	X		
faces direction of oncoming object and/or intended flight	X		
body is perpendicular to line of flight		X	X
body rotates away from intended flight during backswing		X	X
position is too close to object	X	X	
body is positioned appropriate distance from object			X
Arm Action			
1. Preparatory Phase			
arms swing up overhead	X		
arms swing back in horizontal phase		X	X
elbows are held away from the body			X
implement rests on shoulder		X	
implement is held off shoulder			X
2. Action Phase			
movement is primarily in over-the-shoulder action	X		
movement is primarily a sidearm motion in horizontal plane		X	X
elbows extend during forward swing		X	X
contact is made with extended arms			X
Leg Action			
feet are together	X		
feet are shoulder-width apart		X	X
weight transfers to back foot during backswing		X	X
there is no transfer of weight	X		
step is forward toward intended line of flight during swing			X
Control			
total body moves as a unit	X	X	
movement is smooth and sequential with trunk initiating the swing			X

TABLE 8-10 continued

STAGE 1: STRIKING

STAGE 2: STRIKING

STAGE 3: STRIKING

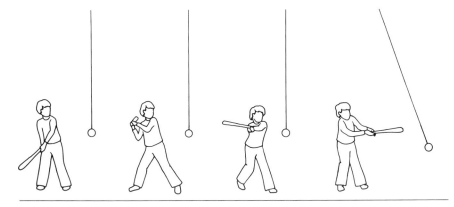

months to 4 years, 4 months) included: (a) an "arm-dominated" pattern with no weight shift or trunk rotation; (b) total body involvement—step and shift of weight, forward inclination of the trunk, knee and hip flexion, and trunk rotation; and (c) "opening up"—movement of one body part forward while another part moved away (the pelvis rotated forward as the arms moved back). Analysis of the boy's progress for one year (from 3 years, 7 months to 4 years, 7 months) indicated that he exhibited the basic characteristics of the mature pattern from the outset; additional progress primarily involved subtle changes in the organization of the timing of the response. These observations clearly suggest that there is a definite developmental sequence in acquisition of the sidearm striking pattern and that, given practice, the mature striking pattern can be achieved at a relatively early age (approximately 4 years).

Ball Bouncing

Few studies have been reported that were concerned specifically with ball bouncing. Espenschade and Eckert (1980) suggest that the development of ball bouncing skill originates when a ball is dropped (accidentally or deliberately), causing it to bounce. From this single bounce the child attempts to tap the ball repeatedly. Control of the ball is not possible, however, until the child learns to place his hand in relation to the center of mass of the ball. In addition the hand must meet the ball as it rebounds from the floor, maintaining contact with it as long as possible while the arm "pushes" the ball back toward the floor. The "slapping" action observed in the young child and/or the unskilled performer is the result of inappropriate timing of the arm and hand action in relation to the rebound of the ball. There are no studies that have systematically assessed the process characteristics of ball bouncing skills in young children. Suggested process characteristics of ball bouncing are given in Table 8-11.

Kicking

Research on the development of kicking skills is somewhat limited; however, the process characteristics of the mature pattern used in kicking a stationary ball have been clearly identified. These characteristics and those that seem to characterize developmental stages in kicking are given in Table 8-12. The stationary kick, i.e., one in which the ball is placed on the floor (motionless) and is kicked while using a limited approach, is the foundation for other kicking skills (e.g., punting, kicking a rolling ball, "power style" kicking, etc.). Thus proficiency in punting or kicking a moving ball is generally not achieved until some degree of proficiency in kicking a stationary ball has been acquired. Kicking a moving ball (including a punt) is a more difficult task because of the additional perceptual demands made on the

TABLE 8-11 Process Characteristics of Ball-Bouncing

Mature Pattern (mastered reasonably well by age 5):
Body is flexed at knees, hips, and waist.
Ball is contacted with fingers spread.
Ball is pushed to floor by elbow extension.
Height of bounce is kept at waist level.
Eyes focus on hands and ball.

DEVELOPMENTAL COMPONENTS	STAGE 1 (3 YRS.)	STAGE 2 (4 YRS.)	STAGE 3 (5 YRS.)
Trunk and Head Position			
trunk is held erect	X		
trunk is flexed slightly forward		X	X
focus is on hand and ball		X	X
Arm Action			
fingers are together; stiff	X	X	
fingers are spread; relaxed			X
action is from shoulder or wrist only, resulting in slapping action	X	X	
hand is retracted from ball at time of contact	X	X	
action is from elbow extension, resulting in pushing action			X
Leg Action			
no action	X		
legs are relaxed; some flexion at hips and knees		X	X
Control			
unable to bounce ball repeatedly	X	X	
ball rebounds to chest level	X	X	
height of bounce is kept at waist level			X

STAGE 1: BALL BOUNCING

STAGE 2: BALL BOUNCING

TABLE 8-12   Process Characteristics of Kicking (Stationary Ball)

Mature Pattern (mastered reasonably well by age 5):
Preliminary step forward is taken on support leg.
Support leg is flexed slightly at contact.
Kicking leg is swung backward with hip hyperextension and knee flexion.
As thigh is nearly perpendicular to floor, knee extends.
Kicking leg swings forward as knee flexion continues.
Trunk is inclined slightly backward upon contact.
Opposite arm swings forward as kicking leg extends.
Kicking leg follows through in direction of kick.
Body is raised on toes of supporting foot during follow through.
Contact is made with toes; ankle is slightly flexed.

DEVELOPMENTAL COMPONENTS	STAGE 1 (3 YRS.)	STAGE 2 (4 YRS.)	STAGE 3 (5 YRS.)
Trunk and Head Position			
erect throughout kick	X		
inclines forward at contact		X	
slightly forward during backswing			X
inclines slightly back at contact			X
Arm Action			
not used	X	X	
used in opposition to kicking leg			
Leg Action			
little or no backswing of kicking leg	X		
backswing is limited; from hip or knee only		X	
a wide-range backswing is used (hip hyper-extension and knee flexion)			X
a step on nonkicking foot is taken		X	X
knee of support leg is flexed at contact			X
hip flexion initiates leg action			X
knee continues to flex as thigh swings forward			X
knee extends at contact			X
there is no follow-through of kicking leg	X		
kicking leg follows through in direction of kick			X
support foot rises on toes during follow through			X
Control			
support foot steps too far from or too close to ball	X		
step is appropriate distance from ball			X

TABLE 8-12   continued

STAGE 1: KICKING

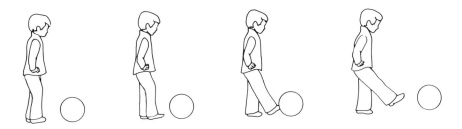

STAGE 2: KICKING

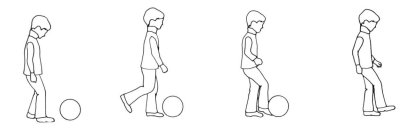

STAGE 3: KICKING

performer. The child must accurately judge the speed and direction of the ball in order to properly time the initiation of the kicking response.

When the child can assume a balanced position on one leg (approximately 2 years of age), the prerequisite ability for beginning the development of kicking skills has been established. The first stage of kicking is characterized by a limited back and forward swing of the kicking leg. In fact, the leg action may not be a swinging action at all, but rather one that "nudges" or pushes the ball away. Contact of the ball may be with the front part of the lower leg rather than with the foot (Espenschade and Eckert, 1980; Wickstrom, 1977). As the child attempts to "kick harder," the range of motion of the leg action increases, and there are compensatory actions in the trunk (lean) and arms (elevation) so that balance can be maintained. As the child makes appropriate adjustment of the position of the supporting foot in relation to the ball and thus is an appropriate distance from the ball, he begins to kick "through" rather than "at" the ball. Additional changes in the process characteristics of the kick are associated with increased force of the kicking action. There is increased action at the knee and hip during backward and forward swing. To achieve a well-coordinated, forceful leg swing forward, the knee continues to flex even as the thigh has started forward; knee extension does not begin until the thigh is approximately vertical, at which time the lower leg "snaps" forward to contact the ball. The increased force of the leg swing requires the compensatory actions identified previously and a follow-through of the action after contact. By the age of 5 or 6, the child demonstrates the process characteristics of a mature kicking pattern. The force of the stationary kick continues to increase as the child grows and practices. When the mature kicking pattern has been established, the child begins to make appropriate adjustments for kicking a rolling or dropped ball.

PRODUCT CHARACTERISTICS OF MOVEMENT: AGE-RELATED CHANGES AND SEX DIFFERENCES

Age-related changes and sex differences in performance based on product characteristics or achievement scores are presented below. The information included has been taken from several sources, including research studies in which performance of various age groups was measured and published normative data associated with motor skill test batteries. As will be noted from the discussion, there is no universal agreement about precise age-related or sex differences in the performance of motor skills. This is due, in part, to differences in procedures used in the investigations (e.g., age groups, task requirements, etc.). Thus apparent trends in age and/or sex differences that are pointed out in the discussion should be considered only as suggestive and not final. To date, no comprehensive longitudinal study has been conducted on age and sex differences in the performance of fundamental motor skills. That is, there has been no investigation in which performance has been assessed by product scores on several skills for the same group of boys and girls over a large age span, e.g., age 3 to age 10.

Walking

Few, if any, studies have investigated the product aspect of the development of the walking pattern. Product measures in general are not a very meaningful way of assessing early walking skill.

Running

Age-related changes in running performance during childhood, as measured by achievement or product scores, are well documented. The time required to run a specific distance (usually 30, 40, or 50 yards) is the measure most frequently used. Although the distance of the dash and the age of the subjects may vary from one study to the next, the general pattern of improvement in performance with age is consistent. For example, Seils (1951) measured the performance of first-, second-, and third-grade children in the 40-yard dash. Data were collected at three-month intervals, and a constant improvement in performance (decreased running time) was observed. Milne, Seefeldt, and Haubenstricker (1971) studied the 30-yard dash and reported yearly improvements in time for children 5 to 11 years of age. Milne, Seefeldt, and Reuschlein (1976) also found differences in performance improvement on the 30-yard dash for kindergarten and first- and second-grade children. Similar results were found by Glassow and Kruse (1960) on the 50-yard dash for girls 6 to 14 years of age and Williams and Breihan (1979) for four-, six-, and eight-year-old children on the 25-yard dash. A "typical" pattern of improvement in running is shown in Figure 8.1. Although running performance generally improves with age, the trend is not a perfectly linear one. That is, improvement does not occur at a constant rate.

Norms provided by the AAHPER Youth Fitness Manual (Hunsicker and Reiff, 1976) on the 50-yard dash indicate that girls' running performances improve until about age 14 and show a slight decline at 16 and 17 years of age. Fifty-yard dash scores improve steadily for boys each year from ages 9 to 17. Whether this sex-related difference is due to differences in physical characteristics, rate of maturation, or some other factor(s) (e.g., interest, opportunity for practice, etc.) is not clear.

One of the major characteristics of the mature running pattern is the ability to change speed and direction. This dimension of running is fre-

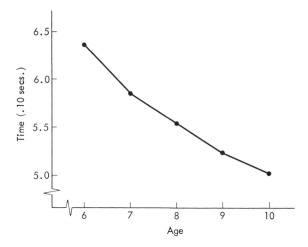

FIGURE 8.1   30-yard dash—Girls (data from Glassow and Kruse, 1960)

quently evaluated through the use of shuttle or agility tasks. Seils (1951) reported that performance on an agility task improved with each succeeding grade for children in grades one, two, and three. Milne, Seefeldt, and Haubenstricker (1971) also observed a year-to-year performance improvement. However, Milne, Seefeldt, and Reuschlein (1976) found that first- and second-grade children were significantly different (performance was better) from kindergarten children in agility performance, but that first- and second-graders were not significantly different from each other on this specific task. Williams *et al.* (1971) found an *overall* improvement in shuttle run performance for children 5 to 10 years of age. Data provided by the AAHPER Youth Fitness Manual (1976) show a pattern of change in agility in which boys improve from ages 9 to 17 whereas girls improve to about 14 years of age and decline thereafter.

Product measures of running performance of children younger than kindergarten age are lacking. DeOreo (unpublished) does suggest that three-, four-, and five-year-old children should be able to complete a 35-yard run in 30, 20, and 10 seconds, respectively. This indicates that product aspects of performance do improve during the early developmental years.

In general, Milne, Seefeldt, and Reuschlein's (1976) data suggest that kindergarten and first- and second-grade boys run faster than girls on both the 30-yard dash and the agility run. Temple (1979) reports that shuttle run performance of prekindergarten boys is clearly superior to that of prekindergarten girls. AAHPER Youth Fitness norms (Hunsicker and Reiff, 1976) also support significant sex differences in running in favor of males. Results of the study by Milne, Seefeldt, and Haubenstricker (1971) indicate that the 30-yard dash performances of boys and girls are not different until after age 9½ years, at which time boys show superior performance; girls performed better than boys until age 8½ years on the shuttle run. Williams *et al.* (1971) reported no consistent sex differences in performance of a shuttle run task (Figure 8.2). Sex differences in running speed of children, thus, are not clearly established at this time.

Jumping

Product measures of jumping performance also indicate improved performance with age. Although the standing broad jump is a more frequently used test of jumping ability, some data on the vertical jump and reach are available. Williams and Breihan (1979) indicated that the score of the jump and reach test increased with age when the performances of four-, six- and eight-year-old boys and girls were compared. Latchaw (1954) also found age-related improvement in performance for fourth-, fifth-, and sixth-grade children. All differences in performance between grade levels were statistically significant except between grades five and six for boys. Although the difference between fifth- and sixth-grade boys was not significant, sixth-grade boys did jump higher. Milne, Seefeldt, and Haubenstricker (1971) also found yearly performance increases in the jump and reach for children 5 to 11 years of age.

Similar improvements in performance of the standing broad jump as a function of age have been recorded by various investigators. Milne, Seefeldt, and Haubenstricker (1971) show such changes from ages 5 to 11 years. Milne, Seefeldt, and Reuschlein (1976) also show age-related changes in performance for kindergarten and first- and second-grade children, as do Glassow and Kruse (1960) for girls 6 to 14 years of age, Williams *et al.* (1971) for boys and girls 5 to 10 years of age, and Seils (1951) for boys in

FIGURE 8.2   Shuttle Run (data from Williams *et al.*, 1971)

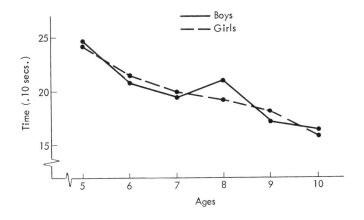

grades one, two, and three. This same steady improvement was not observed by Seils (1951) for girls in the first three grades—third-graders performed better than first- or second-grade girls, but the performance of second-grade girls was not significantly better than that of first-grade girls. Latchaw (1954) also found that performance differences were not significant for fifth- and sixth-grade boys or for third- and fourth- or fourth- and fifth-grade girls. Although performance differences reported in these studies (Latchaw, 1954; Seils, 1951) were not statistically significant, there was evidence of improved performance with increasing grade level.

Broad jump performance data collected by Williams *et al.* (1971) are shown in Figure 8.3 and suggest a rather typical age-related pattern of improvement. The pattern of performance is, however, not a purely linear one. Performance differences between boys and girls are also evident. Other studies clearly support the notion that boys jump farther than girls (Hunsicker and Reiff, 1976; Milne, Seefeldt, and Haubenstricker, 1971; Milne, Seefeldt, and Reuschlein, 1976).

It appears that two conclusions can be drawn from available product measures of performance of the vertical jump and the standing broad jump: (a) performance generally improves with age, at least from ages 5 to 14; and (b) boys usually perform better than girls. Product measures of the performance of jumping skills by preschool youngsters is scanty. DeOreo (1974) suggests that three- and four-year-old children should be able to jump distances of 36 cm. to 60 cm. and 60 cm. to 85 cm., respectively, and that a five-year-old should jump and reach $2^{1}/_{2}$ inches.

Hopping

Hopping performance, in terms of product measures, has been assessed primarily by: (a) determining the number of consecutive hops performed before balance is lost; and (b) the amount of time required to hop a specified distance (usually 25 or 50 feet). Available data suggest that performance, in general, improves with age. Product measures on preschool children indicate that the three and one-half-year-old can execute from 1 to 3 hops, the four and one-half-year-old from 7 to 9 hops, and the five-year-old 10 hops (Wellman, 1937). Williams and Breihan (1979) found that the time to hop a 25-foot distance improved (was faster) from 4 to 6 to 8 years of age. Cratty (1979) suggests that most five-year-olds can hop a 50-foot distance in 10.5 seconds.

Sex differences in hopping are evident. Cratty (1979) indicates that five-year-old girls can hop a 50-foot distance about 3.4 seconds faster than five-year-old boys. Keogh (1970) also indicates that girls perform better than boys on hopping and other footwork tasks. He suggests that girls generally learn to hop sooner than boys and that the quality of their movement is better. Data from the study by Williams and Breihan (1979) indi-

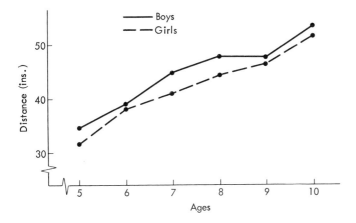

FIGURE 8.3   Standing Broad Jump (data from Williams *et al.*, 1971)

cated that four-year-old boys had a slightly faster 25-foot hop time than girls, but that the girls' performance was superior (faster) to boys at ages 6 and 8 years. The reason for differences in hopping performance by girls and boys at any specific age is not clear at this time. To suggest that it is because girls practice hopping tasks more than boys or because girls are slightly more mature biologically than boys of the same age is reasonable but is only conjecture.

Galloping

Product information on galloping performance of children is very limited. Williams and Breihan (1979) recorded the time required to gallop through a 25-foot distance by four-, six-, and eight-year-olds. The data from that study indicated that performance improves with age, with the greatest improvement occurring between the ages of 6 and 8 years. These data also indicated that, for all age groups, girls performed better (required less time to gallop the distance) than boys.

Skipping

Little research has been conducted on the developmental stages of skipping. Information that is available is based on observations of children of various ages as they attempted to skip. Keogh (1970) has indicated that girls generally learn to skip sooner than boys. This proposed female superiority in skipping performance is not supported by data from the study by Williams and Breihan (1979). Their data indicated that four-, six-, and eight-year-old boys skipped through a 25-foot distance faster than girls of the same chronological age. These data do not reflect the quality of the skipping performance, only the speed with which the child could move through the 25-foot distance. Williams and Breihan (1979) also reported that six-year-old boys performed more poorly than four-year-old boys, whereas eight-year-olds were superior to both four- and six-year-olds. In contrast, girls' skipping performances showed a steady improvement from 4 to 6 to 8 years of age. More research is needed to make the developmental picture of skipping performance more complete.

Throwing (Overhand)

Because an object is projected during the execution of the overhand throw, a readily identifiable and measurable product of performance is available. The measurable product is the trajectory of the object, of which the two major components are direction (accuracy) and force (velocity). "Accuracy of throwing has not been measured in a consistent manner, but . . . improvement occurs with age for both boys and girls" (Keogh, 1973, p. 61). The force component of the overhand throw has commonly been measured by velocity or distance of the thrown ball. Using velocity as the measure of performance, Glassow and Kruse (1960) reported a continuous increase in performance of the overhand throw for girls from 6 to 14 years of age. Williams *et al.* (1971) reported similar results for boys and girls from 5 to 10 years of age. Williams and Breihan (1979) also found age-related improvements in four-, six-, and eight-year-olds' performances of the overhand throw. Using *distance* as the measure of throwing perform-ance, Seils (1951) found that the performance of both boys and girls im-proved for each successive grade for children in grades one, two, and three. A typical age-related performance curve for the overhand throw is pre-sented in Figure 8.4. As these data indicate, product measures of throwing performance generally improve with age. Although improvement in throw-ing is not linear, it is continuous.

Keogh (1973), Dohrmann (1964), and Williams *et al.* (1971) all indicate that boys are superior to girls at all ages in throwing performance. Williams and Breihan (1979), however, reported that eight-year-old girls threw with greater velocity than eight-year-old boys. Keogh (1973) suggested that the boy-girl differences observed in throwing may be due, at least in part, to cultural influences. Support for this position is provided by studies of Eu-ropean children in which boy-girl differences in throwing performance are not evident (Keogh, 1973).

Catching

The only purely objective measure of catching performance is the number of successful catches made in relation to the number of catching attempts. Catching performance, however, is often measured by a rating

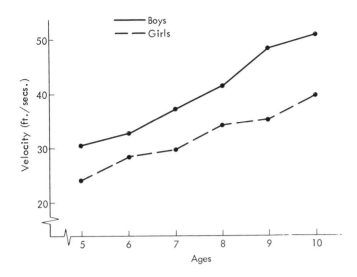

FIGURE 8.4   Overarm Throw (data from Williams *et al.*, 1971)

scale that reflects the quality of the catch. Regardless of the measure used, performance improves with age (e.g., Bruce, 1966; Seils, 1951; Wellman, 1937; Williams and Breihan, 1979). Although there are some age-related data on catching performance available, the age at which performance levels off (no additional improvement occurs) has not been determined.

Sex differences in catching performance are not clearcut. Seils (1951) reported that boys had better average catching performance in grades one and two, but that the average catching performance of girls was better than boys in grade three. Clear sex differences in performance were not evident in the study by Williams and Breihan (1979). Their data suggested that the average performance of girls was better than boys at ages 4 and 8 years; boys' performances were better at age 6. Bruce (1966) found that boys' performances were better than those of girls in second, fourth, and sixth grades. Data collected on prekindergarten children also show that boys perform catching tasks better than girls (Temple, 1979).

Striking

There are a limited number of studies that have assessed the product characteristics of striking performance. Williams and Breihan (1979) measured one-arm striking by having the child project a suspended tennis ball using a racketball racket; performance was measured by a velocity score. Performance improved substantially for both boys and girls from 4 to 6 to 8 years. Two-arm striking performance was measured by the same method

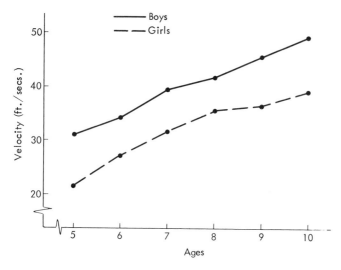

FIGURE 8.5   Striking Suspended Ball (data from Williams *et al.*, 1971)

with similar results. Generally, the one-arm striking performances were better than the two-arm striking performances. Espenschade and Eckert (1980) also suggest that the young child has more difficulty contacting a ball using a two-handed sidearm swing, due to increased difficulty in achieving the proper timing of the movement. Williams *et al.* (1971) also used a two-arm striking task to project a suspended tennis ball. Data on performances of five- to ten-year-olds are shown in Figure 8.5. In general, striking performance improved with age. These data also indicate that boys achieve greater velocity in striking than girls at all age levels.

Ball Bouncing

An early study by Wellman (1937) indicated that the age at which the child could bounce a ball with one hand versus two hands and the distance that was covered while bouncing the ball were related to the size of the ball. Children (27 months) were able to bounce a ball with a $9\frac{1}{2}$-inch circumference a distance of one to three feet before losing control; the distance increased to five feet by 40 months of age. It was not until about 46 months of age that the child was able to bounce a $16\frac{1}{4}$-inch ball for a distance of five feet using a two-hand bounce. Six-year-old children were able to bounce the larger ball, using one hand, for a distance of five feet. The problem with the larger ball, of course, is the size of the hand in relation to the size of the ball. (The hand can contact proportionately less surface on a large ball than on a small ball, and thus less control can be exercised.) The larger ball also requires greater strength to apply the force required for the ball to rebound to an appropriate height to continue the ball bouncing action.

Williams and Breihan (1979) measured ball bouncing performance by having the child repeatedly bounce an 8-inch ball within a 12-inch square on the floor, using one hand. The resulting scores for four-, six-, and eight-year-old boys and girls indicated that performance improved for each succeeding age. As a group, four-year-old children bounced the ball an average of less than two times before control was lost or the ball was bounced outside the square. The six-year-olds achieved an average of four controlled bounces whereas the eight-year-old children averaged slightly more than five bounces. A comparison of the performances of boys and girls of different ages indicated that boys' performances improved gradually with age from two bounces at age 4 years to six bounces at age 8. At ages 4 and 6, boys performed better than the girls; however, at age 8, girls' performances were substantially better than boys'.

Kicking

Little product data on kicking are available. Those which are indicate that kicking performance improves with increasing age for both boys and girls (Williams and Breihan, 1979; Williams *et al.*, 1971). Data from the study by Williams *et al.* (1971) are shown in Figure 8.6. Although both boys and girls improve in kicking from 5 to 10 years, boys show consistently superior performance to girls. Williams and Breihan (1979) found similar

FIGURE 8.6   Kicking Stationary Ball (data from Williams *et al.*, 1971)

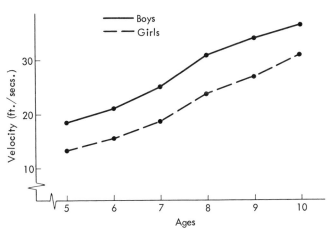

sex differences in four- and six-year-old children but not in eight-year-olds; eight-year-old girls had higher velocity scores than boys of the same age. The reason for the apparent male superiority in ball skills, including kicking, may lie in cultural influences.

SUMMARY

1. *Intertask* motor development is concerned with how children acquire proficiency in a number of different motor skills (e.g., in throwing, catching, kicking, running, etc.).

2. Probabilistic theories of intertask motor development suggest that motor development is bidirectional; that although some general trends in motor development may be observable, the rule is that individual variations in rate and pattern of motor skill development will dominate.

3. There may be five levels of control involved in *intertask* motor development: reflexive and spontaneous control; exploratory control; examinatory and regulatory control; directed, executory control; and refined, automatic control.

4. Several factors may affect the level of motor control exerted by the child in performing a given motor task. These include: the nature of the phases involved in task execution, the kind of movement pattern required of the extremities, and the nature of the environmental interaction.

5. *Intratask* motor development is concerned with changes that take place in body actions as the child gains control in individual motor tasks.

6. The component model of intratask motor development suggests that dramatic changes can and do occur in one body action independent of changes in other body actions.

7. Whole body action descriptions are best used as a guide for observing general levels of intratask motor development on children, and are limited in their value for analysis of sequential changes in motor development.

8. Process characteristics of movement are those characteristics that deal with qualitative aspects of motor performance (e.g., *how* the child moves the body in executing an agility run); product characteristics of movement are those that describe quantitative aspects of performance (e.g., how fast the child runs; how far the child throws the ball).

9. Checklists of process characteristics can be used to analyze individual children's levels of motor development.

10. Process and product characteristics of fundamental motor skill performances of young children improve with age, often in a linear fashion.

STUDY QUESTIONS

1. Identify the major fundamental gross motor skills; indicate which are locomotor and which are ball-handling skills.
2. Differentiate between process and product characteristics of motor skill performance.
3. Differentiate between intertask and intratask motor development.
4. Compare "predetermined" and "probabilistic" theories of motor development. How do they differ? Be specific.
5. List and describe five levels of motor control involved in intertask development. Give a behavioral example of each level of motor control.
6. Describe in detail the following factors that are important in intertask motor development and indicate how they affect such development:
   a. phases in the execution of a motor task (positioning versus manipulative phases);
   b. patterns of development of motor control in the legs;
   c. patterns of development of motor control in the arms, hands, and fingers;
   d. whether the performer is in possession of the object with which he must interact;
   e. stationary or moving characteristic of the object to be interacted with; and
   f. use of an implement.
7. What is the "component" approach to intratask motor development? How is it different from the traditional "stages" approach? Be specific.
8. Of what value are "whole body action" descriptions in understanding motor development in young children?
9. Describe the major "steps" involved in the development of the following fundamental motor skills from a process point of view:
   a. walking
   b. running
   c. jumping
   d. hopping
   e. galloping
   f. skipping
   g. throwing
   h. catching
   i. striking
   j. ball bouncing
   k. kicking

10. Describe differences in sex- and age-related product characteristics of the fundamental motor skills listed above.

REFERENCES

BALTES, P.B., AND GOULET, L.R.   (Eds.) *Life-Span Developmental Psychology: Research and Theory*. Philadelphia, PA: Lea and Febiger, 1970.

BECK, M.C.   The path of the center of gravity during running in boys grades one to six. Unpublished Doctoral dissertation, University of Wisconsin, 1965.

BROER, M.R., AND ZERNICKE, R.F.   *Efficiency of Human Movement*, 4th edition. Philadelphia, PA: W.B. Saunders Company, 1974.

BROWN, E.W.   Biomechanical analysis of the running patterns of girls 3-10 years of age. Unpublished Doctoral dissertation, University of Oregon, 1978.

BRUCE, R.   The effects of variations in ball trajectory upon the catching performance of elementary school children. Unpublished Doctoral dissertation, University of Wisconsin, 1966.

CLAUSE, F.C.   A kinematic analysis of the development of the running pattern of preschool boys. Unpublished Doctoral dissertation, University of Wisconsin, 1959.

COOPER, J.M., AND GLASSOW, R.B.   *Kinesiology*. St. Louis, MO: C.V. Mosby Company, 1976.

CRATTY, B.J.   *Perceptual and Motor Development in Infants and Young Children*, 2nd edition. Englewood Cliffs, NJ: Prentice-Hall, Inc., 1979.

DEOREO, K.L.   DeOreo Fundamental Motor Skills Inventory. Unpublished manuscript, Kent State University.

DEOREO, K.L.   The performance and development of fundamental motor skills in preschool children. In Wade and Martens, eds., *Psychology of Motor Behavior and Sport*. Champaign, IL: Human Kinetics, 1974.

DITTMER, J.A.   A kinematic analysis of the development of running patterns of grade school girls and certain factors which distinguish good and poor performance at observed ages. Unpublished Master's thesis, University of Wisconsin, 1962.

DOHRMANN, P.   Throwing and kicking ability of 8-year-old boys and girls. *Research Quarterly*. 35(1964):464-471.

DUSENBERRY, L.   A study of the effect of training in ball throwing by children ages three to seven. *Research Quarterly*. 23(1952):9-14.

ESPENSCHADE, A.S., AND ECKERT, H.M.   *Motor Development*. Columbia, OH: Chas. E. Merrill Books, Inc., 1967.

FORTNEY, V.L.   The swinging limb in running of boys ages seven through eleven. Unpublished Master's thesis, University of Wisconsin, 1964.

GENTILE, A.M.   The structure of motor tasks. *Mouvement*. October 11-28, 1975.

GESELL, A.   *The First Five Years of Life*. New York: Harper and Row, Pub., 1946.

GLASSOW, R.B., AND KRUSE, P.   Motor performance of girls age 6 to 14 years. *Research Quarterly*. 31(1960):426-433.

HALVERSON, L.E.   A comparison of the performance of kindergarten children in the take-off phase of the standing broad jump. Unpublished Doctoral dissertation, University of Wisconsin, 1958.

HALVERSON, L.E.   Development of motor patterns in young children. *Quest*. VI(1966):44-53.

HALVERSON, L.E., ROBERTON, M.A., LANGENDORFER, S., AND WILLIAMS, K. Longitudinal changes in children's overarm throw ball velocities. *Research Quarterly.* 50(1979):256-264.

HALVERSON, L.E., ROBERTON, M.A., SAFRIT, M.J., AND ROBERTS, T.W. Effects of guided practice on overhand throw ball velocities of kindergarten children. *Research Quarterly.* 48(1977):311-318.

HARPER, C.J., AND STRUMA, N.L. Case studies in the development of one-handed striking. *Research Abstracts.* AAHPER, 1973.

HOTTINGER, W.L. Babyhood: pre and post natal periods. In Corbin, ed., *A Textbook of Motor Development,* Ch. 4. Dubuque, IA: Wm. C. Brown Company, 1973.

HUNSICKER, P., AND REIFF, G.G. (Eds.) *AAHPER Youth Fitness Test Manual.* Washington, D.C.: AAHPER, 1976.

KEOGH, J. Fundamental motor task. Corbin, ed., *A Textbook of Motor Development,* Ch. 10. Dubuque, IA: Wm. C. Brown Company, 1973.

LARSON, R.L. Physical activity and the growth and development of bone and joint structures. In Rarick, ed., *Physical Activity: Human Growth and Development,* Ch. 2. New York: Academic Press, 1973.

LATCHAW, M. Measuring selected motor skills in fourth, fifth, and sixth grades. *Research Quarterly.* 25(1954):439-449.

MALINA, R.M. Ethnic and cultural factors in the development of motor abilities and strength in American children. In Rarick, ed., *Physical Activity: Human Growth and Development,* Ch. 13. New York: Academic Press, 1973.

MALINA, R.M. *Growth and Development.* Minneapolis, MN: Burgess Publishing Co., 1975.

McCLENAGHAN, B.A., AND GALLAHUE, D.L. *Fundamental Movement: A Developmental and Remedial Approach.* Philadelphia, PA: W.B. Saunders Company, 1978.

McGRAW, M.B. *Growth: A Study of Johnny and Jimmy.* Englewood Cliffs, NJ: Prentice-Hall, Inc., 1935.

McGRAW, M.B. *The Neuromuscular Maturation of the Human Infant.* New York: Hafner Press, 1974.

MILNE, C., SEEFELDT, V., AND HAUBENSTRICKER, J. Longitudinal trends in motor performance in children. *Research Abstracts.* AAHPER, 1971.

MILNE, C., SEEFELDT, V., AND REUSCHLEIN, P. Relationship between grade, sex, race, and motor performance in young children. *Research Quarterly.* 47(1976):726-730.

POE, A. Description of the movement characteristics of two-year-old children performing the jump and reach. *Research Quarterly.* 47(1976):260-268.

POE, A. Developmental changes in the movement characteristics of the punt—a case study. Unpublished manuscript, University of Wisconsin.

ROBERTON, M.A. Longitudinal evidence for developmental stages in the forceful overarm throw. *Journal of Human Movement Studies.* 4(1978):167-175.

ROBERTON, M.A. Stability of stage categorizations across trials: implications for the "stage theory" of overarm throw development. Unpublished Doctoral dissertation, University of Wisconsin-Madison, 1975.

ROBERTON, M.A., AND HALVERSON, L.E. The developing child—his changing movement. In Logsdon *et al., Physical Education for Children: A Focus on the Teaching Process.* Philadelphia, PA: Lea and Febiger, 1977.

ROBERTON, M.A., AND LANGENDORFER, S. Testing motor development sequences across 9-14 years. In Nadeau *et al.,* eds., *Psychology of Motor Behavior and Sport,* pp. 269-279. 1980.

SEEFELDT, V.   Developmental sequences in fundamental motor skills. Unpublished manuscript, Michigan State University, 1972.

SEEFELDT, V., REUSCHLEIN, S., AND VOGAL, P.   Sequenced motor skills within the physical education curriculum. Paper presented at the AAHPER National Convention, Houston, Texas, March, 1972.

SEILS, L.G.   The relationship between measures of physical growth and gross motor performance of primary-grade school children. *Research Quarterly.* 22(1951):244-260.

SMITH, S.A.   Longitudinal changes in stride length and stride rate of children running. Unpublished Master's thesis, University of Wisconsin-Madison, 1977.

TEMPLE, I.G.   A test battery for prekindergarten assessment. Unpublished manuscript, Bowling Green State University, 1979.

WELLMAN, R.L.   Motor achievement of preschool children. *Childhood Education.* 13(1937):311-316.

WICKSTROM, R.L.   *Fundamental Motor Patterns,* 2nd edition. Philadelphia, PA: Lea and Febiger, 1977.

WILD, M.R.   The behavior pattern of throwing and some observations concerning its course of development in children. *Research Quarterly.* 9(1938):20-24.

WILLIAMS, H.G.   The perception of moving objects by children. Unpublished paper, University of Toledo, 1967.

WILLIAMS, H.G.   The systematic effects of speed and direction of object trajectory and of age and skill classification upon the perception of moving objects in space. Unpublished dissertation, University of Wisconsin-Madison, 1968.

WILLIAMS, H.G.   Williams process checklist. Unpublished manuscript, University of Toledo, 1973.

WILLIAMS, H.G., AND BREIHAN, S.K.   Motor control tasks for young children. Unpublished manuscript, University of Toledo, 1979.

WILLIAMS, H.G., TEMPLE, I.G., LOGSDON, B.J., SCOTT, S., AND CLEMENT, A.   An investigation of the perceptual-motor development of young children. Unpublished manuscript, Bowling Green State University, 1971.

YARBAS, A.L.   *Eye Movements and Vision.* New York: Plenum Press, 1971.

ZIMMERMAN, H.M.   Characteristic likenesses and differences between skilled and non-skilled performance of the standing broad jump. *Research Quarterly.* 27(1956):353-362.

CHAPTER NINE
BALANCE

Successful performance of motor skills depends in many instances upon the individual's ability to establish and maintain balance. This is especially true for skills that involve intricate body manipulation and projection (e.g., tumbling, agility, etc.). Efficient balance is also integral to performance of skills that involve manipulation and/or projection of an object. For example, the good tennis player always tries to assume a stable position before he executes forehand or backhand drives to ensure that the ball is solidly hit. Tasks that involve pushing, pulling, lifting, or carrying of objects also rely on appropriate use of balance mechanisms. There is little doubt that, for the young child, balance is an integral part of skillful acquisition and performance of many motor tasks.

WHAT IS BALANCE?

Webster's New World Dictionary (1970) defines balance as "bodily equilibrium or stability." Equilibrium is defined as ". . . equality between opposing forces" and stability as "the state or quality of being . . . fixed; steadiness" (Webster, 1970). Similar definitions can be found in textbooks that deal with motor learning and performance, biomechanics, or kinesiology (e.g., Broer and Zernicke, 1979; Cooper and Glassow, 1976; Singer, 1975; Wells and Lutgens, 1976). According to a variety of sources, the terms "balance," "equilibrium," and "stability" may be used interchangeably. Balance, as a state or condition, is achieved through maintaining a specified relationship between the center of gravity of the body and its supporting base. Thus although we may typically think of balance primarily as that activity involved in maintaining an upright, standing position with the feet as the base of support and the center of gravity in the pelvic region, the body can be balanced in many different positions with many different body parts serving as the base of support. Factors that contribute to a state of balance include both external and internal forces that act on the body itself. External forces include gravity, friction, or perhaps another person; internal forces are primarily muscle contractions that act to oppose those forces acting outside the body. "Balance" may therefore be described as a state or condition in which opposing forces are equalized.

Components of Balance

Balance may also be described in terms of the nature of the characteristics or components involved in the balance task itself. Bass' early study (1939) to develop reliable measures of balance indicated that at least two major characteristics of balance tasks exist: *static* and *dynamic*. Static balance tasks require the maintenance of a single position of the body, whereas dynamic balance requires the maintenance of equilibrium while the body is in motion (e.g., the body position is constantly changing). A factor analysis of performance on a large number of balance tasks indicated that nine factors were involved in performance of balance tasks. The names and composition of the factors are not as important as the resulting implication that: (a) static and dynamic balance tasks are different, unrelated forms of balance; (b) balance tasks performed with vision are unrelated to balance tasks performed without vision; and (c) rotation tests measure still a different component or aspect of balance.

Fleishman's studies of the structure of physical fitness (1961, 1963) identified two balance factors: a "gross body equilibrium" factor (that included eyes closed and stick balances) and a "balance with visual cues" factor. Cumbee (1954, 1957) studied the structure of "motor coordination" through factor analysis and isolated two balance factors: "balancing objects" and "total body balance." Her data suggest that balancing of objects is unrelated to balancing the body, *per se*. Ismail and Cowell (1961) identified two balance factors in their study of "motor aptitude" in young boys. The two balance factors identified were "body balance on objects" and "body balance on the floor." Wyrick (1969) also found significant differences between balance on a one inch high beam and balance on a beam four feet above the floor.

Further evidence of the importance of the nature of the task in defining balance ability is provided by Heeschen (1962) and Drowatzky and Zuccato (1967). Heeschen (1962) administered two beam-walking tests, a stabilometer test, and a measure of static balance (Bass stick test) to college-age males and females. Drowatzky and Zuccato (1967) studied a variety of balance performances of junior high school girls. Tasks included stork stand, diver's stand, stick balance, balance beam walk, sideward leap, and Bass' stepping stone test. Both studies report little or no correlation among performances on any of the balance tasks used.

Katzan (1974) has summarized available behavioral research on balance and identified six major components involved in the performance of the majority of balance tasks. They are:

1. *Elevation:* Is the performer asked to balance on the floor or on an object?
2. *Vision:* Is the performer asked to balance with eyes open or eyes closed?
3. *Stability:* Is the performer asked to balance on a stationary or moving object?
4. *Number of Limbs:* Is the performer asked to balance on one or two feet or multiple body parts?
5. *Body Position:* Is the performer asked to balance in an upright or a bent position?
6. *Kind of Locomotion:* Is the performer asked to maintain balance walking, jumping, hopping?

According to Katzan (1974), evidence strongly indicates that rather than being a single, unitary ability, balance is better defined as a set of specific characteristics or components that describe the task to be performed.

Most studies have used adults as subjects (Bass, 1939; Cumbee, 1954; Fleishman, 1961, 1963; Heeschen, 1962; Wyrick, 1969); two studies have used junior high school age subjects (Drowatzky and Zuccato, 1967; Ismail and Cowell, 1961). DeOreo and Wade (1971) found evidence to suggest that balance performances of preschool children were affected by the static and/or dynamic characteristics of the task. Children's performances were quite different when they were asked to balance on a stabilometer (static) rather than to walk across a balance beam (dynamic). The relationship between the two performances was r = .18. The investigators concluded that different balancing abilities were measured by or involved in the two tasks. Lauro (1969) used six- and eight-year-old children and found that the static and/or dynamic task effect in balance found for preschool children did not hold true for older children. In this case children's performances on the static balance tasks (one foot balances) and dynamic balance tasks (jump and turn) were highly correlated. The question of the effect cf task characteristics on balance performances in the young child is far from clearly understood.

Mechanisms of Balance

Regardless of how balance ability is defined or described, it is clear that balance ability involves the successful integration of a number of anatomical and neurophysiological systems. Behaviorally, balance is largely a matter of the proper relationship between the center of gravity of the body and its supporting base; neurophysiologically, it requires complex interactions among vestibular, proprioceptive, visual, and motor systems. Efficient functioning of all these systems is prerequisite to the individual's ability to judge when or if the body is balanced; and if it is not, what adjustments need to be made to obtain and/or maintain balance; and if adjustments are needed, how to carry them out.

The vestibular system includes a number of complex structures located at different levels of the nervous system, all of which provide input for and/or control over sensory and motor information important to balance activities. The vestibular system is particularly sensitive to the position of the head in space. Thus if the performer's head is in any position other than the upright (e.g., tilted, inverted, etc.), the vestibular system signals appropriate brain centers that the position of the head in space has deviated from the vertical. The vestibular system is also sensitive to changes in the speed (acceleration and deceleration) and direction of both head and total body movement. Information is also provided by the vestibular apparatus to the central nervous system to allow for the planning of balance adjustments even before loss of equilibrium due to movement occurs.

The proprioceptive systems carry information derived from stimulation of receptors in muscles, tendons, and joints of the body as it is moved into and out of a balanced position. Proprioceptors in the joints contribute to perception of joint angles (static position of various body parts) and to perception of movement around the joint (changes in position of different body parts). Proprioceptors in the muscles (muscle spindle) and tendons (Golgi tendon organ), both of which respond to stretch of the muscle, are most involved in the subcortical reflex activity necessary for assumption and effective maintenance of posture. For example, there is a tendency for the center of gravity to shift to and fro within the base of support when a person stands upright (postural sway). This results from the alternating reflex contraction of posterior and anterior leg muscles in response to the pull of gravity. As the body sways backward, the anterior muscle groups are stretched and reflexly contract to bring the center of gravity back into proper relationship with the base of support. As the body sways forward, the posterior muscles are stretched and reflexly contract to prevent the center of gravity from going too far forward. These alternating contractions help to maintain the center of gravity over the base of support and are subcortically controlled.

The role of the visual system in balance is not totally clear. There is growing evidence that visual information may be as important, if not more so, than information provided by proprioceptive and/or vestibular systems (Lee and Aronson, 1974; Lee and Lishman, 1975a, 1975b; Lishman and Lee, 1973) in efficient balance performance. Vision provides an objective source of information that the individual can use to judge his position, orientation, and/or movement in space. Objects and/or markings in the environment offer a means by which the performer can "line up" his body in relation to external verticals or horizontals; it also permits him to verify the accuracy of judged bodily position and/or movement as represented through other senses. The extent to which an individual depends on or uses vision to achieve and maintain balance is not well defined. Studies by Witkin and his associates (1948a, 1948b, 1950, 1952) suggest that some people rely quite heavily on visual information to make judgments concerning the upright position of the body; others seem to judge variations in the upright position of the body quite accurately without visual information. More often than not, balance with vision is more efficient and/or skillful than balance without vision.

The function of anatomical and neurophysiological systems in balance is far more complex than indicated here. It is important to recognize, however, that balance ability develops (i.e., changes or improves) concomitantly with accompanying changes in the underlying anatomical and neurophysiological systems of the child. Thus as skeletal proportions, amount of muscle mass, etc. change, the nature of the demands of balance tasks and the ability of the child to cope with them also change. As the nervous system grows in functional complexity, the task of processing information needed for establishing and maintaining balance under a wide variety of different conditions is more rapid and efficient. This no doubt contributes to improvement in balance performance *per se*. The reverse may also be true; deterioration in underlying anatomical and physiological systems may contribute to deficits in balance performance.

AGE AND SEX DIFFERENCES IN BALANCE

Evidence of improved balance performance with age (preschool to at least adolescence) is abundant. Although the precise nature of age differences in balance ability is not totally clear, available data strongly suggest that some important age differences do exist. A summary of some of the major studies of balance development is given in Table 9-1.

Studies reported in Table 9-1 indicate that, in general, balance performances improve with increasing age from 3 to 19 years. Age-related changes in balance performances are more gradual for some tasks than others. Where change is gradual, year to year performance differences are usually small and insignificant (Bachman, 1971; Keogh, 1965). Some studies show significant year to year changes in balance performance (DeOreo, 1975; DeOreo and Wade, 1971; Seils, 1951), whereas others using similar tasks show no such change. Winterhalter (1974) reported significant age differences on 16 different balance tasks when performances of six-, eight-,

TABLE 9-1 Summary of Age and Sex Differences in Balance Performance

INVESTIGATOR	NUMBER AND SEX OF CHILDREN	AGE OF CHILDREN	BALANCE TASKS	AGE DIFFERENCES	SEX DIFFERENCES
DeOreo and Wade (1971)	150 boys and girls	3-, 4-, 5-year-olds	Beam (4", 3", 2") Walk forward distance speed Walk backward distance speed Kneel-stand Stoop turn Stabilometer time errors	Gradual improvement with age; no significant year-to-year differences Gradual improvement with age; no year-to-year differences	No differences Girls generally better
DeOreo (1975)	150 boys and girls	3-, 4-, 5-year-olds	Beam (4", 3", 2") Walk forward distance time Walk backward distance time	Significant year-to-year improvement in distance and time	Boys walk backward farther on 3" beam than girls
Keogh (1965)	boys and girls	5- to 11-year-olds	50' hop Mat hop pattern Static balance on beam Beam walk	Year-to-year age differences not significant; gradual improvement across ages	Did not analyze

Study	Sample	Age/Grade	Task	Age findings	Sex findings
Lauro (1967)	266 boys and girls	6- to 8-year-olds	Beam stand (1½") right foot	Age differences significant (white girls and boys improved)	Not clear
			left foot	Age differences significant (white girls and black boys and girls improved)	
			Jump turn	Gradual improvement with age; age differences not significant	
Seils (1951)	510 boys and girls	Grades 1, 2, 3	Stick balance lengthwise	Age differences significant	Did not analyze
Winterhalter (1974)	90 boys and girls	Grades 1, 3, 5	Static balance	Age differences significant	
			Left leg: eyes open		No difference
			Right leg: eyes open		Girls better
			Preferred leg: eyes closed		Girls better
			Cross stick		No difference
			Lengthwise stick		Girls better
			Standing: body bent eyes open		No difference
			eyes closed		No difference
			Dynabalometer eyes open		Girls better
			eyes closed		No difference
			Dynamic balance Beam walk: eyes open time	Improvement with grade	First grade girls better
			errors	Improvement with grade	No difference

TABLE 9-1 continued

INVESTIGATOR	NUMBER AND SEX OF CHILDREN	AGE OF CHILDREN	BALANCE TASKS	AGE DIFFERENCES	SEX DIFFERENCES
			Beam walk: eyes closed		
			time	Improvement with grade	First grade girls better
			errors	Grades 3 and 5 better than 1	No difference
			Beam kneel		
			time	Improvement with grade	No difference
			errors	Grades 3 and 5 better than 1	No difference
			Hopping pattern		
			time	Improvement with grade	No difference
			errors	Grades 3 and 5 better than 1	No difference
			50' hop	Improvement with grade	No difference
			20' hop	Improvement with grade	No difference
			Seashore beam walk	Grades 3 and 5 better than 1	No difference
Bachman (1961)	320 males and females	6- to 26-year-olds	Stabilometer	Decline from 7–17 yrs; improvement from 17–19 yrs.; females declined after 19	No difference at younger age; at older ages females better
			Ladder climb	Improvement from ages 7–15	Males better
Espenschade (1947)	610 boys and girls	10- to 16-year-olds	Brace tests of motor coordination	Little change for girls; "adolescent lag" for boys	No difference for 10- to 13-year-olds; 14- to 16-year-old boys better
Espenschade, Dable, Schoendube (1953)	287 boys	Adolescent	Beam walking	Improvement except ages 13-15 yrs.	

and ten-year-old children were compared. Performance on all tasks but one improved significantly at each increasing age level. Thus although the specific nature of age-related changes in balance performance is unclear, there is strong evidence of improvement with increasing age.

Although most investigators have found that balancing abilities improve with age, Bachman (1961) reported a decline in stabilometer performance from ages 7 to 17. Espenschade (1947) and Espenschade, Dable, and Schoendube (1953) also observed periods in growth when little or no improvement (and often a decline) in balance performance occurred.

When balance performance is looked at across a wide range of ages and tasks, there is little or no difference between boys and girls in balance performance. If the nature of the task is considered, however, there is a tendency for girls to demonstrate better performance than boys on static balance tasks such as the stabilometer (Bachman, 1961; DeOreo and Wade, 1971; Winterhalter, 1974). Comprehensive longitudinal studies detailing the nature of balance development from a behavioral point of view are needed.

Particular attention needs to be given to two studies conducted by DeOreo (1974, 1975), who studied the process or method that young children (3 to 5 years of age) used in walking or balancing on beams of different widths. Children were asked to walk forward and backward, to kneel down and rise to a standing position, and to perform a stoop turn on beams of different widths. Two distinct patterns of beam walking were identified for these children: shuffle step–mark time and alternate step pattern. More five-year-olds used the alternate step pattern (a more mature method) than did three- or four-year-olds. Most younger children used the shuffle step–mark time method (less mature) for walking the beam. Although some variations in the use of this less mature pattern of beam walking were observed, none of them appeared frequently enough to suggest that there might be an additional stage in performance of this balance task. It should be noted that a sizeable proportion of three-year-old children (about 27%) were unable to perform the beam walking tasks at all. As the beam width decreased, the difficulty of the task increased, and less mature patterns of beam-walking were used by children of all ages. These observations suggest that the development of dynamic balance (e.g., beam walking) may begin with the child shuffling his feet along a relatively wide base (4-inch beam). This stage of development is followed by one in which the child uses an alternating step pattern on a beam the same width. Subsequent stages of development involve increasing the distance and speed of walking and/or progressing to narrower beam widths.

A developmental trend in the process or method used by the child to perform the knee-stand and stoop-turn tasks was also evident. Stages for those tasks were characterized largely by the degree to which the hands were used for support and included the following: (a) hands used on both descent and ascent; (b) hands used on *either* ascent or descent but *not both;* and (c) no hand support involved. A large number of children at each age (three-, four-, and five-years-old) were not able to perform either the knee-stand or the stoop-turn.

BALANCE AND OTHER DEVELOPMENTAL AND/OR LEARNING PROCESSES

A few studies have investigated the relationship between balance and various dimensions of perceptual-motor development, performance of sport skills, and cognitive learning or intelligence.

Perceptual-Motor Development

Experts in child growth and development universally agree that balance is an important aspect of perceptual-motor development. Thus most perceptual-motor training programs, as well as batteries designed to assess perceptual-motor development in children, have emphasized the use of balance activities (e.g., Frostig, 1970; Getman, 1962; Roach and Kephart, 1966; Williams, 1973). To investigate the nature of the relationship between balance and other dimensions of perceptual-motor development, DeOreo (1976) administered a series of tasks to a group of five-year-old boys and girls. The tests included Levels I and II of the Cratty-Martin Gross-Motor Test, a modification of the Purdue Perceptual-Motor Survey, the Frostig Developmental Test of Visual Perception, eight measures of dynamic balance (balance beam), and a stabilometer test of static balance. DeOreo (1976) reported that relationships among measures of balance and other measures of perceptual-motor development were essentially nonexistent. In fact balance items tended to group together on three factors that were separate from factors on which other tests loaded. Fugate (1974) reported similar results in that she found no significant relationship between stabilometer performance and various items on the Purdue Perceptual-Motor Survey. Although such results suggest that balance, *per se,* is not related at a behavioral level to perceptual-motor development, they do not in any way suggest that efficient functioning of balance mechanisms is not an important underlying dimension of perceptual-motor development. It is of course frequently observed that children with perceptual-motor deficits exhibit difficulties with and/or delays in the performance of balance tasks.

Sport and Dance

Theoretically it has been assumed that balance is an important contributor to efficient performance of a variety of sport and dance activities. However behavioral studies that have attempted to investigate the nature of this contribution have reported conflicting results. Pankonin (1966) found balance to be among an important group of predictors of tennis ability, whereas Malmisur (1966) found no significant relationship between dynamic balance performance and tennis ability, as indicated by membership on the Junior Davis Cup team. Haas (1966) reported no significant relationship between balance and bowling performance, whereas Greenlee (1958) found balance to be significantly related to bowling performance. In addition Greene (1962) found no relationship between static balance and badminton skill, but Mumby (1953) reported a significant relationship between balance and wrestling skill and Gross and Thompson (1957) reported a similar relationship between dynamic balance and swimming speed.

Cheney (1965) measured static and dynamic balance of persons described as advanced performers in dance, gymnastics, and sports. Gymnasts and dancers were significantly better than sports performers on both static and dynamic balance tasks; dancers were better than gymnasts on one measure of static balance. Singer (1970) compared stabilometer performances of different groups of college male athletes (participants in basketball, baseball, football, gymnastics, wrestling, and water skiing) and nonathletes. All groups of athletes performed significantly better than nonathletes on the balance task. Of the athlete groups, water skiers had the best balance performances, whereas gymnasts had the second best performances. Other athlete groups were not significantly different from each other in balance performance.

Most studies of balance have used adults (college students) as subjects. Empirical evidence about the significance of balance *per se* to the development or acquisition of motor skills in young children is sparse, if not nonexistent. In fact there are no studies available, to the knowledge of the author, that look at the relationship of balance to acquisition of sport and/or other movement-related skills in children.

Intellectual and/or Cognitive Development

Some mention should be made of studies that have looked at the relationship between balance and intelligence or cognitive development. In general, results of such studies are conflicting. Only a brief sampling of such studies will be given here. Fox (1968) administered 14 balance tests to second- and third-grade boys and girls and found strong relationships among balance items and reading achievement. Zuccato (1966) found a relationship between measures of static and dynamic balance and both mental age and achievement scores of seventh-grade girls. On the other hand Owen (1965) found no significant relationship between "mental maturity" and performance on a dynabalometer task for sixth-grade boys and girls. Goetzinger (1961) found no significant relationship between similar performances of boys and girls ages 8 to 16 years.

The question that must be asked about these conflicting results is how meaningful would such relationships be even if they were consistently reported in the literature? It is possible that development of balance ability and cognitive behaviors in young children are totally unrelated, and that the tenuous relationship reported in some literature may at best represent their possible mutual dependence upon a common underlying set of central nervous system mechanisms. If this is the case, it is unlikely that, at a behavioral level, significant relationships between balance and cognitive development are ever likely to be forthcoming.

EFFECTS OF PRACTICE

Does balance develop solely via maturation or can appropriate experiences be provided that will enhance the development of balance performances in the young child? There is considerable evidence that balance can be improved through practice. Cotten and Lowe (1974), for instance, showed that college males who practiced one minute on each of six static balance tasks for four days showed a significant improvement on three of the six tasks practiced. Improvement was shown on the stork stand and the two-foot-crosswise and one-foot-lengthwise stick balances. No significant change was seen in teeterboard performances or on one-foot-crosswise or two-foot-lengthwise stick balances. Why practice had a positive effect on some balance performances and not others is unclear. Gregory (1974) had groups of third-graders practice balance on a stabilometer under various feedback conditions (tactile and auditory) for three consecutive days. A significant improvement in performance over the three days was evident in all conditions.

Bachman (1961) looked at the effects of practice, that is, changes in performance over ten trials, on stabilometer and ladder-climb tasks. Results indicated that learning did occur over the ten trials for both tasks. The general shape of the learning curves was negatively accelerated; there was a period of rapid change initially that was followed by smaller and smaller changes in performance as practice continued. Learning curves were similar for all ages and for both sexes.

Additional evidence of the effect of practice on balance performance is provided by studies using children (with identifiable developmental lags) enrolled in training programs. Bordas (1971) used two methods of teaching developmental movement and balance to third- and fourth-grade children. Development of balance skills was stressed for all youngsters in the program. The program involved three 30-minute sessions per week for five weeks. At the end of the five weeks balance was remeasured using a stabilometer. Results indicated that both groups of children improved significantly in balance performance. Interestingly, both methods were equally effective in bringing about this change.

Reeve (1976) reported results of a special program designed to improve balance performance in four- and five-year-old "slow learners." This special program, which consisted of one 15-20 minute session per week, was in addition to the regular physical education program. A second comparable group of children (control group) participated only in the regular physical education program. The results showed that at the end of eight weeks, both groups of children improved in dynamic balance as well as in a total overall measure of balance. Children in the special program were significantly better in overall balance performance than the other children. In addition, children in the special program improved significantly in static balance whereas other children did not. These results suggest that practice or experience with balance tasks can and does enhance balance performance.

A THEORETICAL MODEL OF
THE DEVELOPMENT OF
BALANCING ABILITIES

All of the physiological systems associated with balance (i.e., the skeletal, muscular, sensory, and motor systems), although not fully developed, are functional at birth. As the child grows, he begins to interact with the environment and consequently undergoes a variety of experiences. Simultaneously the physiological systems of the child develop and information processing capacities are refined and expanded. As processing of sensory information becomes more efficient, balance-related responses become more effective, and the child gains greater control over his motor behavior.

Perhaps the most meaningful way to describe the *development* of balance is to focus on the relationship between different balance tasks and the demands that they place upon the systems that underlie or support the maintenance of balance. Katzan (1974) suggests that balance tasks and the level of difficulty associated with them can be analyzed by looking at the number and nature of task characteristics. Task characteristics might include body movement, stability of base of support (stable-unstable), use of vision (vision-no vision), body position, body elevation, number of support limbs, and nature of support surface (stationary-moving). The suggested relationship of some common balance task characteristics to underlying physiological systems is shown in Table 9-2. The identification of such characteristics and their relationship to underlying balance systems does not imply that the three systems operate independently of each other or that any given task relies solely upon one system. Rather, it suggests that variations in the type of task to be performed may change the demands placed upon each or all of the systems involved. For example, a simple static balance task may place less demand on the vestibular than the proprioceptive system; i.e., only information relative to head position has to be processed by the vestibular system. A dynamic balance task

TABLE 9-2   Elements of Balance Tasks and Their Relationship to Underlying Physiological Systems

TASK CHARACTERISTICS	MAJOR UNDERLYING PHYSIOLOGICAL SYSTEM(S) INVOLVED
Body Movement (static vs. dynamic)	Proprioceptive and Vestibular Systems
Base of Support (e.g., stable vs. unstable)	Proprioceptive and Vestibular Systems
Use of Vision (e.g., vision vs. no vision)	Visual System
Body Position (e.g., upright vs. bent vs. inverted)	Vestibular System
Elevation (e.g., balance on floor vs. balance on something)	Proprioceptive and Vestibular Systems
Number of Support Limbs (e.g., one foot vs. two feet)	Proprioceptive System
Support Surface (e.g., whole foot vs. knee)	Proprioceptive System

in which the body and thus the head are in motion, however, places greater demands on the vestibular system, because information relative to changes in speed and direction of the body needs to be processed for successful adaptation to that situation. Additional demands are also placed on the proprioceptive and visual systems, as changes in visual and proprioceptive information must also be processed if the task is to be performed successfully. When vision is occluded, removing that source of information concerning orientation in space, demands placed on the vestibular and proprioceptive systems become greater.

As task difficulty increases (greater demands placed on different systems), developmental changes in balance performance may be observed. An example of a proposed model of balance development is presented in Table 9-3. The simplest level of balance development (Level I), and therefore the balancing ability that develops first, involves the maintenance of a stationary position of the body (static) on a large base of support (stable) with the eyes open. The most familiar example of this level of balance development is standing on both feet (wide-spread apart) on the floor with the eyes open. Balancing at this level is largely reflexive in nature and, given adequate strength of the postural muscles, the young child can perform the task easily. At Level II are tasks such as walking, running, standing (two feet) with eyes closed, and standing on one foot with eyes open. The walk and run represent a move toward a variation in demands placed on the proprioceptive and vestibular systems, but are similar to Level I tasks in that they maintain a stable visual framework in which to guide this

TABLE 9-3   Theoretical Model of Balance Abilities

LEVEL		EXAMPLE OF BALANCE TASKS	CHARACTERISTICS	NATURE OF UNDERLYING PROPRIOCEPTIVE/VESTIBULAR AND VISUAL PATTERNS
I		Sit, stand	Static position Stable base Vision used	Proprioceptive/vestibular pattern established in visual framework.
II	A	Walk, run	Dynamic position Stable base Vision used	Visual framework maintained; established proprioceptive/vestibular pattern varied.
	B	Two-foot stand: eyes closed	Static position Stable base No vision	Established proprioceptive/vestibular pattern maintained; visual framework removed.
	C	One-foot stand: eyes open	Static position Unstable base No vision	Visual framework maintained; established proprioceptive/vestibular pattern varied.
III	A	Beam walk	Dynamic position Unstable base Vision used	Building on II-A: Visual framework maintained; proprioceptive/vestibular pattern of II-A varied.
	B	One-foot stand: eyes closed	Static position Unstable base No vision	Builds on II-C: Proprioceptive/vestibular patterns of II-A maintained; visual framework removed.
IV		Beam walk: eyes closed	Dynamic position Unstable base No vision	Builds on III-A: Proprioceptive/vestibular pattern of III-A maintained; visual framework removed.

variation in vestibular/proprioceptive information processing. Standing on two feet with eyes closed reflects the use of a previously experienced or established pattern of vestibular/proprioceptive stimuli, this time without the aid of visual input. Standing on one foot with eyes open represents a further, greater demand on information processing in the vestibular and proprioceptive systems (less stable base of support).

Tasks found at Level III include the balance-beam walk and the one-foot stand, eyes closed. These tasks represent a variation in demands placed on proprioceptive/vestibular patterns experienced or established at Level II. The former task maintains a similar visual framework as in walking, but varies the way in which the established proprioceptive/vestibular pattern may need to be used. The latter task maintains a proprioceptive/vestibular pattern identical to that involved in the one-foot stand, eyes open, but varies the visual framework in which it is performed. At Level IV the exemplary task is that of the balance beam walk with the eyes closed. This task builds on Level III in that it takes a variation in an established proprioceptive/vestibular pattern and removes the visual framework in which it is ordinarily performed.

The discussion of this model hints that balance development may proceed by first establishing a static proprioceptive/vestibular pattern in a stable position with a guiding or supporting visual framework. This basic balance pattern may then be varied in two ways: removing the visual framework or altering the way that the actual proprioceptive/vestibular pattern is used in balancing. The next level or stage of balance development then involves taking the altered pattern of proprioceptive/vestibular functioning and either removing the visual framework in which it is performed or adding a new variation in the proprioceptive/vestibular pattern itself. This reciprocal interweaving seems to continue as balance development proceeds to higher and higher levels and to more and more complex kinds of tasks. As with the development of any specific motor abilities or characteristics, development of one level need not be completed before development of the next level begins. That is, a high level of proficiency need not be demonstrated on Level II tasks and their variations before Level III tasks begin to appear at least at a minimal level of proficiency.

As may be noted, the elements of "body position," "elevation," "number of support limbs," and "support surface" (included in Table 9-3) were not included in The Theoretic Model of Balance Abilities. Any of these elements may serve as the basis for variations of the established proprioceptive/vestibular pattern at Levels II, III, and/or IV. Specifically these elements are closely associated with "stability," i.e., whether the base of support is stable or unstable. It should also be noted that only a small sample of balance tasks is addressed in direct fashion in the model. Other variations that need to be included in any comprehensive model of balance development are directional and speed/acceleration characteristics of dynamic tasks. The model of balance development presented here is only in its early theoretical stages and must await substantial research to determine its validity. The model is, however, based on logic, is consistent with theories associated with other aspects of motor development, and is supported by available (although limited) research in the area of balance.

SUMMARY

1. Successful performance of motor skills depends in many instances upon the individual's ability to establish and maintain balance. Balance may be described as a state or condition in which opposing forces

acting upon the body are equalized. Balance is achieved through maintaining a specified relationship between the center of gravity of the body and its base of support.

2. Evidence strongly indicates that balance may best be described in terms of the nature of the characteristics or components involved in the performance of balance tasks themselves.

3. There appear to be six major components involved in the performance of most balance tasks: elevation, vision, stability, number of limbs used, body position, and kind of locomotion involved.

4. Balance requires complex interactions among underlying neuro-physiological systems and seems to develop concomitantly with changes in these systems.

5. At a behavioral level, balance seems to improve from preschool through adolescent years. Age differences are significant for some tasks but not for others.

6. When balance performance is looked at across a wide range of ages and tasks, there are few if any differences between boys and girls. There is, however, some tendency for girls to be slightly better than boys on static balance tasks.

7. Young children seem to follow an identifiable pattern of development when acquiring dynamic balance skills (e.g., learning to walk on balance beams). This development begins with the child shuffling his feet along a relatively wide base (e.g., a 4-inch beam). This is followed by a state in which the child uses an alternating step pattern on a beam the same width. Subsequent stages of dynamic balance development involve increasing the distance and speed of walking and moving on narrower beam widths.

8. In kneeling on a balance beam, children tend initially to use the hands in both lowering and raising the body; they later use the hands in *either* lowering or raising the body but not both. When the skill of kneeling is mature, no hand support is involved.

9. Overall balance development in young children proceeds by first establishing a static proprioceptive/vestibular pattern of functioning in a stable position with a guiding or supporting visual framework. This basic pattern of balance may then be varied in two ways: by removing the visual framework (e.g., eyes are closed) or by altering the way that the actual proprioceptive/vestibular pattern is used in balancing (e.g., the body is bent or inverted instead of upright).

10. The next level of balance development involves taking this altered pattern of proprioceptive/vestibular functioning and either removing the visual framework in which it is performed or adding a new variation in the proprioceptive/vestibular pattern itself. This kind of re-

ciprocal interweaving effect seems to continue as balance development proceeds to higher and higher levels and to more and more complex tasks.

STUDY QUESTIONS

1. Define the term balance.
2. List and describe the major components or characteristics of balance tasks. What significance do such characteristics have for defining or describing balance abilities?
3. Briefly discuss the role of the following systems in balance performance: the vestibular system, the proprioceptive systems, the visual system.
4. Describe important age and sex differences in balance performance. Be specific.
5. Describe basic developmental trends in balance beam walking.
6. How is balance related to perceptual-motor development? Cite specific evidence.
7. What role does balance play in dance and sports performance?
8. What, if any, is the relationship between balance development and intellectual or cognitive functioning?
9. What is the effect of training or practice on balance development?
10. Critically analyze and describe the proposed theoretical model of the development of balancing abilities.
11. What implications does this proposed model have for motor skill development in young children?

REFERENCES

BACHMAN, J.C.   Motor learning and performance as related to age and sex in two measures of balance coordination. *Research Quarterly.* 32(1961):123-137.

BASS, R.I.   An analysis of the components of tests of semicircular canal function and of static and dynamic balance. *Research Quarterly.* 10(1939):33-52.

BORDAS, E.   The effects of two methods of teaching developmental movement on balance of third and fourth grade children. Unpublished Master's thesis, Springfield College, 1971.

BROER, M.R., AND ZERNICKE, R.F.   *Efficiency of Human Movement,* 4th edition. Philadelphia, PA: W.B. Saunders Company, 1979.

CHENEY, M.K.   A comparison of three groups of skilled performers on a battery of selected tests of balance. Unpublished Master's thesis, State University of Iowa, 1965.

COOPER, J.M., AND GLASSOW, R.B.   *Kinesiology,* 4th edition. St. Louis, MO: C.V. Mosby, 1976.

COTTEN, D.J., AND LOWE, S.   Interrelationships among balance tests prior to and after practice. *Perceptual and Motor Skills.* 39(1974):629-630.

CUMBEE, F.Z.   Analysis of motor coordination. *Research Quarterly.* 25(1954):412-420.

CUMBEE, F.Z., MEYER, M., and PETERSON, G.   Factorial analysis of motor coordination variables for third and fourth grade girls. *Research Quarterly.* 28(1957):100-108.

DEOREO, K.D.   The performance and development of fundamental motor skills in preschool children. In Wade and Martens, eds., *Psychology of Motor Behavior and Sport,* pp. 327–343. Urbana, IL: Human Kinetics Publishers, 1974.

DEOREO, K.D.   Dynamic balance in preschool children: process and product. In Landers, ed., *Psychology of Sport and Motor Behavior II,* pp. 575-584. Proceedings of NASPSPA, Pennsylvania State University, 1975.

DEOREO, K.D.   The relationship between measures of balance and perceptual-motor development in five year old children. Unpublished manuscript, Kent State University, 1976.

DEOREO, K.D., AND WADE, M.G.   Dynamic and static balancing ability of preschool children. *Journal of Motor Behavior.* 3(1971):326-335.

DROWATZKY, J.N., AND ZUCCATO, F.C.   Interrelationship between static and dynamic balance. *Research Quarterly.* 38(1967):509-510.

ESPENSCHADE, A.   Development of motor coordination in boys and girls. *Research Quarterly.* 18(1947):30-44.

ESPENSCHADE, A., DABLE, R.R., AND SCHOENDUBE, R.   Dynamic balance in adolescent boys. *Research Quarterly.* 24(1953):270-274.

FLEISHMAN, E.   The dimensions of physical fitness—a factor analysis of speed, flexibility, balance and coordination tests. Office of Naval Research, 609(32), Technical Report Number 3, Yale University, 1961.

FLEISHMAN, E.   Factor analyses of physical fitness tests. *Journal of Educational and Psychological Measurement.* 23(1963):647-661.

FOX, K.   A study of the relationship between balancing and reading achievement in children. Unpublished Ph.D. dissertation, University of Southern California, 1968.

FROSTIG, M., AND MASLOW, P.   *Movement Education: Theory and Practice.* Chicago, IL: Follett Educational Corporation, 1970.

FUGATE, J.R.   The relationship between a dynamic balance test and perceptual-motor development. Unpublished Master's thesis, Texas Tech University, 1974.

GETMAN, G.N.   *How To Develop Your Child's Intelligence.* Luverne, MN: Author, 1962.

GOETZINGER, P.   A re-evaluation of the Heath Rail-Walking Test. *Journal of Educational Research.* 54(1961):187-191.

GREENE, V.D.   Static balance as a factor in badminton playing ability. Unpublished Master's thesis, University of California at Los Angeles, 1962.

GREENLEE, G.   The relationship of selected measures of strength, balance and kinesthesis and bowling performance. Unpublished Master's thesis, State University of Iowa, 1958.

GREGORY, C.A.   The effect of feedback variations on the acquisition of a novel motor balance skill. Unpublished Master's thesis, Springfield College, 1974.

GROSS, E.A., AND THOMPSON, H.L.   Relationship of dynamic balance to speed and to ability in swimming. *Research Quarterly.* 28(1957):342-346.

HAAS, M.A.   The relationship of kinesthetic acuity to bowling performance for beginners. Unpublished Ph.D. dissertation, State University of Iowa, 1966.

HEESCHEN, R.E.   A comparison of the balanciometer to the Illinois Progressive Balance Beam Test, the Bass Stick Test, and the Springfield Beam-Walking Test. Unpublished Master's thesis, Florida State University, 1962.

ISMAIL, A.H., AND COWELL, C.C.   Factor analysis of motor aptitude of preadolescent boys. *Research Quarterly.* 32(1961):507-513.

KATZAN, M.A.   Generality vs. specificity in the balancing ability of elementary school children. Unpublished Master's thesis, The University of Toledo, 1974.

KEOGH, J.   Motor performance of elementary school children. Unpublished manuscript, University of California at Los Angeles, 1965.

LAURO, G.   Motor performance in primary grade children. Unpublished Master's thesis, University of California at Berkeley, 1967.

LEE, D.N., AND ARONSON, E.   Visual proprioceptive control of standing in human infants. *Perception & Psychophysics.* 15(1974):529-532.

LEE, D.N., AND LISHMAN, J.R.   Visual proprioceptive control of stance. *Journal of Human Movement Studies.* 1(1975):87-95.

LEE, D.N., AND LISHMAN, J.R.   Vision in movement and balance. *New Scientist.* 9(1975):59-61.

KATZAN, M.A.   Generality vs. specificity in the balancing ability of elementary school children. Unpublished Master's thesis, The University of Toledo, 1974.

KEOGH, J.   Motor performance of elementary school children. Unpublished manuscript, University of California at Los Angeles, 1965.

LAURO, G.   Motor performance in primary grade children. Unpublished Master's thesis, University of California at Berkeley, 1967.

LEE, D.N., AND ARONSON, E.   Visual proprioceptive control of standing in human infants. *Perception & Psychophysics.* 15(1974):529-532.

LEE, D.N., AND LISHMAN, J.R.   Visual proprioceptive control of stance. *Journal of Human Movement Studies.* 1(1975):87-95.

LEE, D.N., AND LISHMAN, J.R.   Vision in movement and balance. *New Scientist.* 9(1975):59-61.

LISHMAN, J.R., AND LEE, D.N.   The autonomy of visual kinesthesis. *Perception.* 2(1973):287-294.

MALMISUR, M.   Selected physical characteristics of Junior Davis Cup Players and their relation to success in tennis. Unpublished Ph.D. dissertation, Ohio State University, 1966.

MUMBY, H.H.   Kinesthetic acuity and balance related to wrestling ability. *Research Quarterly.* 24(1953):327-334.

OWEN, J.   Intelligence and its relationship to dynamic balance. Unpublished Master's thesis, Southwest Missouri State College, 1965.

PANKONIN, J.   A study of the relationship of selected measures to tennis ability. Unpublished Master's thesis, University of North Carolina, 1966.

REEVE, E.J.   The effect of the Dayton Sensorimotor Training Activities Program on the balance of children in a developmental kindergarten. Unpublished Master's thesis, Pennsylvania State University, 1976.

ROACH, E.G., AND KEPHART, N.C.   *The Purdue Perceptual-Motor Survey.* Columbus OH: Chas. E. Merrill Co., 1966.

SEILS, L.G.   The relationship between measures of physical growth and gross motor performance of primary-grade school children. *Research Quarterly.* 22(1951):244-260.

SINGER, R.N.   Balance skill as related to athletics, sex, height, and weight. In Kenyon, ed., *Contemporary Psychology of Sport:* Proceedings of the Second International Congress of Sport Psychology, pp. 645-656. Chicago, IL: Athletic Institute, 1970.

SINGER, R.N.   *Motor Learning and Human Performance,* 2nd edition. New York: Macmillan, 1975.

WELLS, K., AND LUTGENS, K. *Kinesiology,* 6th edition. Philadelphia, PA; W.B. Saunders, 1976.

WILLIAMS, H.G. Perceptual-Motor test battery. Unpublished paper, University of Toledo, 1973.

WINTERHALTER, C. Age and sex trends in the development of selected balancing skills. Unpublished Master's project, University of Toledo, 1974.

WITKIN, H.A. Studies in space orientation III: Perception of the upright in the absence of a visual field. *Journal of Experimental Psychology.* 38(1948):603-614.

WITKIN, H.A. Studies in space orientation IV: further experiments on perception of the upright with displaced visual fields. *Journal of Experimental Psychology.* 38(1948):762-782.

WITKIN, H.A. Perception of the upright when the direction of the force acting on the body is changed. *Journal of Experimental Psychology.* 40(1950):93-106.

WITKIN, H.A. Further studies of perception of the upright when the direction of the force acting on the body is changed. *Journal of Experimental Psychology.* 43(1952):9-20.

WYRICK, W. Effects of task height and practice on static balance. *Research Quarterly.* 40(1969):215-221.

ZUCCATO, F. The relationship of selected static and dynamic balance measures to intelligence and scholastic achievement. Unpublished Master's thesis, University of Toledo, 1966.

CHAPTER TEN
THE CONCEPT OF THE PHYSICAL SELF: BODY AWARENESS

The major obstacle to a clearcut discussion of body awareness is the widespread use of vague terminology by individuals who deal with the topic. Body schema or scheme, body concept, body percept, body image, and body awareness are among the most favored terms that have been and are used, often without clear reference or definition. Most of these terms are in fact interrelated, but subtle distinctions among them can and should be made. The one consistent thought throughout the literature on body awareness is that the individual's perception of the body is a very important component of the singularly human characteristic of self-concept or self-image (e.g., Arnheim and Pestolesi, 1973; Ayres, 1972; Cratty, 1979; Nash, 1970). Most authors suggest that the development of the self-concept is, at least in part, a result of or a process parallel to changes occurring in the individual's perception of his body as a physical entity and/or an interactor with the environment. Self-concept or self-image certainly may involve factors other than those related to the body and the physical self; they are not of direct concern here.

COMPONENTS OF SELF-CONCEPT

Body schema and body image are terms used by Nash (1970) to describe body-related components of self-concept. According to Nash (1970) body schema is ". . . the 'diagram' of the body that is built up in the brain (probably in a definite location) by which coordinated purposeful movements are carried out and by which the body parts and the body itself are oriented in space" (p. 461). Body image, on the other hand, is ". . . the image that the individual has of himself as a physical person" (p. 464). Nash (1970) suggests that developmentally, body schema and body image form a hierarchy, with body schema being foundational to and essential for the creation of body image. Nash's definition of body schema implies a neurological substrate; i.e., there is a "diagram" of the body that is constructed through sensory-motor input reaching the brain. His term "body image" infers the involvement of more cognitive-related elements—how the individual "sees" himself or herself in the "mind's eye." This image may be an objective and complete picture, or it may be a more subjective and affective-oriented picture of how one "feels" about oneself. In any event there appears to be a gap between the notion of the schema and its developmental extension, the image. It is possible that an intermediary step between body schema and body image may exist, and it is this intermediate step that we will refer to as body awareness.

Body awareness can be defined as the conscious awareness and identification of the location, position, and movement of the body and its individual parts in space, the interrelationships among those body parts, and the relationship between the body and its parts (moving or stationary) to the external environment. The processes involved in the development of body awareness are dependent upon the earlier sensori-motor processes involved in the development of the body schema and are prerequisite to the development of the more predominantly cognitive body image. Body awareness thus may serve as a connecting link between body schema and body image. The general interrelationships among these dimensions of the physical self-concept are described in Figure 10.1. The placement of the

Figure 10.1 Components of the Physical Self-Concept

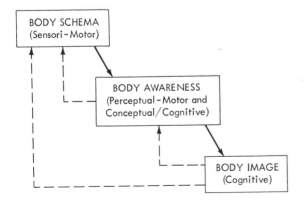

three blocks, representing the major parts of the physical self-concept, suggests that earlier aspects of self-concept development are not completely established before the next begins. The solid arrows indicate the direction of the sequential development of the major parts; the broken arrows suggest that one dimension interacts with, and in fact may facilitate, the development of another.

Body Schema

How does the body schema develop? There is some evidence that the body schema may be, in part, innately determined; that is, as the brain grows (in the neonatal period) a "diagram" of the body is developed (Ayres, 1972; Nash, 1970). This diagram is not static and unchanging, but rather it is constantly modified through sensory-motor experiences that the infant undergoes. Initially the infant treats his body as just another object in the environment. As sensory stimuli, particularly haptic and kinesthetic, are experienced by the infant, he learns that his body parts are not objects in the environment but are a part of a special object, the body itself. In this way the boundaries of the body schema become defined and the body becomes differentiated from the environment. This aspect of the physical self-concept may be thought of as sensory-motor in nature, for it is from the sensory information arising from movements of the infant in his interaction with the environment that the innate body schema becomes altered and further refined (Ayres, 1972).

Evidence in support of the "diagram" notion arises primarily from clinical studies of the effects of brain damage on perception of the body and the "phantom limb" phenomenon (Nash, 1970). For example, patients who have experienced brain damage (e.g., a sudden cerebrovascular accident that has caused paralysis of one side of the body) often ignore the fact that limbs on one side of the body are paralyzed and deny that anything is wrong. This occurs even though no sensations from those body parts are received at conscious levels of the central nervous system.

The phantom limb phenomenon lends credence to the basic notion of the body schema as a diagram contained in the brain. Individuals who have had a limb amputated, for whatever reason, often report that they can "feel" the missing limb as though it were still there. In fact if the last sensation felt before amputation was pain, a painful phantom is often felt. This, of course, suggests that the sensations perceived when the limb was intact are stored in the brain and are related to the "boundaries" of the limb portion of the "diagram." It has been found that, with the passage of time, the phantom-limb phenomenon diminishes and eventually disappears, undoubtedly because no additional sensory information from that limb is available to be stored or to update that which is already stored in the brain. Evidence that the body schema may be innate comes from individuals who are born without a limb or with a limb that is deformed, and who still report phantom limb sensations. Many individuals born without a given limb perceive or feel that body part just as though it actually existed (Nash, 1970). As indicated previously, it has been suggested that the basic mechanism for a body schema is indeed an inherent (innate) part of the nervous system that undergoes change as a result of sensory experiences encountered by the child during development. Nash (1970) suggests that the innate schema is ". . . a kind of standard of the species" (p. 463). The modifications that occur result in a more or less accurate schema for a particular body.

Ayres (1972) emphasizes the developmental nature of body schemes. She suggests that the development of the body scheme is in part dependent on interpretation of sensory information derived from movement of the limbs. Sensory input from the skin (cutaneous/touch), the muscles, and joints (kinesthetic) contribute importantly to the development of the internal model or body scheme in the brain. Ayres (1972) also suggests that the body scheme is not static; that it is the product of intersensory integration or the combining in a functional way of information from several sensory systems. The importance of the body scheme, according to Ayres (1972), is its relationship to "motor plans" or plans of action that are developed through sensori-motor experiences and are stored in the brain. Thus active use of the body helps to build the scheme of the body. Motor plans or plans of action are, in turn, based on the individual's body scheme or awareness of different parts of the physical self, the potential movement capabilities of these parts, and the relationships among such parts during movement. Thus the body scheme is a flexible internal model of the body from which a plan of action or movement can be executed. If the information received in the brain through the somato-sensory system (e.g., haptic, kinesthetic, vestibular inputs) is incomplete or imprecise or is not integrated appropriately with information from other systems, the brain has a poor or incomplete foundation for building a body scheme. Consequently a motor plan cannot be developed, and well-coordinated and skilled performance of a motor task is more difficult, if not impossible, to come by.

Body Awareness in Brief

As the body schema or internal model of the physical self becomes more refined, body awareness begins to emerge. The emergence of body awareness does not terminate the development of the body schema; rather the body schema continues to develop as conscious internal awareness of the body, its parts, and their relationship to the environment becomes apparent through the overt behavior of the child. Dominance begins to be established, and some aspects of the cognitive or conceptual dimensions of body awareness begin to appear.

Body awareness and its subcomponents will be discussed in more detail later in the chapter. Suffice it to say at this point that body awareness development is dependent upon the body schema and involves both perceptual-motor and conceptual/cognitive elements. In addition, it is an important prerequisite to the establishment of the body image.

Body Image

The image one has of oneself as a physical entity includes both the dimension of "body proportion" characteristics as well as the dimension of performance characteristics (Wapner et al., 1965). Judgments of the body as short or tall, fat or thin, strong or weak, etc. are primarily the result of the social interactions the child experiences as he grows and develops. The perception the individual has of himself as a performing being is also formed through interactions with others, for it is during play or the performing of various motor tasks in social situations that the child becomes aware of and judges his own performance in relationship to that of others. To consider his body and/or performance as "good," "bad," or "O.K.," "acceptable" or "unacceptable," the child has to compare himself with other people and/or some standard. A young child generally accepts his body as it is, even if it has some defect (Nash, 1970). It is only through varied social experiences that the child learns to judge whether or not he is similar to or different from other individuals, and whether this difference (if it exists) is good, bad, or irrelevant. Thus initially the body image is formed through sensori-motor processes, but it becomes further defined and refined through cognitive, intellectual, or judgmental processes. These judgmental processes become an integral part of one's total self-concept (Nash, 1970).

Body image research   In recent years there has been considerable interest in the concept of body image. Elementary school teachers, in particular, have turned their attention to helping the child develop an accurate and positive self-image, of which the body image is an important part. Research has focused on such topics as age and sex differences in accuracy of body image, attitudes toward different body types, changes in body image and self-concept through participation in motor activities, and performance aspects of body image. A *brief* review of some of this research will serve to indicate the present "state of the art" with regard to the nature and importance of body image in the development of the young child.

AGE AND SEX DIFFERENCES IN ACCURACY OF BODY IMAGE

Lerner and Schroeder (date unknown) used three stimulus drawings (silhouettes) of different physiques—fat, average, and thin—to determine how accurately kindergarten children could identify their own general physique. The three stimulus figures were shown simultaneously, and the child was told to point to the one that looked most like his body. The children's responses were compared to physique ratings made by the experimenter and the teacher. Only 15% of both boys and girls chose a body type that was consistent with experimenter and/or teacher ratings of that child's body type. These data suggest that kindergarten children, in general, are not very accurate in the perception of their physical selves. That is, they do not have a very precise or well-developed body image. Interestingly, the data also showed that the teacher and experimenter differed in their ratings of the child in 43% of the cases. This indicates that even adults vary in their perception of the nature of the physical characteristics of children.

To assess preference versus aversion for different body types, the children were also asked to point to the figure they would like to resemble and the one they would not want to resemble. Results indicated that a significant proportion of the children showed preferences for the average physique (which society also favors), and that most children exhibited an aversion for (did not want to be like) the fat body type. There were no differences between boys and girls in the accuracy of perception of their bodies or in their preference and aversion choices of body types.

Gellert, Girgus, and Cohen (date unknown) also investigated the accuracy of body image in children ages 5 to 13 years. The methods used were similar to Lerner and Schroeder's (date unknown) with the exception that actual photographs of the children were used. Anterior, posterior, and side views were taken of each child, and the photographs were processed so that height was the same for all children. Each photograph was shown to the child under three different conditions. Under the first condition the photograph was displayed among those of 7 agemates; the heads in all 8 photographs were obscured. Under the second condition the child's photograph was displayed among those of people of noticeably different ages; again the heads were obscured. These conditions thus focused on body shape, proportion, and symmetry for identification. Under the third condition the child's photograph was displayed among those of children of like age, but in this case the heads were visible. The child was asked in all cases to identify or point to the picture that was most like him.

When the heads were visible, children of all ages correctly identified themselves when shown the front view; the majority of children correctly identified themselves from the side view as well. Identification from the rear view was more difficult. In this last case accuracy of identification increased with age to 9 years. Only 52% of the five-year-olds were able to correctly recognize themselves from a rear-view photograph, whereas 88% of the nine- to thirteen-year-olds made correct identifications.

When the heads were obscured, substantial numbers of children were able to identify themselves from all views, but success was largely a function of age. That is, as the age of the child increased, so did his ability to correctly identify the physical characteristics of the body. When the child's photograph was displayed among photographs of individuals of markedly different ages, the success in identifying the body increased more steeply with age than when the photograph was displayed among those of his own agemates. There were no sex differences for any age group. An analysis of the nature of children's incorrect selections indicated that fat and medium-built children tended to select as their own the photographs of thinner peers, and thin subjects tended to select "fatter" photographs, but not photographs of body types at the far extreme.

In general then, if the identification of a self-photograph is used as the measure of accuracy of body image: (a) children ages 5 to 13 tend to have fairly accurate perceptions of the physical characteristics of their bodies; (b) when only body shape and proportion are used for identification, accuracy of the child's perception of his body's characteristics is a function of age; and, (c) boys and girls do not differ in any essential way in the accuracy of their body image.

In an interesting study, Stiles (1975) looked at the accuracy with which six- to ten-year-olds could judge body height and shoulder width. Body image was measured by projecting life-size filmed images of the children onto a screen. Each child looked at the filmed images and tried to judge which image matched his actual height and shoulder width. On film, all images of the children ranged from six inches shorter to six inches taller than their actual height. In general, children of all ages and both sexes made equally accurate judgments about height and shoulder width dimensions of their bodies. The children's shoulder width judgments showed larger errors than their height judgments. This may be because children are more familiar with the concept of body height than they are with the notion of body width.

If developmental or age-related changes in the accuracy of a child's body image do in fact occur, what is the significance of having an accurate body image? That is, is an accurate body image important to development? To successful learning and/or performance of motor and/or cognitive tasks? To establishing a positive self-concept? If so, then individuals working with young children should make a concerted effort to increase or improve the accuracy of the child's body image. If not, then we should deal with the child's body image as it exists and not attempt to change it. Unfortunately answers to these questions are not yet forthcoming.

Although the focus of this text is not on the adolescent years, two studies that have used adolescents to look at the individual's "satisfaction" with various body dimensions and/or physical characteristics merit some mention. Clifford (1971) attempted to measure body satisfaction of junior and senior high school males and females. Two inventories, a "body-satisfaction" scale and a "self-satisfaction" scale, were administered to all individuals. There were no age differences in body- or self-satisfaction reports for these groups of adolescents. Overall, however, boys and girls differed

in the degree of satisfaction they expressed with regard to their bodies and themselves. Girls were generally less satisfied with themselves and with their bodies than boys. Why such sex differences should exist is not clear. A plausible explanation is that adolescent girls have been influenced by a culture that suggests that females should be physically attractive but not necessarily self-confident or self-assertive. In contrast, modern society has not emphasized physical attractiveness in the male but rather has characterized his role in society as one requiring self-confidence, self-assertiveness, and self-sufficiency. Whether or not such differences in body- and/or self-satisfaction are characteristic of the adolescent stage only cannot be determined until similar studies, using children, are conducted.

Wiggins (1973) also investigated sex differences in the self-perception of adolescents (ninth-grade boys and girls). Of particular interest here is the finding that both boys and girls tended to give themselves negative ratings on such physical characteristics as "being the right weight" and having a "good-looking face." Girls tended to be satisfied with their height whereas boys were not. Further, boys judged themselves as better athletes than girls did, but girls perceived themselves as better dancers than boys did.

BODY IMAGE AND MOTOR PERFORMANCE

Effects of participation in motor activities on body image have been studied primarily through investigations that have used a measure of self-concept and not a measure of body image *per se*. Although results of such studies vary somewhat, there is some limited evidence that participation in motor activities does have a positive effect on body image or self-concept. The effect of a perceptual-motor training program on the self-concept of pre-school children with deficits in gross motor skills and self-concept was investigated by Platzer (1976). At the conclusion of a 10-week program (30 minutes daily), children who had participated in the program demonstrated a more positive self-concept (as measured by the Goodenough projective test) than children who had not participated. The precise cause of the differences in self-concept was not clear, since performances on gross motor skills were not different. Since program participation did not produce significant differences in gross motor skills, the differences found in self-concept may be attributed to the Hawthorne effect or to some other unknown by-product of program participation. Using a long period of endurance training (18 weeks), McGowan, Jarman, and Pedersen (1974) did find a significant improvement in the self-concept of seventh-grade boys; peer approval, however, did not change as a result of the program. Sorenson (1974) also found that a special strength training program had a positive effect on the self-concept and peer approval of seventh-grade boys. Children who participated in the program demonstrated a greater increase in peer popularity and a significant positive change in self-concept when compared with children who did not participate.

In contrast to these studies, Maul and Thomas (1975) found no effect of participation in an extracurricular gymnastics program on the movement-related (not academically related) self-concept of third-graders. Fishler (1975) also reported that participation in a six-week conditioning program had little effect on the self-concept of fifth-graders.

Interestingly, Brugel (1972) found that although participation in a competitive baseball league had no effect on the self-concepts of nine-year-olds, it did have a positive effect on the self-concepts of eight-year-olds. These results suggest that there may be important age-related changes in the way in which active participation in motor activities affects self-concept. It should be noted that when eight- and nine-year-olds were grouped on the bases of amount of experience, percentage of participation, and level of skill (rather than age), there were no differences in self-concept scores. In other words those children with *less* baseball experience (eight- and nine-year-olds combined) had self-concept scores comparable to those of children (eight- and nine-year-olds) with *more* baseball experience. This suggests that differences in improvement in self-concept scores between the two age groups were more related to age than to other factors. Certainly additional research is needed to clarify this issue.

Whether it is the teaching method employed or the actual participation itself that affects self-concept (if self-concept is affected) was investigated by Martinek, Zaichowsky, and Cheffers (1977). Two teaching models were used with two groups of first through fifth graders. With the "vertical" model, the teacher made all decisions and initiated the learning process; the "horizontal" model involved the teacher and student sharing decision-making roles. Since there was no difference in self-concept scores between the two teaching models' groups at any grade level, it would appear that the method of instruction in motor activity may not be a significant factor in changing self-concept.

Although the method of instruction may not affect the development of the self-concept, the interaction of the teacher and students and the expectations the teacher has for the students cannot be ignored. Martinek and Johnson (1979) found that significantly greater gains in self-concept were obtained by fourth- and fifth-grade children whose physical-education teachers expected them to achieve at a higher level than by children who were given a low achievement expectancy rating. The positive changes in self-concept thus were, at least in part, a result of the more positive relationship between the teacher and the "high expectancy achievers." Observations indicated that the teachers approached this group of children more frequently, gave more praise and supportive encouragement, and accepted and used their ideas more than they did the ideas of those expected to achieve at a lower level. These data suggest that the teacher may play a significant role in the development of the child's self-concept.

Results of studies that have looked at the correlation between body image and/or self-concept and motor and/or academic performance have also been varied. These studies have not considered how body image or self-concept changes through participation in sport but rather have looked at whether or not motor performance and self-concept are related in some way. The general expectation is that better performers have a better self-concept or body image than poorer performers. In general, research has not supported this expectation.

Mapes (1975) found no significant relationships among measures of physical fitness, self-concept, and academic achievement for fourth-grade boys and girls. Using seventh- and eighth-grade boys and girls, Phelan (1973) also determined the relationships between physical fitness items and self-concept. Although a few significant relationships between individual fitness items and self-concept were found, for the most part physical fitness was not significantly related to self-concept. Albins (1972) used sixth- and eighth-grade girls and college women to determine the relationship between self-concept and perceptual-motor performance. Three tasks were used: the pursuit rotor, mirror tracing, and reaction time. Among the college women and sixth-grade girls, perceptual-motor performance was not related to self-concept. For the eighth graders only pursuit rotor performance was related to self-concept. These data thus provide no support for the notion of a relationship between self-concept and motor performance.

The discussion thus far has focused on that aspect of body image that deals primarily with structural aspects of the physical self; that is, with how one perceives the dimensions and proportions of the body as well as the "feelings" that one has about these aspects of the physical self. Another component of the body image that is important to the young child is that of his perception of himself as a performer. The performer/performance facet of body image has been evaluated primarily by the use of isolated items within the instruments used to measure general self-concept or body image.

Few studies have attempted to assess directly the individual's perception of himself as a performer. Studies that have attempted to look at this aspect of body image have employed, for the most part, the concept of "level of aspiration" (LOA) as a means of determining the performer/performance image the child has of himself. LOA may be more simply referred to as goal-setting or performance estimation. LOA or goal-setting requires that the performer estimate what his performance will be on a given task. The discrepancy between this estimate and the actual performance is then evaluated and used as an indication of the individual's perception of his performing self (Stafford, 1969; Sturtevant, date unknown). Goal-setting or performance estimation obviously must be based on something within the individual's experience. Thus if the individual has performed a task prior to setting his performance goal, then the goal set for his next performance is based on this past experience. If however there is no such past experience, the individual must "imagine" or judge what he is capable of doing based on assessment of his overall abilities (e.g., general feelings of one's adequacy as a performer; judgments of one's ability in relation to peers or siblings; one's perception of the difficulty of the task, etc.). The basis for the individual's estimates of the performing self thus are related to the feelings he has about his physical abilities, i.e., his body image. This aspect of body image is believed to develop, for the most part, through social interactions with peers and "significant others" in performance situations.

Of interest here is the question of whether or not developmental differences exist in the accuracy with which children set performance goals. That is, do older children estimate their performance levels more accurately than younger children? Do boys differ from girls in the accuracy with which they set performance goals? One might predict that this might be the case, if for no other reason than the importance of past experience in the formulation of such estimates. In general, accuracy of goal-setting relative to motor performance is a function of age. That is to say, older children appear to have a more realistic perception of their ability to perform and, therefore, a more accurate performance body image, than do younger children. Also, there is some evidence that boys and girls do not differ in the accuracy with which they set performance goals. For example, Stafford (1969) used third-, sixth-, ninth-, and twelfth-grade boys and girls to study LOA. He reported that on no task (e.g., male-oriented tasks such as grip strength and jump tests versus female-oriented tasks such as hopscotch and stork balance versus neutral tasks such as object replacement and specific group LOA tests) was there a significant difference between boys and girls in accuracy of performance estimates. Thus throughout childhood and adolescent years boys and girls are equally accurate in their estimates of the performing self. Age was, however, a significant factor in the accuracy of performance goal-setting. In general, older children were more accurate in their performance estimates than were younger children. Patterson (1975) also found that older girls (ninth grade) were more accurate than younger girls (seventh grade) in establishing strength and endurance performance goals.

Age differences in the accuracy of performance estimates are not always clearcut. For example, Sturtevant (date unknown) reports that both eight- and nine-year-old boys are unrealistic goal setters, but that eight-year-olds were able to modify their performances more realistically in relation to experience than were nine-year-olds. The tasks used in this study were three distance throws and three accuracy throws. The children were asked to indicate the number of times (in five throws) the ball would travel the designated distance or hit the designated target. In general, although all children were unrealistic in setting performance goals, the eight-year-olds were more accurate (i.e., there was less discrepancy between their estimates of performance and the actual performance itself) after the first of two sets of trials. The nine-year-olds did not show this pattern of change in goal setting. Thus accuracy of estimates of the performing self do not always show steady improvement with age. Differences between eight- and nine-year-olds in this study might be partly explained by the assertion that the older children may have felt that they could or should be able to do better the next time, and thus they saw no need to alter their performance estimates. The younger children may not have known, or been aware, that they would be expected to perform better than they actually had, and thus they reset their performance goals in a more realistic manner.

BODY AWARENESS

In general, body awareness may be thought of as a multifaceted aspect of the physical self-image or self-concept that involves conscious knowledge and/or perception of the body and its parts. Initially, body awareness is evident only through observation of the motor behavior of the young child. As other dimensions of the child's behavior, in particular language, begin to develop, the child communicates this awareness in other ways (Ayres, 1972).

There appears to be a kind of hierarchical order or relationship among the various facets or subcomponents of body awareness. That is, some subcomponents of body awareness are and/or must be developed, at least to some degree, before the next ones can emerge (Kephart, 1964). For the purpose of this discussion, the subcomponents of body awareness will be dichotomized as internal or external. Internal subcomponents of body awareness are those that deal exclusively with awareness of the body and its parts; they include visual attention, awareness of spatial dimensions of the body, lateral dominance, and identification of body parts. External subcomponents are those concerned with the body and its parts in relationship to, and as interactors with, the environment; they include imitation, directionality, and spatial orientation. A diagram of the proposed relationships among these subcomponents of body awareness and among body awareness, body schema, and body image is given in Figure 10.2. The vertical arrangement within and among the components of the physical self-concept (body schema, body awareness, body image) indicates the se-

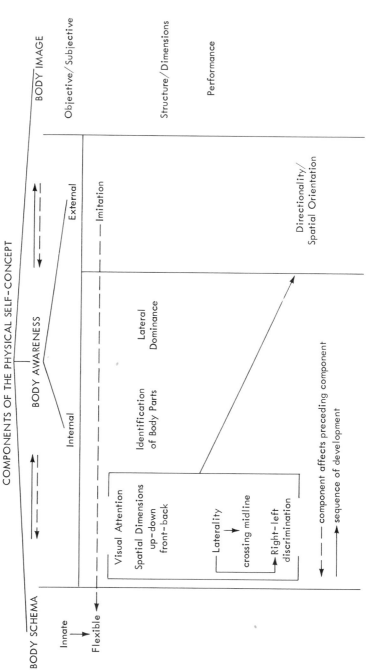

Figure 10.2 A Schematic of the Interrelationships among Various Aspects of Body Awareness and Physical Self-Concept

quence of development of these aspects. The horizontal arrangement highlights those components and subcomponents of the physical self-concept that are developing concurrently. Arrows (solid and dotted) identify important interrelationships among different aspects of the physical self-concept.

Internal Subcomponents of Body Awareness

Visual attention   The first direct evidence that the infant is becoming aware of his body and/or body parts as something other than objects in the environment is gained through observation of the infant's behavior. During the time that he is awake, the infant spends considerable time "studying" or visually attending to his body parts—particularly the hands and feet. The infant watches his own random, thrashing limb movements, focuses on a hand or foot that is held in a static position, and observes his fingers or toes as he moves them in an increasingly controlled fashion. As the infant becomes more aware of his body parts, he begins to voluntarily and consciously initiate movements. This in turn increases his "fascination" with his body and results in increased visual attention activities (Ayres, 1972).

The visual attention subcomponent of body awareness parallels the development of the body schema and is largely sensori-motor based. That is, the visual information gained through attending to or watching the positions and/or movements of the body supports and supplements that gained from the somato-sensory system via the positioning and/or movement of body parts. Thus through integrating visual and tactile-kinesthetic information, the infant begins the long, arduous task of establishing "body boundaries" (which is prerequisite to the development of more precise perceptions of the structural aspects of body image) and a flexible body schema (which is a necessary foundation for skillful motor planning) (Ayres, 1972).

Spatial dimensions of the body   As a result of visual attention, conscious imitation of movements, and other sensori-perceptual-motor activities in which the young child is engaged, several other subcomponents of body awareness begin to develop. Some of these subcomponents are related to the spatial dimensions of the body and therefore are very much interrelated. In fact in some instances the subcomponents overlap to such an extent that a clear differentiation among them is difficult. As will be noted in the discussion to follow, there is a hierarchical order of development among some of the subcomponents. Although the focus of this discussion is on the internal subcomponents, it will be obvious to the reader that external (environment-related) subcomponents are extensions of internal subcomponents concerned with spatial dimensions of the body.

Laterality   A significant step in the development of body awareness comes with the child's increasing awareness that his body has two distinct sides—right and left. Although he may not know the verbal labels "right" and "left," he knows he has two hands, two arms, two feet, etc. He recognizes that although the two sides have a similar shape and size, the parts on the two sides can move independently and/or can simultaneously occupy different positions in space. This conscious awareness of the two sides of the body is referred to as laterality. Spionnek (Cratty, 1979) suggests that from birth to about age $3^1/_2$, the child cannot distinguish between the two sides of the body. Between ages 4 and 5, the child becomes increasingly aware that his two limbs are on either side of his body, but he is not sure of their location or which are called "left" and which are called "right." Recognizing that the body has two sides (laterality) is an important part of the development of the perceptions of spatial dimensions and provides the foundation for the development of other internal spatial subcomponents and for the development of directionality, an external subcomponent of body awareness.

Assessment of laterality typically involves having the child perform activities such as "Angels in the Snow." This task requires the child to execute single- and/or paired-limb movements in the frontal plane while lying in a supine position. Some of the paired movements are ipsilateral (same side) and some are contralateral (opposite side). For example, the child may be asked to move the left arm or the left arm and right leg together or the right arm and right leg together in an arc along the floor. Thus the child is asked to discriminate and coordinate movements of the two sides of the body. Performance of the task does not require verbalization or knowledge of which are the left and which are the right limbs (right-left discrimination), since the evaluator can simply point to or touch those limbs he wants the child to move. Laterality is evaluated objectively in this task by indicating whether or not the child uses the correct limbs and subjectively by noting whether the movement was smooth and within a full range of motion.

The basis for the use of such tests of laterality is that if the child is aware of and can distinguish between the two sides of the body, he will be able to perform the task adequately, and thus laterality will have been established. Whether or not "Angels in the Snow" (or any similar task) measures only the laterality subcomponent of body awareness is questionable. If performance was measured only in terms of whether or not the child used the "correct" limb(s), laterality would be assessed. However the subjective evaluation of the quality of movement may, in fact, be a reflection of the neuromuscular development of the child rather than the perceptual and/or cognitive development relative to the two sides of the body. It may be that laterality is considered by some not to be completely established until the child can demonstrate movements of the two body sides in a coordinated fashion; however, this goes beyond the basic definition of laterality.

Right-left discrimination   The right-left discrimination subcomponent of body awareness is, in essence, an advanced form of laterality. Within this subcomponent the child clearly moves from the sensori-perceptual-motor phase of the development of body awareness to the conceptual/cognitive phase. By definition, right-left discrimination is ". . . the ability to spontaneously label or identify the left-right dimensions of the body" (Ayres, 1969). "Labeling" and "identification" are obviously cognitive activities. Spionnek (Cratty, 1970) suggests that the final stage of development of perception of right and left doesn't occur in most children until age 8 or 9. That is, the child does not come to know precisely which parts of his body are right and left until that age. Spionnek (Cratty, 1979) has shown, however, that by age 5 children can be taught, through conditioning, to identify right and left body parts.

The observed responses of the child to such statements as, "Show me your right hand," "Touch your left ear," etc., are customarily used to assess the level of development of right-left discrimination capacities of the child. The child is evaluated not only on how accurately he responds but also how quickly the response is made.

Figure 10.3 shows developmental data from two studies (Ayres, 1969; Williams *et al.*, 1971). Clearly an age-related change (improvement) in children's ability to discriminate right and left sides of the body exists. The data from Williams *et al.* (1971) show a linear trend whereas Ayres' data (1969) nearly approach linearity. It may be noted that at age 4, children on the average score less than one half of the total possible points on the test (20.0); by age 10, although all children have not obtained a perfect score, accurate and spontaneous discrimination of the left and right sides of the body is evident in most children.

Other available data concerning the development of right-left discrimination in children are reported as the percentage of children at different ages that responded spontaneously and correctly. These data, gathered by Swanson and Benton (1955), are presented in Table 10-1. As the data suggest, by age 6 the majority of children know precisely which parts of their bodies are right and left; however, a large number (approximately 30%) of children at this age are still confused. Consistent with Spionnek's finding (Cratty, 1979), not until age 8 or 9 does the conceptualization of right and left become stabilized in most children. It is interesting to note that, except at age 6, children are more accurate in responding, relative to right-left discrimination of their bodies, with their eyes closed. The reason for this is not entirely clear. Perhaps the best explanation is that closing the eyes permits the child to concentrate on the dimensions of the body without distraction from the environment (e.g., another person).

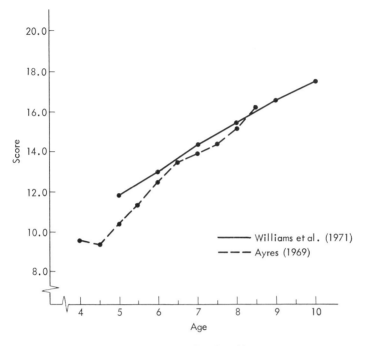

Figure 10.3 Right-Left Discrimination as a Function of Age

At least two test-related factors should be kept in mind when inter-preting right-left discrimination data: (a) the test score is a reflection of spontaneity as well as accuracy of response; and (b) the tests used to gather these data usually involve a few items that are more truly measures of directionality, i.e., left-right dimensions in the environment rather than right-left dimensions of the child's body. Directionality, as it will be seen later, is a more advanced subcomponent of body awareness and is, in fact, an extension of right-left discrimination. Thus what appears to be per-formance that is no better than chance level by children below age 5 (Ayres, 1969) may be a reflection of the child's inability to identify left and right in external space. This same factor should also be considered when inter-

TABLE 10-1   Right-Left Awareness as a Function of Age

AGE	EYES OPEN	EYES CLOSED
6 yrs.	71.5%	64.2%
7 yrs.	86.8%	88.7%
8 yrs.	89.7%	92.5%
9 yrs.	93.6%	95.3%

preting the data at other age levels. This may suggest that right-left discrimination is, in fact, stabilized before age 8 or 9. Certainly additional research which excludes items measuring directionality is called for.

A few studies have looked at some of the factors that may be associated with the development of right-left discrimination. For instance, La-Coursiere-Paige (1974) considered the importance of age, visuo-motor coordination, verbal and nonverbal intelligence, handedness, space relations, and conceptualization of the human figure to the development of right-left concepts. Results of a factor analysis of tests administered to four-through eleven-year-old boys and girls indicated that there was one major factor that contributed to the development of right-left concepts. This factor was labeled "general maturation" and included all of the variables except handedness. Rigal (1974) has also found that handedness is not associated with right-left discrimination.

Craxen and Lytton (1971) considered the relationship between right-left discrimination capacities and reading ability. They found that nine- and ten-year-old retarded readers had greater difficulty on a right-left discrimination test than matched counterparts who were not retarded in their reading. However, the tests of right-left discrimination used involved some directionality items, and therefore the proposed relationship between right-left discrimination is not clearcut. It may be that right-left confusion in relation to the environment (directionality) was more related to difficulty in reading than the distinction between right and left parts of the body.

Crossing the body midline Although individuals have essentially two separate sides of the body that can "work" independently of each other, there are many activities in which the interrelationship of the two sides of the body is very important. In some activities the two sides may operate as separate units, but the temporal or sequential coordination of the two sides is essential to a smooth, efficient performance. For example, skipping involves a step-hop pattern on the right side (this involves a high degree of coordination in and of itself) followed by the same step-hop pattern on the left side. For these two alternate patterns to result in the smooth, rhythmical sequence we call the skip, the transition from right to left to right sides must be smooth and without interruption. That is, the movements of the two sides must be integrated or coordinated in a specific way. Further, in the mature skip, the arms move in opposition to the leg movements. As the right leg moves forward to perform the step-hop pattern, the left arm swings forward. Even though the skipping sequence just described does not actually involve crossing body parts from one side of the vertical midline to the other, there is in essence a crossing of the midline when the sequence as a whole is considered. Activities such as throwing, striking in a horizontal plane (batting), writing on the blackboard, etc. require the actual crossing of the midline by a body part. In this type of activity the child who has difficulty crossing the midline has to make an adjustment either in body position or in the total movement pattern itself.

A developmental trend in the ability to cross the body midline is apparent from available data. Scores on a crossing the midline test (Ayres, 1969, Williams, 1971) for four- to ten-year-old children are shown in Figure 10.4. Crossing the midline tests involve the child copying movements of a model who touches his eye or ear with his contralateral (opposite) or ipsilateral (same side) hand; both right and left hands are used in the test.

Although the actual scores of the two sets of data presented in Figure 10.4 differ slightly, the same general trend of increasing ability to cross the midline as a function of age is reflected in the data reported by both investigators (Ayres, 1969; Williams *et al.,* 1971). It may be noted that the substantial increase in the ability to cross the body midline from ages 4 to $5\frac{1}{2}$ years seems to parallel developmental changes in the ability to perform fundamental motor skills that involve crossing the midline, (e.g., throwing, striking, skipping). Children generally do not demonstrate mature patterns in these tasks until age 5. Prior to that time they tend to position or use the body in such a way that crossing the midline can be avoided. For example, the young child will face the target squarely when throwing and striking rather than assuming a side-facing position and permitting body rotation and arm movement to the opposite side to occur. Skipping attempts

Figure 10.4 Crossing the Midline as a Function of Age

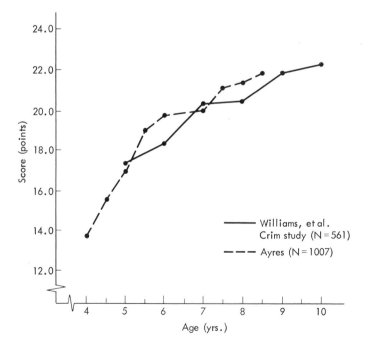

at this stage usually result in a one-sided skip or an uncoordinated, "jerky" transition of the pattern from one side to the other. Thus there appears to be a direct relationship between the ability to cross the body midline and performance on those tasks. That is, crossing the midline develops, although perhaps not fully, prior to the final developmental stages of those tasks. Although this relationship has not been fully documented, Williams (1971) did find that several measures of body awareness, of which crossing the midline was one, were related to performances by five- through twelve-year-olds on an agility task (shuttle run). Even though the specific relationship between performance on the agility task and the crossing the midline task is obscured within the combined body awareness categorization used, it seems reasonable to suggest that the integrated use of the two body sides is important to the quick, efficient change of direction required by the agility task.

Data collected by Williams *et al.* (1971) show that the greatest increase in ability to cross the midline occurs between ages 5 and 7 (kindergarten to second grade) with smaller increases after that (See Figure 10.4). Even at the age of 10 some children still had difficulty crossing the midline.

Is the observed developmental trend in ability to cross the body midline real, or are such differences a reflection of other factors at work? Schofield (1976a, 1976b) has suggested that the lower scores obtained by young children may occur because many children do not understand the significance of using the specific hand used by the tester, and therefore they tend to use the preferred hand for the majority of the movements. Performances of three- to eight-year-old children on such tasks indicated that when the number of preferred or dominant hand responses (ipsilateral and contralateral) was considered, no age, sex, or midline differences were present. That is, all children performed essentially the same when they used the dominant hand to touch the same or opposite eye or ear. However when the nonpreferred hand was used, age differences did exist. All children made fewer responses with their nonpreferred hand than they should have, but younger children made significantly fewer contralateral responses with their nonpreferred hand than did older children. These data suggest that evaluation of the developmental changes in the capacity of the child to cross the midline is far from simple or clearcut. A different, more qualitative way of evaluating "crossing the body midline" may be needed.

Other spatial dimensions of the body   Although most attention has been directed toward the development of right-left discrimination capacities of the child, there are other spatial dimensions of the body that must be considered when discussing the development of body awareness. Awareness of up-down and front-side-back is a significant subcomponent of body awareness and is also related to the development of the structural aspects of the body image.

To date there has been little study of the nature of the development of these other spatial concepts relative to the body. Vernon (1970) has suggested that the order of conceptualization of the spatial dimensions of the body may be the mastery of up-down first, followed by front-back, and finally side (right-left). The fact that the concept of front-back develops before the side concept is borne out in a study by Kuczaj and Maratsos (1975). Children ranging in age from 30 to 49.5 months performed better (were more correct) when asked to place an object in front or back of themselves than when asked to place an object to their side. In all instances older children performed better than younger ones. This study also suggests that the concept of front and back develops, at least in some children, as early as 30 months of age.

Identification of body parts   With the onset of capacity for verbalization, the child is able to communicate her awareness of the body and its structure and functions more directly. The rate at which this more cognitive aspect of body awareness develops varies among children. One of the major factors that affects the development of the capacity to identify body parts is the amount of emphasis placed on it by those with whom the child comes in contact during the early years.

There are some developmental data available, scanty though they may be, that suggest the approximate ages at which most children can identify various body parts. These data are summarized in Table 10-2. The table not only provides a general "timetable" of when specific body parts might be identified by the child, but it also includes the percentage of samples of children who could identify major body parts such as eyes, ears, hands, knees, etc. (Williams, 1973). As with data relative to other developmental parameters, the information should be viewed primarily as a general developmental guideline because of variations in the manner in which data were collected.

As early as age 2 (and earlier for some children), awareness of specific body parts is evident (Cratty, 1979). As mentioned before, awareness of and verbalization about the front and back of the body develop slightly prior to the concept of side. The definite labeling of left and right sides of the body does not occur for the majority of children until age 6 or 7. Again, the age at which a child can label body parts is dependent upon when and how much time is spent with the child in learning body parts. Certainly the child is kinesthetically and visually "aware" of the parts of the body before he can verbalize about them or accurately name them. Thus sensory-perceptual awareness of the body develops before conceptual or cognitive awareness; real evidence of conceptual awareness is not available until verbal behavior begins. With the beginning of formal education (school), those children who have not been able to verbalize about their body parts (because no time has been spent with them in this kind of activity) show

TABLE 10-2 Identification of Body Parts

AGE	PERCENT IDENTIFYING MAJOR PARTS*	PARTS IDENTIFIED**
2 yrs.	No Data	Sometimes verbally identifies gross body parts. Touches "tummy," back, arm, or leg when asked to do so. Aware of toes before leg.
3 yrs.	No Data	Aware of front, back, side, head, hand, foot. Begins awareness of thumb, parts of face.
4 yrs.	No Data	Aware of two sides of body (laterality). Detailed awareness of body parts. Can name little and first fingers.
5 yrs.	55%	Knows there are left and right sides of body; can't name them yet. 90% can name thumb. 80% can name eyes. 50% can name eyebrows. 70% can name hand.
6 yrs.	69%	Can distinguish left and right body parts. Names little and ring fingers.
7 yrs.	88%	70% can name eyebrows.
8-9 yrs.	95%	Concept of laterality well established.

*Williams, 1973; N = 240
**Cratty, 1979

rapid progress. By age 10, errors by normally developing children in identifying at least the gross body parts are indeed rare (Cratty, 1979).

Lateral dominance   Although lateral dominance becomes permanent or fixed after the onset of verbal behavior in the child, it is believed to be sensory-motor based. That is, a child establishes the left or right hand as the preferred or dominant hand without knowing that it is the "left" or "right" hand.

Lateral dominance refers to the preferential use of one of the eyes, hands, or feet over the other (Williams, 1973). Although lateral dominance can also involve the ears, auditory dominance will not be discussed in this chapter. If the child's preference is for use of the hand, eye, and foot on the same side of the body, he is said to have pure dominance. If the preferential use of the hand, eye, and foot involves both sides of the body, the child is said to have mixed dominance (e.g., right hand, right foot, and left eye). If the child does not show a preference for one side of a body part (e.g., right hand) he may lack dominance or be ambidextrous. That is, if he uses the left and right hands interchangeably for the same task, he is ambidextrous. If, however, he always uses one hand for one task and always uses the other hand for another task, he is said to lack dominance (e.g., throws a ball with his right hand, eats with his left hand, writes with his left hand).

How dominance emerges is, at this point, not fully understood. Some theorists have suggested that lateral dominance is linked to cerebral dominance. That is, if one is right-sided, the left hemisphere is dominant (or vice versa). In addition to the cerebral dominance theory, other theories, at least related to hand preference, have been suggested. Some theories suggest a hereditary factor; others suggest that hand preference is related to the position of the fetus in the uterus, unequal distribution of internal organs, or a different rate of development of arteries on the two sides of the body. The most plausible explanation to date seems to be that of cerebral dominance.

Lateral dominance has customarily and most reliably been assessed by observing which side of the body the child uses most frequently in performing a variety of tasks. Hand dominance is usually determined through such tasks as throwing, cutting, writing, handling objects, etc.; foot dominance is assessed through tasks such as climbing, kicking, hopping (which is the lead foot?); eye dominance is assessed through observing which eye is used to look into a microscope, telescope, or in sighting (e.g., aiming a gun). Less frequently a sidedness questionnaire in which the child is asked which hand he uses for writing, which foot he uses for kicking, etc., has been used.

Regardless of the method used for assessing dominance, the specific criterion for determining the dominance of the hand, eye, or foot varies greatly. Sometimes it is defined as the part used "75% of the time," other times it is defined as the part used over 50% of the time, and still other times it is defined as the part used exclusively by the child to perform selected tasks. There is little doubt that there is considerable shifting back and forth on the part of the child from the use of one side to the use of the other. The young child may use the right hand to perform a task one time and the left hand the next. Extensive data concerning the establishment of dominance in children under 4 years of age are not available. However it has been observed that some children do demonstrate consistent use of one hand, eye, or foot before the age of 4. However, the basal or earliest age at which most children show dominance is not known at this time.

Two sets of data are provided and will be referred to in the following discussion of intrapart and interpart lateral dominance. Some caution must

TABLE 10-3 Percent of Pure Dominance by Age

| | AGE | | | |
	4 YRS.	5-6 YRS.	7-8 YRS.	9-11 YRS.
Handedness	92	81	81	94
Eyedness	97	73	68.7	78.8
Footedness	No Data	94	94	98
Hand-Eye	No Data	37.5	41.7	63.5

be used in comparing the two sets of data, however. Table 10-3 presents the percentage of pure dominance related to the hand, eye, foot, and hand-eye combination observed in a population of children 4 to 11 years of age (Williams, 1973, p. 143). Table 10-4, data from Dusewicz and Kershner (1969), indicates the degree of dominance, by means of an average index, for children in grades two through six. An index of 0.00 indicates mixed dominance and an index of 1.00 indicates pure dominance. To arrive at the figures in the table, an index was determined for each child for each body part; these indices were then averaged across all children of a given grade level.

Hand dominance It is apparent that as early as 4 years of age the majority of children demonstrate a preference for using one hand over the other (Table 10-3). The fact that this preference is established before the age of 4 for some children is suggested by Sinclair (1971). She investigated the changes in dominance patterns over a three-year period and found that none of the children who were 5, 6 or 7 years of age at the time of the follow-up had changed hand preference. Thus five-year-olds demonstrated the same hand dominance that they had at the age of 2.

Of particular interest is the decrease in incidence of pure hand dominance for children 5 to 8 years of age as reported by Williams (1973). Whether or not this trend is specific to the sample used or typical of the population is not clear. Since Table 10-4 does not provide data for five-and six-year-olds, no comparison can be made for those ages. Both sets of data show increases in hand dominance for children ages 7 and 8 (grades

TABLE 10-4 Average Dominance Indices for Grades 2-6

| | GRADES | | | | |
	2 (N = 25)	3 (N = 21)	4 (N = 25)	5 (N = 18)	6 (N = 20)
Hand	.86	.87	.96	.88	.88
Eye	.92	.95	.93	.92	1.00
Foot	.32	.51	.52	.66	.47
Interpart	.40	.63	.61	.49	.61

two and three) to age 9 (grade four). Generally, nine- to eleven-year-olds have well-established hand dominance. Horine (1968) also reports that 94% of the ten-year-old boys in his study demonstrated pure hand dominance. In contrast Dusewicz and Kershner's (1969) data suggest a decrease in hand dominance for children in grades five and six (10 to 11 years). An explanation for this decrease is not available. It may simply be related to the size of the sample used.

If the ambivalence in hand use in five- to eight-year-olds (Table 10-3) is, in fact, an actual phenomenon, it may in part be due to the new environment in which the child now finds himself. With the beginning of formal education, the child may go through an experimental stage in which he tries using the alternate hand for some tasks. Another possible explanation suggested by Williams (1973) is that the phenomenon is a "reflection of increased eye-hand coordination capacities of the child" (p. 142). That is, an increase in coordinated use of the eyes and hands allows the child to use either or both hands in simple manipulative tasks. As the tasks performed with the hands become more complex, as for the nine- and ten-year-old, the hand preference becomes more permanently fixed.

Eye dominance   Data from the Williams study (1973) suggest a decrease in pure eye dominance from age 4 to age 8, although Dusewicz and Kers-
hner (1969) report a relatively stable pattern of eye dominance from grades two to five. It should be noted that the average eye-dominance index of 1.00 for sixth graders (Table 10-4) indicates that all children within the sample had pure eye dominance. This is not consistent with the incidence of pure eye dominance in the population at large and is probably a reflection of the small sample used in the study.
a young age because of the relatively few tasks that require the use of only one eye (as compared to the use of the hand). Because fewer tasks involve monocular vision, the need for the development of eye dominance may be reduced. Sinclair (1971) reports that 15% of children studied change eye preference over the three-year period from 2 to 5 years.

Whether or not eye preference is directly related to visual acuity is not clear at this time, because few if any studies have investigated this question. It is conceivable that although one eye may be dominant neurologically, the child may use the neurologically nondominant eye because acuity is better in that eye. Perhaps the decrease in eye dominance seen in Table 10-3 is, in part, a reflection of changes in acuity that may be taking place during that period of development (of course this notion is only speculative at this time). As with handedness, the period from 5 to 8 years may be a time of experimentation, and as more monocular viewing opportunities become available the ambivalence, or lack of clearcut preferential use of one eye, is more apparent.

The incidence of right-eye versus left-eye dominance seems to be less extreme than with handedness. Keogh (1972) reports that one-half of the forty-eight to seventy-one-month-old children in her study were left-eyed. Approximately 30% of the ten-year-old boys in Horine's study (1968) were left-eyed (54% were right-eyed and 16% were of mixed dominance).

Foot dominance   The shift in preference from pure to mixed that occurs with hand or eye dominance does not seem to happen with the feet. Williams (1973) reports a high percentage of pure foot dominance for all ages. Data from Dusewicz and Kershner (1969) do not show as great an incidence of pure foot dominance. These latter authors suggest that there is an increase in the stabilization of preferential foot use from one grade to the next (except for grade six). Horine (1968) reports that 79% of the ten-year-old boys in his study demonstrated pure foot dominance (7% were left-footed). Sinclair (1971) found only one child who changed footedness over a three-year period.

Interpart dominance   Normative data concerning the incidence of pure and mixed dominance among body parts (i.e., pure-sidedness) are scanty. Keogh (1972) found that approximately 50% of the forty-eight to seventy-one-month-old children in her study demonstrated pure dominance; most children (pure or mixed) were right-handed and right-footed. The incidence of mixed dominance (50%) thus was due primarily to eyedness. Williams (1973) found that, across ages 5 to 12, 45% of the children showed pure dominance (hand, foot, and eye). In a sample of fourth-grade children (N = 167), 32% had pure dominance (Williams, 1973). Horine (1968) reports that 35% of the 220 ten-year-old boys were purely right-sided.

The interpart dominance indices presented in Table 10-4 were determined by first averaging the indices for individual parts for each child and then determining the average combined index for each grade level. Thus the change in the interpart index from one grade to the next reflects changes that occurred within the individual part. For example, the considerable increase between grades two and three is primarily due to changes in foot dominance. The apparent fluctuation that occurs between grades three and six may be a reflection of the decrease in pure eye dominance from grades three to four and the decrease in hand dominance from grades five to six (Dusewicz and Kershner, 1969). Table 10-3 shows some data for hand-eye interpart preference. As may be noted, the incidence of pure hand-eye dominance increases steadily from age 5 to age 11.

Significance of lateral dominance   Does it matter if a child has mixed intrapart or interpart dominance, or is right- or left-handed? "The true significance and/or role of sensory dominance in the child's development has yet to be established" (Williams, 1973, p. 144). Some arguments for the importance of pure dominance have been given; others have refuted these arguments and theories in a rather convincing way. A small sampling of some of the evidence available may be of interest to the reader.

The Doman-Delecato system of perceptual-motor training is based on the theory that pure lateral dominance (complete one-sidedness) is essential for proper "neurological organization" to occur. Further, unless the individual establishes complete one-sidedness, he is likely to encounter problems associated with speech, reading, and other perceptual-motor and/or cognitive functions. Thus the establishment of pure dominance is the basis for the treatment of a child in a Doman-Delecato training program. To date, the validity of this theory is far from established through empirical evidence. In other words there is little evidence that one who has mixed intrapart or interpart dominance has, or will have, more difficulty in the classroom or the gymnasium than the child with pure dominance.

In a test of the Doman-Delecato hypothesis, Sabatino and Becker (1971) investigated the relationship between lateral preference (dominance) and several perceptual, perceptual-motor, and cognitive tasks. The children used in their study ($N = 472$) were children who were failing academically—they had failed at least one grade and were underachieving in reading by one or more years. Whether a child had pure dominance (right or left) or mixed dominance was in no way related to her performances on any perceptual, perceptual-motor, or cognitive tasks. Equally important is the fact that only 8% of the total group of children, all of whom had failed academically, demonstrated "confused laterality," i.e., mixed dominance.

Is lateral dominance related to the development of motor capacities in young children? Williams (1973) investigated this question in children from 5 through 12 years of age. After establishing whether the child was of pure or mixed dominance, a battery of perceptual-motor tests was administered to each child. In general, sidedness (mixed or pure dominance) was not related to the children's performance on any of the motor tasks. That is, children with mixed dominance performed as well as those with pure dominance and vice versa. Horine (1968) also reports little or no relationship between patterns of dominance and motor performance in ten-year-old boys.

Rigal (1974) investigated the relationship between handedness and fine motor performance and found some differences between left- and right-handed fourth-grade children. Right- and left-handers did not differ in their performances when the dominant (preferred) hand was used. When the nondominant hand (right for left-handers; left for right-handers) was used, left-handed boys and girls performed better on all tasks than right-handers. These results may be due in part to cultural influences. Until recently manipulative objects that have a distinct sidedness associated with their use have been manufactured with the right-handed person in mind. Thus the left-handed person has had to either use the right hand or adjust the use of the object to the left hand. Scissors are a good example of such an object. Until very recently left-handed scissors were nonexistent. Thus by fourth grade, left-handed children may have had a great deal of experience using the right hand in fine motor tasks. There may be other reasons for these observed differences in performance on fine motor tasks by right- and left-handers.

The lack of a general relationship between dominance and motor performance remains even at the college level. Sinclair and Smith (1967) found no relationship between eye, hand, and foot dominance patterns and the side one breathes on when swimming. Adams (1965) reports no relationship between eye dominance and baseball batting performance (Adams, 1965). Hand-eye dominance patterns were not related to lateral errors in free-throw shooting (Shick, 1974). It appears then that there is little, if any, evidence to suggest that lack of pure dominance is significantly related to successful performance on perceptual-motor or cognitive tasks.

External Subcomponents of Body Awareness

The external (environment-related) subcomponents of body aware-ness develop as a natural consequence of growth in the internal (body-related) subcomponents of body awareness. Thus as the child's awareness of himself as a physical being becomes established, development of the awareness of the body as an object in and interactor with the environment commences. Not all internal subcomponents of body awareness are devel-oped before external subcomponents begin to appear. Usually a given external subcomponent will not manifest itself until the internal subcom-ponent(s) to which it is linked has begun to develop. The clearest example of the relationship between internal and external subcomponents of body awareness is seen in the sequence in which awareness of spatial dimensions of the body (internal) and directionality (external) develop. In general, a child cannot accurately identify left and right dimensions of objects in space (directionality) until she has developed left-right concepts relative to her own body. Not all internal subcomponents of body awareness are directly linked to external subcomponents. Lateral dominance and identification of body parts are body- and not environment-related, and there are no external extensions of these internal subcomponents. The external sub-components with which we will be concerned are imitation, directionality, and spatial orientation.

Imitation   Accompanying the improved capacity of the child to initiate movement of body parts, there is a growing fascination on the part of the infant with regard to examination of objects in her environment. Out of this grows the child's capacity to imitate—to imitate movements and/or positions of objects and people in her external world. The first evidence of this imitation is seen in the smiling response of the infant to a smiling familiar face. This imitative smiling usually occurs sometime between the fifth week and the fifth month (Jersild and Ding, 1932). Thus the imitative voluntary response resulting from interpretation of "something" in the environment begins at a very early age. It has also been suggested that gesture patterns and posture positions by children as young as 2 years of age are imitations of adult behavior (Birdwhistell, 1960).

Assessment of the child's ability for spontaneous and accurate imitation usually involves a model or tester who assumes various positions with the body and/or who performs different gestures with the limbs and hands. The child is then asked to replicate the position or gesture performed. Available evidence suggests that the speed and accuracy with which positions and gestures are imitated by the child increase with age. In general, the three-year-old is half as proficient as the six-year-old in imitating simple hand and arm positions; the four-year-old is 75% as proficient as the six-year-old. When more complex gestures (using two or more body parts simultaneously) are involved, the three-year-old is only one-third as proficient as the six-year-old (Bergés and Lézine, 1965).

Data on performances of children ranging in age from 4 to 8½ years on an imitation of postures task are given in Figure 10.5 (Ayres, 1969). The age-related improvement in the capacity to imitate postures is obvious. A substantial improvement occurs for each six-month period from age 4 to 5½ years. From that point until age 8½ the improvement is more grad-

Figure 10.5   Imitation of Postures as a Function of Age (Ayres, 1969; N = 1004)

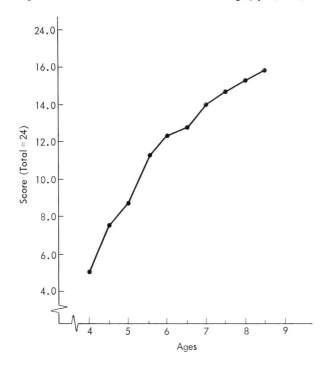

ual; it should be noted that even at 8½, children perform at only a 60% level of proficiency. That is, with the total possible score of 24 points, the average score is only 15.2 points. This suggests that the capacity for imitating body positions is not fully developed until some time after the age of 8 years.

The validity of "imitation tests" as measures of body awareness has been questioned. Opponents suggest that such tests are tests of visual perception rather than body awareness. Certainly a visual perception component is involved in such tasks. However if a subcomponent of body awareness does, in fact, involve the ability of the child to interact with the environment and objects in it, then visual perception plays an important role in the development of body awareness. Further, even though visual perception may be involved in the capacity to imitate, the actual imitative response is motoric and based upon the use of kinesthetic information. Specifically, to carry out imitative behaviors, the young child must perceive what is in the environment and integrate that visual information with the kinesthetic information gained through assuming the positions or executing the gestures. These imitative perceptual-motor activities of the young child contribute to the further development of the flexible body schema and the formation of motor plans as well as to the establishment of body boundaries (a part of body image).

Directionality Directionality is the capacity to identify various dimensions of external space and/or the ability to project spatial dimensions outside the body. Specifically, directionality involves the development of concepts about the location or movements of objects or persons in the environment. The identification of the dimensions of external space involves directional labels such as right-left, up-down, front-back—the same directional labels used in identifying spatial dimensions of the body.

It is speculated that identification of external spatial dimensions (directionality) is dependent upon, and in fact a natural consequence of, the capacity to deal with internal (body-related) spatial dimensions (laterality, right-left discrimination, awareness of front-back-side, and crossing the body midline). Swanson and Benton (1955) provide some support for this notion in reporting that conceptualization of external space lags behind the conceptualization of the spatial dimensions of the body. However their data deal only with the right-left dimensions of space. It has been suggested that the child who has an inadequate conceptualization of the spatial dimensions of his own body will have difficulty with tasks that involve directional dimensions of objects or persons in space. More specifically, it has been suggested that reading and writing skills are dependent upon the use of left-right, up-down, and front-back as spatial references for recognizing shapes, letters, and words, and that these spatial references are developed in relation to one's own body first (e.g., Arnheim and Sinclair, 1975; Godfrey and Kephart, 1969). It seems logical that the child who does not know his right hand from his left will not be able to identify the left-right relationships of objects in space (letters and words, for instance). However although there is some evidence available to suggest that children who have difficulty discriminating among spatial patterns and/or position of letters (e.g., "b" and "d") have associated deficiencies in awareness of spatial dimensions of body, no cause-effect relationship has been shown (Kephart, 1964).

The developmental progression leading to the ability to "spontaneously identify position, dimensions and directions of objects or persons in external space without having first to consciously and deliberately refer to his own body" includes several steps or stages (Williams, 1973, p. 146). Generally the first step in the sequence involves accurate location of objects or persons in relation to one's body (or one's body in relation to objects or other persons). Responding correctly to: "Is this object to the left or right of you?" or, "Stand by my left side," are examples of achievements during this first stage. Thus the accurate location of objects in space is accomplished initially by using the body or self as a reference point. From this initial step, the child begins to identify the relationship between two objects or persons in space and/or the direction of movements in space. Although what has just been described appears, at first glance, to be a two-step process, the perception of spatial relationships within the environment is dependent upon several factors including the nature of the objects (distinct front, back, side features), the nature of the task (identification or placement), and the orientation (facing) of the objects or persons.

Of interest to our discussion is a study by Kuczaj and Maratsos (1975). Children of three different ages were asked to: (a) place objects (doll and toy car) in front, back, and to the side of himself; (b) touch the front and back of several toys that had distinct front-back features (e.g., tugboat, telephone, dog); (c) place a small doll in front, back, and to the side of each of several objects with distinct features; and (d) place the doll in front, back, and to the side of objects that did not have distinct features (e.g., drinking glass, spool, cube). A summary of the results of this study is shown in Table 10-5. Inspection of the data reveals important age differences in the ability to perform various directionality tasks. Steps in the development of mature directionality are also present. In general, the sequence of development in directionality tasks appears to be:

1. placement of objects in front or back of self;
2. identification of front and back of objects;
3. placement of a standard in front and back of a featured object;
4. placement of an object to one's own side and the side of a featured object;

TABLE 10-5 Mean Percent of Correct Responses to Different Directionality Tasks as a Function of Age (Kuczaj and Maratsos, 1975)

AGE GROUP	(A) SELF-REFERENT			(B) TOUCH		(C) PLACEMENT FEATURED OBJECT			(D) PLACEMENT FEATURELESS OBJECT		
	FRONT	BACK	SIDE	FRONT	BACK	FRONT	BACK	SIDE	FRONT	BACK	SIDE
30-37 mos.	83.3	83.3	16.7	64.2	61.7	46.7	40.8	34.2	21.7	22.5	22.5
38-42 mos.	90.0	96.7	43.3	75.0	78.3	55.8	57.5	40.8	37.5	30.8	33.3
43.5-49.5 mos.	100.0	100.0	76.7	93.3	94.2	86.7	86.7	75.8	68.3	72.5	76.7

5. placement of a standard to the front, back, and side of a featureless object using the self as a reference, i.e., in front of the object, between the object and oneself.

It is clear from these findings that, as with awareness of spatial dimensions of the body, concepts about the front-back dimensions of objects in space develop before those relative to side. Further, positional relationships between objects and oneself (directionality) using the self as a referent develop prior to positional interrelationships among objects in space.

It would appear, then, that the initial step in the development of directionality, that is, position of objects in external space in reference to oneself, is well established by the time the child enters school. Although no study has included the up-down dimensions of space, it may be safe to assume that the development of that concept parallels that of front-back. Note also that the directionality component "side" does not, to this point, involve discrimination of left and right. Since the capacity to discriminate left-right dimensions of the body does not appear until about age 6 in the majority of children, identification of left and right of others and of dimensions of space may not appear until age 8 or 9 (Cratty, 1979). Long and Looft (1972) suggest that a linear trend exists in the development of directionality from ages 6 to 12.

By the age of 6 the internal subcomponent of identification of major body parts has been mastered and left-right discrimination has begun. The six-year-old is also aware of vertical and horizontal references and can imitate another's movements, using one side of the body and crossing the body using limbs on both sides when the person being imitated is to the side of the child. The seven-year-old can describe an object as "between" or in the "middle" of two other objects. He can also make reference to both sides of the body simultaneously (Long and Looft, 1972).

By age 8, characteristics of true directionality begin to appear. The child can now describe the position of objects in relationship to himself and to each other when the objects are adjacent to him (e.g., "The key is on my left." "The key is to the right of the coin."). However, when the child moves to a location that is not adjacent to the objects (to the other side of a table for instance) and therefore assumes a different body facing, he still maintains that the objects are in the same relationship to each other ("The key is to the right of the coin."). The eight-year-old is also able to use directional references (rather than position or location) as long as only one direction is involved. That is, he can draw a line to the right but cannot "draw a square at the bottom left-hand corner of the paper." This latter ability does not appear until age 9.

The nine-year-old can objectively (without reference to self) describe relationships among objects. That is, he will accurately respond, "The key is to the right of the coin," when the objects are adjacent to him, and when he assumes the opposite body facing (on the other side of the table) he will respond, "The key is to the left of the coin." At age 9 the child can also imitate movements on one side and crossing the body in face-to-face situations.

The ten-year-old can accurately identify the left and right sides of a person who is facing him. This implies that the child of this age no longer needs to use his own body as a referent when describing the spatial dimensions or relationships within the environment. These directionality capacities develop further in the eleven-year-old until finally, at age 12, children begin to show the ability to use a "natural reference system" (e.g., "The sun rises in the east."). Long and Looft (1972) suggest that the development of mature directionality is not complete for most children until after age 12. It is also apparent from their data that directionality is an external extension of the awareness of spatial dimensions of the body (internal).

Spatial orientation   The final external subcomponent of body awareness to be considered is what is referred to here as spatial orientation. For our purposes, spatial orientation refers to the position of the body in space (e.g., upright, upside down, tilted). Although spatial orientation and directionality are closely related, a distinction between them should be made. Directionality involves the interrelationships of locations and/or direction of objects and/or persons in space; spatial orientation does not. For example, a task of directionality may require the child to locate an object in relation to another object or a person (including himself); spatial orientation refers to the position of one's body in space without reference to another object or another person. Although the child may use cues from the environment to help him make positional judgments, the awareness of one's position or orientation in space does not necessarily require the use of external referents. In addition, while vision is the primary, and in some instances the only, perceptual system used in directionality, body-related sensory information is also used in the perception of one's orientation in space.

The earth's gravitational pull is a major environmental factor affecting judgment of spatial orientation. Ayres (1972) suggests that the basic form of perception of space involves the individual's ability to make accurate judgments about the direction of the force of gravity, and the concepts of "up" and "down" may be derived from interpretations or experiences related to gravity's pull. She further suggests that this basic form of space perception provides the beginning of the establishment of an "environmental scheme"—"... a model or map of the environment to which the body relates" (p. 196). Her environmental scheme is analogous to the body schema (discussed earlier), with the two schemes being interdependent.

How do we judge the position of the body in space, that is, what sensory information is used? In general, it is believed that the somato-sensory system provides the basic information needed for perception of spatial orientation. Specifically, the vestibular apparatus provides information about the position of the head in relation to gravity and is sensitive to sudden changes of movement of the body (direction and speed). Postural information is also gained from the proprioceptors of the neck, so that when the head is not balanced over and/or supported by the shoulders, the proprioceptors of the neck are stimulated. This helps to maintain a balanced, upright position of the head. In addition to the somato-sensory information, visual information concerning the orientation of a "thing" in the environment is used. In the final analysis, it may be the integration of somato-sensory and visual information that provides the basis for making accurate judgments concerning the position of the body in space.

Witkin (1948a, 1948b, 1950, 1952, 1959) has conducted a number of interesting experiments in which he has identified differences among individuals in their perception of "the upright." A variety of experimental situations involving manipulation of the orientation (position) of the person, of the environment, or both the person and the environment have been used. In general, two major categories or classifications of persons have been identified: those who are "field-independent" and those who are "field-dependent." The field-independent individual judges his position (uprightness) using internal, body-related cues more than visual information. Such individuals accurately judge their position as upright (or tilted, whichever the case may be) whether available visual information is accurate or discrepant. This individual is said to be independent of the field—he experiences his body as an entity apart from the environment. The field-dependent person, on the other hand, is more influenced by the nature of the visual information available from the environment. This person judges himself to be tilted if the visual information indicates that "tilt" is present; this is true even though the position of the body is in fact upright. Interestingly, when field-dependent individuals close their eyes and are thus forced to use body-related cues, the accuracy of judgments of the upright improves considerably (Witkin, 1959).

Of interest is Witkin's (1959) work with children and adolescents. Witkin (1959) found that younger children (eight-year-olds) tended to be more field-dependent than older children, but that they became more field-independent with age. Improvement in the accuracy with which children judge uprightness of the body continues until about age 13. Bigelow (1971) reports the same general trend using five- to ten-year-old children. Despite the overall trend from greater to lesser field dependency, however, there are large differences in the degree of field dependency/field independency at all ages. Thus although most younger children tend to be *more* field-dependent, some are field independent. In addition, although there is a greater tendency toward field independency with increasing age, most children and/or adults maintain the same relative position within the group with age. Girls and women also tend to be more field-dependent than boys and men.

In general, it appears that although we may use visual cues in the environment to help us in our perception of our position in space, we can make relatively accurate judgments using only body-related information. In fact, at times visual cues may interfere with the accuracy of the perception of spatial awareness, particularly if the visual information is distorted in some way. There is some evidence that the spatial orientation subcomponent of body awareness may be related to body image. Experiments with ten-year-old boys showed that the field-dependent individuals included little detail and unrealistic proportions in their figure drawings—a task typically used to measure body image. Field-independent individuals, however, produced more articulated drawings and included more detail and more accurate proportions. Even though the evidence is limited, it does suggest a link between the development of body awareness and body image (Witkin, 1959).

SUMMARY

1. The concept of the physical self includes three major elements: body schema, body awareness, and body image.

2. Body schema may be thought of as the innate mechanism within the CNS that allows the individual to be aware of the body, its dimensions, positions, and movement in space. Body schema develops from the child's experience of sensory information arising from movements of the body and body parts.

3. Body awareness development is dependent upon the development of the body schema and is prerequisite to the development of the body image.

4. Body awareness can be defined as the conscious awareness and identification of the location, position, and movement of the body in space, of the interrelationships among various body parts, and of the relationship of the body and its parts to the external environment.

5. Internal subcomponents of body awareness are those that deal exclusively with awareness of the body itself and include visual attention, awareness of spatial dimensions of the body, lateral dominance, and identification of body parts.

6. External subcomponents of body awareness are those concerned with the perception of the body in relationship to the environment, and include imitation, directionality, and spatial orientation.

7. Internal subcomponents of body awareness often (but not always) develop in advance of external subcomponents.

8. In general, body awareness characteristics improve with age, and most reach maturity by the time the child is 8 to 10 years of age.

9. Body image may be described as the image one has of oneself as a physical entity, and includes both "body proportions" and "performance" characteristics. Judgments of the body as short or tall, strong or weak, good, bad, or indifferent are primarily the result of social interactions that the child undergoes as she grows and develops.

STUDY QUESTIONS

1. Define body schema, body awareness, body image.
2. How are these concepts related?
3. How does the body schema develop?
4. What is the "phantom limb" phenomenon? How is it related to the body schema?
5. What is the neurological basis for the body schema?
6. How are "motor plans" and body schema related? What importance does this have for skillful motor performance?
7. How has "body image" been studied?
8. Describe the following aspects of research on body image:
    a. age differences in accuracy of body image
    b. sex differences in accuracy of body image
    c. effects of participation in motor activities on body image
    d. the relationship of body image to physical fitness
    e. body image and level of aspiration (e.g., setting of performance goals)
9. Differentiate between internal and external subcomponents of body awareness. How are they related? Be specific.
10. Define and describe age- and sex-related differences in the following internal subcomponents of body awareness:
    a. visual attention
    b. laterality
    c. right-left discrimination

   d. crossing the body midline

   e. identification of body parts

   f. lateral dominance

   g. hand, eye, foot dominance

   h. interpart dominance

11. What is the significance of lateral dominance to the overall development of the child? Cite specific evidence.

12. Define and describe age- and sex-related characteristics of the following external subcomponents of body awareness:

   a. imitation

   b. directionality

   c. spatial orientation

13. How are specific internal subcomponents of body awareness related to each other?

14. How are specific external subcomponents of body awareness related to each other?

REFERENCES

ADAMS, G.L.   Effect of eye dominance on baseball batting. *Research Quarterly.* 36(1965): 3-9.

ALBINS, G.   The relationship between self concept and motor performance of sixth grade girls, eighth grade girls, and college women. Master's thesis, Texas Women's University, 1972.

ARNHEIM, D.D., AND PESTOLESI, R.A.   *Developing Motor Behavior in Children.* St. Louis, MO: The C.V. Mosby Company, 1973.

ARNHEIM, D.D., AND SINCLAIR, W.A.   *The Clumsy Child.* St. Louis, MO: The C.V. Mosby Company, 1975.

AYRES, A.J.   *Southern California Perceptual-Motor Tests.* Los Angeles, CA: Western Psychological Services, 1969.

AYRES, A.J.   *Sensory Integration and Learning Disorders.* Los Angeles, CA: Western Psychological Services, 1972.

BERGÉS, J., AND LÉZINE, I.   *The Imitation of Gestures,* translated by Parmelee, Arthur H. London: The Spastics Society Medial Education and Information Unit in Association with William Heineman (Medical) Books Ltd., 1965.

BIGELOW, G.S.   Field dependence-field independence in 5 to 10 year old children. *The Journal of Educational Research.* 64(1971): 397-400.

BIRDWHISTELL, R.L.   Kinetics and communications. In Carpenter and McLuhan, eds. *Explorations in Communications.* Boston: Beacon Press, 1960.

BRUGEL, B.A.   The self concept of eight and nine year old boys participating in a competitive baseball league. Master's thesis, Pennsylvania State University, 1972.

CLIFFORD, E.   Body satisfaction in adolescence. *Perceptual and Motor Skills.* 33(1971): 119-125.

CRATTY, B.J.   *Perceptual and Motor Development in Infants and Children,* 2nd edition. London: The Macmillan Company, 1979.

CRAXEN, M.E., AND LYTTON, H.   Reading disability and difficulties in finger localization and right-left discrimination. *Developmental Psychology.* 5(1971): 256-262.

DELECATO, C.H.   *The Diagnosis and Treatment of Speech and Reading Problems.* Springfield, IL: Chas. C. Thomas, 1963.

DUSEWICZ, R.A., AND KERSHNER, K.M.   The D-K scale of lateral dominance. *Perceptual and Motor Skills.* 29(1969): 282.

FISHLER, J.   The effect of a physical conditioning program upon self-concept, peer approval, and physical fitness level of fifth grade students. Master's thesis, Brigham Young University, 1975.

GELLERT, E., GIRGUS, J.S., AND COHEN, J.   Children's awareness of their bodily appearance: a developmental study of factors associated with the body percept. *The Journal Press,* Provincetown, Mass.

GODFREY, B.B., AND KEPHART, N.C.   *Movement Patterns and Motor Education.* Englewood Cliffs, NJ: 1969. Prentice-Hall, Inc.

HORINE, L.E.   An investigation of the relationship of laterality groups to performance on selected motor ability tests. *Research Quarterly.* 39(1968): 90-95.

JERSILD, A.T., AND DING, G.F.   A study of the laughing and smiling of preschool children. *Journal of Genetic Psychology.* 40(1932): 452-472.

KEOGH, B.K.   Preschool children's performance on measures of spatial organization, lateral preference, and lateral usage. *Perceptual and Motor Skills.* 34(1972): 299-300.

KEPHART, N.C.   *The Slow Learner in the Classroom.* Columbus, OH: Chas. E. Merrill, 1964.

KUCZAJ, S.A., II, AND MARATSOS, M.P.   On the acquisition of front, back and side. *Child Development.* (1975): 202-210.

LACOURSIERE-PAIGE, F.   Development of right-left concept in children. *Perceptual and Motor Skills.* 38(1974): 111-117.

LERNER, R.M., AND SCHROEDER, C.   Physique identification, preference and aversion in kindergarten children. Unpublished manuscript, Eastern Michigan University.

LONG, A.B., AND LOOFT, W.R.   Development of directionality in children. *Developmental Psychology.* 6(1972): 375-380.

MAPES, J.L.   The relationship of physical fitness, self-concept, and academic achievement. Master's thesis, Central Washington State College, 1975.

MARTINEK, T.J., AND JOHNSON, S.B.   Teacher expectations: Effects on dyadic interactions and self-concept in elementary age children. *Research Quarterly.* 50(1979): 60-70.

MARTINEK, T.J., ZAICHKOWSKY, L.D., AND CHEFFERS, J.T.F.   Decision-making in elementary age children: Effects on motor skills and self-concept. *Research Quarterly.* 48(1977): 349-356.

MAUL, T., AND THOMAS, J.R.   Self-concept and participation in children's gymnastics. *Perceptual and Motor Skills.* 41(1975): 701-702.

MCGOWAN, R.W., JARMAN, B.O., AND PEDERSEN, D.M.   Effects of a competitive endurance training program on self-concept and peer approval. *Journal of Psychology.* 86(1974): 57-60.

NASH, J.   *Developmental Psychology.* Englewood Cliffs: Prentice-Hall, Inc., 1970.

PATTERSON, L.S.   A comparison of seventh and ninth grade girls on level of aspiration and performance in strength and endurance tasks. Master's thesis, Louisiana State University, 1975.

PHELAN, F.J.   An investigation into the relationship between self-concept and selected physical fitness attributes in seventh and eighth grade boys and girls at University School, Laramie, Wyoming. Master's thesis, University of Wyoming, 1973.

RIGAL, R.A.   Hand efficiency and right-left discrimination. *Perceptual and Motor Skills.* 38(1974): 219-224.

PLATZER, W.S.   Effects of perceptual-motor training on gross motor skill and self-concept of young children. *The American Journal of Occupational Therapy.* 30(1976): 423-428.

SABATINO, D.A., AND BECKER, J.T.   Relationship between lateral preference and selected behavioral variables for children failing academically. *Child Development.* 42(1971): 2055-2060.

SCHOFIELD, W.N.   Do children find movements which cross the body midline difficult? *Quarterly Journal of Experimental Psychology.* 28(1976): 571-582.

SCHOFIELD, W.N.   Hand movements which cross the body midline: findings relating age differences to handedness. *Perceptual and Motor Skills.* 42(1976): 643-646.

SCHICK, J.   Relationship between hand-eye dominance and lateral errors in free-throw shooting. *Perceptual and Motor Skills.* 39(1974): 325-326.

SINCLAIR, C.   Dominance patterns of young children. *Perceptual and Motor Skills.* 32(1971): 142.

SINCLAIR, C.B., AND SMITH, I.M.   Laterality in swimming and its relationship to dominance of hand, eye and foot. *Research Quarterly.* 28(1957): 395-402.

SORENSON, W.J.   The effects of a special strength training program in the self-concept and peer approval of seventh grade boys. Unpublished Master's thesis, Brigham Young University, 1974.

STAFFORD, B.L.   The effects of age and sex on the level of aspiration in selected motor tasks. Doctoral dissertation, Louisiana State University, 1969.

STILES, D.B.   Comparison of self-estimated height and width of children 6 years and 10 months to 10 years and 9 months under static and dynamic conditions. Master's thesis, Purdue University, 1975.

STURTEVANT, S.B.   An investigation of the role of LA and task complexity as evidenced in throwing performances of eight and nine year old boys. Unpublished manuscript, Kent State University.

SWANSON, R., AND BENTON, A.L.   Some aspects of the genetic development of right-left discrimination. *Child Development.* 26(1955): 123.

WAPNER, S., WERNER, H., deAJURIAGUERRA, J., CLEVELAND, S.E., CRITCHLEY, M., FISHER, S., AND WITKIN, H.A.   *The Body Percept.* New York: Random House, 1965.

WIGGINS, R.G.   Differences in self-perceptions of ninth grade boys and girls. *Adolescence.* 8(1973): 491-496.

WILLIAMS, H.G.   Body awareness characteristics in perceptual-motor development. In Corbin, ed., *A Textbook of Motor Development*, Chapter 22. Dubuque, IA: Wm. C. Brown Company, 1973.

WILLIAMS, H.G.   The relationship between motor performance capacities and body awareness characteristics of young children: I and II. Unpublished manuscript, University of Toledo, 1973.

WILLIAMS, H.G., TEMPLE, I.G., LOGSDON, B.J., SCOTT, S., AND CLEMENT, A.   An investigation of the perceptual-motor development of young children. Unpublished manuscript, Bowling Green State University, 1971.

WITKIN, H.A.   Studies in space orientation III: Perception of the upright in the absence of a visual field. *Journal of Experimental Psychology.* 38(1948): 603-614.

WITKIN, H.A.   Studies in space orientation IV: Further experiments on perception of the upright with displaced visual fields. *Journal of Experimental Psychology.* 38(1948): 762-782.

WITKIN, H.A.   Perception of the upright when the direction of the force acting on the body is changed. *Journal of Experimental Psychology.* 40(1950): 93-106.

WITKIN, H.A.   Further studies of perception of the upright when the direction of the force acting on the body is changed. *Journal of Experimental Psychology.* 43(1952): 9-20.

WITKIN, H.A.   The perception of the upright. *Scientific American.* (1959): 51-56.

INDEX

Glassow, R.B., 247, 249, 252
Glia, proliferation of, 39
Godfrey, B.B., 311–12
Goetzinger, P., 271
Goldman, P., 58, 60
Goodenough, F.L., 184, 185
Goodenough projective test, 289
Goodglass, H., 102
Goodnow, J., 148, 149
Grasp mechanisms, 179
  full instinctive, 173
  reaching. *See* Eye-hand coordination
    171–75
Greenlee, G., 271
Gregg, L., 95
Gregory, C.A., 272
Gross, E.A., 271
Gross motor skills, 10, 26, 200–60
  and intersensory integration, 155–57
  intertask motor development, 201–4
  intratask motor development and, 207–9
  process characteristics of. *See* Process
    characteristics of movement
  product characteristics of. *See* Product
    charactersitics of movement
  visually guided reaching behaviors and,
    192–93
Guided placing responses, 176
Guilford, J.P., 16, 18
Guilford model of intellect, 16–18
Gutteridge, 217, 227
Guyton, A., 75, 79, 133

Haas, M.A., 271
Haith, M., 111
Halverson, L.E., 201, 208, 209, 218, 224,
    231, 233
Hand dominance, 181, 305–6
  eye-hand coordination and, 306
  and fine motor control, 308
  pure, 305–6
Handedness. *See* Hand dominance
Hand movement
  developmental sequence of, 205
  flexion/extension, 191
Hand patting, 190
Haptic memory, 131
Harper, C.J., 243
Harris, P., 117
Haubenstricker, J., 247, 248, 249, 250
Hebb, D.O., 21, 22
Hebbian perspective, of perceptual-motor
    development, 21–22
Heel/toe tapping, alternating, 191–92
Heeschen, R.E., 262, 263
Heggelund, P., 58
Hein, A., 20, 176, 177, 192, 193
Held, R., 20, 176, 192
Henderson, S., 120
Heredity, 21–22
Herschkowitz, N., 35, 37
Hillebrandt, 219
Homolateral movement control, 180
Hopping, 224–25
  balance and, 225
  developmental characteristics of, 226–28
  and jumping, similarities and differences
    of, 224–25
  mature pattern of, 226
  process characteristics of, 226

Hopping, (*cont.*)
  product characteristics of, 250–51
  and skipping, relationship between, 230
Horine, L.E., 306, 307, 308
Hsia, J.J., 158
Hunsicker, P., 247, 248, 250, 256, 258
Hypothetical reasoning, 14
Hypoxemia. *See* Asphyxia

Identity matching, 96, 97
Imitation, 13, 309–311
  assessment of, 310
  of postures task, 310–11
  tests, validity of, 311
Information feedback, 3, 7–9, 20
Information pick-up, 68–69
Integration
  intersensory. *See* Intersensory integration
  intrasensory. *See* Intrasensory development
  part-whole, 101–2
  sensory, 5
  visual, 81, 82, 83
Intellect
  balance and development of, 271–72
  figural content of, 16–17
  Guilford model of, 16–17
  nature of, 16
  semantic content of, 16–17
  symbolic content of, 16–17
Intelligence
  abstract, 17
  concrete, 17
Intelligence A, 21
Intelligence B, 21
Intersensory communication, 73
Intersensory integration, 142–67
  auditory-tactile, 150
  auditory-visual, age changes in, 147–50
  and body schema, 285
  and central nervous system development, 157
  and cognitive development, 158–59
  defined, 142
  early development of, 143–46
  and intrasensory development, 146–47
  and motor control, relationship to, 154–58
  other, 153–54
  and paired-associate learning, 158
  prestimulation and, 153–54
  spatial reference system and, 159–62
  types of, 142
  visual, 147–50
  visual-tactile and/or kinesthetic, 150–53
Intrasensory development, 127–41
  auditory abilities, 135–39
  tactile-kinesthetic abilities, 127–35
Intrasensory discrimination, 72
Invariance. *See* Perceptual constancy
Ischemia. *See* Asphyxia
Ismail, A.H., 262, 263

Jahoda, G., 110
Jarman, B.O., 289
Jersild, A.T., 309
Jessen, L.J., 151
Johnson, S.B., 290
Jones, B., 149
Jumping, 217–24
  hopping and, similarities and differences
    of, 224–25
  mature, patterns, changes characterizing,
    218, 224